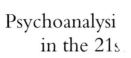

Psychoanalysi
in the 21s Century

MW00655716

Freud described religion as the universal obsessional neurosis, and uncompromisingly rejected it in favour of 'science'. Ever since, there has been the assumption that psychoanalysts are hostile to religion. Yet, from the beginning, individual analysts have questioned Freud's blanket rejection of religion.

In this book, David M. Black brings together contributors from a wide range of schools and movements to discuss the issues. They bring a fresh perspective to the subject of religion and psychoanalysis, answering vital questions such as:

- How do religious stories carry (or distort) psychological truth?
- How do religions 'work', psychologically?
- What is the nature of religious experience?
- Are there parallels between psychoanalysis and particular religious traditions?

Psychoanalysis and Religion in the 21st Century will be of great interest to psychoanalysts, psychoanalytic therapists, psychodynamic counsellors, and anyone interested in the issues surrounding psychoanalysis, religion, theology and spirituality.

David M. Black is a Fellow of the Institute of Psychoanalysis, London, and works as a psychoanalyst in private practice and teaches on a number of professional trainings. He has published widely on psychoanalysis in relation to religion, consciousness and values.

Contributors: David M. Black, Rachel B. Blass, Rodney Bomford, Ronald Britton, Malcom Cunningham, M. Fakhry Davids, Mark Epstein, Stephen Frosh, Francis Grier, David Millar, Michael Parsons, Jeffrey B. Rubin, Neville Symington, Kenneth Wright

THE NEW LIBRARY OF PSYCHOANALYSIS
General Editor   Dana Birksted-Breen

The New Library of Psychoanalysis was launched in 1987 in association with the Institute of Psychoanalysis, London. It took over from the International Psychoanalytical Library, which published many of the early translations of the works of Freud and the writings of most of the leading British and Continental psychoanalysts.

The purpose of the New Library of Psychoanalysis is to facilitate a greater and more widespread appreciation of psychoanalysis and to provide a forum for increasing mutual understanding between psychoanalysts and those working in other disciplines such as the social sciences, medicine, philosophy, history, linguistics, literature and the arts. It aims to represent different trends both in British psychoanalysis and in psychoanalysis generally. The New Library of Psychoanalysis is well placed to make available to the English-speaking world psychoanalytic writings from other European countries and to increase the interchange of ideas between British and American psychoanalysts.

The Institute, together with the British Psychoanalytical Society, runs a low-fee psychoanalytic clinic, organizes lectures and scientific events concerned with psychoanalysis and publishes the *International Journal of Psychoanalysis*. It also runs the only UK training course in psychoanalysis which leads to membership of the International Psychoanalytical Association − the body which preserves internationally agreed standards of training, of professional entry, and of professional ethics and practice for psychoanalysis as initiated and developed by Sigmund Freud. Distinguished members of the Institute have included Michael Balint, Wilfred Bion, Ronald Fairbairn, Anna Freud, Ernest Jones, Melanie Klein, John Rickman and Donald Winnicott.

Previous General Editors include David Tuckett, Elizabeth Spillius and Susan Budd. Previous and current Members of the Advisory Board include Christopher Bollas, Ronald Britton, Catalina Bronstein, Donald Campbell, Sara Flanders, Stephen Grosz, John Keene, Eglé Laufer, Juliet Mitchell, Michael Parsons, Rosine Jozef Perelberg, Richard Rusbridger, Mary Target and David Taylor.

ALSO IN THIS SERIES

TITLES IN THE NEW LIBRARY OF PSYCHOANALYSIS TEACHING SERIES

Reading Freud: A Chronological Exploration of Freud's Writings Jean-Michel Quinodoz

THE NEW LIBRARY OF PSYCHOANALYSIS

General Editor: Dana Birksted-Breen

Psychoanalysis and Religion in the 21st Century

Competitors or Collaborators?

Edited by David M. Black

Routledge
Taylor & Francis Group

LONDON AND NEW YORK

First published 2006

by Routledge
2 Park Square, Milton Park, Abingdon, Oxon OX14 4RN
Simultaneously published in the USA and Canada
by Routledge
711 Third Avenue, New York NY 10016

Routledge is an imprint of the Taylor & Francis Group, an Informa business

© 2006 selection and editorial matter, David M. Black;
individual chapters, the contributors

Typeset in Bembo by
Keystroke, Jacaranda Lodge, Wolverhampton
Paperback cover design by Sandra Heath

British Library Cataloguing in Publication Data
A catalogue record for this book is available from the British Library

Library of Congress Cataloging in Publication Data
Psychoanalysis and religion in the twenty-first century : competitors or
collaborators? / editor, David M. Black.
p. cm. – (The new library of psychoanalysis)
Includes bibliographical references and index.
ISBN 0-415-37943-1 (hbk) – ISBN 0-415-37944-X (pbk)
1. Psychoanalysis and religion. I. Black, David M. II. Title.
III. Series: New library of psychoanalysis (Unnumbered)
BF175.4.R44P786 2006
201'.6150195--dc22
2006006453

ISBN13: 978–0–415–37943–4
ISBN13: 978–0–415–37944–1

ISBN10: 0–415–37943–1
ISBN10: 0–415–37944–X

The subjectivist in morals, when his moral feelings are at war with the facts about him, is always free to seek harmony by toning down the sensitiveness of the feeling . . . Truckling, compromise, time-serving, capitulations of conscience, are conventionally opprobrious names for what, if successfully carried out, would be on his principles by far the easiest and most praiseworthy mode of bringing about that harmony between inner and outer relations which is all that he means by good. The absolute moralist, on the other hand, when his interests clash with the world, is not free to gain harmony by sacrificing the ideal interests . . . Resistance then, poverty, martyrdom if need be, tragedy in a word – such are the solemn feasts of his inward faith . . . Any question is full of meaning to which, as here, contrary answers lead to contrary behavior.

William James

In most interesting subjects we do not want a decision procedure because we want to pursue a deeper level of understanding than that represented by our current questions and the methods we have for answering them.

Thomas Nagel

Contents

Contents

Contributors

David M. Black studied philosophy and eastern religions before training as a psychoanalyst. He is a Fellow of the Institute of Psychoanalysis, London, and a founder member of the Foundation for Psychotherapy and Counselling. He is author of the official history of the Westminster Pastoral Foundation and has written and lectured widely on psychoanalysis in relation to religion, consciousness and values.

Rachel B. Blass is a candidate at the Israel Psychoanalytic Institute and an associate professor and head of the Clinical Psychology Program at the Hebrew University of Jerusalem. She has published and lectured extensively on the conceptual, epistemological and ethical foundations of psychoanalytic theory and practice. Her recent work focuses on the study of the evolution and validity of psychoanalysis' thinking regarding truth and conviction.

Rodney Bomford studied mathematics at Oxford before training for the priesthood of the Church of England at Mirfield Theological College, Yorkshire and Union Seminary, New York. He worked in parish ministry in Deptford and Camberwell and is a Canon Emeritus of Southwark Cathedral. He wrote *The Symmetry of God* (1999), relating the psychoanalytic work of Ignacio Matte Blanco to Christian theology. He retired in 2001 to work further in this area.

Ronald Britton is a well-known psychoanalytic writer, teacher and clinician. His books include *The Oedipus Complex Today* (1989), *Belief and Imagination* (1998) and *Sex, Death and the Super-ego* (2003). He has written on the relationship of psychoanalysis to literature, philosophy and religion. He was chair of the Children and Families Department, Tavistock Clinic, president of the British Psychoanalytical Society and a vice-president of the International Psychoanalytical Association.

Malcom Cunningham is a faculty member of the Psychoanalytic Center of California. He is a graduate of the Medical University of South Carolina. He completed his psychiatric residency at the University of California, Los Angeles, where he is presently a clinical instructor in psychiatry. He has a particular interest in Indian philosophy, yoga and mysticism. He maintains a private practice in Los Angeles.

M. Fakhry Davids practises as a psychoanalyst and adult psychotherapist in London. He is a member of the Institute of Psychoanalysis, London, and of the Tavistock Society of Psychotherapists. He has an active interest in psychoanalytic clinical theory, including its application in adjacent fields, and has previously written on the role of the father and the psychology of racism.

Mark Epstein is a psychiatrist in private practice in New York City. His books include *Thoughts without a Thinker* (1995), *Going to Pieces without Falling Apart* (1999), *Going on Being* (2001) and *Open to Desire* (2005), which explores desire as a subject of meditative awareness. He has undergraduate and medical degrees from Harvard University and is clinical assistant professor in Psychotherapy and Psychoanalysis at New York University.

Stephen Frosh is Professor of Psychology and pro-vice-master at Birkbeck College, University of London. He was previously a consultant clinical psychologist and vice-dean at the Tavistock Clinic. He has written extensively on psychoanalysis and cultural issues. His books include *For and Against Psychoanalysis* (1997), *The Politics of Psychoanalysis* (1999), *After Words: The Personal in Gender, Culture and Psychotherapy* (2002) and *Hate and the 'Jewish Science'* (2005).

Francis Grier is an associate member of the British Psychoanalytical Society, a full member of the Society of Couple Psychoanalytic Psychotherapists and a visiting research lecturer at the Tavistock Centre for Couple Relationships, where he was previously a senior marital psychotherapist. He has a private practice for individuals and couples. He has edited two books: *Brief Encounters with Couples* (2001) and *Oedipus and the Couple* (2005).

David Millar, MA, MSc, C.Psychol, read chemistry at the University of Newcastle upon Tyne and theology at St Catharine's College, Cambridge. He is a training analyst of the British Psychoanalytic Society, head of Adult Psychotherapy Training at the Tavistock Clinic, and chair of the Tavistock Society of Psychotherapists.

Michael Parsons is a training and supervising analyst of the British Psychoanalytical Society. He works in private practice in London. He is the author of *The Dove that Returns, the Dove that Vanishes: Paradox and Creativity in Psychoanalysis* (2000) and co-editor of the collected papers of Enid Balint under the title *Before I was I: Psychoanalysis and the Imagination* (1993).

Jeffrey B. Rubin practises psychoanalysis and psychoanalytically oriented psychotherapy in New York City and Northern Westchester. He has taught at various psychoanalytic institutes and universities including the Postgraduate Center for Mental Health, C. G. Jung Foundation, Object Relations Institute, Harlem Family Institute, Union Theological Seminary and Yeshiva University. He is the author of *Psychotherapy and Buddhism* (1996), *A Psychoanalysis for Our Time* (1998) and *The Good Life* (2004).

Neville Symington has a degree in philosophy, theology and clinical psychology, was chairman of the Psychology Discipline at the Tavistock Clinic and president of the Australian Psycho-Analytic Society. His books include *Narcissism* (1993), *Emotion and Spirit* (1994), *Clinical Thinking of Wilfred Bion* (1996), *Making of a Psychotherapist* (1996), *Spirit of Sanity* (2001), *A Pattern of Madness* (2002), *How to Choose a Psychotherapist* (2003) and *The Blind Man Sees* (2004).

Kenneth Wright studied medicine at Oxford, trained at Maudsley Hospital, Institute of Psychoanalysis and Tavistock Clinic, and practises in Suffolk. He is a member of the British Psychoanalytical Society and Tavistock Society of Psychotherapists. Strongly influenced by Winnicott, he has published and lectured widely. His book *Vision and Separation: Between Mother and Baby* (1991) was awarded the Margaret Mahler Literature Prize. His interests include the development of symbolic usage.

Acknowledgements

I would like to thank Dana Birksted-Breen, General Editor of the New Library of Psychoanalysis, whose idea this book first was, and whose generous interest and invariably prompt emails helped greatly to keep the project moving forward over nearly five years. I am grateful too to all the authors, who worked hard to produce their contributions and have been impressively tolerant of my amateurish attempts to edit them. Special thanks to Rachel B. Blass, Ronald Britton, Mark Epstein and Michael Parsons, who first presented their papers at a conference at the British Psychoanalytical Society in June 2003; those papers became the nucleus of the present book.

Most of the contributions are published here for the first time. I am grateful, however, to the *International Journal of Psychoanalysis*, for permission to reprint Rachel B. Blass's article, and to Karnac, for permission to use Ronald Britton's chapter (a variant of which appeared in *Sex, Death and the Super-ego*). I am also grateful to Dilip Chitre, translator of *Says Tuka: Selected Poems of Tukaram* (Penguin India and Sontheimer Cultural Association), for permission to use the poems quoted in Francis Grier's chapter; to Faber & Faber for permission to use lines from 'Autobiography' in *Collected Poems* by Louis MacNeice in Kenneth Wright's chapter and also for 'Thirteen Ways of Looking at a Blackbird', in *The Collected Poems of Wallace Stevens* by Wallace Stevens in Mark Epstein's chapter.

References to Freud's works (SE) are to the *Standard Edition of the Complete Psychological Works of Sigmund Freud*, translated under the general editorship of James Strachey, London: Hogarth Press.

D.M.B.

INTRODUCTION

David M. Black

This book is entitled *Psychoanalysis and Religion in the 21st Century*, that is, in the second century of the existence of psychoanalysis. In this introduction, I shall attempt to sketch something of the broad currents of thought which flowed into and through the first psychoanalytic century, in which psychoanalysts for the most part either ignored or disparaged religion, and which now makes up the background to our present, very different, situation. Although the detail of the history is complex and entangled, perhaps some larger lines can be glimpsed with reasonable accuracy.

The metaphysical questions to which religions provide an answer have traditionally been summarised as 'God, freedom and immortality'. Immanuel Kant in the eighteenth century wrote a series of 'Antinomies' (1929) demonstrating persuasively that there were irrefutable arguments in favour of all three of these things; he then, no less persuasively, demonstrated that there were equally irrefutable arguments against them. It seemed that philosophy could not settle the questions of religion.

In the century following Kant, the century of Charles Darwin and the formative years of Sigmund Freud, the prestige of religion among educated people shrank at extraordinary speed. The theory of evolution, so long in being formulated and yet, once formulated, so simple as to seem virtually self-evident, left religion without a leg to stand on in the new, compellingly successful, industrial and scientific landscape. Man himself, who in the 'Abrahamic' religions (Judaism, Christianity, Islam) was God's last and most treasured creation, bearer if he lived his life rightly of a unique and sublime destiny, now showed up in the new understanding as just another player in the evolutionary lottery. Man had done well so far, but only because, as it happened, he was well able to adapt to recent planetary conditions. Change the temperature of the oceans or the composition of the atmosphere by a few percentage points, and man would be

replaced by lichens or beetles. The survival of the fittest, as Darwinians never
tired of pointing out, didn't mean the best; it just meant those who happened
to fit the environment. The new science knew nothing of any hierarchy of values.

This was not true, of course, when it came to assess its own achievement.
Freud was 3 when Darwin published *The Origin of Species* (1859); the scientific
world he entered as a teenager was awestruck at Darwin's achievement. All
through the 1880s, while Freud was in his twenties and early thirties, working
as a laboratory scientist and then gradually entering the field of neurology,
Friedrich Nietzsche was pouring forth his astonishing flood of publications,
ending with his tragic collapse into madness in 1889. Nietzsche's perception,
God is dead; everything is permitted!, led to his essentially manic fantasy of an
Übermensch, a 'superman', who would be heroically joyful and defiant despite
the essential futility of life in the godless, post-Darwinian universe. More often,
the implications of Darwin's insight caused religious thinkers to feel profound
anxiety, a state of mind movingly conveyed, for example, in Tennyson's great
elegiac poem *In Memoriam*.

When, from his mid-thirties onward, Freud invented psychoanalysis, he
continually tested his hypotheses against the Darwinian question: how is *this*
(whatever it might be: sadism, masochism, homosexuality, grief, depression,
suicide, war) – how is *this* compatible with evolution? What part might it play
in rendering the species fit for survival, or of what useful function might it be
a distortion?

A great deal of Freud's thought is illuminated when one remains aware of
this fundamental biological preoccupation (which he often verbalises, but not
always). The huge importance of sex in Freud's theory, for example, is not just
some cultural reaction to the manners of late-nineteenth-century Vienna; it
springs from Freud's ever-present awareness that sexual selection is how a species
– any species – comes into being. Sexual intercourse will not happen, and the
next generation will not grow to sexual maturity, unless individual organisms
preserve themselves. Sex and self-preservation, therefore, were the two fundamental drives in Freud's first attempt to formulate drive-theory. (Later,
his attempts to understand narcissism, mourning and the 'death drive' made his
picture very much more complex.)

One of the complicating factors that increasingly preoccupied Freud was
guilt, the spontaneously arising deep pain we can feel about the way we have
treated others (our 'objects' in psychoanalytic language). In his later writings,
Freud comments wonderingly on the power that guilt can have in human life,
even when invisible to the onlooker and unconscious even to the person. The
self-reproaches of melancholics, which can drive them to suicide (so puzzling
to a Darwinian), or the fate of some people to be 'wrecked by success', or to
refuse all help, including psychoanalytic help, because success fills them with
such unbearable guilt that they can't or won't take advantage of it – things of
this kind, the 'deadly power of unconscious morality' (Alvarez 1992), make up

resistances which can be insuperable even by the most patient and skilful psychoanalyst.

It is in this double context, both of his materialistic post-Darwinian science and of the profoundly intractable psychological difficulties he was encountering, that I think we should see Freud's Stoicism. Freud is often described as a pessimist, but that isn't really correct. Freud was a Stoic. Stoicism in its classical form was a religio-philosophical system which insisted that we should know our emotions accurately, not because that would make us any happier, but because otherwise our emotions would lead us astray and cause us to betray our highest values of Truth and Goodness. Freud's famous statement that 'much will be gained if we succeed in transforming your hysterical misery into common human unhappiness' (Freud 1895: 305) has the familiar tone of comfortless truth-telling, the refusal to be seduced by consolation, that we find in classic Stoic writers such as Epictetus and Marcus Aurelius. (Later, with the death of his daughter and his cancer of the jaw, Freud had a great deal to be stoical about, but the roots of that disposition were present from much earlier on.)

So Freud's philosophical attitudes can be mapped, to some extent, on a traditional religious cartography. But his general and very influential view of religion was unambiguously negative. Human beings, and particularly 'our wretched, ignorant and down-trodden ancestors' (1927: 33) have always had to find ways to deal with the reality of their helplessness in countless situations in life. We are like children, said Freud, who long for a strong father to protect them, and this wish can be gratified by believing in a powerful God. The institutions of religion are adapted to meet specific, universal fears: we have to make vital decisions, yet never have any certainty about our rightness in doing so – a set of divine commandments allays our anxiety about right and wrong. We suffer grief and terror in the face of death and transience – religion allows us to believe in an afterlife where we will re-meet those we have lost. We feel bitter resentment that our enemies flourish and go unpunished – religion consoles us by assuring us that *their* afterlife will be one of horrible suffering. In short, as Freud demurely remarked, with so many advantages, no wonder religion has been so successful.

But this left Freud with a problem. For one thing, as Ana-Maria Rizzuto (1979) has pointed out, he was contradicting his own understanding of the lifelong importance of fathers (he always had less to say about mothers). Moreover, he knew that many people he admired, including the Protestant pastor Oskar Pfister and the French writer and pacifist Romain Rolland, were committed religious believers, and yet by no means the ignorant and morally pusillanimous people who, according to Freud's theory, were likely to be attracted to religion. It was Rolland who responded to Freud's highly critical discussion of religion in *The Future of an Illusion* (1927) by saying that Freud had failed to understand the 'oceanic feeling' out of which religion is born. In *Civilization and its Discontents* (1930), Freud mused on Rolland's phrase. He professed himself

3

to have no awareness of such a feeling: he could only conceive it as a wish for 'the restoration of limitless narcissism' – the 'primary narcissism' which Freud believed to be the condition of the newborn baby.

Freud's failure to find anything to respect in religion is puzzling. In all other departments of life, he upholds the fundamental, powerful developmental insight of psychoanalysis, that what we call mature functioning is continuous with what we call immature, and cannot be cut off from it without impoverishment. When it comes to religion, however, he adopts the stance of the conventional nineteenth-century *paterfamilias*: he subjects 'the infantile' to condemnation and ironic mockery. He seems unable to entertain the thought that religious attitudes, like the other components of human psychology, may have their immature, their pathological, and also their relatively mature modes of expression.

Nevertheless, it's probably unfortunate that Rolland, a follower of the Vedantic Hindu teacher Sri Ramakrishna, should have attempted to persuade Freud by using a phrase (the 'oceanic feeling') so open to misinterpretation. As Malcom Cunningham's contribution in this book shows, Vedanta has far more rational arguments in its favour. Freud's proud contrasting of religion with science (religion is an illusion, 'our science' is no illusion) might well have been better challenged by a more direct enquiry as to the basis of such certainty, a questioning of the objective nature of psychoanalytic observations and of the sharp distinction Freud draws between 'reality' and 'fantasy'. More recent philosophers of science have found this distinction much harder to maintain. In the words of Karl Popper:

> Science does not rest upon solid bedrock. The bold structure of its theories rises, as it were, above a swamp. It is like a building erected on piles. The piles are driven down from above into the swamp, but not down to any natural or 'given' base; and if we stop driving the piles deeper, it is not because we have reached firm ground. We simply stop when we are satisfied that the piles are firm enough to carry the structure, at least for the time being.
>
> (Popper 1959: 93–94)

This picture, of science constructed like a sort of mental Venice, is one that would have appealed to Freud, and in his less authoritarian moods he knew well that science cannot deliver certainty. His thinking would have been subtler and richer if he could have borne some such picture in mind when he was reflecting on the complex relations between science and religion.

At the same time, as Pfister and others pointed out, Freud's attack on religion does accurately identify many of its weaknesses. The withers of few believers will remain entirely unwrung by Freud's criticisms. Religions – perhaps the highly mythological Abrahamic religions in particular – do indeed tempt people into the childish postures Freud described. Coming from a Christian background, I remember my own shock once, imagining the terrifying consequences of a nuclear war, when I realised I was entertaining a secret thought to the effect: 'God won't let it happen'! Such fantasies clearly merit Freud's attack.

Why should we be interested in psychoanalysis-and-religion?

Before I comment, necessarily very briefly, on a few of the later analysts who wrote about religion in the twentieth century, I want to address one question which may be in the reader's mind. Why should we be interested in this topic of psychoanalysis and religion? If we are psychoanalysts, or if we are believers, isn't that enough? What do we gain from the dialogue?

I think there are several answers to these questions, and I shall outline two of them.

First, how are we to understand 'religion'? Psychoanalysis has often spoken about it in the singular, as if individual religions are all cut from some uniform cloth, and what applies to one applies to all. Perhaps that may be true of the Abrahamic religions, with their sacred scriptures, intense beliefs about specific historical events, and powerful, often blood-curdling, moral imperatives; but are these the same sort of thing as Buddhism, for example, where the emphasis is put on experience and understanding, honest doubts are welcome, and moral shortcomings are rather matter-of-factly described as 'hindrances'?

Looking more closely, however, one finds that Buddhism too has had a tendency to evolve mythological expressions, massively so in Tibet, and the Abrahamic religions have also developed deeply thoughtful and experiential mystical schools, such as Sufism in Islam, even despite the terrible dangers of being labelled heretical. This dichotomy of mythic and mystical is a key issue in understanding all the major religions, and it's interesting that it's present also in what I shall suggest are the two seminal contributions made by British psychonalysts which have influenced the religious debate: Winnicott's notion of transitionality relates to the mythic level, Bion's O to the mystical.

The theologian Raimon Panikkar used to speak of 'lethal dichotomies' which tempt the logical mind to annihilate one term in favour of the other. 'Free will' and 'determinism' are one such lethal couple, 'mind' and 'body' are another. If we refuse to view them as flat contradictions, such dichotomies can give rise to 'creative tensions'. The logical mind wants to make a 'lethal dichotomy' out of different levels of discourse: the mythic and the mystical, the empirical and the mythic, and so on. Psychoanalysis, with its patient recognition of the ubiquity in mental functioning of unconscious phantasy, can help to protect religion from this tendency, and with it from the stark alternatives of fundamentalism and total disbelief. In that sense, psychoanalysis has a contribution to make to religion, perhaps one of particular relevance today.

The second answer points to a benefit to psychoanalysis. Psychoanalysis, given its roots in the biological sciences, is unable to identify an adequate base for the sense of values. Kleinian–Winnicottian object-relations theory confirms that we live in an irreducibly moral universe, but the desire or lack of desire to make reparation to our objects for the damage we have caused them, in internal or external reality, remains a purely affective story. Important as it is, it leaves values as a wholly subjective category. If someone were to decide, like Shakespeare's Richard III, to set aside thoughts of love and be governed by hatred, we might hate him in return, but we would not be able to say he was wrong. (Some of the statements made by terrorists, or by Nazis such as Heinrich Himmler, allow us to see the outcome of such decisions in brutal reality.)[1] It doesn't seem enough to say that our objection to these attitudes is solely a matter of subjective preference, though neither of course can we claim that our values are wholly objective.

I have attempted elsewhere to examine the claims of 'sympathy' (in the sense of an unavoidable involuntary response to affect, not in the sense of 'sympathising') to give a possible base for what is objective in our sense of values (Black 2004). I think this offers a fundamental guideline, but it remains vulnerable to a riposte, perhaps from a Nietzschean superman, who says: 'I choose to despise my sympathetic reaction'. Even the most morally sensitive individuals must of necessity often override their sympathetic responses: ethical decisions are rarely between 'right' and 'wrong', far more often between options that all have something to be said for them.

For this reason, if we are to get beyond a solely affective, subjective basis for values, a further dimension, to give that basis duration and stability, has to be sought for. This cannot be done by interpreting our objects of conviction as purely 'transitional'; it requires a further step of explicit commitment, conscious 'faith', however that is to be understood. William Meissner, addressing this question later in the century, linked faith to 'the supernatural', a traditional term which can't be used intelligibly in a scientific context. Meissner (1984: 216) spoke of the supernatural as an 'irresolvable point of difference [between psychoanalysis and religion] in that the analytic perspective inherently has nothing to say about it'. But in fact this matter of faith or conviction, its origin, its nature, and its externality to the scientific vision, is of inescapable importance to psychoanalysis, and indeed to science more widely. It is implicit in the sort of philosophical understanding of science represented by my quotation from Karl Popper. Rachel B. Blass, in her chapter, suggests that, by the time he came to write *Moses and Monotheism* (1939), Freud too was becoming aware of a need to account for his convictions, which were passionately held, but not founded on scientifically respectable, empirical observations. Blass addresses this crucial question of religious truth very centrally, and is critical of a widespread tendency among modern psychoanalysts to, in her view, sidestep it.

These arguments, that psychoanalysis can help religion by its insights into the formation and functioning of internal objects, and religion can help psychoanalysis by its understanding of the nature of faith or conviction, point to important ways in which the two disciplines can interrelate. There are many others. As time has gone on, and the scope of psychoanalytic thought has deepened and widened, psychoanalysts have become increasingly aware of the powerfully formative influence of the wider culture (in particular as embodied in language) and of the experience of previous generations. This influence has been especially conspicuous in psychoanalytic work with second- and third-generation survivors of the Holocaust and other episodes of genocide and terrorism. Such work helps us to see that matters of vision (how human life and the universe are 'conceived' or imagined), and the values that flow from such vision, not only crucially affect the individual, but also unconsciously influence the larger issue of transgenerational psychological stability. There are questions here which we are still learning to formulate.

The first generations after Freud: the 1940s and 1950s

The first generations of psychoanalysts, daunted by Freud's authority and submitting too, no doubt, to the Zeitgeist, tended not to question his position on religion. (The fate of Jung did not encourage independence of thought in such matters.) Ironically, while Freud was writing the papers of his final period (say, 1917–1939), two great political systems came into being, based precisely on the rejection of religion and the proclamation, in the one case, of a philosophical materialism, and in the other of a racism based on eugenic ideals derived, however distortedly, from Darwin. The consequences of Communism and Nazism were to preoccupy most of the rest of the twentieth century. In both the Soviet Union and Nazi Germany, the scientific establishment, with rare exceptions, meekly put its expertise at the disposal of its new masters. Nazism exploded the psychoanalytic profession, and sent large numbers of its Jewish practitioners, including Freud himself, out of central Europe into Britain and the Americas.

Following Freud's death in 1939, some of those psychoanalysts who ventured to stand apart from the mainstream, particularly among the Jews who had escaped to the United States, began to assert a more positive valuation of some aspects of religion. Karen Horney towards the end of her life became intensely interested in Zen Buddhism. Erik Erikson wrote studies of Luther (1959a) and Gandhi (1969) that contain some of the most perceptive pictures of the place of religion, as a powerful sensitising factor in an individual life, that psychoanalysis has to offer. Erikson came from a family in which his mother could not or would not declare unambiguously who his father was; when he moved to the United States he adopted the name Erikson and declared himself his own father (Friedman 1999: 147). Writing of the young Luther, he shows profound sympathy for a religious young man, defying an all-too-present and forceful father in a somewhat similar passionate search for identity, this time in the complex cultural world of the late Middle Ages. For a modern Jew to understand a medieval Christian monk with such generosity and imagination is truly remarkable, and a great tribute to the flexibility of psychoanalytic thought.

In his age-based schedule of fundamental developmental tasks, Erikson links religion with the earliest stage of all, that in which the baby develops (or fails to develop) 'basic trust' in the world and in himself. Erikson here provides a striking psychological criterion for the value of religion. 'Whosoever says he has religion', says Erikson, 'must derive a faith from it which is transmitted to infants in the form of basic trust; whosoever claims that he does not need religion must derive such basic faith from elsewhere' (1959b: 65). Later he makes a similar point: 'The clinician can only observe that many are proud to be without religion whose children cannot afford their being without it' (1965: 243). This is again the issue of transgenerational psychological stability.

Of these early, independent-minded psychoanalysts, Erich Fromm came closest to anticipating a thought which has intrigued several more recent analytic thinkers (Grotstein 2000; Eigen 1998), that a 'religious' vision may be the ultimate destination of the road on which psychoanalysis is an important early step. Fromm, a refugee to the United States from Germany, was deeply shocked by the passivity of Catholic and liberal Germans in the face of Nazi oppression; they hadn't condoned it but they had failed to take a positive stand against it. (The similar passive acquiescence of the German scientific establishment likewise awakened another brilliant young scientist, the Hungarian Michael Polanyi (1958), then working in Berlin, to the inescapable centrality of moral issues.) Fromm (1942: 181) thought he found the explanation in the 'state of inner tiredness and resignation, which . . . is characteristic of the individual in the present era even in democratic countries'. He attributed this resignation to the moral corrosions of modern culture, in which true values go unaffirmed, and meaningless desires are fomented by the all-pervading, psychologically informed methods of advertising and the mass media. Such techniques, adopted by the Nazis for their own propaganda, are ubiquitous in the world of capitalism. Pursuit of these over-stimulated desires, said Fromm, leaves one confused, exhausted and dissatisfied – and then irritably vulnerable to the sado-masochistic appeal of authoritarianism.

Fromm ends his most famous book, *Fear of Freedom* (1942), with a call for a new faith: 'a faith', he said, 'that is the strongest the human mind is capable of, the faith in life and in truth, and in freedom as the active and spontaneous realisation of the individual self' (1942: 238). It is hard to dissent from that admirable list of abstractions, but hard too to imagine it persuading anyone onto the barricades. Perhaps recognising this, Fromm, like Horney and many others in the United States, later turned with admiration to a more specific 'faith', namely Buddhism. He was particularly attracted to Zen Buddhism which, following the defeat of Japan, D.T. Suzuki brought to the west in the 1950s with impressive charm and scholarship. Fromm's 'humanistic psychoanalysis' approved especially of the positive value Buddhism sets on well-being (as opposed to the 'negative' psychoanalytic goal of reducing neurotic misery), and philosophically he approved of its elimination of the split between self and object, which he felt led to 'affective contaminations and false intellectualisations' (Fromm 1960: 108).

Fromm writes with an attractive ardour. Read today, his writing seems to suffer from the rather diffuse idealism and abstraction of his time, but the issues he raised continue to be central in any discussion of psychoanalysis and religion.

New developments in the mainstream: the 1950s and 1960s

In the 1950s and 1960s, mainstream psychoanalysis in Britain and the United States took diverging paths. The Kleinian development in Britain generated huge intellectual energy (not only in designated Kleinians); American psychoanalysis, excessively tied to psychiatry, was slower to free itself from the burden of authoritarian postures. Both traditions were then further liberated by the wider cultural changes of the 1960s, the decline in deference to authority, and the ubiquitous challenge of feminist and postmodern thinkers to authoritarian 'discourses'.

In Britain, Melanie Klein emphasised that 'unconscious phantasy' was the underlying element crucially influencing all mental activity. A loyal Freudian, she attempted to derive all such phantasy from the two great drives of Freud's final period, Eros and the death drive, but she came under pressure from a new and powerful theory, developed especially by the Scottish analyst Ronald Fairbairn, who claimed that the individual was primarily 'object-seeking' – i.e. governed by a wish for certain sorts of human relationship – rather than drive-driven. To a large extent, the power of Klein's thinking derived from her refusal to accept that these two pictures were contradictory. Unconscious phantasy, for her, was shaped both by the drives directly and by internalised experiences with others which had in turn been constructed and modified by the drives and by yet deeper layers of phantasy and earlier levels of experience.

This vigorous theory derived from the revolution Freud had set going in psychoanalysis in his last twenty years (death drive, psychic structure created by identifications, a deepening recognition of splitting mechanisms), but in Klein's hands these various inchoate ideas gradually came together to make up a coherent and powerful narrative. Klein herself was indifferent to religion, but her theory radically undercut Freud's rather crude distinction between 'illusion' and 'our science which is no illusion'. Illusion, now renamed phantasy, could of course be delusive, but it was also seen as the necessary substrate for any richness or meaning that life could have. Freud's recognition of the power of 'unconscious morality' was now unpacked into Klein's much more detailed account of our

repeated attacks on the 'good object', and the importance of remorse, destructiveness, mourning and the wish to make reparation. Such themes, of course,
have profound echoes in the preoccupations of mature religions. And although
Klein on the whole preferred not to discuss large philosophical themes, her
psychological theory was more compatible than Freud's with the sort of modern
understanding of science represented by my quotation from Karl Popper.

Seen from a British perspective, the crucial changes that gradually caused
analytic thinking to become more hospitable to religion were made by two men,
Donald Winnicott and Wilfred Bion, both profoundly influenced by Klein.
Winnicott in the 1950s set out to study what, in a resonant phrase, he called 'the
substance of illusion'. He introduced his notion of 'transitionality', initially as
part of an account of development in infants and toddlers (Winnicott 1958).
A 'transitional object' is an object, perhaps a soft toy or a strip of blanket, which
for the baby can be the target of any projection he or she currently needs to
make. In the baby's mind, the transitional object is neither 'internal', in Klein's
sense, nor external, in the ordinary adult sense; its reality is, so to speak, the baby's
invention. The possibility of transitional phenomena, said Winnicott, emerges
out of the mother's special capacity for relating and adapting to the needs and
wishes of her infant. This enables the infant to have 'the illusion that what the
infant creates really exists'.

A transitional object is 'created', as Winnicott puts it, by the infant's phantasy;
its reality, external to phantasy, can be disregarded and must not be challenged.
To ask factual questions about the object – 'Did you conceive of this or was it
presented to you from without?' – is to annihilate it as a transitional object. To
ask if the teddy bear is *really* what the child treats it as – a lovable friend, a safe
protector, a bad child to be punished, an unwanted child to be abandoned, etc.
– is to make a category mistake. The value of the teddy bear lies in the phantasy
that comes to life in its presence; its eventual fate is to be 'decathected' – its
function diffuses itself more widely into the child's environment, over which the
child is now beginning to have more control, and the transitional object itself
drifts into limbo. 'It is not forgotten and it is not mourned.'

Out of this experience with one or more transitional objects, the wider
'transitional space' of play and, increasingly, shared play develops. Once again,
play is intensely important, is based in illusion, and cannot be challenged in reality
terms without destroying it. Winnicott thought that in these transitional phenomena we see the roots of adult creativity and shared culture – ultimately of
all the cultural worlds of art, religion and creative scientific activity (Winnicott
1971). This idea, as we shall see, has influenced many subsequent psychoanalysts
concerned with religion (including Kenneth Wright and Mark Epstein in the
present volume).

The other British analyst whose theory was to become especially influential
in thinking about religion was Wilfred Bion. Perhaps more than any other
psychoanalytic thinker, Bion struggled to find an accurate language to describe

the different sorts of operation that take place in the mind. Oppressed by the multitudinous associations which all our ordinary language for mental experience carries, he invented a sort of mathematical notation which would convey in an abstract diagram ('the Grid') the different types and levels of mental event. Artificial as this sounds, Bion used his notation very creatively to get a grasp on how thoughts become 'thinkable' in three domains: in psychoanalytic sessions, in mother–child interaction, and in psychotic functioning.

Like Freud, Bion was influenced by Kant, and he adopted Kant's fundamental belief that 'things-in-themselves' are unknowable: we can only know phenomena, never 'noumena'. To describe unknowable ultimate reality, Bion chose the symbol O, standing for Origin (the point at which the axes of a graph intersect; he was concerned that O should not be read as zero). O, said Bion (1965), can never be attained or put into words, but in our attempts to 'tell the truth' of our experience, whether as patient or as analyst, we are attempting to get closer to O. He sometimes speaks of O as the 'absolute facts' (of an analytic session, for example) (Bion 1965). These absolute facts can to some extent become known if certain 'invariants' are preserved between O and our attempts to represent it.

In this theory, O seems to have moved some way from Kant's 'things-in-themselves', and it's hard to know what to make of Bion's 'invariants' that are somehow present in something unknowable. Perhaps, however, we should embrace this difficulty as a necessary paradox. Seen from a religious angle, Bion appears to be dealing with the same puzzle that religious thinkers struggle with, of having different levels of truth that must (surely?) map on to one another; but how is that possible, if they are really on different levels? The Hindu upanishadic notion of *maya*, a world that is illusory but not exactly unreal, perhaps resonates with the relativised world of truth that Bion's O leaves us inhabiting. (Parallels with Indian thought may not be accidental. Bion was born and spent the first eight years of his life in India. When he died aged 82 he was within two months of returning for the first time to his native country (Bleandonu 1994). In his autobiography, Bion (1982) spoke of the ineradicable pain of his early exile.) Recent psychoanalytic thinkers on religion, particularly those drawn to Indian thought like Jeffrey B. Rubin, Mark Epstein and Malcom Cunningham in this book, have often found in Bion's ideas a valuable point of entry.

There has been no consensus among Bion's commentators on what to make of O. Neville Symington, who speaks of psychoanalysis as a 'spiritual activity', and Michael Eigen, who describes himself as a 'psychoanalytic mystic', have both based themselves in important ways on Bion's ideas; James Grotstein (2000: 290) perhaps goes furthest, believing that when he wrote of O, 'Bion was implying that the immanent "incarnate Godhead" is the thinker of "the (alleged) thoughts without a thinker"' – it being part of Bion's theory that thoughts can arise in our minds prior to the existence of an apparatus with which to think them.

In contrast to such writers, Rafael Lopez-Corvo, author of *The Dictionary of the Thought of W.R. Bion*, writes. 'I am unable to find any religious position in any of [Bion's] formulations . . . even when he seems to defend the position of the mystic, he is just appreciating the attitude behind the human act . . . not [the mystic's] beliefs' (2003: 316). Perhaps all one can say is that when a thinker introduces into his or her thought the concept of 'the unknowable', there is no way of controlling what we may imagine it contains.

For our present purposes, however, we may note that there is a difference between an account of *transitionality*, in which the question of objective truth is not to be raised, and Bion's account of O, in which there is an objective truth, but it remains forever beyond our grasp. I understand this contrast to parallel the contrast between mythic and mystical ways of thinking, discussed by Rodney Bomford, in particular, in this book.

Developments in America: the 1970s and 1980s

Out of these two theories, Winnicott's of transitionality and Bion's of O, most subsequent psychoanalytic writing on religion has emerged. (I regret that I am having to confine my remarks to the world of English-speaking psycho-analysis, and even with that limitation I am very aware that this brief sampling unfairly omits many thinkers who are very worthy of inclusion.) In the changed climate of the 1970s, American analysts such as Ana-Maria Rizzuto and William Meissner were able to speak with a profound understanding of religious matters.

I shall mention each of these at more length, but it is of interest to note that older analysts too were liberated by the new atmosphere. The highly respected senior analyst Hans Loewald, in a lecture given at Yale in 1978, focused once again on Freud's exchange with Romain Rolland about the 'oceanic feeling'. Loewald's comments are tantalisingly brief but extremely penetrating. He suggested that what Rolland was getting at was a different way in which time can be experienced. 'Eternity', not meaning everlastingness, but in the traditional sense of a *nunc stans*, a timeless moment, may represent, Loewald (1978: 65) suggested, a new construction of consciousness which can occur when 'primary and secondary modes of mentation may be known together'. He links such moments with babyhood, with dream, and also with profound emotional and mystical experience.

Loewald thought that experiences of this kind may be profoundly disturbing. Far from religion being an escape from reality, as Freud contended, perhaps, says Loewald, our pursuit of 'the active conduct and direction of a reasonably successful life' shields us from much more disturbing reality. Freud, says Loewald (1978: 72), 'by avoiding a further understanding of religion remained in this respect on the safe ground of the rational ego'. And he ends his lecture rather movingly: 'Some of the things I have discussed I have wanted to say for a long time'. I think in this courageous lecture we glimpse the oppressiveness of the conformist culture of psychoanalysis which at last was lifting.

In 1979, Ana-Maria Rizzuto published *The Birth of the Living God*, the first major empirical and clinical study by a psychoanalyst of the forces involved in shaping what she called the 'God image' or the 'God representation'. Using Winnicott's concept, she emphasises that, from a psychological point of view, God can be only an 'illusory transitional object', but she then goes on to make a very important distinction from the ordinary application of such terms. The child may indeed go out from home with 'his pet God under his arm', but he will then encounter an official God supplied to him by his culture. The resulting complex conflation, she says, goes on being altered and modified throughout life, even if the individual believes he has put religion behind him – just as the internalised parents are never finally abandoned. 'For most people, the occasion for deciding on the final representation of their God comes in contemplating their own impending death' (Rizzuto 1979: 8).

Rizzuto stays clearly in her role as psychoanalyst, commenting on religious phenomena in her patients. She is less concerned with what people consciously 'think they believe' than with the way they use their religious objects. Often, she says,

> when the human objects of real life acquire profound psychic meaning, God, like a forlorn teddy-bear, is left in a corner of the attic . . . A death, great pain or intense joy may bring him back for an occasional hug or for further mistreatment or rejection, and then he is forgotten again.
>
> (Rizzuto 1979: 179)

At the end of her beautifully written book, Rizzuto declares her relation to Freud (who often seems, in these religious discussions, to be like the undiscardable teddy bear). She has had to disagree with him, she said – but only with one Freud, 'the Freud who *believes* that man lives on the bread of knowledge alone' (her italics). She follows 'the other Freud . . . the Freud of object-relations' and the Oedipus complex, the Freud who said: 'The idea of a single great god – an idea which must be recognised as a completely justified memory . . . has a compulsive character: it *must* be believed' (Rizzuto 1979: 212). (She is quoting from *Moses and Monotheism*.)

Five years later, in 1984, William Meissner published *Psychoanalysis and Religious Experience*. Meissner, a Jesuit and a professor of psychiatry, is perhaps, of all the psychoanalysts who have written about religion, the one most fully qualified to do so. His writing has an authority and scholarly grounding in both disciplines which is inevitably rare.

After looking in detail at elements in Freud's personal psychology that may have affected his attitude to religion, and after examining Freud's theory and his

13

exchange with Oskar Pfister following publication of *The Future of an Illusion*, Meissner comes to his own views. He outlines a five stage developmental schema for 'faith' (based broadly on Kohut's account of the integration of narcissism). So far as I am aware, this remains the most detailed attempt by a psychoanalyst to picture religious development. It finds a place for experiences of mystical vision (which he distinguishes cautiously from psychotic regression), for animism and magical thinking, for intense anxieties to do with rectitude and punishment, for attitudes of responsible moral concern within restricted groups, and (the final stage) for attitudes of balance, understanding and wisdom in which the limitations of one's own group and tradition can be recognised and the validity of other traditions and groups can be evaluated and acknowledged with good humour. Although Meissner's attitude towards religion is almost opposite, in this final 'modality' he is addressing the same concern that Ronald Britton discusses in this book: how does a person come to be his or her own authority and reclaim the capacity for judgement from the superego and (Meissner would add) from the group?

Commenting on his own schema, Meissner writes:

> In this light, Freud's account [of religion] can be seen as presenting critical insight into a narrow range of the dynamics of belief, artificially isolated from the full range and complexity of human religious experience. The broadening of the psychoanalytic account to include the full range of that spectrum is a major task for the future.
>
> (Meissner 1984: 158)

Basing himself on Winnicott, and quoting Rizzuto, Meissner aligns himself with those who view 'illusion' as a vehicle to gain access to reality. 'It is through illusion . . . that the human spirit is nourished' (1984: 177). He discusses the fact that religious symbols 'work' only for those within the cultural group they belong to; few believers would be able to maintain their belief, for example in the real presence of Christ in the Eucharist, if participation in the liturgy 'were not surrounded with a panoply of concrete symbolic expressions of what is basically a highly theological and suprasensory understanding' (1984: 181).

Meissner brings us here to the nub of the issues about religious truth and about using Winnicott's ideas of transitionality in matters of religion. For while the 'God representation' may well be transitional, what about the theological understanding of which it is the symbolic expression? Is that illusion too? If so, what is the relation of the believer to it?

These questions go beyond anything psychoanalysis can answer, and Meissner addresses them only briefly, though with his customary steadiness. 'The assertion of faith', he writes, 'carries with it a transcendent element . . . it is not merely a reassertion of basic trust; it is, rather, a creative assertion of something beyond trust and far more significant' (1984: 183). He leads us to the edge of a realm of irreducible mystery. 'The religious view of man', says Meissner, 'is specifically supernatural' (1984: 226). No science in his view, not even psychoanalysis, can have anything to say about it.

Meissner's writing has great profundity, and no other psychoanalyst has written of religion with comparable thoroughness. Nevertheless, his comments on the supernatural will only satisfy those who are able to believe in a 'revelation' that cannot be subjected to psychological examination. Most psychoanalytic thinkers would probably be unable to accept the idea of such a revelation; but, if not on that, on what can 'faith' be based? When I first encountered the word 'supernatural' in Meissner's writing, I had a sort of instinctive revulsion from it. On reflection, however, I think it is true that faith cannot be based on what science has the power to assess. In my own chapter, I attempt to look at whether 'transcendence' can have any meaning, in the absence of supernatural revelation.

The contributions in this book

In the later 1980s, the trickle of psychoanalytic interest in religion began to broaden, and during the 1990s and early 2000s it has become something of a flood. Edwin Wallace, Stanley Leavey, Moshe Halevi Spero, Neville Symington and many others have written about religion thoughtfully and from many angles. The interest in eastern religions, Buddhism in particular, which had been incubating in the west since the 1950s, and which following the Japanese influence was greatly stimulated by the arrival of refugee teachers from Tibet, also emerged into psychoanalytic thinking during this period. Excellent writers, including Jack Kornfield, Jack Engler, Nina Coltart, Mark Epstein, Michael Eigen and Jeffrey B. Rubin, led the way in finding understandings that could do justice to both Buddhist and psychoanalytic readings of mental experience. (For a useful anthology of writings on Buddhism and psychoanalysis, see Molino 1998.)

This period is that of the contributors to this volume (who include Symington, Epstein and Rubin), and this volume is intended to give some overview of the variety of ideas that are now current. It is not intended to present a 'school' or to suggest that there is any sort of consistent account of religion in modern psychoanalysis, and the reader should be prepared for radical divergencies.

I have divided the chapters into four parts. The groupings are rather arbitrary, but I hope the division will help to bring certain issues into focus. Part One addresses directly the issue of religious truth: is there such a thing, and if so what might it look like? Part Two discusses religious stories with an eye to the psychological truths they may contain. The largest group, Part Three, considers the ways in which religions (or, in one case, 'spirituality') function: what is the nature of religious experience, and how does it link with what psychoanalysis knows? Finally, in Part Four are chapters that discuss echoes between psycho-analysis and specific religious traditions, including Freud's own tradition of Judaism.

I have put Rachel B. Blass's chapter first because it makes a fundamental challenge to much current psychoanalytic thinking about religion: she asks what is happening to the claim of the ordinary believer that his or her religion is 'true'. The rise of fundamentalisms all around the world, in all three Abrahamic religions and also bizarrely in Hinduism (whose capacious appetite for schools and deities might seem to conflict with the very notion of fundamentalism) represents a passionate assertion by practising religionists of their belief that they are not just talking about 'transitional objects' or cultural signifiers but about supremely important reality. The phenomenon of the religiously motivated suicide-bomber has drawn our attention to this fact in recent years in the most powerful and shocking way. Blass thinks we can best understand such depth of feeling by reflecting on the source of our own convictions, whatever these may be. She suggests that in *Moses and Monotheism* Freud, towards the end of his life, was grappling with the fact that he too was governed by convictions – for example, in the value of the pursuit of truth – which were not arrived at for scientific, objective reasons. Perhaps Freud was starting to ask himself the kind of questions that would later preoccupy Karl Popper and Michael Polanyi.

In the following chapter, M. Fakhry Davids uses clinical material to examine the question of the relation between the 'religious object' of God and the ordinary internal objects that a child derives by projection and introjection from his personal history. In a way somewhat reminiscent of Rizzuto, but from a Kleinian point of view, Davids shows how the individual's conception of a God may be deeply coloured or wholly distorted by personal experience. He anato-mises the building of the necessary 'illusion' on which trust is based, pointing out that mere mathematical realism will never make room for an emotional tonality that is essential if life is to be lived satisfactorily. He addresses the fact that religious objects have a nature that is derived from the community of believers, and it will be very much an individual matter how far the particular believer will want to enquire into this.

I have put my own contribution into this first group. It raises the question of whether we can give any meaning to the religious use of the word 'transcendent' without departing from a scientific stance. I suggest that if we are to do so both psychoanalysis and some religious aspiration may have to adapt a bit. I have cast the chapter in the form of a 'thought experiment'; borrowing some ideas from neuroscience, I suggest that there may be a place for a 'contemplative position' analogous to the paranoid–schizoid and depressive positions.

In Part Two are two chapters, by Ronald Britton and David Millar, in which familiar religious stories are examined to see what psychological truths (or untruths) they may convey. Britton, of all the contributors to this volume, probably comes closest to Freud's view of religion. He discusses the biblical Book of Job with a lively concern for the health of Job's ego. He sees God as acting the role of a crushing superego, seeking like much religion to make Job feel guilty for thinking his own thoughts about his experience. Britton has written a psychoanalytic contribution, not a general indictment of religion, but like Freud he draws attention to an important and widespread way in which religious piety may be psychologically damaging. Psychoanalytically, the focus of his chapter is on the crucial question of the place of 'judgement' and whether it is to be seen as a function retained by the superego or available for full adoption by the ego.

David Millar looks at the Christian story of Christ's birth, which he understands psychologically as dealing with issues to do with the arrival of the 'new baby': how do we allow it to exist, what do we do with our hatred and murderous impulses, and how can we maintain our relation to a good object? Via consideration of the psychological functions of the Virgin birth, Herod's massacre of the innocents, and so on, he goes on to examine in detail Dickens's novel *A Christmas Carol*; he looks in particular at the changing role of the superego in governing Scrooge's behaviour and perception of his history.

Part Three has five chapters, all dealing in various ways with the question summarised in Michael Parsons' title: 'Ways of Transformation'. These authors are concerned with the effects on religionists of their religious experiences. Parsons himself finds meaning in a very wide range of traditions, and is content to put on one side the wish to think about them in terms of ascertainable truth or falsehood. His careful discussion of religious language reminds us what a rich and thought-filled history the great religious traditions have. More than any other contributor to this volume, Parsons draws attention to the huge cultural variety of religions; despite his hospitality to them he is aware of how deep-rooted the different traditions are, and how different they are from one another.

Jeffrey B. Rubin is well known as a psychoanalyst who has written specifically about psychoanalysis in relation to Buddhism. Here, however, he writes more generally about 'spirituality', a popular term whose several meanings he carefully anatomises. Rubin writes out of both clinical and personal experience, emphasising in particular how spiritual experiences can seem to overcome our sense of separateness from others and from the natural world. (He begins his chapter with a vivid story from his own experience, of an episode in which time seemed to change its nature.) He argues that both spirituality and psychoanalysis have been impoverished by their failure to enter into mutually respectful dialogue.

With Francis Grier and Kenneth Wright we return to the central psychoanalytic territory of adult experience and its relation to infancy. Francis Grier uses clinical examples to discuss 'adoration' – a word that occurs spontaneously to baby-observers watching certain sorts of mother–baby interaction. Grier suggests that early experiences of adoration (and of being adored) are of great value to the developing infant, but as a clinical practitioner, working with couples as well as individuals, he also shows ways in which in later life adoration or the longing for it can derail adult relationships. He uses poems from ecstatic mystical traditions to illustrate some of the many forms religious adoration can take.

Kenneth Wright speaks of the passionate need of the baby to be brought into emotional existence by the mother's recognition. He emphasises the importance of a preverbal depth of experience which will never be verbalisable. (This theme, which appears most vividly I think in Wright's chapter, is one of the linking themes throughout the book: it appears in Neville Symington's chapter, and also in Francis Grier's and my own, and perhaps it is a latent presence in almost all of the chapters.) Rejecting Freud's attempts to derive altruistic love (*agape*) from libido (*eros*), Wright suggests that the mother's face is the central object in a quite separate developmental line, linking with experience of the sacred. He shows how attempts to put preverbal experience into words lead naturally to the use of language with 'religious' weight and depth.

Neville Symington speaks of religion as the guarantor of 'civilisation' (meaning, as I understand him, not the mere development of city-dwelling but a set of moral and emotional attitudes). In this chapter, he discusses religion as a system developed by human beings to enhance their capacity for mental representation of their experience, and as such crucial to full humanity. Symington has written extensively and from a very original angle on religion and psychoanalyis: his chapter is a further contribution to what is now a substantial body of work. He has also (together with Joan Symington) written on Bion (Symington and Symington 1996), and the concept of 'existence knowledge' that he develops here is part of the fruit of his deep engagement with Bion's thought. Symington's moral passion, and his concern for the values of 'civilisation', sometimes give his writing an urgency comparable to that of Erich Fromm in the 1940s.

In Part Four are four chapters that each offer a view of psychoanalysis in relation to a particular religious tradition. Stephen Frosh examines ways in which Freud's Jewish identity may have influenced the science he created. Frosh suggests that despite Freud's overt repudiation of Judaism, psychoanalysis has retained fundamental qualities that characterise the Judaic tradition. Questioning some of the specific parallels that have been proposed, for example by David Bakan, he nevertheless finds ways to formulate certain deep similarities of shape and style that perhaps make the Nazi epithet for psychoanalysis, 'the Jewish science', more insightful than its anti-Semitic originators knew.

Frosh is an academic psychologist who has written widely on Freud and psychoanalytic issues. Mark Epstein is one of the pioneers in writing about psychoanalysis and Buddhism, from the standpoint of a practitioner of both disciplines. Here, he compares the Buddhist 'no-self' teaching with Winnicott's notion of 'unintegration'. He tracks the development of this idea in Winnicott's thought, noting that in his earlier writings Winnicott spoke of the unintegrated state as frightening and almost psychotic. By the end of his life, he came to see it as one of the preconditions of 'feeling real'. Epstein's discussion also has the effect of demythologising Buddhist Enlightenment and making its value recognisable in an understandable way.

Malcom Cunningham contributes a lucid introduction to Advaita Vedanta, linking it with psychoanalysis and in particular with Bion's thought. (Bion, as I have suggested above, might not have thought this entirely strange.) Vedanta has a special place already in psychoanalytic history because of Romain Rolland's connection with it. It became well known in the west in the 1890s, after Sri Ramakrishna's disciple Vivekananda travelled to Chicago to the World Parliament of Religions; later, Aldous Huxley and Christopher Isherwood were both members of the movement. Cunningham's account gives a philosophical background that helps us to understand what may have been in Rolland's mind when he used the phrase 'oceanic feeling'.

I have put last a chapter by Rodney Bomford, a theologian who has written of psychoanalysis using the thought of Ignacio Matte Blanco. He writes here of a crucial theme, relevant to almost all the contributions to this volume: that of the different levels of religious discourse, in particular the empirical, the mythic and the mystical. Much of the difficulty rational and scientific thinkers have with religion has to do with the confusion of these three levels (and religious believers themselves regularly confuse them). Fundamentalism, that tragically important theme of the first years of the twenty-first century, springs essentially from the failure of religious believers themselves to remember the 'level' they are thinking at. Eastern religions are often thought to have a more elaborated philosophical understanding of these matters, but Bomford's informed historical exposition shows how intelligently and thoughtfully they have been discussed in Christianity.

I present the following contributions with an awareness that they are very various, both in their religious and in their psychoanalytic preoccupations. They represent an honest and deeply thoughtful attempt by their authors to address matters of fundamental importance. The reader will find they make up a diverse tapestry, but one in which, as he or she examines it, more threads than one might expect glint and echo each other from different parts of the fabric.

Note

1 Consider, for example, the phrase 'a correct attitude' in the following:

> If 10,000 Russian women die of exhaustion in digging an anti-tank ditch, this is of no interest to me except to the extent to which the ditch is readied for Germany . . . We Germans, who are the only people in the world who have a correct attitude towards animals, also have a correct attitude towards these animal human beings.
>
> (H. Himmler, speech to the Nazi Gauleiters, 4 October 1943, quoted in Sereny 2000: 28)

References

Alvarez, A. (1992) *Live Company: Psychoanalytic Psychotherapy with Autistic, Borderline, Deprived and Abused Children*. London: Routledge.

Bion, W.R. (1965) *Transformations*. London: Heinemann.

Bion, W.R. (1982) *The Long Week-end 1897–1918*. Abingdon: Fleetwood.

Black, D.M. (2004) Sympathy reconfigured: Some reflections on sympathy, empathy and the discovery of values. *International Journal of Psychoanalysis* 85(3): 579–595.

Bleandonu, G. (1994) *Wilfred Bion: His Life and Works 1897–1979*, trans C. Pajaczkowska. London: Free Association Books.

Darwin, C. (1859) *The Origin of Species*. London: John Murray.

Eigen, M. (1998) *The Psychoanalytic Mystic*. New York: ESF.

Erikson, E.H. (1959a) *Young Man Luther*. London: Faber and Faber.

Erikson, E.H. (1959b) *Identity and the Life Cycle*. New York: International University Press.

Erikson, E.H. (1965) *Childhood and Society*, revised edition. Harmondsworth: Penguin.

Erikson, E.H. (1969) *Gandhi's Truth: On the Origins of Militant Non-Violence*. New York: Norton.

Freud, S. (1895) *Studies in Hysteria*. SE 2.

Freud, S. (1927) *The Future of an Illusion*. SE 21.

Freud, S. (1930) *Civilization and its Discontents*. SE 21.

Freud, S. (1939) *Moses and Monotheism*. SE 23.

Friedman, L. (1999) *Identity's Architect: A Biography of Erik H. Erikson*. Cambridge, MA: Harvard University Press.

Fromm, E. (1942) *Fear of Freedom*. London: Routledge.

Fromm, E. (1960) *Psychoanalysis and Zen Buddhism*. Harmondsworth: Penguin.

Grotstein, J. (2000) *Who is the Dreamer, who Dreams the Dream?* London and Hillsdale, NJ: Analytic Press.

Kant, I. (1929) *Critique of Pure Reason*, trans. N. Kemp Smith. London: Macmillan.

Loewald, H. (1978) *Psychoanalysis and the History of the Individual*. New Haven, CT: Yale University Press.

Lopez-Corvo, R. (2003) *The Dictionary of the Thought of W.R. Bion*. London: Karnac.

Meissner, W.W. (1984) *Psychoanalysis and Religious Experience*. New Haven, CT and London: Yale University Press.

Molino, A. (ed.) (1998) *The Couch and the Tree: Dialogues in Psychoanalysis and Buddhism*. New York: North Point Press, Farrar Straus and Giroux; London: Constable.

Polanyi, M. (1958) *Personal Knowledge: Towards a Post-Critical Philosophy*. London: Routledge and Kegan Paul.

Popper, K. (1959) *The Logic of Scientific Discovery*. London: Routledge (2002).

Rizzuto, A-M. (1979) *The Birth of the Living God*. Chicago: University of Chicago Press.

Sereny, G. (2000) *The German Trauma*. Harmondsworth: Penguin.

Symington, J. and Symington, N. (1996) *The Clinical Thinking of Wilfred Bion*. London: Routledge.

Winnicott, D.W. (1958) Transitional objects and transitional phenomena, in *Through Paediatrics to Psychoanalysis*. London: Hogarth Press.

Winnicott, D.W. (1971) *Playing and Reality*. Harmondsworth: Penguin.

PART ONE

The possibility of religious truth

1

BEYOND ILLUSION

Psychoanalysis and the question of religious truth

Rachel B. Blass

The relationship between psychoanalysis and religion has been changing since the mid 1980s. During this period numerous psychoanalytic books and articles have appeared that reject what is commonly presented as Freud's reductionistic understanding of religion and his negative evaluation of it as an expression of infantile needs. While the view that religion should not be so simply reduced may have entered the mainstream of psychoanalysis, many of these newer writings on religion go further to claim that, from a psychoanalytic perspective, certain forms of religious belief and practice should be positively evaluated as a healthy development, an expression of a kind of achievement – emotional, moral, spiritual and cultural – that could be expected to emerge through a successful psychoanalytic process. The names associated with this shift are Michael Eigen, James Jones, Sudhir Kakar, William Meissner, Ana-Maria Rizzuto, Neville Symington and others, all of whom, interestingly, rely on the thinking of Donald Winnicott, although not exclusively so. The degree to which this positive evaluation has become integral to psychoanalytic thinking may vary according to geographical location, but I think one finds that, overall among analysts today, there is a much greater openness to and acceptance of certain religious beliefs and practices than ever before. In this chapter I will argue that this shift towards conciliation between psychoanalysis and religion is misleading. The conciliation is between psychoanalysis and religion in a specific sense of the term only. In this specific sense of religion the question most central to the traditional Judeo-Christian believer, the question of God's existence, is not only bracketed, but also no longer considered relevant or meaningful. Religion is regarded not as an expression of knowledge or truth pertaining to the nature of reality, the transcendent reality of God, but more as a kind of self- or relational experiencing within a realm of illusion. Conciliation thus becomes possible because, in this postmodern, non-realist sense of religion, there is no longer room for the concern (which troubled Freud) that religious belief is a distortion of reality. I think, however, that, in focusing on religion in this new and limited sense, differences and tensions between psychoanalysis and religion are concealed and the distinct nature of psychoanalysis as concerned with reality and a search for truth is blurred. Paradoxically, perhaps, by blurring this distinct nature of psychoanalysis a meaningful common ground for psychoanalysis and religion in its traditional sense is also lost. My argument is composed of two parts. In the first and main section of the chapter, I describe the major shifts that have taken place in psychoanalysis's approach to religion and some of the problematic implications and consequences of these shifts, both for psychoanalysis and for religion. I show how, in these shifts, the analytic concern with truth gets lost and how it is this concern that underlies the tension between psychoanalysis and religion from Freud's time onwards. I go on to show that this concern can also meaningfully connect between psychoanalysis and religion. In the second section, by bringing to the fore a neglected dimension of Freud's thought in his *Moses and Monotheism* (1939), I point to a deeper connection between the two. Through Freud's attempt in that book to understand what underlies our conviction in ideas that are beyond scientific demonstration, a more complex understanding of psychoanalysis's notion of truth evolves. Through this notion of truth, psychoanalysis and religion may be regarded as two opposite perspectives on the nature of the reality that lies at the foundations of our sense of an ethically compelling 'Otherness' within us. While both perspectives strive to grasp this truth, they will, according to Freud, inevitably fail to do so. I argue that it is in this shared failure that a place for dialogue between psychoanalysis and religion emerges without blurring the fundamental differences between them.

Freud's notorious rejection of religion

Freud's negative attitude towards religion is clearly stated and often cited. The basic text most commonly referred to in this regard is his *The Future of an Illusion* (1927). There, he points to the illusionary nature of religion – in other words, that the foundations and origins of belief lie in wishful thinking. And, while he acknowledges that this in itself does not put in question the value or truth of religion, he emphasises the infantile nature of the wishes involved. He writes that, when 'a psychologist who does not deceive himself' assesses the process of human development,

> the idea forces itself upon him that religion is comparable to a childhood neurosis, and he is optimistic enough to suppose that mankind will sur-

mount this neurotic phase, just as so many children grow out of their similar neurosis.

(Freud 1927: 53)

Moreover, Freud does ultimately put in question the validity of religious claims:

Religious doctrines will have to be discarded . . . in the long run nothing can withstand reason and experience, and the contradiction which religion offers to both is all too palpable. Even purified religious ideas cannot escape this fate.

(Freud 1927: 54)

A few years later, in his *Civilization and its Discontents* (1930), he refers to religion most explicitly as delusionary. There, he speaks of the case in which 'a considerable number of people in common . . . attempt to procure a certainty of happiness and protection against suffering through a delusional remoulding of reality' and he adds that 'The religions of mankind must be classed among the mass delusions of this kind' (Freud 1930: 81).

The new psychoanalytic approaches to religion

Ever since the time these critical views were initially put forth, there have been voices coming from within psychoanalysis (in addition to the numerous ones coming from without) that have taken issue with Freud. The first of these analytic voices is that of Oskar Pfister, the Swiss psychoanalyst and Lutheran minister who was a major interlocutor of Freud's on matters of religion. Pfister's objections were made public at Freud's request in his article 'The illusion of a future', published in German in *Imago* in 1928 (and significantly republished in English in the *International Journal of Psychoanalysis* sixty-five years later: Roazen, 1993). It is possible to follow a continuous, albeit rather thin, stream of critical writings that ensued in the following fifty years. Zilboorg, Erikson, Fromm and Loewald are the most prominent of the writers who explicitly rejected what was considered to be Freud's central view of religion as illusionary, delusionary, infantile and neurotic. The more dominant trend, however, was the acceptance of this Freudian view (Kakar 1991: 56). Beginning approximately in the mid 1980s, a change in this trend began to take place. Among some of the more provocative book titles directly addressing the issue of psychoanalysis and religion that have appeared since then are *The Birth of the Living God* (Rizzuto 1979), *The Psychoanalytic Mystic* (Eigen 1998), *The Analyst and the Mystic* (Kakar 1991), *Soul on the Couch* (Spezzano and Gargiulo 1997), *Emotion and Spirit* (Symington 1994), *Ecstasy* (Eigen 2001), *Terror and Transformation* (Jones 2002), accompanied by some more low-key titles such as *Psychoanalysis and Religious Experience*

(Meissner 1984) and *Psychoanalysis and Religion* (Smith and Handelman 1990). In these books, and in the numerous articles that have appeared during these years, religion is understood in the light of psychoanalytic theory (and especially through some of its recent developments) as a normal, healthy, positive phenomenon. The understanding expressed in these books reflects a broader sentiment within the psychoanalytic field in general of tolerance and acceptance of religious belief and believers. While psychoanalysis is, perhaps, one of the most atheistic professions in terms of official religious affiliation and practice of its members, there has nevertheless evolved a prevalent analytic attitude that considers religious belief and practice to be not beyond interpretation, but something not to be questioned by analysis – a kind of private, personal decision, which may be positively regarded if it allows for growth and well-being. This is in sharp contrast to an attitude that prevailed in the shadow of Freud's *The Future of an Illusion*, an attitude in which Otto Fenichel (1938: 316), for example, could write of how, as his patients progressed in their analyses, they became gradually liberated from their religion and Helene Deutsch had to conclude, regretfully, that a Catholic nun she had treated so effectively for her obsessional neurosis was unable to accomplish a real cure since she remained within her religious order (1951: 189, cited in Leavy 1990: 50). I think that today, even if an analyst held such views on the success and failure of analyses, he may not feel completely free to state them openly in front of a contemporary psychoanalytic audience.[1] Why not? What changed? On the basis of a close study of all the recent books and articles that have appeared on psychoanalysis and religion, I think that it is possible to point to two basic changes that have taken place. First, new criteria and new findings are introduced, which allow for the conclusion that there is a connection between religion in some senses of the term and psychic well-being. What I refer to here is how many of the recent analytic writings on religion determine its value on the basis of the fact that religion may allow for the expression, and even reinforcement, of various desirable human capacities for relationship, such as trust, intimacy, care and community (Wallwork and Wallwork 1990: 161), and provide an important means for articulating basic aspects of self-experience. As James Jones, the very prolific American writer on psychoanalysis and religion, states,

> religious moments . . . allow us to enter again and again into that timeless and transforming psychological space from which renewal and creativity emerge . . . [there,] we gain access again to the formative (and reformative) experience at the heart of selfhood.
>
> (Jones 1991: 134)

These writings suggest that such capacities and experiences can be regarded as relevant factors in determining the value of religion only in the light of post-Freudian psychoanalysis, which replaces oedipal notions of maturity with notions of maturity that focus on interpersonal relatedness and self-experience (with varying degrees of differentiation and intensity). But the new, positive appreciation of religion rests not only on the evolution of psychoanalytic notions, but also, at times, on the evolution of religious ones. At the far end of the spectrum of changes that are introduced, spiritual development and encounter with the sacred become synonymous with analytic kinds of transformation of intentions and self-experiencing. For example, Symington, in his 1994 book on psychoanalysis and religion, redefines religion and spirituality so that, in their mature forms, they are compatible 'with the denial of God's existence' (p. 88) and equated with willing the good, disciplining one's intentions and upholding a morality based on freedom and responsibility for the other. Thus he can ask, 'If the goal of psychoanalysis is the transformation of bad actions into good, [and he does argue that this is indeed its goal] is it not right to call this a spiritual aim?' (p. 181). And he can readily answer positively, adding that both theology and psychoanalysis have yet to recognise that 'the greatest spiritual encounters' (p. 130) occur between patient and analyst. Moreover, being a practice geared towards the transformation of narcissism into concern for others, psychoanalysis is the pinnacle of mature religiosity and a much-needed substitute for the failed primitive religions of revelation (p. 75). Coming from a very different angle and seemingly relying on the writings of Lacan, Bion and Winnicott, Michael Eigen speaks of the 'holiness' of therapy (1998: 42), and the 'mystical' and 'sacred' (2001: 37) nature of psychoanalysis and the self-experiencing that these allow for. He tells us that psychoanalysis is, for him, at times 'a form of prayer' (Eigen 1998: 11). Never really defining what holiness, mysticism, sacredness and prayer are, it becomes apparent that he is using these terms to refer to a general and vague kind of openness to experiencing. In a rather ecstatically written (albeit typical) section of one of his books, he responds to the question of what he means by God, and states, 'God could be anything . . . to blank oneself out and be totally open to whatever currents pulse this way or that . . . whether you're into body, or emotion . . . Taoist or Buddhist, whatever, it feels good' (Eigen 1998: 193, the last two ellipses appear in the original). The second change that has taken place in the psychoanalytic understanding of religion is of a more epistemological kind, and focuses on the issue of illusion. What is argued is that what stood in the way of Freud's acceptance of religion was his negative and limited attitude to illusion, which allowed him to slide too smoothly from illusion to delusion. The problem, according to this view, was not only that Freud failed to appreciate the value of the wishes contained in the illusory religious beliefs (this would be tied to the first kind of change that I have just noted), but also that Freud did not fully grasp the meaning of illusion. This point is very central to the basic thesis of this chapter. According to the new literature on religion, when illusion is fully grasped – that is, when it is properly understood in terms of transitional space and phenomena – the question of the validity of religious belief that seemed to trouble Freud becomes irrelevant. Not only is there no possible move from illusion to delusion, in the sense that the fact that religious belief is founded on a wish does not allow one to conclude that the belief is false, but also the fact that a belief is an illusion implies the irrelevance of the question of falsity. Perhaps the statements most cited in this context are taken from Winnicott's article 'Transitional objects and transitional phenomena' (1953). There, he describes how the mother allows

> the infant the illusion that what the infant creates really exists. This inter-mediate area of experience, unchallenged in respect of its belonging to inner or external (shared) reality, constitutes the greater part of the infant's experi-ence, and throughout life is retained in the intense experiencing that belongs to the arts and to religion.
>
> (cited in Winnicott 1971: 16)

In other words, what characterises illusion is its necessity, its positive valuation as the ground of culture and creativity and, most importantly in this context, the fact that 'the question: "Did you conceive of this or was it presented to you from without?" . . . is not to be formulated' (Winnicott 1971: 14). Here, the question of the objective reality of God is not bracketed for the sake of understanding the personal meanings attributed to him, but rather there *is* no such question. While to insist on the objective reality of a religious illusion would be, according to this Winnicottian perspective, a kind of dogmatism that verges on madness, to insist on the relevance of the *question* of the objective reality of such illusions (as did Freud) would be ignorance that verges on positivism, here meaning a kind of misguided belief that there is value to the distinction between true and false in such matters.[2] Both the change in terms of the criteria that determine the value of religion and the change in terms of its epistemo-logical status allow for a dramatic change in psychoanalysis's general attitude towards religion. On the one hand there is a pervasive tolerance of religious belief associated with its lying in a realm of personal participation that can never be questioned, and on the other there is, among some analysts, a special appreciation of religion as a realm for the expression of higher individual and cultural capacities and experiences. However, all of this is only towards religion in the mature sense of the term and maturity here becomes increasingly associated with what is viewed as valuable by the analytic theories that come to reassess religion. In other words, it may be seen that analytic theories that consider maturity in terms of self-experience value only those kinds of religion that focus on experiencing. Analytic theories that consider maturity in terms of interpersonal or cultural relatedness of various forms value religions of the kind that stress these forms of relatedness. And, most importantly from my per-spective, analytic theories that stress the value of illusion can appreciate religion only in so far as it does not demand our belief that what the religion posits is really true. Reconciliation between psychoanalysis and religion comes with a transformation both of the nature of psychoanalysis and the nature of religion. They begin to resemble each other, with psychoanalysis coming to sound, in some of its writings, much more mystical than it did in the past.[3] Consequently, alongside the tolerance of all belief – because judgement is limited in the realm of illusion – one often finds a continued psychoanalytic antagonism towards religion in its more traditional sense. As Hinshelwood (1999) explains in his foreword to an edited book entitled *Beyond Belief*, which presents contemporary views on the nature of the relationship between psychoanalysis and religion, he feels a kind of aversion towards religion, but he goes on to explain that this is only towards religion in its institutionalised form. He adds that he thinks he shares the viewpoint of all the contributors to the volume (twelve in number), who 'more or less all repudiate "organised religion". They reject dogma and (mostly) rituals. They revert simply to "natural religion", the deeply personal religious experience of a mystical kind' (1999: xvi–ii). Indeed, in the other chapters as well, the ideal religion becomes more of a personal, self-determined mysticism, devoid of history, ritual, authority, obligation and mediation, a kind of westernised Buddhism,[4] while strong words are levelled at the dogmatism, fundamentalism, primitiveness and wrong-mindedness of religion that does not fit this mould. As I will argue, the religion of many believers nowadays, as in the past, does not fit this mould and it is a problem posed by the religion of *these* believers with which Freud struggled in his time and which continues to pose a problem for contemporary psychoanalysis. The problem is concealed, not resolved, by the spirit of conciliation that currently prevails. I will now try to highlight the difficulty of conciliation between psychoanalysis and religion in its more traditional sense by first returning to Freud and explaining why his attitude towards religion would not be affected by the considerations put forth by the newer approaches. By recognising that the fundamental tension between psychoanalysis and religion that Freud posited is not mitigated by these con-siderations, and that Freud's position was not based on naïveté and ignorance of them, but rather on dialogue *with* them, we are given the opportunity for a deeper understanding of the fundamental nature of this tension. In this way, it also becomes apparent that the positive attitude to religion characteristic of contemporary psychoanalysis is not a necessary outgrowth of the evolution of psychoanalytic thinking from the simplistic or limited positions of Freud's time. Rather, it involves a shift away from a concern integral to psychoanalysis as put forth by Freud.

Freud's rejection of the new approaches

It is my view that the contributions of the new approaches to the psychoanalytic understanding of religion would have necessarily been discarded by Freud and would have had little impact on his thinking. This view is, in part, based on the fact that the arguments set forth by the new approaches are not always so novel. Freud was, indeed, aware of many of the arguments and, to this extent, he did reject them. At the heart of this rejection lies the issue of truth and reality. For Freud, as he explains in *The Future of an Illusion*, 'Religious ideas are teachings and assertions about facts and conditions of external (or internal) reality which tell one something one has not discovered for oneself and which lay claim to one's belief' (1927: 25). Consequently, according to Freud, what should determine one's attitude to such assertions is only the question of whether or not they are indeed factually, realistically true. Changing the criteria for evaluating religion, finding that religion allows for the expression of all sorts of positive intra- and interpsychic developments, or changing the notion of religion in such a way that the question of truth is obliterated, does not draw us closer to an acceptance of the idea that the assertions of religious belief regarding reality (external or internal) may, in fact, be true. Freud was not naïve in this context. He rejected religion, knowing full well that the question of the truths of religion, primarily the truth of the existence of God, is not for psychoanalysis to determine. While psychoanalysis has been repeatedly reminded of its limits in this regard, I do not think that Freud needed a reminder. He openly acknowledges this – for example, in his reference to the fact that there is no direct tie between illusion and delusion (1927: 31). And over a quarter of a century before Freud's strongest repudiation of religion, William James made this fact and other limits of psychological explanation common knowledge in *The Varieties of Religious Experience* (1902). I would like to suggest that Freud rejected religion because his analytic stance pulled him towards a philosophical stance that entailed a rejection of religion. Or, in other words, there is something about the assumptions of religion that poses a problem for Freud's analytic stance, which required him to adopt a philosophical view that denies the validity of religion. The main problematic assumption here is that God is a reality, is real, but transcends external objectivity. This is problematic for Freud and, I think, more broadly for psychoanalysis in general if psychoanalysis is seen as concerned with acknowledging reality as it is, internal and external. To explain, psychoanalytic knowledge addresses a very limited area of reality; primarily it is concerned with the nature of psychic reality. While it can point to psychic processes involved in other areas, such as the arts and various sciences, it is not within its scope to make pronouncements regarding what is true or false in those fields *per se*. For example, while psychoanalysis may tell us of the motivations involved in the acceptance of the law of gravity or the theory of relativity, it does not inform us of the truth or falsity of such laws and theories, nor does it add new physical laws of its own. I am not saying anything new here. But then we must ask ourselves, why, when it comes to the issue of the existence of God, does the idea that psychoanalysis is not theology – that it cannot make pronouncements on the truth of the matter, but can only point to the psychic processes involved – become a kind of novelty that need be repeated time and again? How does the claim regarding God differ from the claims of physics? I maintain that it differs in that it contains not only an extra-analytic claim, a claim about reality that cannot be determined by psychoanalysis – psychoanalysis deals regularly with this – but also a claim that there are aspects of reality that cannot be determined; that is, cannot be objectively determined at all. The existence of God is real and true, according to the believer, but is beyond ever being demonstrated, because it stands as a non-objective fact. This is different and this is a problem. It is a problem because psychoanalysis understood as an endeavour geared towards acknowledging reality relies on the notion of the objectivity of reality. It cannot determine what is true and what is false in regard to most dimensions of this reality, and has no real intention to do this. It is not, according to many views, particularly focused on determining the actual facts of the patient's early history, so much as the meanings experienced. It is not concerned with whether or not the law of gravity is true. It is, however, concerned with the fact that there is an objective truth of the matter in these regards, no matter how complexly formulated. For the understanding of psychic reality and the acceptance of the external as it is take place in the light of such objectivity. Just imagine a patient who denies the law of gravity. Our focus on the psychic meaning of this is strongly determined by what we know regarding the existence and acceptance of this law. And were the patient to claim that all that we know is irrelevant to the truth of his denial because his knowledge in this regard, although certain, is not open to any form of potential verification, what then? In this case, to bracket the question of the truth of the patient's claim is to bracket what we know about the world and what is accepted as true, and in this, without reason, there is a limit put on the analytic process and the exploration of what is real. This is, in a sense, what the believer asks of us. He asks that we accept as true, but in a sense without reason (acceptable to a non-believer), a reality that is not open to consensual validation, and that we regard the personal meanings that he expresses in the light of this reality (Leavy 1990: 59).[5] For Freud, this meant limiting his search for truth. This was inimical to his analytic stance, and so had to be rejected (and to this end he applied available philosophical arguments). As he states in his rejection of religion in 'The question of a *Weltanschauung*', 'It is simply a fact that the truth cannot be tolerant, that it admits of no compromises or limitations . . . and that it must be relentlessly critical if any other power tries to take over any part of it' (Freud 1933: 160). By changing the nature of what is referred to by both the terms 'psychoanalysis' and 'religion', the newer analytic approaches to religion could tolerate such deviation from the pursuit of truth. Freud could not. Already in his time the view was gaining force that religious beliefs are merely a kind of fiction accepted as true for their great practical significance, both culturally and in terms of the needs of mankind that cannot be fulfilled by 'cold science' (1927: 35). However, such a view, Freud states with clear disdain, could be proposed only by a *philosopher*. No serious believer would accept this. Nor could he. In a letter to Oskar Pfister in 1930, Freud writes, 'The question is not what belief is more pleasing or more advantageous to life, but of what may approximate more closely to the puzzling reality that lies outside us' (Meng and E. L. Freud 1963: 132–133).[6] Freud's wish and concern were to draw near to this reality. It should be noted that emphasising my view that *the* factor that determined Freud's attitude to religion was his concern with truth does not render all other factors insignificant. For example, I do not mean to deny the significance of Freud's negative view of what he considered to be the infantile roots of religious belief.[7] But these infantile origins only complement, support and contribute to Freud's position that religious beliefs are not really true. In effect, by pointing to infantile roots Freud explains how it is that people believe such beliefs, given that it cannot be because of the actual existence of the realities that these beliefs refer to. However, it is the truth and not the infantilism that is the crucial point here for Freud. This may be seen, for example, from the fact that other activities that are infantile in origin are not intolerable to Freud. Adult sexual activity also has infantile roots but, as long as it does not make false claims regarding reality, Freud did not feel that it should be overcome. Similarly, art, although expressing phantasy life and turning away from reality, could be viewed as valuable because it made no claims to universal truth.[8] 'Art', Freud writes, 'does not seek to be anything but an illusion . . . it makes no attempt at invading the realm of reality' (1933: 160). It was only the invasion of reality, of truth, that was intolerable to Freud, and which he thought to be taking place in the case of religious belief. As long as religion is viewed in terms of assertions regarding reality (and this, Freud affirmed, is what serious traditional believers maintain) the newer psychoanalytic perspectives on religion that shift away from the concept of truth through reliance on the notion of illusion and other merits of belief could, thus, not convince him to abandon the criterion that stood at the basis of his approach to religion – the criterion of the truth of religious claims. Prophetically, perhaps, Freud knew that his position on the truth of religion would not be welcomed by modern defenders of the faith. He remarked that, as a consequence of his stance, he would now 'have to listen to the most disagreeable reproaches for my shallowness, narrow-mindedness and lack of idealism or of understanding for the highest interests of mankind' (1927: 36). He 'consoled' himself with the thought that at least in our day and age such reproach would not bring with it 'a sure curtailment of one's earthly existence and an effective speeding-up of the opportunity for gaining a personal experience of the after-life' (p. 36).

Traditional believers and the new approaches

What I would like to suggest now is that the newer psychoanalytic approaches to religion, clearly much more positive than Freud's approach in their religious understanding, would not be wholeheartedly welcomed by all believers either.

While all believers would be happy to hear that being a believer does not necessarily entail involvement in infantile, regressive, neurotic processes and practices, and on the contrary could reflect and contribute to one's psychic well-being and adaptive living within society, these good tidings have a price. These benefits are associated with religion only if religion is first transformed in the way I have described. As I have noted, the psychoanalytically ideal religion becomes more of a personal, self-determined mysticism, devoid of history, ritual, authority, obligation and mediation. Experience becomes central and truth, in the original sense of corresponding to something real, is no longer particularly relevant. One may argue about the number of believers who have adopted belief of this kind. In any case, there exists a large body of traditional believers who have not; for whom the essence of religion lies in acknowledging the reality of a supernatural or divine being (Vergote 1990: 76), a being who uniquely, although really existent, transcends objectivity and sense experience (Leavy 1990: 47, 50). In what follows, I am concerned with belief as held by this large body of traditional believers. These believers maintain that there is no meaning or value to religion if its assertions are not true, not real. Real here does not mean real in the sense of their being expressive of real inner experience, a psychic reality that lies behind the religious stories and practices, but rather real in the sense that the assertions made about the nature of God, his existence and transcendence, his actions and his promise, his message and his demands, are actual. In the Judeo-Christian tradition, we are speaking here of a unique being who intervenes actually in the course of human history. As the theologian Hans Kung summarises,

> The man who believes . . . is primarily interested . . . in the reality itself . . . He wants to know whether and to what extent his faith is based on illusion or on historical reality. Any faith based on illusion is not really faith but superstition.
>
> (Kung 1984: 418)

It is from such an understanding of religion that Cardinal John Henry Newman (1864) referred to 'religion as a mere sentiment' as 'a dream and a mockery'. And he explains, 'As well can there be filial love without the fact of a father, as devotion without the fact of a supreme being' (*Apologia pro vita sua*, Chapter II, [1864] 1995: 39). This does not mean, of course, that all traditional Judeo-Christian believers accept each word of the Bible in its literal sense. They do not all believe that the world was created in seven days in the literal sense of the term, or that Jonah actually spent some time in the belly of a fish. Commentary, Midrash, biblical tradition and exegesis guides believers towards the actual meanings that lie behind these stories. But, in their view, what lies behind are actualities pertaining to God, to a God who is independent of human existence, a God who created and loves humankind and expresses this love through his actual continued participation in history, awaiting our more full participation in his reality. For traditional believers, this is not a metaphor, nor is it an illusion. It is, rather, a reality for which they would (ideally) be willing to die.[9]

The dialogue between Freud and the traditional believer

Freud rejected the truth of this reality and, in so doing, took a stance diametrically opposed to that of traditional theistic religion. However, it is my view that in that very opposition he was closer to the concerns of the traditional believer than those who adopt the much more friendly attitude characteristic of the new psychoanalytic thinking on religion. This is because Freud's opposition, his rejection of religion, is founded on a love of truth. His desire to know, discover, reveal – in other words, to encounter truth – was passionate and unrelenting, not merely scientific in the modern use of the term. Explaining the dynamics of Leonardo da Vinci's passion to know, Freud quotes Leonardo's statement that 'in truth great love springs from great knowledge of the beloved object' (1910: 74). Freud's identification with Leonardo in this context is clear. More directly, Freud speaks elsewhere of the 'submission to truth and rejection of illusions' as the only consolation that psychoanalysis has to offer (1933: 182) – a view and sentiment that lies at the foundations of psychoanalysis and has reverberated throughout its history. Oskar Pfister thought that this love of truth not only pointed to an affinity with the believer, but also was, in fact, a religious stance. Shortly after the publication of *The Future of an Illusion*, Pfister wrote to Freud that 'Anyone who has struggled so powerfully for the truth and fought so courageously for the redemption of love as you have is, whether he admits it or not, a true servant of God according to scripture' (1928: 149–150; in Meissner's translation 1984: 75). But, perhaps Pfister goes too far and he, too, conceals in this way a meaningful collaboration between Freud and the traditional believer that is, in fact, founded on the opposition, on the recognition of the fundamental differences, between the two. Both Freud and the traditional believer belong to what the American philosopher and contemporary social critic Allan Bloom (1987) has called 'the community of those who seek the truth'. According to Bloom, in this community true friendship takes place through disagreement. Writing of Plato and Aristotle he states, 'The common concern for the good linked them; their disagreement about it proved they needed one another to understand it. They were absolutely one soul as they looked at the problem' (Bloom 1987: 381). As Freud rejected religion in the name of truth, he not only maintained that religion consisted of assertions that made claims of truth, but also shared in the passionate desire for truth with which traditional believers, in their faith in an ultimate reality, would readily identify. But Freud and the traditional believer share another concern. This has to do with the more specific characteristics of the religion that Freud comes to explain.

The religion that Freud has in mind retains its traditional nature not only because it focuses on an actual and yet supposedly transcendent reality, but also in other ways. At the centre of the religion that Freud tries to explain are not individualistic experiences of openness to one's self and to the world, but rather the presence within us of a paternal figure, an 'Other' that protects and demands, and is at the source of our ethical prescriptions and our guilt when we fail to fulfil them. It is a religion of ritual and remembrance, authority and dogma. In his final work on religion, *Moses and Monotheism* (1939), this religion is especially also one of community, tradition and sacred text. In other words, the dialogue between Freud and the traditional believer (at least in the west) can be meaningful because their disagreement is about a phenomenon recognised by both. This is not the case when the nature of the religious phenomenon to be understood is modified, as it often is in the newer analytic approaches. I would now like to suggest that, towards the end of his life, Freud's dialogue with the traditional believer goes beyond that of simple disagreement or opposition over the truth behind a commonly acknowledged phenomenon. In *Moses and Monotheism*, as he returns to study the sacred text of the Bible, in a somewhat traditional Talmudic fashion – although explicitly noting that he hoped to avoid what he referred to as the unattractive ingenuity of the Talmudists (Freud 1939: 17) – as he seeks to find in that text some answer to the question of the source and meaning of his own personal sense of Jewishness, a deeper and more complex conception of truth emerges. Through this conception, Freud comes to some understanding that his view of religion – perhaps like the religious view itself – is only an attempt to describe a reality that will always remain to some extent beyond description (although, as we shall see, not for mystical reasons). Thus, both share not only a concern with truth, but also an inevitable failure to grasp it fully. Through this shared failure, a new arena for dialogue between the opposing views can emerge. It is here that another dimension of the ongoing relevance of Freud's perspective on religion becomes apparent. I turn now to explain this final point. (In the course of this explanation I will, at points, refer the reader to an earlier study of mine of Freud's *Moses and Monotheism*, where further justification and elaboration of some of the ideas put forth here are found: Blass 2003.)

Historical truth and its value for dialogue

Moses and Monotheism, which was ultimately published in full as a book in 1939, is often viewed as yet another one of Freud's anti-religious texts (for example, Meissner 1984: 106; Gay 1987: 44) – although I maintain that this is far from being the case (Blass, in preparation). In that book, Freud explains the origins of Judaism and monotheism through a very complex analysis of religious and historical writings. Freud's explanation centres on a story regarding the relationship between Moses, an Egyptian prince and follower of the mono-theistic beliefs of Akhenaten, and the problematic Jewish people whom Moses chose in order to carry on his religion. This relationship was ultimately a fatal and painful one, as the Jews for various reasons and needs were to rise up and kill Moses, only to afterwards feel remorse and guilt reminiscent of the experiences of the sons who killed the primal father in *Totem and Taboo* (1913). Freud's story of this relationship and the historical events surrounding it is presented as a product of careful scrutiny of relevant texts, and as a valid explanation of the source of many of the particular characteristics of the Jewish people, their beliefs and the attitudes that they have aroused and continue to arouse in others. In the course of this exposition, Freud presents his notion of 'historical truth'. He does so in the context of his concern, and I have argued that this is the major concern of the book (Blass 2003), to understand the source of the believer's conviction, the power of certain ideas to compel us to believe in them even though they are not only unverified by reality, but also incom-patible with it. Freud wonders, for example, why such ideas are not 'listened to, judged, and perhaps dismissed, like any other piece of information from outside' (1939: 101). In dealing with this question in *Moses and Monotheism*, Freud more seriously than ever before is willing to examine the pious religious suggestion that these ideas, though strange and unverified, are accepted because they are simply true (pp. 128–129). That is, believers are convinced because they meet in these ideas what they somehow know to be true; much in the same way that we believe there is a blue chair in front of us for the simple reason that it so happens that this is the case. For example (and this is Freud's main example), the believer accepts the idea of there being a *single* God, although it is a strange and unverifiable proposition, because as a matter of fact there is a single God. The believer accepts the idea because, upon hearing it, the believer's mind recognises its truth. Freud acknowledges that such an explanation does have explanatory power but, of course, it would require us to also accept that the human mind has a 'special inclination for recognising the truth' (p. 129). Freud concludes that knowing that our intellect is very easily led astray by our wishes – that is, we tend to recognise as true that which we wish for – the claim that we have such a special inclination for truth is obviously mistaken and consequently the pious explanation must be rejected. Nevertheless, very interestingly at this point, Freud does not suggest (as he has at others) that what the believer recognises as true is, therefore, merely illusion and in turn delusion, and here the notion of historical truth is introduced.[10] He writes, 'We too believe that the pious solution contains the truth – but the *historical* truth and not the *material* truth' (p. 129, original italics). This historical truth, as Freud goes on to describe and define it, does not refer to the historical facts; it is not the objective reality (as it is often wrongly taken to mean). But it is not merely an internal, psychical reality either. Rather, it is a special kind of impression in the mind of a past reality. Its origin is in the real world; real events left the impression. But the impression is not identical to the real world, to the actual events. The source of the relevant distortion in this context is not our wishful tendencies, but rather the primal nature of the impression.[11] Something from the outside was registered in our minds at a time when it was impossible for us to create an accurate image of it, or to understand it in a way that is accurate in terms of our present understanding of reality. It is this historical truth, buried in the depths of our minds, according to Freud, that explains the believer's acceptance of religious ideas. These ideas are false propositions regarding objective reality, but they are in a sense true to the internal impression of what was once external reality. As such, they are what Freud refers to as 'justified memor[ies]' that demand to be believed (1939: 130). In other words, the believer is compelled to accept religious ideas because upon hearing them his or her mind recognises their truth, but what takes place here is not a simple correspondence between mind and reality as such (as when my mind recognises the existence of a chair that is there), but rather between mind and the vestiges of a past primal reality. To the extent that religious ideas are shaped by the limitations of our mind to have accurately perceived and registered this reality, and, to the extent that they are further influenced by our wishes, these ideas are false. However, to the extent that they convey the great truths of 'the earliest experiences of the whole of humanity' that return and find revived expression in our minds and in our lives, they are also true – true to a past external reality (p. 130). Here, there is a radical shift in Freud's position regarding the truth of religious ideas and their relationship to his own. Indeed, Freud had always maintained that there exist some real events at the foundations of religious belief, whether it be a primeval patricide or a loving relationship that did, in fact, exist in the past with one's own father. But now there is a difference. I mention here just two points. First, Freud's focus is now on the truth and the justification of these ideas, not on their distortive nature. There are good and real reasons to believe. As he notes in the postscript to *An Autobiographical Study* (written while he was preparing his *Moses and Monotheism*): 'In *The Future of an Illusion* I expressed an essentially negative valuation of religion. Later, I found a formula which did better justice to it . . . granting that its power lies in the truth which it contains' (1935: 72). Second, while religious ideas are distortive of the objective material reality, Freud now, in effect, contends that *all* ideas that attempt to grasp the common primal realities of mankind will inevitably be so. It is in the very nature of that early reality that we encounter it only through the traces that it leaves in our mind. We can then retrospectively form propositions regarding the material reality that engendered these traces, but these propositions are always only conjecture. Our minds have never really fully met that early reality, nor, being prehistorical and external in origin, could we ever meet it now. And while these propositions are only conjecture they are still the best we have in the way of truth, since it is through these conjectures that the traces of an earlier reality can now find some expression (Blass 2003: 676). But then what of Freud's theory itself, his own ideas regarding the origins of the traces of past reality? Is Freud's explanation of the origin of these traces not an attempt to go beyond the religious conjectures, to reveal the 'true', in the sense of 'materially true', story behind them? Isn't that what *Moses and Monotheism* is all about? Elsewhere, I have argued that it is indeed an *attempt* to describe the reality behind the biblical story, but it is an attempt that was doomed to fail (Blass 2003). Moreover, to some extent Freud, himself, knew this. While putting forth *Moses* as a careful piece of historical work guided by analytic attunement to the texts, Freud knew of all the historical criticisms that could be levelled at his work and, indeed, ultimately were time and again. Freud knew that, as real history, his theory was not well grounded. Throughout the writing of *Moses*, within the text and in related correspondences, Freud speaks of a pervading doubt regarding the truth of his findings. He repeatedly notes that he expects to be told that he 'brought forward this structure of conjectures with too much positiveness, for which there is no basis in the material' (1939: 31), and to be blamed for 'unjustified certainty' (p. 41). Rather than refute these potential criticisms, Freud, at points, acknowledges that they 'find an echo in [his] . . . own judgement' (p. 41) and that he, himself, feels 'uncertain in the face of . . . [his] own work' (p. 58) and burdened by his feelings of doubt (p. 17). He knows that 'the historical foundations of the Moses story . . . are not solid enough' (letter of 6 January 1935, cited in Pfeiffer 1966: 205). However, such doubts regarding the veracity of his findings do not point to the fictional nature of Freud's story of *Moses* either. While many interpreters of the book have opted for such an under-standing in the light of its dubious historical value, there is clear evidence that this is not how Freud perceived it. Alongside the doubt, Freud repeatedly speaks of his conviction in the reconstruction that he is offering and the justification of his ideas in this regard (Blass 2003: 671–672). Thus, for example, after setting forth his feelings of uncertainty in the face of his work he can immediately add that 'It is not as though there were an absence of conviction in the correctness of my conclusion' (Freud 1939: 58). It is my view that Freud's *Moses* is neither fact nor fiction. The book (perhaps, one may argue, like religious conjectures themselves) is presented as a piece of historical truth. It attempts to capture the traces of a past reality left in our minds, but through a story, through a set of propositions regarding the world, which do not correspond to material reality *per se*, and which could never be confirmed as true (Blass 2003: 679). In other words, the book aims for truth, to describe reality as best possible. But the kind of reality that it comes to describe is such that the propositions that are put forth in order to describe cannot directly represent the facts, but are not fiction either. For, in this instance, the propositions that are materially false are nevertheless the medium that draws our minds closest to the truth. In an earlier draft of *Moses and Monotheism*, Freud subtitles the book a 'historical novel' (Bori 1979). This has been brought as evidence that he had actually recognised the fictional nature of his writing (see, for example, Kermode 1985: 4; Richardson 1992: 437). However, a closer look at what Freud *says* about this subtitle (which he also noteworthily abandoned) confirms the unique status of the book. He explains (in the introduction to that earlier draft) that in *his* use of the term 'historical novel' a new definition is required that excludes the notions of fiction and invention, which are 'associated with the blemish of error' but at the same time allows for the depiction of a truth that has 'no proven reality' (cited in Yerushalmi 1991: 17). Freud's thesis regarding *Moses*, like the biblical story itself, has no proven reality and yet is not fiction or invention. Like the traditional religious view, it is an attempt to be true to a reality that, to some extent, will always remain beyond immediate description, and its justification can come only from the truthfulness of the attempt. It, too, comes to explain the sense of our being bound by traditions and ethical prescriptions coming from the past and specifically from a paternal all-loving and all-powerful sense of 'Otherness' that resides within us; it explains what Freud now recognises in human experience as the monotheistic pull towards intellectuality, truth and justice – what Lou Andreas-Salomé referred to as 'the most triumphant vital elements of the past [now recognised by Freud as] . . . the truest possession in the present' (cited in Pfeiffer 1966: 206). In the writing of *Moses*, Freud struggled with his doubts as he continued to seek material truth and proof, but ultimately he allowed himself to go with his convictions. Noting the lack of sufficient evidence for his conclusions, he confides to Andreas-Salomé that 'It suffices me that I myself can believe in the solution of the problem' (letter of 6 January 1935, cited in Pfeiffer 1966: 205). Freud's belief was *not* religious. He continued to reject the idea of the existence of God and the supernatural throughout. Only human reality lies at the foundation of his explanation of our experiences and tendencies. But in this opposition to the religious perspective in *Moses and Monotheism* a new arena for dialogue is forged. Both Freud's own perspective and the religious one are now understood as two opposing attempts to truthfully grasp, through ideas that could never be proven true, a common inner reality that comes from the past in a way that leaves it always to some degree inaccessible to our minds. While remaining opposed, the grounds for the outright rejection of the alternative perspective are, here, clearly moderated and, thus, a more humble dialogue and exchange become possible. This moderation does not entail any blurring of the concern for truth and reality as we find in some of the newer analytic approaches to religion. It is not by creating a common ground of illusion, by putting aside distinctions between truth and fiction, religious ideas and those of psychoanalysis, experience of the sacred and experience of the self, that meaningful bridges between perspectives emerge. Rather, what I have been proposing here is that it is by understanding the unique nature of one's own convictions, and by struggling to ensure that, indeed, they are emerging through a sincere search for truth, that new possibilities are sought and opened up for the respectful and meaningful recognition both of the other and of reality, internal and external, as it is and was.

Further implications

In this chapter I have focused on the relationship between psychoanalysis and religion, but it may be seen that it contains implications that extend beyond this issue. These implications refer to the relative place of experience and knowledge, of illusion and reality, of freedom from the past and recognition of its binding influence in the process of being and becoming ourselves. It also has implications for the possibility of dialogue between opposing perspectives. It suggests that, when the concern is with discerning truth and reality, the focus on differences rather than on areas of harmonious coexistence may be not only a source of tension, but also an important way of finding meaningful common ground. These implications are being developed in forthcoming works.

Acknowledgements

An earlier version of this chapter was presented as an invited lecture at the 'Competitors or collaborators? Psychoanalysis and religion in the 21st century' conference, held at the British Psychoanalytical Society, June 2003. The preparation of this paper was funded in part by a grant from the International Psychoanalytical Association's Research Advisory Board, awarded in 2003.

Notes

1 There are some exceptions here. Julia Kristeva (1987), for example, writes of religion in a seemingly positive tone, but nevertheless speaks of renouncing one's religious faith as a positive step in the course of an analysis in a way somewhat analogous to these earlier writings.

2 These ideas regarding the necessity of illusion are, at times, accompanied by the idea of the necessity and value of the irrational (for example, Ostow 1988: 209). It should be noted here that their relevance of the question of objective reality refers only to the content of the illusion. From this perspective, the capacity to form illusion and the relational conditions that enable this are considered to be objective realities of great relevance and an important focus of analytic concern. It should also be noted that not all writers who have promoted the notion of illusion and transitional space for the understanding of religion have dismissed the objectivity of the content of the illusion. Notable exceptions are William Meissner and Ana-Maria Rizzuto. However, others have made use of their writings to support the general trend.

3 This may be seen to be part of a broader cultural trend, which has allowed for a new respect for the sacred by changing the meaning of the term (see Bloom 1987: 216).

4 This religious ideal often does away with the notion of the existence of a transcendent object to the point that the self becomes the object of religious experience (Blass 2005).

5 Moreover, in the case of religion, the truths proposed are intimately related to personal meanings in contrast to the truths of physics.

6   It is important to recognise that the fundamental tension that Freud refers to here is not merely between religion and science, but in a more essential way between religion and truth (see Freud 1933: 170, on the relationship between science and truth).

7   I also do not wish to downplay the importance of Freud's negative view of the consequences of religious teachings for personal and cultural developments. However, this again points to a secondary issue.

8   This understanding stands in contrast to some of the newer analytic interpretations, which maintain that Freud held a generally antagonistic attitude towards illusion, except in the realm of art, and that, were this attitude to change for the better, so would Freud's attitude towards religion (Meissner 1984: 162; Kakar 1991: 59).

9   It should be clear that there is no implication here that the reader need assume that this traditional Judeo-Christian perspective is the most authentic form of belief. What is posited is merely that it is one dominant form of belief, and one that is particularly relevant to the understanding of Freud's ideas on religion and on truth, as well as to the shift away from these ideas in contemporary psychoanalytic perspectives.

10 This may be in part because Freud presents a much more elaborate picture of belief in *Moses* and thus it is more difficult to discern latent wishes that lie behind its various specific aspects.

11 This impression could be referred to as preverbal, but to use such a term in this context may frame the impression as part of a developmental process, or make it into a more typical form of registration of early experience in a way that is not completely congruent with what Freud has in mind here. In this context Freud, in fact, contrasts his proposition regarding historical truth with impressions received by the individual child (1939: 132) and does not consider it to be such a general process as has been recently suggested (for example, Green 2001: 31). Here, my understanding of Freud is in line with that of Laplanche (1995: 675), who notes that, when it came to the study of phenomena related to religion, Freud considered it especially necessary to look beyond the personal history of the child to the prehistorical events of the childhood of humanity.

References

Blass, R.B. (2003) The puzzle of Freud's puzzle analogy: Reviving a struggle with doubt and conviction in Freud's *Moses and Monotheism*. *International Journal of Psychoanalysis* 84: 669–682.

Blass, R.B. (2005) Attachment and separateness and the psychoanalytic understanding of the act of faith. In J. Auerbach, K. Levy and C.E. Schaffer (eds) *Relatedness, Self-definition and Mental Representation: Essays in Honor of Sidney J. Blatt*. New York: Routledge.

Blass, R.B. (in preparation) *From Seduction Fantasy to Faith: The Evolution of Freud's Concepts of Truth and Reality between 1895 and 1939*.

Bloom, A. (1987) *The Closing of the American Mind*. New York: Simon and Schuster.

Bori, P.C. (1979) Una pagina inedita di Freud: La premessa al romanzo storico su Mosè [An unknown page of Freud: The premise to the historical novel of Moses]. *Rivista di Storia Contemporanea* 7: 1–16.

Deutsch, H. (1951) *Psychoanalysis of the Neuroses*. London: Hogarth Press.

Eigen, M. (1998) *The Psychoanalytic Mystic*. New York: Free Association Books.

Eigen, M. (2001) *Ecstasy*. Middletown, CT: Wesleyan University Press.

Fenichel, O. (1938) Problems of psychoanalytic technique. *Psychoanalytic Quarterly* 7: 303–324.

Freud, S. (1910) *Leonardo da Vinci and a Memory of his Childhood*. SE 11.

Freud, S. (1913) *Totem and Taboo*. SE 13.

Freud, S. (1927) *The Future of an Illusion*. SE 21.

Freud, S. (1930) *Civilization and its Discontents*. SE 21.

Freud, S. (1933) The question of a *Weltanschauung*. SE 22.

Freud, S. (1935) Postscript to *An Autobiographical Study*. SE 20.

Freud, S. (1939) *Moses and Monotheism: Three Essays*. SE 23.

Gay, P. (1987) *A Godless Jew: Freud, Atheism and the Making of Psychoanalysis*. New Haven, CT: Yale University Press.

Green, A. (2001) *Time in Psychoanalysis: Some Contradictory Aspects*. London: Free Association Books.

Hinshelwood, R.D. (1999) Foreword. In S.M. Stein (ed.) *Beyond Belief: Psychotherapy and Religion*. London: Karnac.

James, W. (1902) *The Varieties of Religious Experience: A Study of Human Nature*. New York: Longmans, Green.

Jones, J.W. (1991) *Contemporary Psychoanalysis and Religion: Transference and Transcendence*. New Haven, CT: Yale University Press.

Jones, J.W. (2002) *Terror and Transformation: The Ambiguity of Religion in Psychoanalytic Perspectives*. Hove: Brunner-Routledge.

Kakar, S. (1991) *The Analyst and the Mystic: Psychoanalytic Reflections on Religion and Mysticism*. Chicago: University of Chicago Press.

Kermode, F. (1985) Freud and interpretation. *International Review of Psychoanalysis* 12: 3–12.

Kristeva, J. (1987) *In the Beginning was Love: Psychoanalysis and Faith*. New York: Columbia University Press.

Kung, H. (1984) *On Being a Christian*. New York: Image Books.

Laplanche, J. (1995) Seduction, persecution, revelation. *International Journal of Psychoanalysis* 76: 663–682.

Leavy, S. (1990) Reality in religion and psychoanalysis. In J.H. Smith and S.A. Handelman (eds) *Psychoanalysis and Religion*. Baltimore, MD: Johns Hopkins University Press.

Meissner, W.W. (1984) *Psychoanalysis and Religious Experience*. New Haven, CT: Yale University Press.

Meng, H. and Freud, E.L. (eds) (1963) *Psychoanalysis and Faith: The Letters of Sigmund Freud and Oskar Pfister*. New York: Basic Books.

Newman, J.H. (1864) *Apologia pro vita sua* [A defence of his life]. New York: Penguin (1995).

Ostow, M. (1988) Psychoanalysis and religious experience. *Journal of the American Psychoanalytical Association* 36: 206–209.

Pfeiffer, E. (ed.) (1966) *Sigmund Freud and Lou Andreas-Salomé: Letters*. New York: Harcourt, Brace, Jovanovich.

Pfister, O. (1928) Die Illusion einer Zukunft [The illusion of a future]. *Imago* 14: 149–184.

Richardson, W. (1992) Love and the beginning: Psychoanalysis and religion. *Contemporary Psychoanalysis* 28: 423–441.

Rizzuto, A. (1979) *The Birth of the Living God: A Psychoanalytic Study.* Chicago: University of Chicago Press.

Roazen, P. (1993) The illusion of a future. *International Journal of Psychoanalysis* 74: 559–579.

Smith, J.H. and Handelman, S.A. (1990) *Psychoanalysis and Religion.* Baltimore, MD: Johns Hopkins University Press.

Spezzano, C. and Gargiulo, G.J. (eds) (1997) *Souls on the Couch: Spirituality, Religion and Morality in Contemporary Psychoanalysis.* Hillsdale, NJ: Analytic Press.

Symington, N. (1994) *Emotion and Spirit: Questioning the Claims of Psychoanalysis and Religion.* London: Karnac (1998).

Vergote, A. (1990) Confrontation with neutrality in theory and praxis. In J.H. Smith and S.A. Handelman (eds) *Psychoanalysis and Religion.* Baltimore, MD: Johns Hopkins University Press.

Wallwork, E. and Wallwork, S. (1990) Psychoanalysis and religion: Current status of a historical antagonism. In J.H. Smith and S.A. Handelman (eds) *Psychoanalysis and Religion.* Baltimore, MD: Johns Hopkins University Press.

Winnicott, D.W. (1971) *Playing and Reality.* London: Penguin.

Yerushalmi, Y.H. (1991) *Freud's Moses: Judaism Terminable and Interminable.* New Haven, CT: Yale University Press.

2

'RENDER UNTO CAESAR WHAT IS CAESAR'S'

Is there a realm of God in the mind?

M. Fakhry Davids

Introduction

My title is from the Gospel according to St Matthew.[1] To the kingdom of God, Jesus tells the Pharisees, many are called but few are chosen. Antagonised by this idea, they try to 'entangle him in his talk' with a trick question: is it lawful to pay taxes unto Caesar? Perceiving their 'wickedness', however, Jesus calls for the tribute money to be brought to him: whose image, he asks, is on the coin? 'Caesar's' they reply, whereupon Jesus tells them to 'Render therefore unto Caesar the things that are Caesar's, and unto God the things that are God's' (Matthew 22: 1–22).

It is a sad fact that God is often invoked in human affairs in unhelpful or downright destructive ways, mostly to the dismay of the sincere believer (e.g. Pfister 1993) to whom these are instances where God has been dragged, inappropriately, into the realm of Caesar. But this raises the thorny question, where does God properly belong?

Jesus' idea that our relationship with God belongs to a realm other than where our worldly transactions are located is echoed in the words of the Prophet Muhammad. A companion had left his camel untethered outside, which, he felt, reflected a trust in God so complete as to dispel worldly concerns. It also implied a sort of moral high ground – an unspoken belief that his exemplary faith would in itself ensure the safety of the camel. The Prophet, however, advised that he should first tie the camel securely and then trust God to protect it.

The incident adds to the idea of the realms of Caesar and of God as separate in an interesting way, implying that God is not there to do things that humans can do for themselves. Psychically, the expectation that God should carry out a human task involves the mindset of young children who take for granted that their parents will look out for them. Infantile omnipotence – the infant's earliest view of itself as omnipotent – is implicated in this. As the infant matures, growing awareness of its limitations challenges this omnipotence, which is, early on, projected into the parent whose greater competence is now idealised. To an outside observer it is this adult competence that allows the parent to provide care absolutely vital for the infant's survival. In the infant's eyes, however, nothing at all is beyond the idealised parent, and the security of having such a parent in place banishes all worry. It is this, the infant's picture of a parent, that the companion confused with God. Recognising that his companion was under the sway of infantile omnipotence, the Prophet acted as an auxiliary ego, pointing him back to ordinary reality (by assessing risk and urging appropriate action). Attending to material concerns – rendering unto Caesar what is Caesar's – has the effect of restoring an adult mindset, which is, evidently, a prerequisite for trust in God to be properly grounded – to render unto God what is God's.

Al-Hakim al-Tirmidhi, a renowned scholar from the third century of Islam, explicitly extended the idea of two distinct realms to the inner world (Al-Tirmidhi 2003).[2] He distinguished between *qalb*, literally the heart, and *nafs*, which he located physically in the stomach. *Qalb* contains the spirit, which responds directly to God (Qur'an 17:85), and is inborn. An angel, acting on God's command, installs it into the foetus during the second trimester of pregnancy (Al-Bukhari, vol. 8, book 77, no. 593). One's relationship with God is thus mediated via *qalb*, and the process of refining it – as far as one can – is the special preserve of the mystics, who would see themselves as the few chosen, from time to time, to dwell in this inner kingdom of God.

Nafs, usually translated as self, is the seat of passion and desire, which originate in the flesh, in the animal body we inhabit. The psychology of the *nafs* contains not only the vicissitudes of those impulses – as our innermost wishes – but also the complex inner world of thought, feeling, phantasy and relationships associated, ultimately, with their gratification or frustration. While the impulses that set things in motion are at root constitutional, it is the individual's particular history of interchanges with the environment, in the service of wish-fulfilment, that accounts for the unique diversity and richness of each inner world. Since its content bears the mark of real interchanges with others, past and present, in the external world, without which it would not have come into existence, this inner world may be spoken of as the realm of Caesar in the mind.

Firmly rooted in religious tradition,[3] Tirmidhi's picture of the mind thus specifically postulates a realm of God within, and delineates it sharply from the realm of Caesar. This is quite different from psychoanalytic conceptions of the inner world. Psychoanalysis, too, holds that real impulses rooted in individual biology, in interaction with actual experiences of gratification and privation, form the essential substrate on which the inner world is constructed. However, where Tirmidhi confines this to *nafs*, psychoanalysis views the *entire* inner world, including the object 'God', as fashioned out such experiences:

> we do not have to conceal the fact that this discovery [that religious belief is, psychologically, an illusion] . . . influences our attitude to the question which must appear to many to be the most important of all. We know approximately at what periods and by what kinds of men religious doctrines were created. If, in addition, we discover the motive that led to this, our attitude to the problem of religion will undergo a marked displacement. We shall tell ourselves that it would be very nice if there were a God who created the world and was a benevolent Providence, and if there were a moral order in the universe and an after-life; but it is a very striking fact that all this is exactly as we are bound to wish it to be.
>
> (Freud 1927: 33)

Later in the book Freud argues that humankind itself has invented the notion of God in order to fulfil deep-seated unconscious wishes.[4] With religious belief claimed for the realm of Caesar, he anticipated that the new psychoanalytic tools, by fully illuminating the neurotic wishes underpinning belief in him, would reveal God as a wish-fulfilling illusion. With no place of his own in the mind, God therefore had no future.

It is this psychoanalytic proposition that I want to revisit in this chapter. The question I want to explore is whether a realm of God may be said to exist in the mind as suggested by Tirmidhi. In his lucid re-evaluation of psychoanalysis' approach to the religions David Black argues that Freud's conclusions in *The Future of an Illusion* set psychoanalysis on a false start in its explorations of religious phenomena in the mind. He thinks that an object relations perspective, which is less preoccupied with origins and more with the meaning of subjective experience, makes it possible to approach the subject of religion in a new way (Black 1993). I shall follow this lead by conducting my inquiry within an object relations frame.

Relating to God

God as refuge

I would like first to look at the emergence of the idea of God in the analysis of a patient, Mr A.

Mr A would properly be described as agnostic; religious sentiment had neither positive nor negative meaning to him. In the course of the analysis he had had a breakdown, but at this point he had achieved greater stability in his mind. This was accompanied by progress in his outside life; for instance, he began to undertake small pieces of work so that a future career now seemed possible.

He reported, with some embarrassment, that when he delayed in the lavatory after the previous session he was on his knees praying to God that he might find the strength to keep going at the various embryonic tasks he had begun. At that time we were working on the problem of how to keep alive forces of growth in the face of concerted attacks from an intensely destructive part of himself. This 'voice' maintained that he was entitled to a protected life on account of past deprivation, and any slight setback was mercilessly exploited to prove that it really was not worth embarking on anything new.

At first I saw the incident in the lavatory as a positive development, thinking that God represented an internal figure who might support him when, away from his sessions, he was so exposed to merciless destructiveness. This would have been a significant development, but interpreting along these lines gave rise to an excessively cosy and smug atmosphere. He now sang my praises, but material in the sessions became deadly repetitive and there was no progress on the career front.

The impasse forced me to reconsider and, with outside help, I began to see the lavatory incident as a negative therapeutic reaction. It was not so much an appeal for support from an object felt to be separate from him, as I had thought; instead, it undid the analytic progress by reinstating an earlier version of me, now much idealised, on whom he was *totally* dependent. It was the act of kneeling before this god-me that had, for him, literally re-installed a unity between us that he had been moving on from (towards a career of his own). It was therefore a regression, an attack on progress made thus far, and when I interpreted this the intense violence associated with awareness of himself as a separate being (rather than in a symbiotic/parasitic existence with me) was once again mobilised. Alongside this, however, things in his life gradually began to move forward once more.

God as guide

My second example is from a friend who knew of my interest in dreams.

M, a Muslim, was planning to marry and, anxious at taking such a momentous step, prayed for God's guidance using specific, ritualised prayers recommended by the Prophet. That night he dreamt:

> He and his fiancée were at a gathering, like a small celebratory dinner party, where the atmosphere was companionable and friendly. They entered a triangular room with two doors. At the far end was an open fire, with an attractive woman seated across from it, who momentarily caught his eye with a seductive look. He felt extremely awkward, and slightly compromised by the secret meeting of their eyes.

47

He took the dream as God's answer to his prayer. At first he thought God was telling him that the woman he intended to marry was really two people, a devoted partner on his arm, and a dangerous seducer of men. To marry her would be like playing with fire. However, this interpretation did not allow him to find inner peace, and he took his discomfort as a sign that the interpretation was incorrect: it was too literal. If the dream was indeed an answer to *his* prayer for guidance, why was the message exclusively about her? This line of thinking led to a different interpretation. He now took the triangular shape as referring to three person relationships, and saw the whole dream as addressing *his own* difficulty in living with the awareness that being married to her would not mean owning her: he would have to live with the fact that she had important ongoing relationships with others. He knew he could be possessive, and in this frame of mind might experience others as seducing her away from him. This understanding brought greater peace of mind – he felt that he had been answered with guidance, concerning himself in the prospective marriage, that he could both understand and use.

Psychoanalysts usually rely on the clinical situation as a whole to help illuminate the meaning of dreams. How did he deal with this problem? Could God, in his omniscience, not be telling him that the prospective marriage was indeed a serious mistake, as suggested by his first interpretation? Was he not simply settling for the interpretation that condoned a marriage he himself had set his heart on (sharing the responsibility for that decision with God) rather than one that might force him to reconsider?

M said that he had a rule of thumb regarding these dreams. If he were on a destructive course, the dream would usually signal this urgently and unambiguously. For example, at one time when he was planning to undertake the pilgrimage to Mecca (which is compulsory for Muslims when they can afford it) his prayer yielded a dream in which a crack opened up in a flyover, followed by the entire structure collapsing, causing death, destruction, injury and mayhem all around. Unusually for him, his recall of the dream was also broken up and patchy. The vivid theme of destructiveness, echoed in the broken–up recall, made him look at his plan as a kind of a flyover (we would say a manic plan) that was not properly grounded. He reconsidered, and eventually abandoned it on the grounds that there were too many other stressful events in his life at that time that required his undivided attention. (This decision was particularly difficult since it flew in the face of accepted *legal* opinion that religious obligations enjoy priority over all else.)

According to M's rule of thumb, the absence of such obvious negative content probably indicated that the marriage dream was not warning of a destructive course of action. Instead it provided guidance as to the implications that the marriage might have for him. God was reminding him that one has to work at a marriage, and offering guidance as to what, for him, such work might entail. His first interpretation of the dream was mistaken since it simply made the problem his fiancée's, not his own.

God as ultimate other

My third example is an amalgam drawn from the experience of mystics. While all believers take for granted that God exists, and then serve, worship or consult him in different ways, the mystics move beyond this in trying to develop their *relationship* with God. It is the self-consciousness of this attempt to relate to an omnipotent and omniscient internal object that sets it apart from the ways of relating to God that I have described thus far.

The *sufis*, who form the mystical tradition within Islam, define their god as follows: God is omnipotent; God can be known though his attributes, but not in his true nature; God's nature is beyond human conception; he is neither man nor woman; his form is unlike that of any of his creation; he sees, hears etc. but does not have human sense organs; he is not bound by time and space; his power knows no limit; he is not accountable to anyone for his actions (Al-Haddaad 1992). Margaret Smith, an eminent western student of gnosis, draws the following description of God from the Qur'an:

> 'Sole Maker of the Heavens and the Earth! He hath created everything and he knoweth all things! This is God your Lord. There is no God but He, the Creator of all things; therefore worship Him; for He watcheth over all things. No vision comprehends Him, but He comprehends all vision, and He is the sublime, the All-informed . . . He is the Hearer, the Knower'.(Qur'an 6:96ff). God is Omnipotent, Omniscient, Present everywhere, All-seeing yet unseen, the First and the Last, the Mighty and the Wise, the Gracious, the Merciful, the Forgiving.
>
> (Smith 1976: 143)

Omnipotence means not only that God has powers beyond that of the human subject, but also that the finite capacity of the human mind limits the extent to which God can be perceived and known. Only God can know himself fully; humans, in moments of enlightenment, may get a glimpse of this or that aspect of God, and the *sufis* hold that such moments are really priceless encounters with 'truth' that transform the 'seeker' for the better. However, the process of relating to such an object involves an intense inner struggle, which a *sufi* described as follows.[5]

Frustrated at trying to relate to one who cannot really be known, he drew comfort from the idea that God gains pleasure from being sought (which can be inferred from the Prophet's description of the journey to God, quoted below). On reflection he realised that he had now conceived of God in a human form – God gained satisfaction from having a wish fulfilled – and he reminded himself that God is free of desire. He started afresh, but each time this same sequence repeated itself: he saw products, qualities and attributes of his own in God: the realm of God was being appropriated by his 'ego'. He saw that he was trying to apprehend something infinite using the finite resources of his mind. He despaired of being able to find God, castigated his mind for being so limited, and became furious at his shortcomings. He came to see this as rage at God for the mind he had been given. This made matters worse: how could a heart sullied by rage and ingratitude hope to approach God? The gloom of despondency descended upon him, and in the midst of this abject state God's words, 'I have not granted you knowledge, except for a finite amount' (Qur'an 17:85) came to him. Instantly, an intense emotional experience, hard to describe, took him over. Overwhelmed by feeling, he 'saw' himself as he was, a limited human, in his proper relationship to God, the limitless. All he had been given by his generous Lord passed, as it were, before his eyes: his life, his family and friends, his achievements in the world, his faith, his mind, as well as his failings and shortcomings. His heart filled with an indescribable humility and gratitude. In that moment God's words had touched and enlivened all of him, putting things into perspective. He felt reconciled, at peace.

There is a paradox at the heart of the *sufi* experience: God is 'found' at the very moment that one accepts, intellectually and emotionally, that it is possible to see only one's own projections. By creating a space for engaging with God, the omnipotent, *sufis* try to do something that stretches them to the limit of mental capacities that, by definition, cannot encompass that object. The moment it has a conception, what is conceived is not the truly omnipotent object but an object of infantile omnipotence. In recognition of this paradox *sufis* often quote the Prophet Muhammad: 'He who knows his own self (*nafs*) truly knows his Lord'.

It is the act of engaging with this inner struggle (being on 'the path') that seems to create the space in which a link with God might emerge. Its difficulty is acknowledged in the Prophet's description of God as veiled from his servant in seventy veils of light (Smith 1976). Yet,

> Those who seek God in truth will find that He comes to meet them on the way and guide them to the goal . . . In the Traditions there is a saying ascribed to the Prophet, which runs, 'God has said: "I am present when My servant thinks of Me: I am with him when he remembers Me . . . whosoever seeks to approach Me by a span, I will approach him by a cubit; and he who seeks to approach Me by one cubit, I will seek to approach him by two fathoms; and whoever walks towards Me I will run towards him."'
>
> (Smith 1976: 145)

Discussion

The question I am trying to address is: are these three internal relationships with God simply particular instances of more general ways of relating to an object, which, psychoanalytically, we could say emanate from the realm of Caesar? Or is there something that might set them apart from such 'ordinary' object relationships? I want to suggest that the first two are versions of object relating well documented and understood within the realm of Caesar – the object just happens to be called God[6] – while the third represents something different.

My patient A kneeled to the same God that Freud recognised in his analysis of the 'oceanic feeling' (Freud 1927). God represented the object of an earlier, merged relationship. In the transference, this was his experience of analytic care at a time when, too ill to work, the analysis was the main focus of his days. Internally, this support was felt as (and probably corresponded to) an early infantile state – such as the sensation of being held in his mother's arms – now much idealised. Work, on the other hand, was equated with the parental intercourse that excluded him, provoking rage and intensely destructive impulses, which mental immersion in the earlier infant–mother relationship had, in the past, shielded him from; it was this protection that he sought to reinstate.

Discovering God and recruiting him to the template of this object relationship allowed my patient to buy time for his defence. As I indicated, at first I mistakenly thought God was a new development. Because the new guise succeeded, for a time, God was, therefore, a good choice. Psychoanalytically, however, God was but the current incarnation of the analyst with whom he wished to merge; that he chose God for this purpose had little to do with qualities felt to be specific to God, in his own right, as a real other. God had been recruited to the realm of Caesar.

My friend M's God was a more sophisticated internal object with whom he had a real relationship. Unlike A, M did not seek to merge with God, nor did he feel that, as a believer, he had a direct line to God,[7] that would spare him the anxiety involved in facing his own problems. Proximity to God, through belief in general and the prayer for guidance in particular, would not result in omniscience seeping into him. Separate from him, God was perceived as willing to make available another perspective, opening up a store of knowledge usually unavailable, in order to help him reach a thought-out decision. God's help was in addition to his own mental work, not instead of it. He seemed to accept, without undue resentment, that decoding God's message was hard work; and that he might get it wrong.

As far as psychic structure is concerned, M's experience of consulting God is indistinguishable from that of any healthy individual who consults an other – externally or internally – for advice and guidance. Although M calls that object God, the process he employs is not unlike that of a non-believer who allows his unconscious to speak directly to him through dreams. This calls on a healthy capacity for object relating, which A, for example, did not have in place. In addition, judgement is required to evaluate the advice proffered,[8] retaining responsibility for decisions in the subject's own hands. From the point of view of my theme, therefore, the capacities involved are the outcome of normal psychological development; M's request for guidance is channelled to God, rather than to any other object, because religion is a significant part of his inner world. To understand the psychic processes involved we could say that, having learnt how to ask real parents (or their equivalents) for help, M has moved on to consulting an inner 'parent' called God. There is, I think, no reason to suppose that the relationship between M and God-as-guide involves psychic capacities that go beyond those acquired, honed and utilised in the realm of Caesar.

These two ways of relating to God reflect the quality of object relating that A and M were each capable of. The inner capacities involved are the products of experience with people in the real world, beginning with primary caregivers and extending into later life. As such, those capacities stem from the realm of Caesar, and when we relate to God in these ways we are, psychically, in the realm of Caesar. In addition, as an object God is indistinguishable from other, material objects. A psychoanalyst might say that God, in such instances, is but a contemporary version of a primary object: A's God seductively held him back, like his mother once did, while M's God helped him, as his parents and teachers once did.

Before examining the *sufi*'s God it is worth underlining that the question of God's existence (in external reality) lies beyond the scope of psychoanalytic inquiry, as Freud notes at the beginning of *The Future of an Illusion* (1927: 31). The *sufi*, of course, believes that God exists. For our inquiry, however, it is the nature of the unseen God (as an internal object) and the relationship with him that are at issue. God is clearly separate from the *sufi*, from whom he is sharply distinguished by omnipotence, his defining characteristic. This fundamental starting point – that God is separate and distinct from the humans – underpins the *sufi* quest.

To psychoanalysts omnipotence in an object is problematic. It is thought to be characteristic of early infancy, where it counterbalances in phantasy the fact of the infant's utter helplessness and its dependency on others for survival. Infantile omnipotence usually involves the retreat to a phantasy world, in which infant and object are immersed in a longed-for, pleasurable involvement, and which serves as a refuge from difficulties encountered in their real relationship. For instance, the psychic problem of accepting the end of a pleasurable feed can be avoided by the phantasy that the infant feeds itself, giving rise to further problems e.g. in development of the awareness of dependency. Normal in early infancy, in later life such phantasy is mostly a dangerous manic defence that easily triumphs over awareness of ordinary reality. In phantasy things can be as one wishes, and the omnipotence of infantile phantasy stems from the belief that phantasy and reality are equivalent and hence interchangeable. Any difficulty arising in an ordinary relationship can be evaded, without cost, by simply replacing it with a phantasy one; not facing difficulties is thus felt to be of no consequence. Because of the seriousness of these considerations, the presence of omnipotence in later object relationships must raise the question of whether infantile dynamics are involved.

Is the *sufi's* God omnipotent in this infantile way, as Freud thought? I think not. Although *sufis* do indeed believe God to be omnipotent, careful interrogation of their *relationship* with him yields a number of observations that suggest something more complex. First, as I have already indicated, God is seen as a separate being with whom merger is not the aim. Since God is self-sufficient, the need to be in a relationship with him is not mutual, but located firmly in the subject. Merger, on the other hand, predates separateness and the wish of the subject is thus not differentiated from that of the object; they too are merged. Although *sufis* do sometimes speak of their goal as a longing for unification with God, detailed examination of what this entails reveals a quite different process. It is a longing to develop a relationship with an object whose being cannot be comprehended, but whose presence can evidently be experienced.[9] However, to claim to have become one with God is regarded as heresy.

Second, the process involves grappling with one's projections into God. This not only acknowledges the danger of unconsciously recruiting God into wish-fulfilling phantasy, but also suggests it is inevitable. The process of self-examination, which brings projections into consciousness, may be seen as an attempt to take them back, and is reminiscent of the psychoanalytic process. However, unlike the analysand, the *sufi* aims not to make contact with his inner world; he wants to locate himself properly as subject to power that, in external reality, lies in the hands of an other. This is not an abstract notion; it is based on the recognition that humans have no control over some things that are absolutely vital to them, especially life itself. The *sufi's* attempt to enter into a relationship with God, who is regarded as having ultimate control, may be seen, psycho-analytically, as an attempt to come to terms with this fact; not only to recognise it, take it for granted, or accept it, but to reconcile his entire being, as far as possible, with it.

Are the qualities called upon in this relationship ones honed in the realm of Caesar, as I have argued with respect to the other two ways of relating to God? In so far as the capacity to relate to any object is founded upon the experience of proper early developmental care, the answer is yes. Likewise, the capacity for self-scrutiny that brings one's projections into awareness is utilised in other, ordinary, relationships. Unseen objects are also not new, but an object that, in essence, cannot be conceived of is; it is not encountered in object relationships within the realm of Caesar. *Sufis* maintain that the experience of trying to relate to God ('the creator') involves them in something quite different from what is encountered in relationships with the world – either people or things ('the created'). In ordinary relationships failure to find a desired object ushers in the dynamics of mourning (Freud 1915), which results either in acceptance of the limitations of the object, or abandoning of the object in pursuit of a more satisfactory one. At this very point, however, the *sufi* is confronted by his own limitations and has to give up the idea that his pursuit of God can bring about the desired outcome. If he is able to engage fully with this fact, something paradoxical seems to happen: what is sought does indeed come about. *Sufis* see this as dwelling at the walls of the 'ego' – that is, at the limit of human possibility – and report that occasionally seemingly solid walls give way, as if by the will of an Other, to open up a different experience. When the walls close in again, they feel immensely enriched. Since the core experience lies beyond the ego, words are not up to the task of describing it. Al-Aydarus, a fifteenth/sixteenth century *sufi*, offers the following:

> The zephyr of reunion has blown!
> with neither connection nor separation;
> By virtue of a hidden rising place,
> in which knowledge has no scope.
> For it is the fruit of certainty,
> and the attainment to the rank of perfection.
>   (Quoted by Al-Haddaad 1992: 50)

Anxiety, illusion, truth

If the distinctive relationship with an omnipotent object lies at the core of the realm of God within, are there specific anxiety situations that call this object into being?

I would like to approach this question through a brief account of work with a second patient, Mr B.

In the penultimate week before his first summer break (the longest in the analytic year) he arrived for the Friday afternoon session in mid-morning. It turned out that he had been unable to sleep the previous night, and had become convinced that lights flickering in the distance were really coded messages inviting him to come to a session in the morning. I was not in, but he gained access to the building through a service entrance, and turned back only when confronted by the locked door of my consulting room suite. As he left the voice of God gave him an ultimatum: die or go mad. He missed his actual session later in the day, and on the weekend became progressively more paranoid. When he returned the following week he was in the grip of florid delusions. In-patient psychiatric care was arranged, and he remained beyond the reach of analytic work until well after the end of the break.

Some four years later, on the Friday before a long weekend, Mr B complained of feeling depressed. He considered things that might have brought it on – events of the previous day, the continuing miserable weather etc. A surprise had come through the post that morning, he suddenly recalled, which he intended to share with me. Recently he told an acquaintance of a new creative project he had begun. The surprise was a short essay on this very theme that she happened upon. It was unbelievable how in tune the essay was with his own thinking. Their encounter was exceedingly brief, yet amazingly she picked up exactly where he was at; and what an extraordinary coincidence that she should find an essay that precisely articulated this. He mentioned, in passing, that his own thoughts had now been eclipsed by the written piece, but continued enthusing about the many aspects of the 'almost mystical connection' between the two of them.

I felt drawn into the story, and saw that excitement about the 'mystical connection' had eclipsed the earlier focus on his own project i.e. approaching separation in a different way, through awareness of a depressed feeling. I interpreted that he was preoccupied with the impending long weekend, which made him anxious; solved this by trying to become one with me in the session so that he and I shared everything. This almost mystical connection replaced the whole problem caused by my shutting him out, including the depressed feelings stirred in him.

He remained silent. At first this felt comfortable and thoughtful, but after a little while I became anxious lest I had spoken too directly of separation.[10] However, he eventually replied that he could see what I meant; if this is how he reacts to one missed session, how much worse must it be when I go away for longer? Although seemingly thoughtful, the remark contained a hint of self-accusation: how hopeless he was at managing separation, nothing had really changed etc. He had, in fact, made progress over the years, so I said that he expected me not to notice that it was now possible for him to see that the prospect of a long weekend made him depressed. He replied that he saw what I meant, and moments later asked quietly, 'How can I know for sure that I will see you again on Tuesday?'

I was on the verge of interpreting that separation results in so complete a loss of his object that he needs reassurance etc., when I hesitated, realising that this would be repetitive. His mother, I recalled, had suffered from a prolonged post-puerperal psychosis, and I wondered whether I was experienced as such a mother. When close to real feelings about object loss ('depression') was I felt to be emotionally absent, leaving him alone with them? I therefore said that his question raised a grave matter: he could not be certain he would see me again on Tuesday, but neither could I. I thought, though, that he fully expected me not to want to face that awkward fact. Instead he anticipated an interpretation aimed at covering things up. Following this intervention he was more grounded: the manic flavour gave way to a depressed atmosphere, from which he moved to a realistic engagement with issues that faced him in the immediate future.

In the session my patient voices an anxiety that when he leaves his object the loss might be permanent. At the beginning of his analysis Mr B could not tolerate this anxiety, hence his breakdown. Faced with a fear – that he might not see me again – that could not be mentalised, the feared situation came alive as something real: the middle of the night brought an unconscious conviction that his analyst was dead. He defended himself against this by splitting his internal object into an analyst who was always with him, sending him coded messages when he was in trouble etc, and the

55

harsh, punitive God he encountered later. The light of day allowed a glimmer of anxiety back in, so that he could now come to check whether I was, in fact, alive. My unavailability, however, served to re-amplify his fear to psychotic proportions.

Two observations about this use of God are relevant here. First, what he calls God – in fact, a harsh, punitive superego whose word is all-powerful – is only one side of a coin. The other half is equally omnipotent, not bounded by time, space or other reality constraints, and is always with him; this is the internal analyst who, when he is away from me in reality, sends him coded messages. Second, and at a deeper level, the patient's hatred of reality (i.e. of the fact that he could not know whether he would see me again) was so intense as to be intolerable, and was projected into God, the one responsible for everything. This freed him to act on the impulse to investigate whether I was alive or not, but it also transformed God into a fearsome, vengeful figure. Four years later he had internalised the kernel of a containing object, which enabled this anxiety to come to the fore in a less threatening way. One could say that Mr B had now learnt to trust a little more, and it was therefore more possible, with some help in the session, to verbalise this profound anxiety. He has begun to find a way out of his earlier dilemma.

Mr B raises the problem of facing the fact, mentioned earlier, that life is not under human control. It is a gift from without, and remains subject to ultimate external control. The fear that we, or a loved one, may lose it is a realistic one that we all have to face. To do so we rely on the existence of an internal containing object. Earlier on such a figure was absent from Mr B's mind (probably on account of his mother's less than optimal availability during early infancy), and his difficulties then illustrate graphically the crippling anxiety that the presence of such a figure protects us from. It is the existence of this *internal* object that provides the foundation of trust that the *external* one will return, thus containing the anxiety voiced in his question.

The true answer to Mr B's question is that we do not know, but had I put this to him I would probably have driven him psychotic once more. The answer that promoted his psychological development involved helping him to experience me as an object able to contain his anxiety in the here-and-now. My psychoanalytic answer was thus:

> if you experience me as able to tolerate that anxiety, it will bring relief. If you internalise this containing me, I can be with you always, able to comfort you when, apart from me, you so fear that I have died. You will have me inside your mind, and that will enable you to trust that I shall return.

In fact, he will have internalised a containing capacity, but its association with me will mean it is experienced as an internal version of me.[11] It is this fertile association that invites a link between internal and external object, such that the survival of the internal object is felt to reassure that the external one is alive too, even though we have no direct proof of it. Normally we tolerate the ambiguity of *believing* this to be so while at the same time *knowing* it to be untrue. The emergence of the stable internal object, a necessary developmental step, is thus also used to fulfil our wish that the external object should continue to exist. In this sense it conforms to the definition by which Freud judged belief in God to be an illusion: it is so precisely because that is how we wish it to be (Freud 1927).

The fear that a loved one might die underlines the fact that the gift of life is not in human hands. Since the source of this fear cannot be realistically overcome, the anxiety it generates is so profound that we could not live with it in its naked form.[12] The human way of mastering it invites an ambiguous and illusory equation between internal and external object. However, illusion does not face the truth head-on and I think religious systems, at their most elementary, try to do so. Fundamental, unavoidable and insoluble anxiety, I think, constitutes the emotional substrate upon which religious entities are built; they drive the individual to invest religious objects with meaning so that they become psychologically alive and real.

The realm of God

A Muslim child is taught to recite the following prayer before going to sleep at night:

> Oh God, in thy name do I die and live,

and on waking in the morning:

> All praise be to God,
> He who revived us to life after giving us death,
> and to whom we shall return.
> (Siddiqi 1968: 21)

These prayers acknowledge the anxiety I have been speaking of, connect the experience of loss to death, and assert that life and death emanate from God's realm, not Caesar's. If neither she nor her parents are in charge of life and death, at least *someone* is. Psychoanalytically, we could say that this demarcates a space in the mind for God as an object connected to a real issue crucial to the child. In her subjective experience, however, things are likely to be more complex.

At first, she is likely to picture God as a quasi-human figure – for instance as a person who lives up above, and towards whom she might have any number of feelings. The qualities attributed to this 'person' will have much in common with her experience of real others in her life: our early conceptions of God are determined by individual psychology. Mr A's was a god inside of whom he wished to live as a refuge from life's struggles; M saw God as a helpful figure who could be consulted, and would help, in his moment of real indecision and doubt; and to Mr B God was a ferocious, punitive figure who exacted a terrible punishment for his wish to check whether his analyst was alive. All of these conceptions of God bear the unmistakable mark of primary object relationships (Klauber 1974); put another way, our picture of God is utterly suffused with emotional baggage from the realm of Caesar.

This may be observed in a child in whom weaning generates intense resentment and hatred towards a deeply loved mother. If the hatred cannot be tolerated, a phantasy that her father ordered the weaning might allow the child to redirect it towards him. But if he is not particularly hateful, the idea that God has power over everything (emerging, say, after these events) allows a new compromise in which hatred can be displaced onto God. Later, the story of Abraham being ordered to sacrifice his son might reinforce an unconscious perception of God as narcissistic, arbitrary, cruel and heartless. If, however, in her world God is spoken of as loving and compassionate, he might be transformed into an exacting and demanding internal figure, whose love is conditional on obedience and is swift in punishment, a conception that might easily be confirmed by a particular reading of scripture. Hatred would have been displaced from mother to father to God; then projected into God where it is blended with his love to yield a compromise – conditional love followed by cruel punishment. The price paid for such an arrangement is that other aspects of God's omnipotence – his compassion and mercy in this instance – are sacrificed.

Normally, I think, each element in a religious system is saturated with the scars of emotional battles waged in the real, material world, which gives religion a highly personal inner meaning.[13] It implies, too, that in the mind what belongs to the realm of Caesar starts off as inevitably mixed in with what belongs to the realm of God. A corollary of this observation is that a psychologically healthy upbringing, in which affects belonging to real external objects can be experienced in relation to them and so attach to their internal representations, is likely to minimise such saturation. It is probably also a factor in enabling projections into God to be recognised as such, and taken back, a step necessary if religious objects are to claim their distinctive space in the mind.

A community of believers share a set of beliefs that, at root, address directly the unanswerable questions that are an inherent part of life. Shaped by individual psychology, their answers are individual and varied, yielding a range of religious understanding and experience. Some settle for a clear-cut approach, such as knowing that God caused everything to be, that he will look after us provided we do 'good', and that we will end up in heaven on account of it. Unconscious hatred generated by God's arbitrariness, unpredictability and inscrutability may then be projected into non-believers (using more or less racist mechanisms), who will earn God's wrath. Others able to tolerate more inner conflict may catch a glimpse of contradictions between their own emotionally coloured view of God and the one formally held by their religion. Tension, debate and disagreement about these issues might follow, allowing individuals' personal understanding of their religion to evolve. Yet others will have a burning desire to be actively involved with the being felt to play such a crucial – though taken-for-granted – role in their lives, in search of something deeper and truer. Each level of involvement with religion is more sophisticated than the preceding one, but the more sophisticated do not negate those less so; they add a level of complexity, yielding a rich and varied community in a dialogue built around shared beliefs.

What motivates the believer to have a deeper involvement with God? I think three psychological factors are crucial: inherent curiosity, the capacity to bear anxiety, and willingness to face the unknown.

The foundations of curiosity can probably already be noticed in infancy – some babies are more alert to, and involved with, their surroundings than others – and clinically, patients differ with respect to the wish to know their minds.[14] Curiosity is not always welcome as it is easily associated with infantile phantasies of getting inside the feeding breast, when the motive of getting to know becomes confused with that of getting inside in order to possess and control the object of one's dependency. Internal and external factors can exacerbate this, for instance excess hatred at being shut out of the parental bedroom may interfere with one's curiosity about what goes on inside. Answers that suffice for one person may, therefore, leave the next burning with curiosity.

Mostly those who seek God hope to find inner peace. However, when the answer to every pressing question is that God is not as imagined, that he knows but we do not, the resulting frustration easily generates hatred and resentment. People have different capacities to tolerate hatred – the *sufi* I described earlier could bear to see his aggression towards God; others struggle more with this. If it cannot be borne, then deeper curiosity about God may itself become its victim. As a result of a projection of hatred/destructiveness into the process, excessive inquiry about God may come to be seen as dangerous. Or it may manifest as a fear of the unknown. The amount of uncontained hatred within is therefore a further factor directly related to how forbidding the prospect of drawing close to the unknowable God is.

The interplay between these factors – inherent curiosity, the capacity to bear hatred and anxiety, and the related willingness to face the unknown – allows for the variation in individuals' experience of God. Let us imagine that my hypothetical child, in adulthood, were content not to delve too deeply into who her God is (i.e. to her personally), nor try to develop her relationship with him. She will have acknowledged God as responsible for life and death, and she might feel genuinely grateful to him for her life and be motivated to be a good person in return. However, psychoanalytically she will have settled for a contradiction: although acknowledging God's omnipotence, trust in her objects nonetheless involves clinging to the omnipotent illusion that I have argued equates an inner object, a product of her mind, with the external one. This perpetuates a fertile and murky transitional area of functioning (Winnicott 1953) in which something is both true and untrue: the object is simultaneously recognised as separate (with a fate not subject to our will) and experienced as belonging to one, i.e. as internal (and under our own control). Crucial for the development of trust early on, it is this solution that the *sufi* revisits in adulthood.

The recognition that in trusting that his object will reappear he 'forgets', momentarily, that control over this is in God's hands troubles the *sufi*. He sees it as an omnipotent assumption, which he tries to put right through the engagement I described earlier. Psychoanalytically, we could say that recognising he has not fully come to terms with the fact that life and death are not under his control, he tries now to do so. In so far as it is true such control is indeed vested externally, the *sufi* quest may be said to be in touch with reality. It is an attempt to move beyond taking this for granted (which we all do), to reconciling his whole being with it. I am suggesting that this emotional work goes beyond what is addressed in ordinary object relationships in the realm of Caesar. When things go well in this engagement, the believer's awareness of the fact, with all its implications, does not diminish the sense of wonder at the magnificence of all that is within and around him; instead it puts it into a proper perspective, resulting in a deeper level of gratitude for what one has. For some the object in relation to which all of this is experienced is called God, and the place where this engagement happens could therefore be thought of as the inner realm of God.

A final question relevant to the *sufi* quest is this: why do only some choose to relate self-consciously to an omnipotent object? The early achievement of a stable internal object is a crucial step in mental health; it establishes the primacy of real relationships over phantasy ones by making a link between a good internal parent and the external one. This achievement keeps alive the idea of the object in the face of frustration, and is vital in the move from narcissistic phantasy ('I feed myself'), an aspect of infantile omnipotence, to object relatedness ('My mother feeds me'). Since this puts us vitally in touch with reality, failure to do so results in serious psychopathology. All of us, therefore, except the most severely mentally ill, traverse this path: we might say that the psychic work involved is located on a terrain to which all are called and almost all are chosen.

However, I have argued that this solution is fashioned in a murky transitional area where the parent is simultaneously recognised as separate *and* felt to be part of the infant's mind. The *sufi* addresses directly the fact that this solution fudges the truth. By recognising fully that the existence of the internal object is independent of the external one, whose life is not in human hands, the *sufi* tries to come to terms with human limitation. Unlike the psychic work involved in establishing the internal good object, however, mental health does not depend on this work; failure to embark on it means simply that we have to live with an inner contradiction. We might therefore say that the psychic work involved in this is located on a terrain where many are called but few are chosen.

Conclusion

Freud was aware that he passed over the mystical aspect of religion:

> Critics [of his view that the notion of God is an unsustainable illusion which must give way to reason] persist in describing as 'deeply religious' anyone who admits to a sense of man's insignificance or impotence in the face of the universe, although what constitutes the essence of the religious attitude is not this feeling, but only the next step after it, the reaction to it which seeks a remedy for it.
>
> (Freud 1927: 32)

Given that deity is central to religion, what Freud calls 'man's insignificance or impotence' cannot be properly understood outside of the relationship between believer and deity, which I therefore placed at the heart of my inquiry. I have suggested that at the outset the deity is inevitably seen through the lens of our relationships with objects in this world; emotional colouring from the realm of Caesar suffuses our picture of God. I have gone on to suggest that by attempting to clarify the nature of God in relation to himself the mystic tries to address this difficulty head-on. From a religious point of view it may be seen as an attempt to bring his unconscious, inner 'picture' of God in line with who God really is. From a psychoanalytic point of view, it may be seen as an attempt to come to terms with a fact of life that had, in infancy, necessarily been glossed over through the use of illusion.

Notes

1 This is a revised version of a paper presented at a day conference on Psychoanalysis and Religion, organised by the Freud Museum, London, on 1 June 1996.
2 Tirmidhi died in the year 300 AH/912 CE (Heer, in Al-Tirmidhi 2003).
3 Tirmidhi's treatise focuses mainly on the inner journey towards God.
4 Briefly, the parents, perceived as omnipotent in early infancy, are not fully forgiven their limitations. A version of a parent is then re-cathected as an omnipotent god.
5 I have brought together a number of accounts from the late al-Haj Sulaiman da Costa, a seeker after 'the path of God's friends (awliyaa)'.
6 That is, there is a difference between the subject's experience and the analytic understanding of it.
7 This might represent a disguised wish for merger.
8 In this case the dream had to be decoded.
9 See Al-Aydarus' poem on page 54.

10 Briefly, Mr B understood intellectually that separations were difficult. Mention of it easily engaged an intellectual, cooperative mode e.g. he would bring associations, dreams etc. on the subject, none of which deepened his involvement with it.

11 Often patients experience it as the analyst's voice in their minds.

12 Although I shall confine my discussion to this fact, there may be others (e.g. the strength and relative proportion of life and death drives within) that may also be pertinent to religious objects.

13 I have confined my discussion to the internal object 'God'. Each entity in a religious system – God, the devil, angels, heaven, hell, rituals, an after-life, spirits etc – may be regarded as an object in its own right, which the believer conceives of and relates to in a particular way. Internally, one's religion is thus a complex affair.

14 Melanie Klein, for instance thought of this capacity as deriving from an epistemophilic instinct, and Wilfred Bion later proposed that certain psychotic patients have an excess of something that drives in the opposite direction (-K).

References

Al-Bukhari, M. (n.d.) *Sahih Al-Bukhari Volume 8*, trans. M. M. Khan. Madinah: Islamic University. Also at http://www.islamicity.com/mosque/sunnah/bukhari/

Al-Haddaad, A.A. (1992) *Gifts for the Seeker*, trans. M. al-Badawi. London: Quilliam Press.

Al-Tirmidhi, A-H. (2003) *A Treatise on the Heart*, trans. N. Heer. In *Three Early Sufi Texts*. Louisville, KY: Fons Vitae Press.

Black, D.M. (1993) What sort of a thing is a religion? A view from object relations theory. *International Journal of Psychoanalysis* 74: 613–625.

Freud, S. (1915) *Mourning and Melancholia*. SE 14.

Freud, S. (1927) *The Future of an Illusion*. SE 21.

Klauber, J. (1974) Notes on the psychical roots of religion, with particular reference to the development of eastern Christianity. *International Journal of Psychoanalysis* 55: 249–255. Reprinted as The psychical roots of religion: A case study. In J. Klauber (1986) *Difficulties in the Analytic Encounter*. London: Free Association Books/ Maresfield Library.

Pfister, O. (1993) The illusion of a future: a friendly disagreement with Prof Sigmund Freud, edited by P. Roazen. *International Journal of Psychoanalysis* 74: 557–579.

Siddiqi, M.A.H. (1968) *Prayers of the Prophet*. Lahore: Sh. M. Ashraf.

Smith, M. (1976) *The Way of the Mystics*. London: Sheldon Press.

Winnicott, D.W. (1953) Transitional objects and transitional phenomena. In *Collected Papers: Through Paediatrics to Psychoanalysis*. New York: Basic Books.

3

THE CASE FOR A CONTEMPLATIVE POSITION

David M. Black

> Two birds, companions always united, perch in the same tree. One eats the ripe fruit, the other looks on without eating.
>
> Svetasvatara Upanisad

Introduction

It is clear that there are many ways in which the component elements of religion – worship, ritual, doctrine, group membership, ethical values, and so on – have their analogues in the affective world that psychoanalysis recognises. It is comparatively easy, therefore, for psychoanalysis to stage a takeover of the entire domain, and to say (as Freud did) that religion is made up of nothing but phantasy and a projection of our wishes and fears into the heavens. We can thus comfort ourselves in relation to our fear of our own or others' death (by believing in an afterlife), in relation to our badness (by believing in our goodness when we perform the ritual or obey the rules), in relation to our insignificance (all souls are infinitely precious to God), and so on. We can even keep our children in line, by scaring them out of their wits by a description of the fires of hell. The great sermon on damnation in Joyce's *A Portrait of the Artist as a Young Man* is, in its perverted way, a psychological masterpiece.

An approach of this sort, very familiar to psychoanalysis, keeps religion firmly subordinate to psychology. And there is a paradox in the wish to speak respectfully about both religion and psychoanalysis, because both disciplines aspire to offer the dominating vertex: from the perspective of analysis, religion can only be a department of 'phantasy', and from the perspective of religion, psychoanalysis can only be a this-worldly practice which religion transcends.

This is so even if the religion, like Zen Buddhism, asserts that ultimately the world of Enlightenment is the same as the world of un-Enlightenment – nevertheless, there has been a journey to take to discover it as such. And the motives of the Enlightened are no longer the same as those of the un-Enlightened.

The notion of 'transcendence' is, I think, the key to the difference between religious and scientific thought. By 'transcendence' in this context I mean only that one value can be 'higher' than another, not merely as a matter of subjective preference, but 'in reality'. From what standpoint can such a reality be assessed? Ordinary materialist scientists can believe in extraordinary things such as the realm of quantum physics, the astounding innate precisions of instinct in the insect world, the monstrous irrational cruelty and destructiveness of which human beings are capable, and so forth, and they can sort-of concoct all these things together into a single picture of the world (though the discontinuity between quantum and classical physics is a profound worry to many physicists) – but they can give no meaning to the idea of a value-system which is other than subjective and an expression ultimately of the *Realpolitik* of evolution.

This inability to give a meaning to 'transcendence' is not, for materialist scientists, just a contingent incapacity, from which they happen to suffer; it is necessary, and it derives from conservation principles and from the fact that all our apprehension, whether of quantum particles, insects, terrorist actions or, indeed, of what purports to be religious experience, is ultimately dependent on electro-chemical activity in the brain. That is the inescapable vertex from which science conceives our experience, and there's no getting past it. Mystical union, Buddhist Enlightenment, divine revelation, colossally moving or over-whelmingly persuasive as they may be to those who experience them, are and can only be the subjective correlate of certain sorts of brain event. If so, in what way can they be supposed to have any superiority over other sorts of brain event?

What I shall attempt to do in this chapter is to explore one possible way in which, without departing from the broad consensus of current psychoanalytic and neuroscientific understanding, the idea of 'transcendence' might find a meaning – not quite the meaning of traditional religious thought, but not a meaning, either, that is wholly subordinate to our current psychological under-standings. Whether my argument is entirely convincing I am uncertain; but it seems likely that the debate between scientific and religious modes of thought will not be resolved unless each side is willing to adapt a bit in response to the other. In saying this I am differing from another position which I very much respect: that which Stephen Jay Gould (2001) and many others have adopted, which says that science and religion are 'non-overlapping magisteria', two domains of human thought, both authoritative and both necessary, which exist in different dimensions and in no way impact on one another, either in support or in contradiction. In my approach, by contrast, there must be some overarching picture which enables us to see the two things as part of a single coherent universe.

I begin by proposing an experiment in how we think about consciousness.

The impact on consciousness of 'conversation'

The first issue I want to address is this: what are the consequences of the fact that our conscious experience comes to be structured so strongly by language that it is hard, perhaps impossible, to imagine living in a world which is not differentiated and structured by formulas of a linguistic and grammatical kind; and yet, initially, in infancy, our conscious experience was not verbally structured? There is a persistent strand in our thinking, in philosophy, art, and also in religious mysticism, which suggests that language imposes a distortion on experience, but that it is difficult, perhaps impossible, to escape from the many-layered webs that language lays over the world. We are intrigued by stories such as those of Kaspar Hauser, or the wild boy of Aveyron, in which a human being has developed without language, as if somehow they might give us access to some truth that language hides from us – but in fact, of course, what we encounter are human beings who are sadly impaired in their social and cognitive capacities. The fascination for children of stories in which animals speak – like the Dr Dolittle books – is perhaps a variant on this, capturing a sense of loss the child feels on entering the human social world.

The philosopher Thomas Nagel, in a famous paper entitled 'What is it like to be a bat?' (1979a), came to the conclusion that we have no idea what it is like to be a bat. We can only, he says, imagine conscious states that we might in principle experience ourselves, and since we do not have a bat's nervous system and sensorium, its experience is quite simply beyond our ken.

If so, perhaps we have to give the same answer to the question, what is it like to be a baby? After all, a baby's brain, with no capacity for episodic memory, and minimal communication between the two hemispheres, is extremely unlike our own, and the internal stream of verbal consciousness which is so familiar to us can be no part of a baby's awareness; yet we have all been babies, and our interaction with babies is compelling and feels intelligible, at any rate sometimes – it would seem strange to think we have no imaginative access at all to a baby's states of mind.

As an experiment, I shall approach this question by provisionally setting aside the familiar account from Freud of two mental states, Conscious and Unconscious, with their various subdivisions of Preconscious, Repressed unconscious, System unconscious, and so on. These divisions, the so-called First Topography, are extremely useful from the point of view of therapeutic practice, but they nicely demonstrate precisely the problem that using words inflicts on us: they focus the light of consciousness from a particular angle, and what they illuminate they reveal very clearly, but what they put in shadow they hide from us. For the sake of this 'thought experiment', I shall propose, therefore, a different model: that we have several grades of consciousness. These grades of consciousness can each be inhabited by ego or the sense of 'I', though ordinarily at any given moment one of them is particularly the location of ego. How many of these grades are there? Well, perhaps indefinitely many, but certainly more than one.

On this model, what happens in psychoanalytic work is that the analyst's understanding and interpretations allow the patient to inhabit a different consciousness. Suppose, for example, a patient in individual therapy who is also in a group, whose conscious motives are entirely benign – he 'only wants to help the group reach a deeper level' – recurrently describes episodes in the group in which he has spoken in ways that create resentment and anger, and leave him feeling misunderstood and unaccountably isolated. The analyst is initially puzzled: the patient's account of his contribution sounds anodyne, or perhaps genuinely insightful. But then it occurs to the analyst to wonder about the nonverbal signals which may have accompanied the contribution – its timing, tone of voice, underlying motivation, etc. The analyst suggests to the patient that, when he made these contributions, perhaps he was in fact angry himself, was feeling outside the net of communication in the group, and his 'desire to help' concealed another set of motivations, to attack angrily, to be noticed, and so on. One patient (let's call him A) might respond to such an interpretation by refusing to 'go there'; he denies that anything of the sort was going on, and he stays with his own account. Another patient, B, might agree, on reflection, that something like that was happening, and might agree that it played a part in the disappointing response he received.

Interpretation of this sort is the small change of any analytic session; it is essentially to do with change of focus. Patient B, who accepted the interpretation (unless he was merely being compliant) was changing his focus from one part of the remembered episode to another, and also consenting to *really attend* to something that was not unconscious but from which attention had been withheld. (It was preconscious, in Freud's language.) With an extra-transference interpretation, this can often take place at a mainly cognitive level; the same thing done in the immediacy of the transference brings in the more disturbing, affective elements.

We now know (Gabbard and Westen 2003) that cognitive and psychoanalytic interpretations – and I am assuming that every analytic practitioner inevitably uses both – affect different parts of the brain, cognitive work affecting mainly cortical layers, long-term psychoanalytic work also affecting subcortical structures. If in the course of therapy patient B becomes able to be more consistently in touch with his own motives for his actions, and able to take them seriously, he comes to inhabit his brain in a somewhat new way, regularly drawing on a larger range of the information it makes available to him.

The point in terms of our present question is that such changes are initiated by verbal interaction. I shall use the word 'conversation' as a general term for verbal interaction, stretching its ordinary meaning a little to include all sorts of verbal interactions including social chat, analytic sessions, lectures, listening to the radio, reading, etc. All such verbal interactions result in continual modification and stimulus to mental structure, and presumably to actual brain-structure as well.

Conversation is a necessity, and is intensely desired. Edwin Wallace (1991: 269) writes: 'language does not merely express the psyche, but is constitutive of it; it is the very vehicle by which one presents oneself to the world and by which one receives and responds to it'. Deaf children without deaf peers invent their own sign-language (Economist 2004). Babies blind from birth, who have never seen hands, either their own or anyone else's, spontaneously make expressive gestures using their hands (Trevarthen and Aitken 2001: 6).

What happens when a psychoanalytic interpretation 'works' is that the consciousness of the patient is enlarged and to some extent relocated by the interaction with the analyst. What we speak of as the goals of analysis, the greater capacity for intimacy, the increased tolerance of ambivalence, the withdrawal of projections and expulsion of introjections, the more accurate drawing of the boundaries between self and other — all these things are testimony to the power of 'conversation' in shaping awareness and thereby modifying the world the patient invests with affect-and-cognition. A patient's use of language is reshaped to some extent in the course of an analysis, hopefully in a way that creates a more accurate 'fit' with his experience, and encompasses a larger range of it.

What we do in psychoanalysis is a local variant of what happens at 15–42 months

The child's entry into the web of human conversation begins overtly at the age of 12–18 months, when he or she begins to use recognisable words. The take-up of new language then occurs at prodigious speed until about age 5, after which it slows up, but it continues throughout childhood and adolescence and, more slowly, throughout the rest of active life. To learn a new language is, at least temporarily, to adopt a somewhat changed personality, as well described by Eva Hoffman (1991) in her autobiography.

Prior to the age of 12 or 15 months is the stage usually described in psychoanalytic writings as preverbal. This term is not really satisfactory, as there is no stage of babies' lives in which they are not interacting with adults and older children who use words to them, and they respond, if not to the precise semantic meaning of the words, to the musical and gestural components of the communication. Already by the age of 2 weeks babies show clear signs of recognising specific words used by their mothers (Share 1994). Babies in general are highly responsive to communications couched in words, particularly in 'motherese', that is, words spoken with dramatic variations of pitch and emphasis, and accompanied by highly expressive facial and gestural signals. The developmental psychologists Colwyn Trevarthen and Kenneth Aitken (2001) use the term 'proto-conversational readiness' to describe the posture of the baby in relation to such interactional possibilities. Analogously, the term 'protoverbal' is preferable to the term 'preverbal' when describing the developmental stages prior to active language-use.

What is changing, as the infant moves through the protoverbal stages and enters the overtly verbal phase? We could, of course, describe it in many different dimensions. Freud initially, constructing a one-person model of the psyche, spoke of the changing bodily locations of desire. Later, as he became more aware of the huge role played by aggression, mourning, guilt, etc., the fundamental importance of object-relations forced itself upon his attention (Freud 1917, 1923). Melanie Klein accommodated these insights more systematically by giving a central place to anxiety and phantasy, and projected back into protoverbal babyhood a picture of phantasy activity based on what could be learned from children who had reached the stage of verbal functioning.

Nowadays, with ever more precise observation of babies, it has become clear that classical psychoanalysis tended to underestimate the extent of the infant's capacity both for self-organisation and for intersubjective awareness. There is now abundant evidence that babies are born anticipating a sympathetic inter-personal environment in which they will be proactive as well as responsive, and without this they are traumatised. Filmed studies of mother–baby interaction reveal orderly age-related transformations in the baby's interaction throughout the first year, intricately coordinated with the mother's reciprocally changing patterns of play and communication (Trevarthen and Aitken 2001; Stern 1985). As Trevarthen and Aitken emphasise, attachment alone is not enough; the baby also requires companionship.

The outcome for the infant of these intense interactions with one or more companions is a set of 'implicit relational expectations' (Daniel Stern's phrase) which will affect him, for better or worse, throughout life. The expectations derived from the first year are 'implicit', that is to say, unconscious and nonverbal, and are very difficult if not impossible to change in later life, no doubt because they are imprinted in complexly embedded patterns of synaptic connections in the brain. For this reason, the tendency of much recent research is to emphasise the continuities between protoverbal and verbal functioning. In this chapter, however, I want to foreground some of the *differences* created by the shift from protoverbal to verbal mental functioning. It involves a profound change in the *sort* of consciousness with which children apprehend their external and internal world. I want to ask two questions of this transition. First, what is gained by it? And second, what is lost by it? I also want to keep in mind the view that many religious practitioners express, of language as a potential obstacle to some sorts of awareness.

What is gained by the transition to verbal consciousness?

Essentially, one crucial gain results from this transition: children join as active participants in the ever-changing web of 'conversation' which unites human beings into society. There are, in any society, certain agreements about what constitutes meaningful behaviour, what it makes sense to be interested in or to attend to, and children who are to be successful members of the society need to enter comfortably into these agreements. In psychoanalytic language, they internalise and identify with objects which affirm these skills and goals and approve their pursuing them. Neuroscience tells the same story in terms of neuronal pathways which are enriched and strengthened, or alternatively deleted, in response to social interaction (Edelman 1992). 'The ball' in so many childhood games – football, baseball, cricket, tennis, and so on – is a symbol of such social consensus. Children have to learn to 'keep their eye on the ball', and also to catch, throw, kick, use a bat or racquet – and the majority of children learn to do so adequately without too much difficulty. Autistic children, however, do not see the point: they may attend no more to the ball than to any other point in their visual field. They fail to enter the social consensus, and are not set to succeed at society's goals. Less pathologically, children from immigrant families often suffer a related confusion: goals that are 'obvious' to their school-mates are not obvious to them.

Language, the instrument that grasps and gives clarity to conscious experience (Freud 1923), is the medium in which these goals are set up and communicated, and the charm of verbal communication is a very large part of the bonding that holds together friendship-, work- and family-groups, which together generate, designate and pursue these socially understood goals. Reciprocally, shared exercise of social skills and shared pursuit of social goals reinforce in turn the bonding of these groups. It is hard to overstate the importance, therefore, of the transition to verbal consciousness. When a child learns language, people are only half-joking when they say he or she is joining the human race.

Precisely because of its power, however, the transition carries a great danger. It is that society's goals distort or supplant the child's own biological goals. The child comes to have essentially a double definition: he or she is both a member of society and a biological unit, and while the child has to succeed as the one, he or she must also succeed as the other. If the society the child joins – which in the first instance is the couple of baby and primary care-giver, but then rapidly widens out to the family as a whole and then in a range of further directions – if this initial society exerts influences which take the child away from his or her biological goals, psychological damage results.

If we tell this story in neuroscientific terms, we are speaking here of the development of the neural networks of the two hemispheres of the brain. Until about the age of 18 months, the largely nonverbal right hemisphere is dominant; from 18 months, prefrontal callosal axons begin to grow across from the left hemisphere, and dominance begins to shift from the right hemisphere to the left, which is primarily associated with verbal activity. From the age of about 3½ years, the left, verbal hemisphere has become dominant, and it will remain so for the rest of life (Schore 2003; Solms and Turnbull 2002).

The age of around 3½ years figures in a number of developmental schemas. It was the age at which Freud, though not Melanie Klein, reckoned the Oedipal phase to begin, and it is also the age identified by Peter Fonagy and Mary Target (1996, 2000; Target and Fonagy 1996) as marking the start of the capacity to 'mentalise', i.e. to imagine others as having minds which can have different content from one's own. According to the neuroscientist Allan Schore (2003), it is the age at which psychic conflict, between the verbal self-representations of the left hemisphere and the nonverbal self-representations of the right hemisphere, becomes a possibility. Part of what psychoanalysis has described under the heading of the Oedipus complex can perhaps equally be understood in terms of struggling towards some reconciliation of left and right hemispheric functioning.

The picture is, therefore, that in the first 18 months of the child's life, brain development is occurring at prodigious speed and predominantly in the nonverbal right hemisphere. Just as the chemical composition of breast-milk changes according to the developing baby's needs, so too the emotional and gestural responses of the mother adapt unconsciously and with great subtlety to the changing capacities of the growing infant. The word 'attachment' is used to describe the result. Attachment to the primary care-giver is the medium in which the development of the right hemisphere takes place and it strongly influences the patterning of the synapses which become established or deleted.

To pick out one suggestive point. Allan Schore (2003) emphasises in particular that the internalisation of a capacity for affect regulation is one of the fruits of the mental structure that results from this protoverbal conversation. Affect regulation, he says, 'is not just the dampening of negative emotion. It also involves an amplification of positive emotion, a condition necessary for more complex self-organisation' (2003: 4). This will be worth recalling when we come to think of the functions of religious activities.

All subsequent emotional development takes place on the basis of this profound unspoken inwardness of right-hemispheric consciousness. Learning to keep an eye on the social ball makes huge demands on the developing child, which require so much attention that they can become serious causes of distortion or derailment. Psychoanalysis describes patients who use what we call intellectual or manic defences. These are people who have learned to speak with some coercive quality of intelligence or exuberance, which at the same time puts them out of touch with crucial aspects of the emotional reality of their situation. Winnicott (1960) wrote of the 'false self' which develops when children are unfree to express their own needs, and learn instead to comply with the apparently greater needs of the mother. Distortions of this sort may be introduced whenever internal conflict becomes unbearable, often because of quite ordinary requirements, for example the need to fit in to the psychic structure of the sibling set. Frank Sulloway (1996) has made a comparison of a large number of the scientists at times of scientific revolution, who either rapidly came to support the new theory, or who adamantly opposed it – i.e. those who were adaptable and those who remained conservative. His very consistent finding was that conservative scientists are predominantly first-born siblings, more flexible ones later-borns. A fact of this sort is highly suggestive of the pressures within sibling sets that lead in the long run to profoundly different character-structure.

The gain of the transition to a verbal consciousness, if things go reasonably well, is a capacity to unite social and biological aims and to live satisfyingly in the social world without forfeiting or frustrating the fundamental biological motivations that are the bedrock of personal fulfilment. The painful adjustments that these often contradictory requirements entail are one way of describing the content of what Melanie Klein called the depressive position. It is significant that the depressive position is conventionally described in terms of the capacity to unite parts into wholes, parts of the self as well as parts of the object.

What are the losses of the transition?

The losses of the transition to verbal consciousness are above all to do with the immediacy and vividness of experience. What Freud described as the 'primary process', characteristic of mental functioning in the System Ucs, includes many elements of Klein's paranoid-schizoid position, with its relating to parts of objects and its chaotic turmoil of 'deep unconscious phantasy'. Freud I think had in mind the blind unconscious 'will' or 'striving' of Schopenhauer, which was the ultimate reality of the 'inwardness' of a world given to us in two modes, from the inside (first-person) as 'will' and from the outside (third-person) as 'representation' (Schopenhauer 1819). The unconscious can do nothing but wish, as Freud put it.

This (relatively speaking) immediate contact with 'wishing' or willing is the joy and misery of the protoverbal stages of development. This is where we meet what Freud called 'the initial pleasure-ego', with its peremptory judgements on reality, 'It shall be inside me' or 'It shall be outside me'. As Freud (1925) says, the ego-alien, the external, and the bad are initially synonymous, and they are matched by the ego-syntonic, the internal and the good. These judgements in turn constitute the mechanism that establishes what Klein (1946) later described as the primary (healthy) splitting of the world and the self into good and bad.

The uninhibited vividness of this present-tense experience is lost with the transition to a verbal consciousness. The attraction of hallucinogenic drugs is perhaps that they reinstate some of the infantile experience of physical sensation – both in its clarity and in its 'timeless' (and intensely interesting) quality. The 'adhesive identification' that Esther Bick described (Bick 1968; Harris 1982) also belongs to this protoverbal consciousness, a defensive manoeuvre against onward development and change by attaching oneself without thought to an experience of perceiving.

A confusion of states of consciousness with *stages* of conscious development has led some thinkers to believe that primary-process thinking, with its 'symmetrical' or reversible grammar, is characteristic of infancy, and that ego states such as the paranoid-schizoid position are representative of protoverbal stages of development. This is to underestimate the 'normality' of protoverbal functioning. There are several senses in which the protoverbal consciousness is in outstandingly accurate contact with its experience and these are obscured if it is judged by the standards of later consciousness.

One of these senses is the 'vividness' of its physical sensations. Another is, I suggest, the quality of its contact with certain sorts of emotional experience. Freud in *Moses and Monotheism* (1939) returned to the philogenetic argument he had first put forward in *Totem and Taboo* (1913), and claimed that 'an experience in the primaeval ages of the human family' had left 'permanent traces' in the human mind. This argument reads oddly nowadays and is generally rejected by modern biologists, who believe that changes in DNA can occur only at random and uninfluenced by the experience of the organism. If they are correct, that leaves homeless Freud's idea that such 'permanent traces' might become the basis of religious conviction. However, it is possible to reinstate his thought if we think that, instead of relating to the past experience of the species, the conviction carried by religions, etc, may depend on vividly experienced episodes in the protoverbal stages of the development of the individual – not remembered in verbalisable form (episodic memory depends on the maturation of the hippocampus, which occurs subsequent to the 18-month threshold), but nevertheless stored in implicit memory in the structures of the right brain.

Clinical evidence suggests that even very early experiences may be carried through in some way into verbal consciousness, though not in the form of episodic memories.

Mr S, a competent 50-year-old man, whose treatment I supervised, would become extremely angry with his female therapist. He would be first very withdrawn, and then contemptuous and despairing. What he said repeatedly was: 'You don't pick me up!' Both she and he were at a loss to know how to understand this statement, and the passionate hatred into which it carried him. It was only after the therapist had quietly stayed for many sessions with the fact that this was his experience, that he happened to mention that he had been born prematurely and had been in an incubator for the first week of his life. His mother had been allowed to watch him through the glass screen, but not to touch him. (As the therapist subsequently commented: 'the preverbal communication went both ways . . . he was also able to put me in touch with being an angry inadequate mother who was completely helpless, as she must have been'.) Whether his enormous despair, hatred and contempt were directly connected with this early situation we had, of course, no means of knowing, but the therapist's careful interpretation of his passionate feeling of 'not being picked up' in terms of that early experience proved remarkably successful in resolving what had threatened to become an impasse.[1]

What I am suggesting is that the baby's experiences in emotional interaction may be particularly clear, and not gainsayable. The rapture of the 2-month-old baby during interactions to do with feeding and changing with a loving, lively and sympathetic mother may be conceived as laying down in the right brain a 'knowledge' – a certainty – which if it were verbal we might summarise as a knowledge that to be loved and to love are wonderful and life-giving. Subsequent experiences with loved and loving others serve to confirm that primal certainty, and in adult life the compelling delight and liberation of falling in love, and the conviction of the goodness of self and other that is part of it, re-contact that early irrefutable, non-ambivalent emotion. On the other hand, if the mother is ambiguous, fearful of the intensity of her own passions, or doubtful of her own worthiness to receive love, the baby may be given a confusing and aversive signal, which causes him too to become in later life ambivalent or avoidant in the presence of ardour and the possibility of love.

Similarly, there can be moments of great peace in mother–baby interaction, moments when there is nothing to be done, when the baby experiences the maternal reverie without excitement or apparent content. At such times, perhaps the breathing of the two parties is the central object of conscious awareness. Such moments are not infrequent, and like experiences of more excited loving they may carry with them an unquestionable quality of 'goodness'.

Rachel Blass (2003) suggests that in *Moses and Monotheism* Freud was wondering about the origin of his own (non-religious) convictions, such as his belief in the pursuit of truth, which he held powerfully and independently of observable 'evidence'. We may speculate that some of the characteristics of the mother's early communication with the baby are relevant here too. Perhaps the open face and uncomplicated emotional expression in 'motherese' are a source of great joy to the baby (and by contrast emotionally complex or shaded expressions may be a source of pain or sadness), and the origin of the love of truth may lie in these responses. We are speaking, in all these cases, of qualities of feeling which may be experienced with great clarity and accuracy by the baby, for which our later language is too blunt and imprecise an instrument.

This account of the origin of conviction in later life depends on the assumption that certain sorts of later experience can make a bridge between protoverbal and verbal consciousness. To establish a unity between the two sorts of consciousness has perhaps a very special power, felt to be 'significant'. Hans Loewald (1978) has suggested that experiences of 'eternity' reported by mystics – eternity not in the sense of everlastingness but in the sense of a 'timeless moment', a *nunc stans* – may derive from an enlarged construction of consciousness when 'primary and secondary modes of mentation may be known together'. Perhaps the power of art also has to do with this bridging across between verbal and protoverbal consciousness – a successful work of art being one that communicates in some way similar or harmonious messages both to the verbal, thinking brain and to the nonverbal, sensuous, emotional right brain. This would help us to understand the reciprocal importance of 'form' and 'content' in a successful work of art, and its peculiarly satisfying, stabilising quality that can be present even when the subject-matter is tragic or harrowing.

I think such an account gives a reasonably persuasive picture of why certain subjectively experienced moments of conviction, conversion, or aesthetic satisfaction occur. However, it fails to give an adequate basis for responsibly held, enduring convictions. Experiences, however impressive, are merely experiences and like other experiences they are open to interrogation as to their meaning, their relation to our existing values, our larger world-view, and so on. Exciting moments of insight may prove, on reflection, hollow, trivial or dangerously misleading. We need to be able to distinguish between excited, transient moments of 'certainty' – some conversion experiences are of this kind – and enduring, responsible, principled convictions, such as the concern for truth of a Giordano Bruno or a Darwin, or the religiously based concern for justice of a Martin Luther King or a Dietrich Bonhoeffer.

This question takes us beyond the scope of this chapter, because to answer it would bring in the importance of validation by a like-minded group. There are myths of solitary seekers, but the reality is likely to be that great principled achievements take place in dialogue, internal or external, with others who share one's concerns. However, I want to focus here on the inward template that influences such dialogue, and we may glimpse its origin when we think of early experience in the protoverbal stages, laid down in some way in the right hemisphere of the brain. Such experiences can support later 'convictions' of many kinds, including of course not only negative ones such as settled murderous hatred or pathological jealousy, but also positive ones such as convictions of the importance of truth, justice and compassion. Where the connection is made to moments of peace between mother and baby, moments when nothing needed to be done, then perhaps the way lies open to a conviction of 'goodness' of an ontological rather than a passionate kind. Such a conviction seems to resemble those described by religious people as deriving sometimes from informal, spontaneous events, and sometimes from more formalised experiences attained through prayer and meditation. It's perhaps also this nonverbal re-contact with early experience which allows the individual some degree of independence from the glamour of group membership. Bion (1992: 152) in one of his *Cogitations* suggested that Plato's famous image of humankind as a group, seated in a cave with their backs to the light, essentially expresses a recognition that the entice-ments of group membership may be so compelling that they prevent us from turning to look at what we could 'see' to be true.

What is at stake in this thought-experiment, and how does it relate to our starting-point?

What have we achieved by this thought-experiment? We set out to conceptualise some sorts of what Freud called 'unconscious', and Melanie Klein called 'positions', as different sorts of consciousness. Doing so brings into view the possibility that consciousness exists in a layered series, of which the paranoid-schizoid and depressive positions are two members (or two large classes of members). What characterises each member of the series is that it includes the data of its predecessor in a more economical synthesis, allowing a larger overview of the subject's total situation and a wider extension of sympathy to the denizens of the subject's world (usually in psychoanalytic language referred to as his 'objects'; this is odd, however, in respect of sympathy because sympathy is with the other perceived as a subject: Black 2004a).

If, in addition to our various theoretical models, designed to cope with different dimensions of psychic development, we include this layered, hierarchical picture, it becomes possible to conceive of a further layer, a contemplative layer or 'contemplative position', which can be accommodated without prejudice to the existing developmental and structural models which psychoanalysis employs. This 'contemplative position' is one from which the experience of being alive in the world can be perceived and thought about without the need for imme-diate action. A developmental and neurological origin for this contemplative position can be glimpsed in times of tranquillity with the mother in the earliest phases of babyhood, which are then inscribed in implicit form in the nonverbal structures of the right hemisphere.

What happens in some sorts of meditation, such as Buddhist mindfulness meditation (*vipassana*), is that the compulsive action and response that character-ise the relationship world is stilled and seen increasingly by way of non-verbal, more steady experiences of consciousness which are hard to access (and harder still to maintain). These more steady experiences of consciousness reach deeper than the verbal levels to contact implicit emotional memories of a stable 'contentless' togetherness with the mother during the protoverbal phases at times when there was nothing needing to be done. There has been much discussion in recent years of the relationship between psychoanalysis and meditational experiences. (For example by James Grotstein (2000). Grotstein's argument takes a different form from my own, but his suggestion of a 'transcendent position' parallels in certain respects my proposal of a 'contemplative position'.) There is little doubt now that meditation causes significant and measurable effects, for example in improving recovery times from physical trauma, in enhancing the working of the circulatory and immune systems and in creating stable and repeatable patterns of neural activity measurable by fMRI scans (Benson 1976; d'Aquili and Newberg 1999; Goleman 2003; Guardian 2004). It has been hard to find a place for these findings in the psychological picture given by psychoanalysis. However, the fact that meditation has benign consequences for body and emotional functioning suggests that it should be taken seriously as creating an identifiable structure and contributing to 'health' in the widest sense. It is possible that this state also gives access to a more accurate or far-reaching ontological perception as recently discussed by Engler and Mitchell (2003) in terms of the Buddhist no-self doctrine.

The 'contemplative position' is a position comparable to the depressive and paranoid-schizoid positions, that is to say, an ego-state or series of ego-states with definable characteristics including above all tolerance of frustration, anxiety and excitement and a willingness to contemplate rather than to act on motives that arise. Remembering Allan Schore's emphasis that successful affect-regulation involves an amplification of positive emotions, we may note that positive emotion is often deliberately enhanced by meditations that set out to create a 'compassionate' state of mind. (It is of interest that in Indian religions the Sanskrit word translated as 'compassion' implies an affect that is directed first towards the self and then towards others: Goleman 2003.) No doubt the emphasis on devotion and love in other religions performs a similar function.

Like other states of mind, the contemplative position can be idealised. We may recognise this when we meet the not uncommon picture of a meditator who becomes rather dismissive of ordinary relationships and responsibilities. Unidealised, however, experience of this position may enable him or her to become more reliable and in a profound sense more 'accessible'.

Finally, to come back to our starting-point, the contemplative position allows us to find a possible meaning for the word 'transcendent'. The contemplative position 'transcends' the ordinary motives of pleasure-seeking and pain-avoidance, in favour of contemplation and understanding. Coupled with a recognition of the generalisable nature of sympathy (Black 2004a), it makes comprehensible that there can be a positive wish for motives of justice and compassion, rather than seeing justice as desirable solely as a consolation for unfulfilled narcissistic longings (Freud 1921). We may understand it as another position too in relation to the representations of the two hemispheres of the brain – a position from which the 'fit' between verbal and nonverbal awarenesses may be considered and, perhaps, somewhat improved.

The contemplative position is *not* transcendent, however, in the sense of giving access to some 'higher reality' or ultimate truth, and in this respect it may be disappointing to some religionists. We can't escape from what the neuroscientist Francisco Varela called 'the intrinsic circularity in cognitive science wherein the study of mental phenomena is always that of [i.e. a study done by] an experiencing person' (Varela 1996; see also Black 2004b). We remain in the phenomenal world, and the world of 'noumena' remains closed to us. Nothing a scientific thinker can say, therefore, can dispense with the need for conscious 'faith', an act of subjective commitment beyond what can be guaranteed by evidence, if convictions are to be maintained or values securely underpinned. This is seen vividly with the large-scale values, such as justice and compassion, which clearly compete with our ordinary drive-based motives, but in fact it is true even in the more intimate sphere of values which has been so well described by psychoanalysis in its account of the depressive position and the role of envy, gratitude, cruelty, remorse, etc. in our treatment of our objects. 'Faith' is the product of an act of commitment by a 'subject' prepared to entrust himself to his own subjective conviction; it cannot be guaranteed by objective evidence because, in the last analysis, subjectivity cannot be discovered in objective evidence objectively considered (Nagel 1979b; Velmans 2000; Black 2004b). The furthest the scientist can go is to describe the conditions in which decisions with regard to faith may be made, and may deserve intellectual respect.

This picture of a contemplative position also makes room for the reservation that many psychoanalysts feel towards religious ways of thinking, that they can serve as an escape from the real conflicts of the patient's social and biological life. It does so by emphasising that the 'higher' levels of consciousness can indeed be used defensively, to bypass conflict on the lower levels, and if so the result is weakness and incompleteness, sometimes of catastrophic dimensions, in the patient's life as a whole. We see this, for example, when a patient attempts to bypass the paranoid-schizoid struggles of adolescence and adopts attitudes of precocious 'depressive position' maturity which lead on to breakdown in early adulthood or midlife. Something of the same sort is seen sometimes in those who aspire too one-sidedly to a spiritual development.

Note

1   I am grateful to Mrs Dot Phillips for permission to use this material.

References

Benson, H. (1976) *The Relaxation Response.* New York: HarperTorch.

Bick, E. (1968) The experience of the skin in early object relations. *International Journal of Psychoanalysis* 49: 484–486.

Bion, W.R. (1992) *Cogitations*. London: Karnac.

Black, D.M. (2004a) Sympathy reconfigured: Some reflections on sympathy, empathy and the discovery of values. *International Journal of Psychoanalysis* 85(3): 579–595.

Black, D.M. (2004b) 'A fact without parallel': Consciousness as an emergent property. *British Journal of Psychotherapy* 21(1): 69–82.

Blass, R. (2003) The puzzle of Freud's puzzle analogy. *International Journal of Psychoanalysis* 84: 669–682.

d'Aquili, E. and Newberg, A. (1999) *The Mystical Mind: Probing the Biology of Religious Experience*. Minneapolis, MN: Fortress Press.

Economist (2004) Signs of success, 21 February.

Edelman, G. (1992) *Bright Air, Brilliant Fire*. New York: Basic Books.

Engler, J. and Mitchell, S. (2003) Being somebody and being nobody: A reexamination of the understanding of self in psychoanalysis and Buddhism. In J. Safran (ed.) *Psychoanalysis and Buddhism: An Unfolding Dialogue*. Boston, MA: Wisdom.

Fonagy, P. and Target, M. (1996) Playing with reality, I: Theory of mind and the normal development of psychic reality. *International Journal of Psychoanalysis* 77: 217–233.

Fonagy, P. and Target, M. (2000) Playing with reality, III: The persistence of dual psychic reality in borderline patients. *International Journal of Psychoanalysis* 81: 853–873.

Freud, S. (1913) *Totem and Taboo*. SE 13.

Freud, S. (1917) *Mourning and Melancholia*. SE 14.

Freud, S. (1921) Group psychology and the analysis of the ego. SE 18.

Freud, S. (1923) The Ego and the Id. SE 19.

Freud, S. (1925) Negation. SE 19.

Freud, S. (1939) *Moses and Monotheism*. SE 23.

Gabbard, G. and Westen, D. (2003) Rethinking therapeutic action. *International Journal of Psychoanalysis* 84: 4.

Goleman, D. (2003) *Destructive Emotions: A Dialogue with the Dalai Lama*. London: Bloomsbury.

Gould, S.J. (2001) *Rocks of Ages*. London: Jonathan Cape.

Grotstein, J. (2000) *Who is the Dreamer, who Dreams the Dream?* London and Hillsdale, NJ: Analytic Press.

Guardian (2004) Yoga benefits body, soul and blood vessels. *Guardian* 8 November: 6.

Harris, M. (1982) Growing points in psychoanalysis inspired by the work of Melanie Klein. *Journal of Child Psychotherapy* 8: 165–184.

Hoffman, E. (1991) *Lost in Translation: Life in a New Language*. London: Minerva.

James, W. (1902) *The Varieties of Religious Experience*. Harmondsworth: Penguin (1985).

Klein, M. (1946) Notes on some schizoid mechanisms. In *The Writings of Melanie Klein* vol 3: 1–24. London: Hogarth Press (1975).

Loewald, H. (1978) *Psychoanalysis and the History of the Individual*. New Haven, CT: Yale University Press.

Meltzer, D. (1967) *The Psycho-analytical Process*. Perthshire: Clunie Press.

Nagel, T. (1979a) What is it like to be a bat? In *Mortal Questions*. Cambridge: Cambridge University Press.

Nagel, T. (1979b) Subjective and objective. In *Mortal Questions*. Cambridge: Cambridge University Press.

Schopenhauer, A. (1819) *The World as Will and Representation*, trans. E.F.J. Payne. New York: Dover (1969).

Schore, A. (2003) The human unconscious: The development of the right brain and its role in early emotional life. In V. Green (ed.) *Emotional Development in Psychoanalysis, Attachment Theory and Neuroscience: Creating Connections*. London: Brunner-Routledge.

Share, L. (1994) *If Someone Speaks It Gets Lighter*. London: Analytic Press.

Solms, M. and Turnbull, O. (2002) *The Brain and the Inner World*. London: Karnac.

Stern, D. (1985) *The Interpersonal World of the Infant*. New York: Basic Books.

Sulloway, F. (1996) *Born to Rebel: Birth Order, Family Dynamics and Creative Lives*. New York: Pantheon.

Target, M. and Fonagy, P. (1996) Playing with reality, II. The development of psychic reality from a theoretical perspective. *International Journal of Psychoanalysis* 77: 459–479.

Trevarthen, C. and Aitken, K. (2001) Infant intersubjectivity: Research, theory, and clinical applications. *Journal of Child Psychology and Psychiatry* 42(1): 3–48.

Varela, F. (1996) Neurophenomonology: A methodological remedy for the hard problem. *Journal of Consciousness Studies* 3(4): 330–349.

Velmans, M. (2000) *Understanding Consciousness*. London: Routledge.

Wallace, E. (1991) Psychoanalytic perspectives on religion. *International Review of Psychoanalysis* 18: 265–278.

Winnicott, D.W. (1960) Ego distortion in terms of true and false self. In *The Maturational Process and the Facilitating Environment*. London: Hogarth Press (1965).

PART TWO

Religious stories that tell psychological truth

4

EMANCIPATION FROM THE SUPER-EGO

A clinical study of the Book of Job

Ronald Britton

> I heard it in a yellow wood.
> If God is God he is not good.
> If God is good he is not God.
> Archibald MacLeish, *JB*

These lines are from Archibald MacLeish's verse drama *JB* in which he places the Book of Job in a modern setting. He wrote it in 1958 when he was 64 and with it won one of several Pulitzer prizes that came his way. Born in Illinois he graduated from Yale in 1915 and died in 1982 at the age of 90, having written a considerable amount of first-class poetry and prose beginning in the 1920s, when he lived for a time in Europe. He practised as a lawyer and was Boylston Professor at Harvard. He served in the First World War, was Librarian of Congress throughout the Second World War and Assistant Secretary of State at the end of it. He is not my subject however but he is a man who, having lived through the twentieth century, not surprisingly identified with Job.

It is the Book of Job that I will use in this chapter to help illuminate a problem in psychoanalyis. MacLeish's lines focus on the theological 'problem of evil' but my chapter is in no way theological nor is it concerned with a religious issue; it is a clinical contribution about the relationship of the ego (Job) with the super-ego (God). The ego is the English translator's Latin term for Freud's German word 'Das Ich', the I, the person of the personality one might say. The Latin makes it sound impersonal, which probably suited English standoffishness and appears to have appealed to an American fondness for mechanics, hence ego psychology. The French translator's choice sounds thoroughly subjective: 'Le moi', as in 'Après moi le deluge'. So even in our translators' language we bring to this concept our different cultural stereotypes: the English gentlemanly ego as a schoolboy struggles to express himself in Latin, the American ego, a lusty foreign immigrant now technologically equipped to subdue the wilderness, and the French 'Le Moi' whose essential existence confronts a world that wants to deny it. Freud's Das Ich is like Odysseus, the masterful navigator through life's perilous journey, the arbiter of belief and judgement, the recipient of perception and desire, hence also the seat of anxiety. In 1923 he added to fear of the external world and fear of being overwhelmed from within by instinct a third *Gewissensangst*, fear of conscience. 'A poor creature', he said of the ego, 'owing service to three masters', external reality, internal instinct and the 'severity of the super-ego' (Freud 1923: 36). It is this last relationship I want to talk about, best expressed in religious terms as in Psalm 135: 20 'You that fear the Lord, bless the Lord!'

Much has been written about the concept of the super-ego, and the ego-ideal, from many psychoanalytic viewpoints: from the United States, notably by Otto Kernberg and Roy Schafer and from France by André Green. However, for the sake of clarity I will not give a history of the concept as it evolved in Freud's mind nor of the writings of current authors. I will confine myself to a simplified account of my view of the situation between ego and super-ego when their relationship is markedly adversarial. It derives from my own reading of Freud, Melanie Klein and Bion shaped, I like to think, mainly by my clinical experience. I am also suggesting that it can be illuminated by some postmodern commentaries on the Book of Job. Other analysts have been drawn to the Book of Job as a source of psychoanalytic understanding, notably Owen Renik (1991).

The fear of the super-ego as described by Freud is no small matter of qualms of conscience but in some individuals takes the form of fear of disease, death or annihilation. 'The ego gives itself up because it feels hated and persecuted by the super-ego, instead of loved' (1923: 54), he wrote.

> If we turn to melancholia . . . we should say that the destructive component had entrenched itself in the super-ego and turned against the ego. What is now holding sway in the super-ego is, as it were, a pure culture of the death instinct.
>
> (Freud 1923: 53)

He went on, 'To the ego, living means the same as being loved – being loved by the super-ego' (1923: 58). This last statement I think makes sense if one looks at Melanie Klein's ideas of the origin of the super-ego. She wrote: 'In my view, the splitting of the ego, by which the super-ego is formed, comes about as a consequence of conflict in the ego, engendered by the polarity of the two instincts' (Klein 1958: 240). Klein here is referring to the opposing destructive and libidinal drives towards objects and postulating that from the outset we divide ourselves in order to accommodate them. It means that there is at the core of the infantile super-ego, before its reorganisation in the Oedipus situation, an inherent hostility to external reality and a latent accusation of betrayal against the ego for its attachment to things as they are. The perception of the object of desire is similarly split and that part of experience that is good is initially taken into the ego forming a sense of self as containing something valuable, in religious terms called the soul. Both good and bad experience personified as an ideal or persecuting object is on the other hand introjected into the super-ego. Actual experiences of the parental figures are recycled through projection and re-introjection. It is on these actual experiences that we rely for modification of the super-ego so that fearsome though may be the archaic creatures that underlie it and haunt our dreams we can have benign internal figures protecting us. Such as those repeatedly appealed to in the Psalms (number 28); 'To thee, O Lord, I call; my rock, be not deaf to me, lest I become like those who go down to the Pit'.

Melanie Klein repeatedly stressed that this original hostile super-ego is modified and mitigated only by love. In her model therefore the introjection of a loving mother and father is *necessary* in order to modify the potentially destructive super-ego. Even in favourable circumstances if we follow this theory of Klein's, there remains in the core of the super-ego something hostile to the ego. Klein, because of her insistence on love and hate as innate primary factors in the personality, was often described as underestimating the effect of the child's actual environment. In fact as I see her theory the actual quality of parenting is absolutely crucial as it has to remedy innate endowment. *Love is necessary for survival.* Christian theology repeatedly expresses this in the form of the notion of redemption from original sin whether through faith, as in Protestant thinking, or the gift of grace as in Catholic theology.

Bion enlarges further on the danger of an unreconstructed super-ego in his theory of containment. He emphasised that the result of a major failure of maternal containment in infancy 'is an object which, when installed in the patient, exercised the function of a severe and ego-destructive superego' (Bion 1959: 107). That is a super-ego dedicated to destroying the ego. He was thinking of the physical and mental self-mutilating attacks that he saw in some psychotic and severely borderline patients.

I would like to mention two adverse developments of the super-ego, producing what Fairbairn called the 'internal saboteur' (Fairbairn 1952: 105). One such as that Bion described, in which the super-ego is really committed to murdering the ego, and another in which, though it is not bent on its destruction, it is hostile to the ego's independent development. It is the latter that I want to talk about in this chapter. I have written about the destructive super-ego elsewhere (Britton 2003). Its counterpart in theology is the hypothetical theistic solution offered by Bertrand Russell to the problem of evil, that the Universe is created by a Fiend. The clinical situation which I want to talk about today however is analogous to that of Job in which the ego is confronted with an ostensibly supportive super-ego demanding worship as well as subservience.

In his article on mutative interpretation written in 1934, James Strachey proposed that a therapeutic effect of analysis was a modification of the super-ego. Basing his idea on Melanie Klein's description of the cycle of projection and re-introjection he suggested that a severe super-ego can be modified by the recycling of projections onto the analyst and their subsequent re-introjection modified by their sojourn in the analyst. This idea underlies a great deal of analytic practice and has remained a useful rationale for therapeutic change. What I want to discuss however concerns the relationship of the ego to the unreconstructed super-ego and not simply the character of the latter. Even when the super-ego retains its adverse character, analysis can help the patient, I believe, by changing the relationship between the ego and super-ego. In particular it can help to wrest from the super-ego the function of judging both internal and external reality that it has usurped. Even Freud mistakenly reallocated this function and corrected himself subsequently. 'I seem to have been mistaken in ascribing the function of "reality testing" to this super-ego – a point which needs correction' (1923: 28). He had from his earliest writings said that 'Belief (and doubt) is a phenomenon that belongs wholly to the system of the ego' (Freud 1897: 255–256). This reclamation I think of as the ego's *emancipation* from the super-ego and I will suggest that it is accomplished by the ego making a judgement on the super-ego.

Freud first introduced the term ego-ideal, later using it interchangeably with super-ego. When he used only one or other term singly in this way he attributed two functions to it. Namely as an ideal model and as the critical agency that judged how the individual measured up to this ideal. I think it is simpler to refer to the first as ego-ideal and the second super-ego. Also the origins of this entity have been described differently at different times. In its first appearance as the ego-ideal in 1914 Freud suggested that it was the psychic remnant of the ideal self of infancy (Freud 1914). Much later, in the *New Introductory Lectures*, (1933: 67), he suggested that it was 'the precipitate of the old picture of the parents, the expression of admiration for the perfection that the child attributed to them'. By this time the super-ego had become well established in his thinking as the internalisation of parental authority, 'a precipitate', he wrote in 1923 '. . . of these two identifications [father and mother] in some way united with each other . . . as an ego ideal or super-ego' (Freud 1923: 35).

What then has become of the idealised infantile self of the ego-ideal? I suggest that the ego-ideal is the successor to the ideal child that once existed *in the parent's mind*; now it lives on internally in the individual as a would-be self, repeatedly sought after and recurrently mourned. The super-ego as the psychic residue of the critical parents continues to judge the actual ego by how it measures up to the ego-ideal. This regular source of internal reproach, that most of us are used to, is in some a painful scathing assault on self-regard in others a delusional assurance of perfection.

By 1930 the concept of the super-ego was securely established as the seat of conscience and its punitive nature was emphasised. Freud now attributed the aggression of the super-ego to the projection of aggression by the young child onto its parental precursors, acknowledging this to be a suggestion of Melanie Klein and others in London (Freud 1930: 130).

The complexity of the concept of the super-ego was increased by the work of Melanie Klein on the early, or archaic, super-ego of infancy which some regard as the origins of the super-ego and others as its precursor. When she developed her concept of the depressive position she made a crucial distinction between guilty fear and guilty feeling. Guilty fear as the persecutory anxiety resulting from an internal accusation of the super-ego directed towards the ego; whereas guilty feeling, such as pain and remorse, is directed from the ego to the object. I would like to emphasise in the context of this discussion that in the first situation guilt is experienced as internal accusation, that is from super-ego to ego, but in the latter case, in the depressive position, guilt is an affect of the ego. It is an instance of the ego reclaiming a function for itself by taking responsibility and thereby diminishing the power of the super-ego: another act of emancipation. As Freud commented, 'it may be said of the id that it is totally non-moral, of the ego that it strives to be moral, and of the super-ego that it can be super-moral and then become as cruel as only the id can be' (1923: 54).

The study of the nature of the super-ego in psychoanalysis has been preceded for centuries by the study in theology of the nature of its external representation, God. The existence of evil in a world ostensibly created by an omnipotent God who is also wholly good has been a particular problem. The Book of Job has been said by Christians to address this question, 'the problem of evil'. Like Milton's *Paradise Lost* it can be seen as an attempt to justify the ways of God to men. When I was at school we studied the Book of Job, which I was assured was important because it answered the problem of evil in the world. Try as I would I could not see how it did that, and so the Book of Job remained a preoccupation as a paradox. To me the answer it gave to the question seemed to make the problem worse. I was therefore particularly interested in postmodern scholarship that reframed the text and made it possible to take different meanings from its paradoxes. I would like to look at it in this context because I view it as an account of the emancipation of man, from Divine, arbitrary, injunction by the reclamation of his right to form judgements. In our terms it is the ego claiming that *it* is the proper location of judgement. Initially even Freud mistakenly reallocated that function to the super-ego. In the Book of Job I take Job to be the ego and God the super-ego, and though he is cruelly treated and threatened, Job claims the right to form a judgement.

The story begins with Job described as blameless and upright, a man who feared God and turned away from evil. God said to Satan, 'Have you considered my servant Job, there is none like him on earth'. Satan replied, does Job fear God for naught? He prospers and is safe, attack all that he has and he will curse you. God accepted this challenge and in effect made a wager with Satan that Job would remain steadfast. He said to Satan, everything he has is in your power but don't harm him. Promptly within one day all Job's cattle were stolen, his servants killed, his sheep, shepherds and property struck by lightning and burnt in a fire. The same day a tornado destroyed his eldest son's house and killed all Job's children (Revised Standard Version (RSV) I: 1–19). His response was not to curse but to worship: 'Naked I came from my mother's womb, and naked shall I return; the Lord gave, and the Lord has taken away; blessed be the name of the Lord' (RSV I: 20).

God renewed his boast to Satan about his exemplary servant Job and Satan renewed his challenge to God. A man will give all he has for his life but if you touch his bone and flesh, he will curse you. So God said: it is in your power to afflict his body as you will but spare his life. Satan afflicted Job with loathsome sores from head to toe and left him sitting in the ashes of his property scraping himself with a piece of broken pottery (RSV II: 1–7). Job's wife suggested to her husband that he should curse God and die. Job said she was a foolish woman. 'Shall we receive good at the hand of God, and shall we not receive evil?' (RSV II: 10). But, though he did not curse God, as his suffering continued he cursed the day of his birth.

> Let the day perish wherein I was born, and the night which said 'A man-child is conceived' . . . Why did I not die at birth, come forth from the womb and expire? Why did the knees receive me? Or why the breasts, that I should suck.
> (RSV III: 3–12)

Job's comforters, his three friends, were appalled by his condition and his losses but they preached to Job on the subject of God's justice, and implied that he must have done something wrong and that when he became blameless he would be rewarded. They proposed only one solution: to defend ourselves from God, we must be spotless and above reproach. They offered in other words the obsessional solution to fear of persecution from the super-ego, that of endless cleansing and re-examination.

Job said to them, why do you not pity me but instead tell me that if I am righteous God will restore me (RSV IX). To God he says, 'If I wash myself with snow, and cleanse my hands with lye, yet thou wilt plunge me into a pit' (RSV IX: 30). Provoked by his comforters Job reiterates that God destroys both the blameless and the wicked but still he does not curse God nor renounce him. He continues to believe that God is omnipotent but does not claim he is a bad god or an evil spirit. What he does do, however, is to challenge God to justify what he has done to him. He now complains that God remains silent and invisible and that he does not believe that God listens to him.

There is a pivotal moment in the story when Job says 'let not dread of him terrify me into silence'. He determines to speak his mind. 'I loathe my life; I will give free utterance to my complaint', he says, and seriously asks God to justify himself.

> I will speak, and let come on me what may. I will take my flesh in my teeth, and put my life in my hand. Behold, he will slay me; I have no hope; yet I will defend my ways to his face.
>
> (RSV XIII: 13–15)

In the course of his complaint Job begins to imply that God is deficient, that he lacks empathy, that he is less than a man.

> Does it seem good to thee to oppress, to despise the work of thy hands and favour the designs of the wicked? Hast thou eyes of flesh? Dost thou see as man sees? Are thy days as the days of man, or thy years as man's years, that thou dost seek out my iniquity and search for my sin, although thou knowest that I am not guilty, and there is none to deliver out of thy hand?
>
> (RSV X: 3–7)

Job begins to characterise God as unrelenting, incapable of change, 'But he is unchangeable and who can turn him? What he desires, that he does'. These would be serious faults in a man.

At this point enters Eli'hu, a young man, perhaps a recapitulation of a young confident Job, speaking for God. He claims to know better than Job and his old comforters because it is not experience that makes men wise but closeness to God. He goes on to say that God does not need justification because he is greater than man, and ineffable, 'For God speaks in one way, and in two, though man does not perceive it'. One of the points made by God's young advocate is that it is immaterial to God what Job thinks. This is plainly not true. God by making Job a test case has put himself in a position that he requires Job's unquestioning obedience to demonstrate the devoted servitude of humankind.

So we move into the finale. God appears in a whirlwind and proceeds to impress and intimidate Job into submission. In effect he says, I made you; I made everything you see; I taught you everything you know; I made the monsters, Behemoth and the Leviathan, that frighten you in your dreams and the natural and unnatural events that terrify you. How dare you judge me by man's standards: I am incomprehensible to you and my ways are a mystery.

It is Job's response to this that has been the focus of much discussion and religious questioning. It is a postmodern account of this by Jack Miles that makes most sense of the paradox in the Book of Job for me. I think it also opens the door to applying this to our efforts to understand the relationship of the ego to the super-ego. Miles makes a point that other postmodern critics have made:

the original text has been wrongly translated to make it fit Jewish and Christian religious assumptions. He wrote, 'Unfortunately, a tradition of interpretation based on a silent correction of the Hebrew text has managed to change into repentance a reply that should properly be heard as irony' (Miles 1995: 314). As Miles points out, God speaking from the whirlwind makes no claim to Job on moral grounds and no effort to justify himself, only to demand worship and obedience on a basis of power – might is right. The traditional Jewish and Christian view has been that Job repents, presumably for his lack of unquestioning obedience, and is rewarded with long life and newly found prosperity.

To make the point clearer I will give the key lines in the translation used in the Revised Standard Version of the Bible of Job's brief reply, 7 verses, to God's 123 verse rhetorical question. His first response to God's demonstration of ultimate power is to say

> I am of small account;
> What shall I answer thee?
> I lay my hand on my mouth.
> I have spoken once, and I will not answer
> Twice

After a further demand for a reply he says:

> I know that thou canst do all things,
> And that no purpose of thine can be thwarted

He continues in the familiar Revised Version:

> I had heard of thee by the hearing of the ear,
> But now my eye sees thee;
> Therefore I despise myself,
> And repent in dust and ashes

Miles offers a more accurate, theology-free translation of these last crucial lines:

> Word of you had reached my ears,
> But now that my eyes have seen you,
> I shudder with sorrow for mortal clay

Job says, as I read it, 'now I know what you are like I have nothing more to say, you have made your point that you can do anything and that you will do what you want'. It is an answer full of irony; in a situation where Job's enthusiastic voluntary worship and duty were supposed to be demonstrated to defeat Satan's claim that self-interest was Job's real motive, we have his acquiesence and silent judgement. The word satan in the Book of Job, unlike the Book of Daniel, means simply the Adversary, one might say the sceptic. Satan, like Job's wife, the other sceptic, has by this point in the story disappeared altogether. That triangle has collapsed, there is only God and Job. I suggest that the Adversary now has been incorporated into Job, who thus, while subjectively functioning as God's obedient servant, contains within a silent objectively observing self. An internal triangle is formed that gives Job freedom of thought while he is denied freedom of action.

There are various postmodern views on the meaning of Job's response to God in the whirlwind if it is not an act of contrition. Stephen Mitchell's essentially Buddhist view is that Job surrenders his narrow insistence on morality and achieves enlightenment, realising that the physical body is dust and personal drama insignificant (Mitchell 1987). Edwin Good (1990) says that Job repents for having thought that sin is important in construing the world. Miles' argument is different, he thinks that Job's response is to acquiesce to God's power but to retain his own judgement on God's actions. 'If,' as he puts it, 'God can force Job to stop blaming God and start blaming himself, God wins. If God cannot do that, God loses' (Miles 1995: 430). Miles in his book *God: A Biography* is engaged in examining the emergent character of God in the Tanakh, the original Hebrew bible. I am looking at it from the other perspective, not the development of God, the super-ego, but that of Job, the ego. Taking it to be the ego and the super-ego in this story it represents a crucial moment in development when the ego takes the super-ego to task and while still afraid of its power claims the right to question its judgement and to doubt its motives. This is I think also a crucial moment in some analyses when the individual can question the authenticity of the voice of adverse judgement whether it is experienced as coming from within as self condemnation or by projection as coming from the analyst.

However the Book of Job found its way into the Bible and into Jewish and Christian religion because it vindicates God, and reassures the faithful. It does this in a postscript, a short passage of prose that follows the powerful poetic ending. In this postscript, God praises Job and gives him long life and good fortune for the rest of his days, and Job surrounded by a new family praises the Lord. I see this as the necessary happy ending added by the religious. If it had been a film script in our own day, the studio management would have insisted on an upbeat ending of a similar kind. In psychological terms it represents what Melanie Klein called manic reparation. Unlike true reparation, in which one confronts loss, feels pain, bears guilt, and accepts reality, in manic reparation all is restored, no one is guilty and nothing has been mourned. Job's wife, who lost all her children and suggested cursing the person responsible for killing them, is silent and invisible in the postscript. If unlike the biblical version it were to end with Job's dialogue with God, it becomes either a tragedy in the Greek sense where, 'As flies to wanton boys, are we to the gods / They kill us for their sport' or the celebration of Job as a Stoic hero, determinedly seeing things as they are.

This latter figure I think strongly resembles Freud's characterisation of the ego, enslaved to three masters but triumphantly able to pass judgement on them including moral judgement. As he put it, 'it may be said of the id that it is totally non-moral, of the ego that it strives to be moral, and of the super-ego that it can be super-moral, and then becomes as cruel as only the id can be' (Freud 1923).

The customary identification of the Divine figure in the Tanakh is as 'the Lord, the God of your fathers' (1 Chronicles 29: 20). This emphasis, reiterated in the liturgy with considerable frequency, fits well with Freud's hypothesis that it is the super-ego of the parents rather than the parents that is the introjected basis for the child's super-ego. Is this always the case? Or is Freud describing a particularly forbidding super-ego that afflicts some unfortunate individuals? Is this parental super-ego handed on because it has never been effectively judged or challenged within the parent who is still its servant? It is my impression that this figures in the personality of some people where it produces a particular pattern of internal submission to an alien spirit.

It did I believe in the case I will describe, a patient Mr P, who needed analysis to reach the position I have attributed to Job, that of becoming the judge of his own super-ego.

Prior to that Mr P was afflicted by an internal judgement that he was defective; the judgement itself crippled him, as he consequently had difficulty in believing in his own capacities. He was clear in the analysis that this idea that he was inadequate was not what he *really* thought of himself but nevertheless he felt weighed down by it. In addition, he would have said with Job, 'And if I lift myself up / Thou dost hunt me like a lion'. He was in exactly the position that Freud described in the Ego and the Id, and it made itself clear in the transference. He believed I was saying, 'you must be like me' and that I was also saying 'you must never presume to be like me'. The God of Job says that he has made man in his own image; William Blake represents this in his illustrated version of the Book of Job by making God above in heaven and Job below on earth identical in his opening drawing. And yet the thrust of God's argument with Job is that he must never presume to think he is remotely like God. Mr P felt defective because he could never fulfil his mother's aspirations. She had based her ego-ideal on that of her father and lived perennially disappointed to be a woman. Mr P, as her son, felt there was something his mother did not like about him and yet that there was an affinity between them based on some defect he shared with her. He also felt that he must never rejoice in his emergent masculinity as that would have made him superior to her.

Mr P is a middle-aged biological scientist who came to me for analysis some years ago because he was troubled, unable to flourish and subject to depression. He had a previous quite long analysis that ended when his therapist, a woman, retired from practice. This left him with a feeling of failure and unable to get clear what he thought about her.

Mr P was happily married with three children and had a good job in his chosen academic field. Nevertheless, despite high qualifications and obvious ability, he felt inferior to his colleagues and was professionally diffident. In particular once he had completed his doctoral thesis, he never published in his field. Once we began analysis it became clear to me that he was more troubled in his relationships at work than in any other part of his life. In particular he seemed to me to be intimidated by women colleagues, even when he was meant to be in the leading role. If he asserted ideas of his own he became very anxious, lest some terrible unspecified reprisals might follow. He, despite his analytic sophistication, did not link the eruptions of fear of his colleagues with the small instances of his self-assertion that preceded them. And though he made it obvious to me, he seemed to be unaware of the immediate source of his anxieties.

This was a pattern in the analysis. He would make clear to me, by describing in detail, situations at work without defining them or his feelings about them. I would, in the course of interpreting something to him, summarise in a few words the situation so described. It was that part of the interpretation to which he would relate and treat it as if I had told him something he did not know about his colleagues and his feelings about them. For example, he told me of a work group of which he was in charge that was dominated by his assistant, who was a woman. In detail he gave an account of a project proposal and his efforts to offer an opinion and to raise questions, all of which were ignored by this woman. He described acquiescing to this. To my ear, it sounded very painful and he sounded frustrated and defeated but he said nothing of these feelings.

I interpreted that he felt that he was ignored and that his thoughts were disregarded by someone who was uninterested in anything other than her own ideas and I suggested that this was what he expected from me in the analysis.

The interesting thing was that Mr P treated my description of his colleague, whom he had so vividly described, as news. Not only was it news to Mr P but he took it to be my knowledge, an opinion of mine formed independently of him. He responded by saying, 'I see what you mean. Of course any ideas like that about you is just projection. But I think you might be right about Mrs X, your idea of her sounds very convincing'.

So it was safe for Mr P to have an idea about Mrs X if his analyst *appeared* to be the author of it. This, it became apparent, was true of ideas in general. Mr P could not complete his thoughts. The observations, reflections, associations were all present, but the conclusions were missing, which gave a spurious impression that Mr P was not very bright. As we progressed I began to realise how intelligent he was. My comment that he was unable to use his intellectual assets, and that I wondered how much he could not use fully any of his assets, produced a surprise. Mr P had often complained of being hard up and how the expense of interest payments and bank charges that incurred because of his overdraft added to it. Now he revealed he actually had another property that he had inherited from his mother but he didn't sell it, he never used it and he never thought to raise money on it. Meanwhile he struggled to make ends meet.

As the analysis moved on another pattern succeeded this, one in which I, as the analyst, appeared to play a more central role. I noticed that my interpretations were all paraphrased and repeated to himself by Mr P. His paraphrase subtly transformed what I hoped might be enlightening comments into criticisms, of a carping kind, or expressions of dissatisfaction with him. These he was clearly prepared to accept. In other words he was building a relationship with me in his mind in which he would submit to a critical, carping analyst and he would feel dejected and unappreciated, privately complaining but acquiescent. This seemed to be his 'psychic retreat' (Steiner 1993). What seems particularly interesting about it is that this was not a place of illusory satisfaction but of dissatisfaction sustained at a bearable level. It was not a place of pleasure but a place of safety.

As his analysis progressed and he was dislodged from this enclave, he became more anxious and afraid that I would attack him in his sessions for presumptuousness. If this abated and he experienced me as encouraging him, he would become afraid that I was exposing him to terrible risks in his work from other people by demanding that he assert himself more. A dream he brought at this time threw more light on the feared situation.

In his dream he was in his team at work and the other members were all female with Mrs X the leader. He was holding forth to the group when he realised that he was not fully dressed and that his penis was exposed; he tried to hide it with his papers.

His associations to this dream were initially to his experiences of Mrs X at work and then to a screen memory of his childhood, which I had heard several times before. It concerned him as a young boy, being told off by his mother at the behest of a neighbouring family for riding his bicycle too fast near 'the girls', that is, the daughters of the neighbouring family. These same girls seemed to him to be approved and regarded as acceptable by his own mother in a way that he never felt he was. It made him think he would have been acceptable to his mother if only he had been a girl. This ushered in a period of recollection and reflection in his analysis on aspects of his adolescence which, although he had mentioned them when he came to me for consultation, had not found a place in his analysis or significance up to this point. As a young boy he had been quite vigorous but when puberty approached he became at his mother's behest more passive and avoided what she called rough boy's games.

In the period of analysis that followed this dream, his writing inhibition was considerably relieved. There were other changes: he renewed his involvement in physical sports and he used his inheritance. Mr P, however, became apprehensive about some unspecified ill fortune that might follow such hubris and felt guilty towards all those on whom he had depended in the past, particularly his mother. He felt that benefiting from his analysis might be construed as a criticism of her. He also thought that it would be an implicit criticism of his previous therapist. He believed that his self-assertion would have been seen by her as narcissistic self-aggrandisement. He imagined adverse judgements from all and sundry: what he was having difficulty doing was making critical judgements of others. It became clearer to both of us that his mother had been chronically depressed. Also that his father kept quiet and urged his son to agree with his mother. As a child he had thought a good deal about his mother's state of mind and her beliefs and these ideas returned. He was sure she was very disappointed in her relationship to her father and felt that as a girl she lacked what he admired and respected.

My reading of this was that Mr P's mother had projected her defective self onto her son and consequently saw him as in some indefinable way wrong. He always sensed this and in order to get close to her would identify with her picture of him. In other words to be recognised he thought he had to conform to his mother's idea of him. For someone like this analysis carries a considerable risk of providing a perfect opportunity for re-enactment. The analytic super-ego both in the person of the analyst and as a religion of which the analyst was high priest was present in the transference from the outset. The usefulness of the analysis depended on the development of the patient's scepticism. The temptation for the analyst was to crush it. Job was accused of scepticism, of 'drinking up scoffing like water' (Job 34: 7). My patient expected similar accusations and tempered his critical comments accordingly. His judgement was good and his natural scepticism was not malevolent but he would subordinate it to any opinion I might be thought to have, or that the ancestors might have whose words I was presumed to worship. It was this way of being that was to change in the course of analysis but at each step when he challenged me to justify myself as Job did to God, he had to say to himself, like Job: 'Let not that dread terrify me into silence'. The emancipation of his ego from the adverse judgement of a potentially envious super-ego was achieved only by the reclamation of his right to form a judgement on this internal critic.

To do this Mr P had to find a place from which he could view the relationship between himself and his super-ego, whether the latter was represented by me in the transference, his former analyst, his colleagues at work, and his mother in the past, his wife in certain modes and most significantly the inner voice of self-reproach.

The third position of self-observation belongs I believe within the ego and not the super-ego. In more normal language that position from which we can view ourselves while being ourselves we need to find within that part of our personality that we identify as our own person. If we vacate it we become the creatures of our conscience. We cannot avoid having a conscience, we cannot abolish the super-ego but we need to be able to put it in its place. And that is not as the final arbiter of what is real and what is true. Freud said that analysis helped to reclaim for the land of the ego parts of psychic life lost in the sea of the id: 'where id was ego shall be'. I am suggesting that it can help reclaim for life on earth functions attributed to the heavens: where super-ego was ego shall be.

References

Bion, W.R. (1959) Attacks on linking. In *Second Thoughts*. New York: Jason Aronson (1967).

Britton, R. (2003) *Sex, Death and the Super-ego*. London: Karnac.

Fairbairn, W.R.D. (1952) *Psycho-analytic Studies of the Personality*. London: Routledge.

Freud, S. (1897) Draft N, Letter 64, 31 May 1897, Extracts from the Fleiss papers. SE 1.

Freud, S. (1914) On narcissism. SE 14.

Freud, S. (1923) The Ego and the Id. SE 19.

Freud, S. (1930) *Civilisation and its Discontents*. SE 21.

Freud, S. (1933) *New Introductory Lectures*. SE 22.

Good, E.M. (1990) *In Turns of Tempest: A Reading of Job*. Stanford, CA: Stanford University Press.

Klein, M. (1958) On the development of mental functioning. In R. Money-Kyrle, B. Joseph, E. O'Shaughnessy and H. Segal (eds) *The Writings of Melanie Klein*, Volume 3. London: Hogarth (1975).

Miles, J. (1995) *God: A Biography*. London: Simon and Schuster.

Mitchell, S. (1987) *The Book of Job*. Berkeley, CA: North Point Press.

Renik O. (1991) The Biblical Book of Job: Advice to clinicians. *Psychoanalytical Quarterly* 60: 596–605.

Steiner, J. (1993) *Psychic Retreats*. London: Routledge.

Strachey, J. (1934) The nature of the therapeutic action of psychoanalysis. *International Journal of Psychoanalysis* 15: 127–159.

5

THE CHRISTMAS STORY
A psychoanalytic enquiry
David Millar

> Everything is what it is: liberty is liberty, not equality or fairness
> or justice or culture, or human happiness or a quiet conscience.
> If the liberty of myself or my class or nation depends on the
> misery of a number of other human beings, the system which
> promotes this is unjust and immoral. But if I curtail or lose my
> freedom, in order to lessen the shame of such inequality, and do
> not thereby materially increase the individual liberty of others, an
> absolute loss of liberty occurs. This may be compensated for by
> a gain in justice or in happiness or peace, but the loss remains,
> and it is a confusion of values to say that although my 'liberal'
> individual freedom may go by the board, some other kind of
> freedom – social or economic – is increased.
>
> Isaiah Berlin, *Two Concepts of Liberty*, 1958

I

In the western world, Christmas is hard to ignore even if we come from a family
or tradition that does not keep Christmas. Many readers will share memories of
Christmas as a very special time. As children, Christmas is magical. As adults, the
seasonal holiday with family, with its long build-up, can be stressful and problematic. Yet probably the most difficult feelings come from separation and loss.
There is an idealization of putting things right, but Christmas is a way of bringing
people together that is very important for them. It can bring a painful loneliness
if we are excluded.

I think that Christmas expresses a deep wish for a truce – that enmity might be put aside. This is poignantly illustrated by the 1914 Christmas truce on the western front some five months after the start of the First World War, on parts of the front not yet subject to the most bitter fighting. Men, including some officers, climbed out of their trenches, and shook hands in no man's land. Each side buried their dead who lay there, played football together, exchanged souvenirs and thought and talked about home and families. The German historian Michael Jurgs (2003) describes how the ceasefire began at a part of the front where many of the German soldiers spoke good English – involving mostly Catholic Saxon and Bavarian regiments. Some had worked before the war as cab drivers and barbers in places like Brighton, Blackpool and London. When war had broken out they had had no option but to return to Germany, some of them leaving families behind. At parts of the front the informal truce lasted quite some while before the authorities ensured that hostilities were resumed.

In this chapter I hope to show that the Christmas story, a myth about God becoming man, has a complex layering in which certain deep human problems are part addressed and part evaded. I want next to look at the stories about the nativity of Jesus in the gospels. These stories include an old couple, a father, a virgin mother, God, angels and a crafty, jealous king. The stories are about birth and hope but also, less often recognized, include the idea of the death of the baby. As with dreams, the nativity stories contain patterns of 'transformation' at many different levels. For example, when the gospel writers do not know something about Jesus' life, they turn to the scriptures – believing that what happened before will have happened again. The description in the gospels of Matthew and Luke of Bethlehem as Jesus' birthplace is clearly derived from the book of the prophet Micah: 'But you, Bethlehem in Ephrathah, small as you are to be among Judah's clans, out of you shall come forth a governor for Israel' (Micah 5: 2).

In the nativity stories, God communicates with men and women through angels and dreams. In Luke's gospel the angel Gabriel appears to the priest Zechariah to tell him that although he and his wife Elizabeth are old, his wife will conceive and have a son – John the Baptist. This is a transformation of a visit by God to Abraham (Genesis 17), in which God tells Abraham that although he is 100 years old and his wife Sarah 90 years old, his wife will conceive and bear a son who is to be called Isaac. The miraculous birth is a sign of God's choice of Israel, the descendant of Abraham, as his son.

The birth of John the Baptist is a sign of another special son – the one who is to come. The angel Gabriel speaks to Mary, a kinswoman of Elizabeth, a virgin who is betrothed to a man named Joseph, about these expectations:

He will be great; he will bear the title 'Son of the Most High'; the Lord God will give him the throne of his ancestor David, and he will be king over Israel for ever; his reign shall never end.

(Luke 1: 32–33)

After the birth of Mary's son, an angel appears to shepherds out in the fields, keeping watch over their flock by night, saying: 'Today in the city of David a deliverer has been born to you – the Messiah, the Lord. And this is your sign: you will find a baby all wrapped up, in a manger' (Luke 2: 10–12).

A sign of what? Luke says a sign of peace on earth (Luke 2: 14). But Matthew also tells us, a sign of trouble. King Herod, stirred up by the news, searches for the child to do away with him (Matthew 2: 13).

II

The nativity stories are part of the Bible story, which is the sacred myth for Christians. The majority of the books making up the Bible, those that Christians call the Old Testament, form the sacred myth for Jews. No single approach tells the whole truth about myth. Myths are collective creations, touching many conscious and unconscious thoughts, feelings, anxieties and defenses in those who hear them. Like dreams they are notoriously ambiguous. The anthropologist Edmund Leach, following Claude Lévi-Strauss, sees myth as mediating between categories that are irreconcilable. He writes:

> The problem is not resolved because it is irresolvable, yet it seems to be resolved . . . Myths serve to provide an apparent resolution, or 'mediation' of problems which are by their very nature incapable of any final resolution.
>
> (Leach 1969c: 54)

A virgin cannot be a mother, and a mother cannot be a virgin. The Virgin Birth is anomalous – as are the pregnancies of Sarah and Elizabeth, both women long past the age of childbearing. But what, more exactly, is being mediated by the Christmas story with its parental-intercourse-denying myth of the Virgin Birth of a special son? Leach argues that beliefs in supernatural birth, from whatever culture, do not stem from innocence or ignorance of the facts of physiological paternity (Leach 1969b: 85). He writes:

> If we put the so-called primitive beliefs alongside the sophisticated ones and treat the whole lot with equal philosophical respect we shall see that they constitute a set of variations around a common structural theme, the metaphysical topography of the relationship between gods and men.
>
> (Leach 1969b: 85–86)

I need next to develop a further stage of my argument. As I see it, the 'meta-physical topography of the relationship between gods and men' concerns the relationship between the ego and the superego. Freud (1917, 1923) describes the superego as an inherent structure of the mind, one part of the ego that sets itself over the other, observing and judging it critically. Britton (2003) writes that the judgement of the ego may be distinguished from that of the superego as follows.

> Judgement based on experience is the business of the ego: through its belief system and function of reality testing, it speaks with the authority of the individual's own experience. The superego, in contrast, claims authority by virtue of its position and its origins: it is claimed on the basis of the principle of parental authority, bolstered by ancestral authority.
>
> (Britton 2003: 71)

Recognition of the parents' relationship, in whatever partial form, challenges further the child's belief that he occupies a throne giving him sole and permanent dominion over the good object. Manic phantasies earlier used to control the breast are used to control the internalized parents (Klein 1935: 287). Stereotypically, the omnipotent self invades the mother, and takes the father's place – triumphing over the loss of the mother that the child believes he possesses forever and ever. However, the mania of having it all one's own way makes a tear in the boundaries of reality – a catalyst for annihilating persecution and internal chaos, intensifying the mania. The cycle leads to a form of 'psychic retreat' (Steiner 1993) – the bondage of a pathological organization, where the superego throne is occupied by an idealized bad object that threatens annihilation and which the child also identifies with. This sort of superego is described by Jacques (1965) as 'the perfect object'. He writes:

> These [unconscious] phantasies [of immortality] are equally as persecuting as the chaotic internal situation they are calculated to mitigate. They contain omnipotent sadistic triumph and increase guilt and persecution as a result. And they lead to feelings of intolerable helplessness through dependence upon the perfect object which becomes demanding of an equal perfection in behaviour.
>
> (Jacques [1965] 1988: 236)

However, the superego is not a unitary conception (O'Shaughnessy 1999). The reorganization of the superego under the influence of the Oedipus situation that Freud describes involves an intervention that helps to pull the ego out from its bondage – an internalization, alongside earlier figures derived from the maternal relationship, of an awesome father who is feared for his capacity to castrate but loved for his strength. This normal superego is strict and perhaps tyrannical, but is a guide and the ego can enter into dispute with it.

'The perfect object' and the normal superego correspond, it seems to me, to Birksted-Breen's (1996) description of two irreconcilable categories which alternate in the unconscious mind: on the one hand, the ubiquitous phantasy of the phallus, that is felt to be immortal, all powerful and lacking nothing, and 'an attempt away from triangulation' and, on the other hand, the internalized masculine structuring function of the 'penis-as-link', which links mother and father, promotes mental space, thinking and recognition of interdependence, and gives new meaning to previous perceptions. As I see it, the Christmas story mediates these two irreconcilable categories, seeming to provide a solution. Countless individuals down the generations have put themselves into the Christmas story, while also looking on. Stereotypically, what is being looked at is mother and her new baby. The looker-on is the sibling above. The 'one that is to come' which is perceived is a realization of a 'not us' mother and baby in the mind. Stirred up is a yearning for the lost good mother–infant relationship, but also Herod-like murderous hatred that the source of good experience does not return to the looker-on in its earlier form. At the threshold of what Klein (1935) called the depressive position – with its anxieties for the good object, guilt and remorse – dependence on the object as the source of good experience, and triumph over the object's free life, form two 'dissonant cognitions' (Festinger 1957). My hypothesis is that the Christmas myth mediates, on the one hand, the idea of an intervention that encourages movement towards relinquishment of omnipotence, loss of the idea of one's own immortality, and acceptance of new risks, and on the other hand, the retreat of an illusional Oedipal system (Britton 1989), represented by the parental-intercourse-denying story of the Virgin Birth, that triumphs over the masculine structuring function of the 'penis-as-link' and covers the persecution of a bad superego. The appearance of resolution in the Christmas myth disguises the painful conflicts at the threshold of the depressive position, and the need to own dissonant cognitions, to become more able to stand guilt and responsibility for one's actions. Segal (1997) writes:

> The battle between perception of reality and omnipotent imposition of phantasy onto reality is a long battle which proceeds in small stages. In part, this battle is a constant attack on perception by the omnipotent self, and it is not only an attack on external perception but also an attack on perception of one's inner states, and on the inborn phantasies such as those of parental intercourse, which interfere with omnipotence.
>
> (Segal 1997: 30)

In this chapter I will next outline how I see the Christmas story as a retreat – a pattern of loss of the good object, euphoria, and a tightened bondage of 'the perfect object'. I then want to make use of some material from Charles Dickens' very popular Christmas book, *A Christmas Carol*, which Slater (Dickens 2003: xiii) calls a 'modern fairy-tale', to illustrate movement out of retreat and the countervailing forces. I hope my readers will read the *Carol* for themselves, if they have not already done so, so to judge better my interpretation of it.

III

The Jewish scriptures underwent a major redaction during the fifth and sixth centuries BC, the period which saw loss of the land under the neo-Babylonian empire, 'the exile', and 'the return'. Loss and grief are followed by euphoric expectations about 'the return' (e.g. Isaiah 40: 3), and then by tightening measures to avoid exposure to the loss of 'the perfect object's' good favour (Millar 2001).

Leach (see e.g. 1969a, 1969c) describes how many of the Old Testament stories were edited at this time to support what he calls the 'post-exilic myth' – with its assertion of an immortal possession of the land (the land representing, I think, the good object), and belief that the strength of the group lies in endogamy. It does seem pretty certain that it was during the post-exilic period that belief in the wrongness of marriage to foreigners became strong in some influential Jewish groups. Leach illustrates the clever editorial work that draws the reader away from the inconsistencies they can observe, towards these beliefs the redactors want to propagate. He writes:

> the Biblical story of the succession of Solomon to the throne of Israel is a myth which 'mediates' a major contradiction. The Old Testament as a whole asserts that the Jewish political title to the land of Palestine is a direct gift from God to the descendants of Israel (Jacob). This provides the fundamental basis for Jewish endogamy – the Jews should be a people of pure blood and pure religion, living in isolation in their Promised Land. But interwoven with this theological dogma there is a less idealized form of tradition which represents the population of ancient Palestine as a mixture of many peoples over whom the Jews have asserted political dominance by right of conquest. The Jews and their 'foreign' neighbours intermarry freely.
>
> (Leach 1969c: 31)

The social, economic and political factors and tensions connected with the post-exilic occupation of the land, of which we have extremely fragmentary knowledge, will have contributed in complex ways to the development of the 'post-exilic myth'. However, I have suggested that marriage to foreigners in the external world may be viewed unconsciously in the internal world as a parental link involving the masculine structuring function of the 'penis-as-link'. Hatred and jealousy likely to be stirred up by this sort of parental link can be placated by adherence to a theory of an idealized endogamous marriage, guaranteeing affiliation to a superior line of descent (even though in external reality such a marriage may not be practical). In this 'hardened myth' guilt is evacuated into a near-foreign group, the northern brothers, who are especially blamed for loss, seen as ignorant, and hated with a virtuous hatred.

The Christmas story can be seen as a transformation of this 'post-exilic myth'. In the gospel nativity stories, the many comings and goings (via angels and dreams) between God and man – concerning 'the one who is to come' – reflect turbulence, disturbance and uncertainty, but also the expectations of an omnipotent self who believes himself king forever. The emergence of the Christian group is marked, I think, by a pattern similar to that seen in the formation of the post-exilic myth: loss of the leader and loss of the capital city Jerusalem (both destroyed by the Roman Empire), the euphoria of the resurrection stories, and a new rigidification. There is again triumph over the father. The Christian sons make Jesus' Jewish father Joseph a saint in their own calendar, while stealing his books to back up their story. The 'one who is to come' is now the one and only omnipotent son of a mother exclusively possessed by the Christian sons. As with the post-exilic myth, hatred and jealousy stirred up by the parental link can be placated by adherence to a theory – that the believer is part of a Church, symbolized by the Virgin Mother, that offers affiliation to a superior pure line of descent (even though in external reality celibacy may not always be practical). Again there is a ganging up on a near-foreign group. Guilt is now evacuated into the Jews, who are blamed for loss and hated with virtuous hatred.

IV

The central character in *A Christmas Carol* is a miser called Ebenezer Scrooge.

> Nobody ever stopped him in the street to say, with gladsome looks, 'My dear Scrooge, how are you? When will you come to see me?' No beggars implored him to bestow a trifle, no children asked him what it was o'clock, no man or woman ever once in all his life inquired the way to such and such a place, of Scrooge. Even the blindmen's dogs appeared to know him; and when they saw him coming on, would tug their owners into doorways and up courts; and would wag their tails as though they said, 'No eye at all is better than an evil eye, dark master!'
>
> (Dickens 2003: 34)

In this story we again find an ignorant group held in contempt – the urban poor – justified in terms of one of the more unpleasant economic doctrines of the day.

'If they would rather die,' said Scrooge, 'they had better do it, and decrease the surplus population' (p. 38). At the beginning of the *Carol* it is Christmas Eve. Scrooge's clerk Bob Cratchit, a member of the poor group, leaves his employer's office to spend Christmas with his family. He is devoted to Tiny Tim, his weak, crippled son. Scrooge resolutely refuses, as ever, the Christmas invitation made to him by his young married nephew Fred. Scrooge takes 'his melancholy dinner in his usual melancholy tavern; and having read all the newspapers, and beguiled the rest of the evening with his banker's-book, went home to bed' (p. 41).

Scrooge lives in a 'gloomy suite of rooms', 'in chambers which had once belonged to his deceased partner' (p. 41). It is in these melancholy chambers that the haunting described in the story takes place. It begins with the appearance, at Scrooge's front door, of the Ghost of Jacob Marley. Dead for seven years, Marley was Scrooge's business partner. The narrator also tells us that Scrooge has experienced a 'terrible sensation' from earliest years, alluding to some infantile terror.

> And let any man explain to me, if he can, how it happened that Scrooge, having his key in the lock of the door, saw in the knocker, without it undergoing any intermediate process of change: not a knocker, but Marley's face . . .
>
> As Scrooge looked fixedly at this phenomenon, it was a knocker again. To say that he was not startled, or that his blood was not conscious of a terrible sensation to which it had been a stranger from infancy, would be untrue.
>
> (pp. 41–42)

Braving his fright, Scrooge enters his own front door. Marley's Ghost again appears, now dragging heavy chains. The Ghost, by his own account, had lived, like Scrooge, as a miser. The Ghost tells Scrooge:

> My spirit never walked beyond our counting house – mark me! – in life my spirit never roved beyond the narrow limits of our money-changing hole.
>
> (p. 48)

However, Marley has appeared to help Scrooge. He tells Scrooge that if he is to be freed from the chains of bondage he has to face Three Spirits.

> You will be haunted . . . by Three Spirits . . . . Without their visits . . . you cannot hope to shun the path I tread.
>
> (p. 50)

In the *Carol*, Scrooge's father is portrayed as abandoning and cruel, but I think that the intervention of Marley's Ghost, though the spirit of a flawed character, represents a good internal father that Scrooge has triumphed over. Scrooge himself acknowledges to Marley's Ghost: 'You were always a good friend to me' (p. 50).

Then, the first of the Three Spirits of Christmas announces itself as the Ghost of Christmas Past – Scrooge's past. The Ghost of Christmas Past, which I think is a normal superego, shows Scrooge what he calls 'shadows of the things that have been' – shadows that 'have no consciousness of us' (p. 57). These concern both good and also very sad experience. The Ghost shows Scrooge the place where he was 'bred' and where he was a boy. Scrooge becomes 'conscious of a thousand odours floating in the air, each one connected with a thousand thoughts, and hopes, and joys, and cares long, long forgotten' (p. 57).

In the next shadow we read about an excruciatingly painful early separation from his family. We see Scrooge as a boy excluded from home and family, left at boarding school over Christmas. Nonetheless, Scrooge has strengths and capacities that help him to endure. We see the young Scrooge use his imagination to bring alive various characters in the children's stories he reads. I think that in this way the young boy helps to keep alive the good mother he is missing.

The Ghost then shows Scrooge another shadow of himself at the school, on another Christmas Eve:

> [Scrooge] was not reading now, but walking up and down despairingly . . .
>
> [The door] opened; and a little girl, much younger than the boy, came darting in, and putting her arms about his neck, and often kissing him, addressed him as her 'dear, dear brother'.
>
> 'I have come to bring you home, dear brother!' said the child, clapping her tiny hands, and bending down to laugh. 'To bring you home, home, home!'
>
> 'Home, little Fran?' returned the boy.
>
> 'Yes!' said the child, brimful of glee. 'Home, for good and all. Home, for ever and ever. Father is so much kinder than he used to be, that home's like Heaven! . . . I was not afraid to ask him once more if you might come home; and he said Yes, you should; and sent me in a coach to bring you.'
>
> (pp. 59–60)

We are not told why Scrooge was neglected and abandoned. We may think, perhaps, that his mother died after the birth of the 'one who is to come', his sister, little Fran. Or was it that his mother left the father to live with a lover? Or perhaps Scrooge's mother remained at home, but was unable to stand up for him.

Whatever the external reality, in this shadow we have sight of the risk to Scrooge of the loss of his mother, who he needs to help him with his feelings. What 'came darting in' – in a state of increasing despair – is, I suggest, an omnipotent phantasy. Fran, the infant sister that in unconscious phantasy I think Scrooge condemns to death at birth, is transformed into a virgin mother who will rescue him – bring him to a 'home [that's] like heaven'.

However, a continuing sense of good experience remains. In the next shadow, we see Scrooge's feelings of love and gratitude towards the good parents, represented by Old Fezziwig, to whom Scrooge is now apprenticed, and Mrs Fezziwig. It is again Christmas Eve. The couple, with their family, give a domestic ball for those who work for them. As the two Fezziwigs dance to the fiddler, the narrator says,

> As to *her*, she was worthy to be his partner in every sense of the term. If that's not high praise, tell me higher and I'll use it. A positive light appeared to issue

105

from Fezziwig's calves. They shone in every part of the dance like moons. You couldn't have predicted, at any given time, what would become of 'em next.

(p. 63)

This passage has a warm atmosphere. Scrooge's gratitude to and admiration of this couple seem real, but at the same time the narrator sounds a warning note – referring to Scrooge's 'agitation' as he observes this shadow, which I think is a state of euphoria. Scrooge's 'heart and soul were in the scene, and with his former self. He corroborated everything, remembered everything, enjoyed everything, and underwent the strangest agitation' (p. 64).

The Ghost of Christmas Past, being a superego, even a normal one, is somewhat contemptous of Scrooge's gratitude, suggesting that Fezziwig 'has spent but a few pounds of your mortal money' (p. 64). However, Scrooge is strong enough to stand up to his guide. He replies to the Ghost:

heated by the remark, and speaking unconsciously like his former, not his latter self. 'It isn't that, Spirit. He has the power to render us happy or unhappy; to make our service light or burdensome; a pleasure or a toil. Say that his power lies in words and looks; in things so slight and insignificant that it is impossible to add and count 'em up: what then? The happiness he gives, is quite as great as if it cost a fortune.'

(p. 64)

Scrooge can also bear to feel a little remorse. He tells the Ghost of Christmas Past that he has had the thought that he 'should like to be able to say a word of two to his clerk' (p. 64).

However, there is something within Scrooge that interferes with further integration of feelings, and anxieties around good experience. In the next shadow we see Scrooge, as a young man, unable to establish a happy relationship with a 'fair young girl'. Rather than growing stronger, and more able to let go some of the inevitable grievance he carries, instead grudge and resentment gathers strength. The painfulness of Scrooge's disparagement of the girl who might have been his own partner is described in one of the book's most finely drawn scenes. When she describes how things are between the two of them, Scrooge reacts impatiently, but the girl confronts him:

'I have seen your nobler aspirations fall off one by one, until the master-passion, Gain, engrosses you . . .

Our contract is an old one. It was made when we were both poor and content to be so, until, in good season, we could improve our worldly fortune by our patient industry. You *are* changed. When it was made, you were another man . . .

... you who in your very confidence with her, weigh everything by Gain ...

You may – the memory of what is past half makes me hope you will – have pain in this. A very, very brief time, and you will dismiss the recollection of it, gladly, as an unprofitable dream, from which it happened well that you awoke. May you be happy in the life you have chosen!'

She left him; and they parted.

'Spirit,' said Scrooge, 'show me no more! Conduct me home. Why do you delight to torture me?'

(pp. 65–66)

Sodre (unpub.) writes that in the miser there is

an idealization of an object which has been transformed into faeces – and which is held in sadistic captivity.

Avarice can thus be seen as a form of perversion of the melancholic's wish to totally possess the object; as he corrupts the nature of the object by making it unusable, in an ordinary way, even for himself.

It is, I think, this corruption of avarice that the fair young girl calls 'Gain' – bringing severe persecution. No longer does omnipotent phantasy just come 'darting in' (p. 60). There is the hold of an omnipotent organization, ruled by a very bad superego. Slater points out that 'the brilliantly named figure of Scrooge, evok[es] the sense both of "screw" and of "gouge"' (Dickens 2003: xix).

There is an earlier reference in the text (Dickens 2003: 65) to the fair young girl having tears in her eyes, wearing a mourning-dress. Otherwise unexplained, I think this suggests a condensation of Scrooge's loss of the fair girl with another loss, mentioned a little earlier in the text – the death of little Fran, the infant sister who, I suggested above, Scrooge in unconscious phantasy condemns to death at birth. Little Fran, 'always a delicate creature, whom a breath might have withered' (p. 61), died after the birth of her first child, Fred. I think persecution tightens with her death. Scrooge cannot marry the fair girl. He cannot even allow himself a child in the form of his nephew Fred, who Scrooge goes on to neglect so badly.

With this last shadow persecution mounts.

'One shadow more!' exclaimed the Ghost.

'No more!' cried Scrooge. 'No more. I don't wish to see it. Show me no more!'

But the relentless Ghost pinioned him in both his arms, and forced him to observe what happened next.

(pp. 66–67)

In this next shadow, we see the fair young girl as a grown woman, on a later Christmas Eve. She has a family including

> a beautiful young girl, so like the last that Scrooge believed it was the same, until he saw *her*, now a comely matron, sitting opposite her daughter.
>
> (p. 67)

The increased persecution is matched by an extended euphoric account of this family, where the narrator tells us 'there were more children there, than Scrooge is his agitated state of mind could count' (p. 67).

It is interesting to note that unlike the earlier shadows, Scrooge would not have actually perceived what is described. Behind this shadow is, I think, the primal scene. When the husband arrives home, and the daughter sits with her parents by the fireside, the narrator tells us in sentimental tones that Scrooge 'looked on more attentively than ever' and his 'sight grew very dim'

> when he thought that such another creature, quite as graceful and full of promise, might have called him father.
>
> (p. 68)

The manic denial of the parental link breaks down, however, when Belle's husband tells his wife how he has observed Scrooge 'quite alone in the world'.

> 'Belle,' said the husband, turning to his wife with a smile, 'I saw an old friend of yours this afternoon.'
> 'Who was it?'
> 'Guess!'
> 'How can I? Tut, don't I know,' she added in the same breath, laughing as he laughed. 'Mr. Scrooge.'
> 'Mr. Scrooge it was. I passed his office window; and it was not shut up, and he had a candle inside. His partner lies upon the point of death, I hear; and there he sat alone. Quite alone in the world, I do believe.'
> 'Spirit!' said Scrooge in a broken voice, 'remove me from this place.'
> 'I told you these were shadows of the things that have been,' said the Ghost. 'They are what they are, do not blame me!'
> 'Remove me!' Scrooge exclaimed. 'I cannot bear it!'
>
> (p. 68)

With his good friend and partner now lying 'upon the point of death', Scrooge is left terribly exposed to persecution and despair. He tells the Spirit of Christmas Past, 'Remove me! . . . I cannot bear it'. The normal superego, being no more than a superego, says 'Do not blame me' (p. 68). The next haunting gives Scrooge a respite, before he is plunged into terror.

V

I think in this next haunting the Ghost of Christmas Present represents 'memories in feeling' (Klein [1935] 1975: 180) of good parents and the world they introduce to the child. The Spirit

> was clothed in one simple deep green robe, or mantle, bordered with white fur. This garment hung so loosely on the figure, that its capacious breast was bare, as if distaining to be warded or concealed by any artifice . . . Its dark brown curls were long and free: free as its genial face, its sparkling eye, its open hand, its cheery air, its unconstrained demeanour, and its joyful air. Girded around its middle was an antique scabbard; but no sword was in it, and the ancient sheath was eaten up with rust.
>
> (Dickens 2003: 74)

In this Ghost's presence everything takes on a peculiar intensity and size. The incense and drops of water from the Ghost of Christmas Present's 'very uncommon kind of torch' (p. 77), enriches life, and may make bearable what is otherwise unbearable. Scrooge cannot get enough of the Ghost of Christmas Present. Watching his nephew Fred's family play their Christmas games, Scrooge begs the Ghost 'like a boy' (Dickens 2003: 90) to be allowed to stay longer, despite the unkind comments that Fred's family make about him. The Ghost of Christmas Present also stirs some guilt and concern.

> 'Spirit,' said Scrooge, with an interest he had never felt before, 'tell me if Tiny Tim will live.'
> 'I see a vacant seat,' replied the Ghost . . . 'If these shadows remain unaltered by the Future, the child will die.'
>
> (p. 82)

However, the Ghost of Christmas Present lives for just one day. At a quarter to midnight there appears two hateful and hated children.

> From the foldings of its robe, it brought two children; wretched, abject, frightful, hideous, miserable . . . They were a boy and a girl. Yellow, meager, ragged, scowling, wolfish; but prostrate too, in their humility . . . Where angels might have sat enthroned, devils lurked; and glared out menacingly . . . No change, no degradation, no perversion of humanity, in any grade, through all the mysteries of wonderful creation, has monsters half so horrible and dread . . .
> 'Spirit are they yours?' Scrooge could say no more.
> 'They are Man's,' said the Spirit, looking down upon them . . . 'This boy is Ignorance. This girl is Want. Beware of them both, and all of their degree,

but most of all beware this boy, for on his brow I see that written which is Doom, unless the writing be erased.'

(pp. 92–94)

The boy, Ignorance, is Scrooge, who condemns his infant baby sister to die from Want. However, the monster boy is also an infant Scrooge who is himself dying from Want – in bondage to a very bad superego that works to corrupt him.

The bell struck twelve. Scrooge looked about him for the Ghost [of Christmas Present], and saw it not . . . He beheld a solemn Phantom, draped and hooded, coming, like a mist along the ground, towards him.

(p. 94)

This Phantom, the Ghost of Christmas Yet to Come,

was shrouded in a deep black garment, which concealed its head, its form, and left nothing of it visible save one outstretched hand. But for this it would have been difficult to detach its figure from the night, and separate it from the darkness by which it was surrounded.

(p. 95)

Led by the Phantom, Scrooge overhears some business men in the city talking. One of them says: 'Well! . . . Old Scratch . . . has got his own at last' (p. 97). Slater writes that Old Scratch was a nickname for the devil from Old Norse *skratta*, a goblin (Dickens 2003: 289, note 57). Scrooge cannot think of any person connected with himself to whom this conversation could apply. The Phantom leads him, however, to an appalling corrupt place:

an obscure part of the town, where Scrooge had never penetrated before . . . The ways were foul and narrow . . . the people half-naked, drunken, slipshod, ugly . . . Far in this den of infamous resort, there was a low-browed beetling shop . . . Secrets that few would like to scrutinise were bred and hidden in mountains of unseemly rags, masses of corrupted fat, and sepulchures of bones.

(pp. 98–99)

A trio, a charwoman, a laundress and an undertaker's man bring various possessions belonging to a dead man, to which they have helped themselves, to sell to the shop's proprietor, old Joe, who I think represents Old Scratch. The charwoman has stripped the bed-curtains, blankets and the shirt that 'somebody was fool enough' (p. 101) to put on the man to be buried, leaving the body lying under a ragged sheet.

'He, ha!' laughed the . . . [charwoman], when old Joe, producing a flannel bag with money in it, told out their several gains upon the ground. 'This is the end of it, you see! He frightened every one away from him when he was alive, to profit us when he was dead! Ha, ha, ha!'

(p. 102)

The scene describes, at one level, an external circle of enmity, where despised groups, Ignorance and Want – whether at institutional, national or international level – slip their chains of 'humility' and may threaten civilization. But, at another level, this 'obscure part of the town, where Scrooge had never penetrated before' portrays the topography of terror in his mind. The 'masses of corrupted fat, and sepulchures of bones' in old Joe's shop, that Scrooge observes, represent his 'Gain'. It is sometimes said, and I do not agree with this, that the Phantom is death. I think that the Phantom 'draped and hooded, coming, like a mist along the ground' represents Scrooge's very bad superego. The implacable phantom silently lords it over Scrooge, interfering with mourning, and the contemplation of mortality.

A pale light, rising in the outer air, fell straight upon the bed; and on it, plundered and bereft, unwatched, unwept, uncared for, was the body of this man.

Scrooge glanced towards the Phantom. Its steady hand was pointed at the head. The cover was so carelessly adjusted that the slightest raising of it, the motion of a finger upon Scrooge's part, would have disclosed the face. He thought of it, felt how easy it would be to do, and longed to do it; but had no more power to withdraw the veil than to dismiss the spectre at his side . . .

He lay, in the dark empty house, with not a man, a woman, or a child, to say that he was kind to me in this or that, and for the memory of one kind word I will be kind to him. A cat was tearing at the door, and there was a sound of gnawing rats beneath the hearth-stone. What *they* wanted in the room of death, and why they were so restless and disturbed, Scrooge did not dare to think.

'Spirit!' he said, 'this is a fearful place. In leaving it, I shall not leave its lesson, trust me. Let us go!'

(pp. 102–103)

This 'fearful place' is the melancholic shadow that has fallen upon Scrooge's ego (Freud 1917: 249). The shadow is quite different from the shadows shown to him by his normal superego, in which there is always a component of wanting to put things right. The Phantom's 'steady hand' points at the head of the dead man. Scrooge is left 'quite alone in the world' with his accuser's single viewpoint – Scrooge is to blame.

111

This accuser is not good, its hand is not kind, and the nature of the fate it seeks to impose is irrevocable. Just the slightest raising of 'the veil' (p. 102) and Scrooge's ego may be overwhelmed with his unconscious belief that he is, and nothing but, the unloving monster boy, Ignorance, who deserves to die with no one to remember him with one kind word. Only the devil will receive him. Sophocles' Oedipus wishes for the withdrawal of a similar veil and pays a terrible price. Scrooge is no Sophoclean hero. Although he says he wants to move the veil, he holds that he has 'no more power to withdraw the veil than to dismiss the spectre at his side' (p. 102).

> 'Good Spirit,' he pursued, as down upon the ground he fell before it: 'Your nature intercedes for me, and pities me . . .'
> The kind hand trembled . . .
> Holding up his hands in a last prayer to have his fate reversed, he saw an alteration in the Phantom's hood and dress. It shrunk, collapsed, and dwindled down into a bedpost.
>
> (pp. 108–110)

I think the story here brings a reverse movement, back into retreat. This miraculous transformation of the Phantom into a 'good spirit', whose hand is kind and which is capable of pity towards Scrooge's terror, is a trick of self-deception. The visit of the third Spirit, the Ghost of Christmas Yet to Come, confronts Scrooge with his avarice and his bad superego that aims to reduce everything to nothing – with its murderous hold over his perception of his need for his good objects to help him with his feelings. The salvation that begins with the intervention of Marley's Ghost now falters. There is renewed appeasement of and collusion with 'the perfect object'.

VI

In the final chapter Scrooge awakes from his haunting.

> Yes! And the bedpost was his own. The bed was his own, the room was his own. Best and happiest of all, the Time before him was his own, to make amends in! . . .
> He dressed himself 'all in his best' and at last got out into the streets. The people were by this time pouring forth, as he had seen them with the Ghost of Christmas Present; and walking with his hands behind him, Scrooge regarded everyone with a delighted smile. He looked so irresistibly pleasant, in a word, that three or four good-humoured fellows said, 'Good morning sir! A merry Christmas to you!' And Scrooge said often afterwards, that of all the blithe sounds he had ever heard, those were the blithest to his ears.
>
> (pp. 111, 114)

The *Carol* does end with a wish that enmity might be put aside, but it is a temporary truce. The melancholic shadow is the 'lesson' (p. 103) Scrooge shall not leave. When the narrator says that Scrooge 'did it all, and infinitely more; and to Tiny Tim, who did NOT die, he was a second father' (p. 116), we recognize this for the euphoria it is.

A Christmas Carol conveys a picture of an enmity to life that convinces. I have suggested that the haunting involves the intervention of a flawed but good internalized father that Scrooge has triumphed over in the Oedipus situation. Haunted by the Three Spirits of Christmas, Scrooge is pulled in a direction out of retreat. Dickens movingly portrays Scrooge's struggle – with its risk that loss of omnipotence, remorse and terror will lead to Scrooge's remaining links with his good objects (represented also by Tiny Tim and the struggling Cratchit family) being quite overwhelmed. Dickens takes the reader in imagination to the psychic truth of a place in the mind where mother and baby really may be destroyed – identifying in horror and pity with Scrooge's forsaken state.

I have also suggested that, at the end of the story, the hold that the Ghost of Christmas Yet to Come has on Scrooge pulls him back into retreat – away from the possibility of more lasting psychic change with grief and sadness for what is irreparably lost, a sense of good internal parents re-found (resurrected in the ego), and recognition that all serious choice brings loss and the relinquishment of something treasured. The evasion is also, I think, part of the way Dickens' story works for the reader.

Connections between the *Carol* and the life of Dickens would go far beyond the limits of my present enquiry. Those who are interested may consult a number of biographers and essayists (e.g. Ackroyd 1990; Tomalin, 1990; Smiley 2002). However, it may be noted that in Ackroyd's view 'for the first time in his published writings, the whole nature of Dickens' childhood informs the little narrative' (p. 432). At the end of the *Carol* Scrooge is left in old age wealthy but childless and, notwithstanding the euphoria, lonely. At the time the *Carol* was published on 17 December 1843, Dickens was aged 31, married with a growing family, and enjoying growing fame. But he had choices ahead of him.

Acknowledgements

I wish to express my gratitude to David M. Black, Michael Brearley and Ignes Sodre for their helpful and valuable comments and suggestions at various stages in the preparation of this contribution.

References

Ackroyd, P. (1990) *Dickens*. London: Vintage.

Birksted-Breen, D. (1996) Phallus, penis and mental space. *International Journal of Psychoanalysis* 77: 649–657.

Britton, R. (1989) The missing link: Parental sexuality in the Oedipus complex. In J. Steiner (ed.) *The Oedipus Complex Today*. London: Karnac.

Britton, R. (2003) *Sex, Death, and the Super-ego: Experiences in Psychoanalysis*. London: Karnac.

Dickens, C. (2003) A Christmas Carol. In M. Slater (ed.) *A Christmas Carol and Other Christmas Writings*. London: Penguin.

Festinger, L. (1957) *A Theory of Cognitive Dissonance*. Stanford, CA: Stanford University Press.

Freud, S. (1917) *Mourning and Melancholia*. SE 14.

Freud, S. (1923) The Ego and the Id. SE 19.

Jacques, E. (1965) Death and the midlife crisis. In E. Spillius (ed.) (1988) *Melanie Klein Today: Developments in Theory and Practice*, vol. 2. London and New York: Routledge.

Jurgs, M. (2003) *Der Kleine Frieden im Grossen Krieg*. Munich: Bertelsmann.

Klein, M. (1935) A contribution to the psychogenesis of manic–depressive states. In *Love, Guilt and Reparation and Other Works 1921–1945*. London: Hogarth Press (1975).

Leach, E. (1969a) Genesis as myth. In *Genesis as Myth and Other Essays*. London: Jonathan Cape.

Leach, E. (1969b) Virgin birth. In *Genesis as Myth and Other Essays*. London: Jonathan Cape.

Leach, E. (1969c) The legitimacy of Solomon. In *Genesis as Myth and Other Essays*. London: Jonathan Cape.

Millar, D. (2001) A psychoanalytical view of biblical myth. *International Journal of Psychoanalysis* 82: 965–979.

O'Shaughnessy, E. (1999) Relating to the superego. *International Journal of Psychoanalysis* 80: 861–870.

Segal, H. (1997) Phantasy and reality. In J. Steiner (ed.) *Psychoanalysis, Literature and War*. London: Routledge.

Smiley, J. (2002) *Charles Dickens*. London: Weidenfeld and Nicolson.

Sodre, I. (unpub.) Avarice. Tavistock Public Lecture.

Steiner, J. (1993) *Psychic Retreats: Pathological Organisations of the Personality in Psychotic, Neurotic and Borderline Patients*. London and New York: Routledge.

Tomalin, C. (1990) *The Invisible Woman: The Story of Nelly Ternan and Charles Dickens*. London: Penguin.

PART THREE

The nature and psychological functioning of religious experiences

6

WAYS OF TRANSFORMATION

Michael Parsons

How we perceive the relation between psychoanalysis and religion will depend on how we think about each of them in the first place. Certain conceptions of psychoanalysis will probably not show much interest in religion, and certain religious attitudes are unlikely to appreciate psychoanalytic thinking. Some analysts, for example, view psychoanalysis as an empirical science, to be validated by objectively verifiable observations. This approach will seek a theoretical base in disciplines, like attachment theory or neuropsychology, that favour empirical research of that sort. Those who hold this view of psychoanalysis may not be very concerned with its relation to religion unless, like Freud (1927) in *The Future of an Illusion*, to see religion as replaceable by the scientific values of psychoanalysis. For others, however, psychoanalysis is a matter of unique subjective experience. In this case, what matters most cannot be empirically validated or quantified, or even, perhaps, precisely articulated in words. From such a perspective the relation between psychoanalysis and religion may appear more worth considering.

There are corresponding differences where religion is concerned. One standpoint emphasises the transcendence of the divine, sees the source of knowledge as external, in the form of dogma and revelation, and locates authority in scripture and religious institutions. On the other hand there are those for whom the ground of being is to be sought within, who for knowledge and authoritative conviction look to the authenticity of their own spiritual experience, and whose sense of responsibility is based in that experience rather than in obedience to external structures. Those inclined to the former attitude may find psychoanalysis, with its impetus towards self-determination and internal autonomy, a threat to the authority of revealed truth and prescribed morality. The latter kind of spiritual temperament may be more interested in a discipline like psychoanalysis that is also, in its own way, concerned with inwardness.

117

So if we ask whether psychoanalysis and religion are 'competitors or collab-orators', the answer will depend on our own position. We can align them, oppose them to each other or make them mutually irrelevant, by the view we take of them. If we imagine religion and psychoanalysis as two intersecting circles, then in either one we can choose where to place ourselves. We may stay well away from the area of overlap and there will not be much dialogue with anyone anywhere in the other circle. My interest, on the other hand, is in the part of the diagram that belongs to both circles, and in exploring how widespread, among the various spiritual traditions, are the possible points of contact with psychoanalysis.

In Psalm 142 the Psalmist complains to God about his miseries, including his persecution by enemies who 'privily lay snares' for him. No man wants to know him and he has nowhere to flee to. He cries out:

> O deliver me from my persecutors: for they are too strong for me.
> Bring my soul out of prison, that I may give thanks unto thy Name.
> (Psalm 142: 6–7)

The psalm as a whole might sound like a standard sort of complaint, asking God to step in and put down the ungodly, and see to it that as a good believer the Psalmist gets a fairer deal out of life. But what about the verse just quoted? If the Psalmist truly believes in God's ways, why does he not give thanks to Him anyway, even if he is in prison? Evidently this is a kind of prison that makes it impossible to do that. 'Bring my *soul* out of prison'. The Psalmist is talking about a state of mind, one in which he is not capable of giving thanks to God; and that is what makes it a prison. The persecutors who are 'too strong for me' may be understood psychoanalytically as belonging to the Psalmist's own inner world. The reason why he cannot give thanks to God is that he is caught in a state of mind where there is such a sense of persecution that it is impossible to feel gratitude at all. It is this internal prison from which he needs to be freed.

It is an important aspect of psychoanalytic understanding to know that a description of something external – an event, a state of affairs, a set of commands – may also represent an internal psychic situation. If a patient complains of feeling attacked and interfered with by someone, the analyst might interpret this as a way of conveying how persecuted the patient feels by a demanding and con-trolling aspect of his or her own personality. Elsewhere I have given the example of a patient who described how business people in one locality were getting together to improve their amenities and environment, in contrast to another area where people did not seem able to mobilise themselves and cooperate like that. I took this as referring to the patient's internal state, and his concern about whether different aspects of his own self could come together to mobilise his resources and bring about change in him (Parsons 2000: 173). There is a striking example of this shift from external to internal awareness in the biblical book of Jeremiah. After much denunciation of Israel for forsaking God, and warning of God's punishment, Jeremiah prophesies a new phase in the relationship between God and his people.

> Behold, the days come, saith the Lord, that I will make a new covenant with the house of Israel, and with the house of Judah:
> Not according to the covenant that I made with their fathers in the day that I took them by the hand to bring them out of the land of Egypt . . .
> But this shall be the covenant that I will make with the house of Israel; After those days, saith the Lord, I will put my law in their inward parts, and write it in their hearts; and will be their God, and they shall be my people.
>
> (Jeremiah 31: 31–33)

This passage is echoed, and its emphasis on inwardness is highlighted, in the traditional form of the Anglican Communion Service. The priest rehearses the Ten Commandments, and after each commandment the congregation replies 'Lord, have mercy upon us, and incline our hearts to keep this law'. The inclination of the heart matters, but the emphasis is on obedience to the law. After the final commandment, however, the response is 'Lord, have mercy upon us, and write all these thy laws in our hearts, we beseech thee'. This marks a shift from external behaviour to internalisation, and to a changed internal state that results from that.

The passage in Jeremiah makes it clear that this shift implies a spiritual, or psychological, progression. The same thing appears in St Paul's Epistle to the Romans. The early Christian Church was divided about whether its members should be required to convert to Judaism. This would mean, of course, that non-Jewish men who became Christians would have to be circumcised. Paul thought that belief in Christ was for everybody, whether or not they were Jews.

> He is not a Jew, which is one outwardly; neither is that circumcision, which is outward in the flesh:
> But he is a Jew, which is one inwardly; and circumcision is that of the heart, in the spirit.
>
> (Romans 2: 28–29)

This seems an attitude well in accord with psychoanalysis. Both psychoanalysis and religion are interested in a shift in understanding, from external to internal. But whether this shift will lead to true inner growth and development depends on the nature of what is internalised. A relationship with a good internal object is one thing. But it is also possible to internalise oppression, and install a harsh, moralistic superego. The importance of the quality of internal life appears in Jesus' complaint against the scribes and Pharisees.

Hypocrites! for ye are like unto whited sepulchres, which indeed appear beautiful outward, but are within full of dead men's bones, and of all uncleanness.

(Matthew 23: 27)

The word 'sepulchres' is specific. Christ is talking about a kind of deadness of the spirit. The opposite state, and the transformation from one to the other, is what St Paul points to when he says:

For as in Adam all die; even so in Christ shall all be made alive.

(1 Corinthians 15: 22)

In the Church's Easter anthems this affirmation celebrates the resurrection of Christ. But Paul is clearly talking also about an internal process of moving out of a state of deadness into one of being spiritually alive. Christ himself said: 'I am come that they might have life, and that they might have it more abundantly' (John 10: 10).

Helping someone towards a more abundant kind of aliveness is also what a psychoanalyst is there for. This attitude shows, for example, in Marion Milner's comment on 'the astounding experience of how it feels to be alive' (Milner 1950: 159). Winnicott began his autobiographical fragment *Not Less than Everything* with a prayer 'Oh God! May I be alive when I die' (Winnicott, C. 1989: 4). These are not specifically psychoanalytic utterances: Milner and Winnicott were not 'doing psychoanalysis' when they made them. But both Winnicott and Milner are notable for the interrelation in their work between profound personal experience and psychoanalytic thinking, and coming from them such statements are at once human and psychoanalytic. An analyst who has been especially concerned with what it means to be psychically alive, or not, is Michael Eigen. A chapter of his book *Psychic Deadness* (Eigen 1996: 69–87) is devoted to Winnicott's ideas, and in the introduction he says that 'Winnicott's work is a kind of biography of the sense of aliveness as it unfolds in infancy and throughout a lifetime' (p. xxi). We can see what Eigen means in Guntrip's (1975) account of his analysis with Winnicott. Guntrip's brother died in infancy when Guntrip was 3½ years old, and Winnicott said that after this Guntrip had

collapsed . . . but managed to salvage enough of yourself to go on living, very energetically, and put the rest in a cocoon, repressed, unconscious . . . Your problem is that that illness of collapse was never resolved. You had to keep yourself alive in spite of it. You can't take your ongoing being for granted . . . You know about 'being active' but not about 'just growing, just breathing', without your having to do anything about it.

(Guntrip 1975: 152)

Guntrip writes that Winnicott once said to him: 'We differ from Freud. He was for curing symptoms. We are concerned with living persons, whole living and loving' (Guntrip 1975: 153). I do not think Freud was concerned only with curing symptoms, but Winnicott was making a particular point about the nature of psychoanalysis – the same point that Thomas Ogden (1995) articulates very precisely as follows:

> I believe that every form of psychopathology represents a specific type of limi-tation of the individual's capacity to be fully alive as a human being. The goal of analysis from this point of view is larger than that of the resolution of unconscious intrapsychic conflict, the diminution of symptomatology, the enhancement of reflective subjectivity and self-understanding, and the increase of sense of personal agency. Although one's sense of being alive is intimately intertwined with each of the above-mentioned capacities, I believe that the experience of aliveness is a quality that is superordinate to these capacities and must be considered as an aspect of the analytic experience *in its own terms.*
>
> (Ogden 1995: 696, original italics)

In Winnicott's book *Playing and Reality* there is a chapter called 'The place where we live' (Winnicott 1971: 104–110). For years I understood that phrase to mean 'the area where our experience is located', reading it in the same way as 'the house where I live'. But I have realised it can also be read as 'The place where we LIVE' – meaning the place in which, when we manage to be in it, we become fully alive. This place is what Winnicott calls the intermediate area, the potential space that persists in various forms throughout life, as an evolution of the transitional space of childhood. The defining characteristic of this space is that it is neither inside nor outside. In this intermediate area external reality, which is other than ourselves, independent of our wishes and feelings, and internal reality, which is our own imaginative creation, do not exclude each other. It offers a space in which the world may continually be both discovered and originated by us, on condition that one does not rule out the other.

External and internal reality are matched in spiritual language by the ideas of transcendence and immanence. The transcendent is that which is totally other than ourselves, beyond our grasp so that we struggle to conceive how we might relate to it. The prophet Isaiah says:

> To whom then will ye liken me, or shall I be equal? saith the Holy One.
> For my thoughts are not your thoughts, neither are your ways my ways, saith the Lord.
> For as the heavens are higher than the earth, so are my ways higher than your ways, and my thoughts than your thoughts.
>
> (Isaiah 40: 25; 55: 8–9)

The immanent is that which is so deeply internal to us that it seems to form the ground of our being. This understanding of God's nature has been notably articulated in our own times by Paul Tillich. In the fourteenth century the Eastern Orthodox theologian Nicolas Cabasilas wrote that the person of Christ 'is closer to us than our own soul' (quoted in Ware 1997: 70), while the Qur'an says that Allah is 'closer to man than his neck vein' (50:16). Spiritual teaching, in all religious traditions, points to the need to comprehend both these perspectives without either negating the other. A key verse of the Qur'an says: 'We [Allah] will show them our signs on the horizons and in themselves' (41:53). There are certain sayings of Muhammad, called *hadith*, which have a semi-scriptural authority, and one of these reports Allah as saying: 'The heavens and the earth cannot contain Me, but the heart of my believing servant does contain Me' (Burckhardt 1959: 115). The Psalmist in the Bible puts the two aspects together like this:

> O Lord, thou hast searched me out and known me: thou knowest my down-sitting and mine uprising, thou understandest my thoughts long before.
>
> For lo, there is not a word in my tongue: but thou, O Lord, knowest it altogether.
>
> Such knowledge is too wonderful and excellent for me: I cannot attain unto it.
>
> If I climb up into heaven, thou art there: if I go down to hell, thou art there also.
>
> I will give thanks unto thee, for I am fearfully and wonderfully made: marvellous are thy works, and that my soul knoweth right well.
>
> (Psalm 139)

This sublime language might seem to imply what is called 'believing in God', and some religious language does jump to speaking of 'God transcendent' and 'God immanent'. But in a back-handed way I have chosen these scriptural examples exactly because I want to dig beneath this kind of vocabulary. The fundamental text of Taoism, the *Tao Te Ching* (1963), declares that the Tao, the underlying principle of existence, fills the universe and is the origin of the ten thousand things. Yet the Tao is also small, inward and unobtrusive – 'the spirit of the valley' (Chapter 6). The *Katha Upanishad*, a Hindu sacred text, says that Atman, meaning Self, That Which Is, 'is not born, does not die, is not the effect of any cause; is eternal, self-existent, imperishable'. But as well as being 'greater than the greatest' it is 'lesser than the least'. It 'lives in all hearts'. 'The individual self and the universal Self [live] in the heart like shade and light' (Shree Purohit and Yeats 1937: 30–31). Formulations such as these make it clear that transcendence and immanence do not have to be matters of doctrine about God. They are *dimensions of experience*. In the verses quoted, the Psalmist puts the axis of immanence and the axis of transcendence into relation with each other, just as Winnicott did with internal and external reality, and the purpose is the same.

As Winnicott delineated in this way the intermediate area in which we are most imaginatively alive, so the Psalmist creates a new space in which the wholeness of his being may be more fully known.

Psychoanalysis is a process, and spiritual disciplines too envisage a process of internal evolution. A classic account is the Persian poem *The Conference of the Birds* written in the twelfth century by Farid ud-din Attar, one of the greatest Sufi mystics. His poem describes the journey of a group of birds to meet a mysterious creature called the Simurgh. The Simurgh is not explicitly described as divine, but his transcendence seems absolute. 'He is the sovran lord and is bathed in the perfection of his majesty' (Attar 1961: 12). He exists on a plane far beyond anything that the birds could aspire to. Despairing, they say to their leader, the hoopoe:

> We are feeble . . . so how shall we be able at last to reach the Sublime Simurgh? If we should arrive it would be a miracle. Tell us something about this marvellous Being . . . or, blind as we are, we shall understand nothing of the mystery. If there were some relation between this Being and ourselves it would be much easier for us to set out.

The hoopoe replies:

> When the Simurgh manifested himself . . . radiant as the sun, he produced thousands of shadows on earth. When he cast his glance on these shadows there appeared birds in great numbers. The different types of birds that are seen in the world are thus only the shadows of the Simurgh . . . When you understand this you will understand exactly your relation to the Simurgh.
> (Attar 1961: 29–30)

Thousands of birds set out, but at the end of the journey only thirty are left. The literal meaning of the word 'Simurgh' is 'thirty birds'. Attar writes:

> The sun of majesty sent forth his rays, and in the reflection of each other's faces these thirty birds (si-murgh) of the outer world, contemplated the face of the Simurgh of the inner world . . . When they gazed at the Simurgh they saw that it was truly the Simurgh who was there, and when they turned their eyes towards themselves they saw that they themselves were the Simurgh . . . The Simurgh [said]: 'The sun of my majesty is a mirror. He who sees himself therein sees his soul and his body, and sees them completely'.
> (Attar 1961: 131–132)

What was presented as a journey to meet an unknown transcendent Other, is revealed as a journey from one inward state of being to another inward state of being.

The Simurgh as a mirror, revealing to the birds their own true nature, reminds us of Freud's (1912: 118) description of the analyst as a mirror reflecting back to his patients what they show him of themselves. It has been important, since Freud wrote that in 1912, for psychoanalytic technique to recover from its implication of a withholding sort of anonymity. But something different about it remains true. André Green (2002: 50), for example, has written that what characterises the psychoanalytic exchange is 'to achieve a return to the self by a detour through the other'. *The Conference of the Birds* was written within the tradition of Islam, and the idea of 'return' resonates through the Qur'an like a leitmotif:

> They shall meet their Lord and unto him they are returning.
> (2:43)

> . . . those who, when a misfortune befalls them, say: Surely we are Allah's and to Him we shall surely return.
> (2:152)

> And whatever is in the heavens and whatever is in the earth is Allah's; and to Allah all things return.
> (3:105)

> As He brought you forth in the beginning, so shall you also return.
> (7:28)

Sufism is known to its followers as 'The Path of Return'. One aspect of Islam is that of an outwardly orientated, activist kind of religion, and the idea of returning, by death of the body, to an external deity who created and operates the material world, does not have much connection with psychoanalysis. But a work like *The Conference of the Birds* indicates that the Allah to whom all things return is also the Allah who is closer to man than his neck vein. The majesty of the Simurgh reveals to the birds that their journey has not been a way to the obliteration of their selves in some external divine Other, but a path of return to their own selves, which they recognise transformed through the mediation of the Other.

One more schema of spiritual transformation is the Tree of Life, in the Kabbalistic tradition of Jewish spirituality. This is a remarkable diagram which sets out ten *sephiroth*, or centres of energy, to describe different elements in the nature of man. It is potentially of special interest to psychoanalysts, because more than any other spiritual tradition that I know of, this offers a clearly worked out, indeed a highly elaborated, account of psychic structure. To compare psychoanalytic conceptualisations of psychic change with the dynamics of the Kabbalistic Tree of Life would be a fascinating enterprise. By studying the multifaceted meanings of each centre, and their relations to each other within the structure of the Tree of Life, the student of Kabbalah is led to a deepening understanding of what it means to be human. The Tree can also be layered on to itself, the top half of one Tree forming the bottom half of the next, to produce a ladder, traditionally linked to the ladder between earth and heaven in Jacob's dream at Bethel (Genesis 28: 12). The ladder as a whole represents the totality of created being, known in this tradition as Adam Kadmon. Adam Kadmon is reflected in the biblical Adam, who represents man in his ordinary state, Jacob asleep at the foot of the ladder. At the top of the ladder, having progressed through the worlds of spiritual experience represented in the Tree of Life, is Adam transformed by the realisation of his potential. There is a clear connection between the Tree of Life and the Christian tradition already noted, of Christ as the second Adam, in whom what was dead in the first Adam, 'shall all be made alive'.

Running through all these spiritual traditions are, first, the idea of a developmental movement in which a person's original identity is not lost, but persists through a process of transformation; and second, the idea of an object that promotes this process of transformation. Both of these are essential psychoanalytic concepts as well. The spiritual object may be a godhead, an exemplar of the absolute such as Christ or the Buddha, a particular spiritual pathway, a sacred text, or an individual teacher. The object and the process cannot be separated. Winnicott, having described the transitional object, immediately says 'It is not the object, of course, that is transitional' (1971: 14). The transitional object represents development from one state to another. That is why it is called 'transitional'. But it is the unfolding of the developmental process that constitutes the object (Parsons 2000: 160–162). Christopher Bollas' concept of the transformational object conveys the same insight. The mother in early infancy, he says,

> is less significant and identifiable as an object than as a process that is identified with cumulative internal and external transformations.

> (Bollas 1987: 14)

The spiritual object is constituted as a spiritual object by the transformational process that it is called on to make available. That is a dense statement, so I shall unpack it. The subject is in a state of readiness for some kind of developmental movement. We might be talking about a baby, or an analytic patient, or someone seeking a spiritual path. For the developmental process to take place, a particular sort of object is needed – one with the potential to be a transformational object. We might be talking about a mother, or an analyst, or a spiritual object of the sort I have mentioned. The subject has to call this object into existence; that is to say, into an existence that will be meaningful for the subject. In that sense, the subject has to create the object for himself or herself. But for that to be possible, the object must already be there. In Winnicott's language, this is a transitional object.

125

The object, once called into meaningful being, makes possible the transformational process. The need for this process, though, is what allows it to become a transformational object in the first place.

Different spiritual traditions have their own identities, and it is important not to try to reduce them to a lowest common denominator. But one could perhaps describe their kinship to psychoanalysis by saying that they, and psychoanalysis, are alike concerned with processes of transformation that work to bring people into deeper contact with the *sources of meaning* in their lives. A patient who was developing a successful career said that his professional life seemed to consist of episodes. They might be major ones for him, like a successful presentation at an important conference, or being sought out for his opinion by leading figures in his field. But then the episodes were over and done with, and he would be drawn on to whatever the next thing might be. He knew his career looked successful, but he missed any feeling of a thread running through it. He had no sense of continuity, no feeling of 'This is what I'm about'; and he went on to talk of how the same thing might be true in his emotional life. It is easy to see how someone could think religion was exactly what this man needed. He should believe in God this way, or follow those observances, and that would give him a sense of meaning. A psychoanalyst might question whether this would be an escape from looking at his internal conflicts, and say that his repeated idealisations are bound to disappoint him so long as he is trying to avoid the ambivalence that is part and parcel of life. The religious person might agree that accepting the imperfection of life could make it feel less like a rollercoaster, but still ask how that would provide the sense of meaning which this man is looking for. The psychoanalyst might reply that it is not the job of analysis to provide meaning, but to help a person see life in a more real way, so that whatever meaning he finds for himself can be real.

Behind such a discussion of difference, it is worth noting a similarity between what this patient is doing and how the birds begin their journey in Attar's poem. In fact he is further along than they were at first, because he is making use of the therapist actively to question himself. Attar's birds start by questioning the hoopoe about the journey. They say it sounds completely impossible and make excuses for not embarking on it. These questions and excuses reveal the characters and qualities of the individual birds, and the hoopoe responds with advice and teaching-stories designed to help them reflect on their difficulties and weaknesses. Both psychoanalysis and spiritual disciplines depend on a person's being willing to talk, or think, in a way that can reveal those things they would rather not have to confess to themselves.

'Confessing', even to oneself, does not seem a very psychoanalytic notion. The linked concept of 'repentance' is even more alien to psychoanalytic thinking. These ideas are redolent of exactly why psychoanalysis has traditionally objected to religion, with their appearance of submission to oppressive, antilibidinal codes of conduct, and guilt in the face of those codes internalised as a punitive, moralistic superego. One reason why the sixteenth-century English Church establishment could not bear William Tyndale's translating the Bible into English (to the point of executing him for it) was that he went back to the original language (Daniell 1989: xvi–xxi; 1994: 93–100). The word for 'repentance' in the Latin Bible, in universal use up to Tyndale's time, was *poenitentia* – 'penitence', with implications of pain, penalty, compensation, and so on. This concept allowed the Church to exercise a powerfully moralistic control over its people, often benefiting from the 'penances' that it imposed. Tyndale translated the New Testament into English directly from the original Greek. The Greek word that was translated into Latin as *poenitentia* is *metanoia*, which has a very different significance. It means 'change of mind', an inward shift of viewpoint, not an external action to compensate for a fault. When John the Baptist preached, 'Repent ye: for the kingdom of heaven is at hand' (Matthew 3: 2), he was not saying 'Own up to how bad and wicked you are'. He was saying, in St Matthew's Greek, *Metanoeite*, 'Find a different internal perspective on yourselves'. *Meta* means change, and the root word behind *-noia* and *-noeite* is *nous*, meaning 'mind'. 'Paranoid' describes a mind that is beside itself ('para-' as in 'parallel lines'), and *nous* has entered the English language as 'common sense'. But in the spiritual vocabulary of Christianity *nous* has a specific meaning. It refers to a capacity for inward perception that can discriminate that which has a quality of truthfulness. When St Paul says 'Be ye transformed by the renewing of your mind' (Romans 12: 2) he is making precise use of a technical term. What the Greek says is *metamorphousthe tē᷄ᵢ anakainōsei tou noos*, 'by the renewing of the *nous*', meaning that a transformation of one's being depends on renewing the capacity to distinguish internal truthfulness from self-deception.

In Islam there is an exactly comparable term, the Arabic word *qalb*, which means 'heart'. For Sufis the *qalb* is both a capacity for perception of what is psychologically and spiritually truthful, and the point of contact with the profoundest depth of one's being (Burckhardt 1959: 115). *Nous* and *qalb* are close to the quality of psychic honesty that the analytic process calls for in patients. It is by developing this capacity for discrimination of their own internal states that both analytic patients and followers of a spiritual path gain deeper knowledge of themselves.

Spiritual disciplines and psychoanalysis both make demands on those who pursue them which are acknowledged to be impossible. In spiritual terms, the attempt to bring oneself into closer alignment with the divine, the Tao, Atman or the Buddha-nature, exposes the impossibility of attaining this in a person's habitual, automatic state of being. Every tradition offers its own way of change towards a new spiritual condition, in which development of that closer alignment will be achievable. The psychoanalytic situation, whether or not the fundamental rule of saying whatever comes to mind is explicitly stated, constitutes a demand on patients for total honesty about themselves. It is recognised that this demand cannot be met. The analytic process works by accepting that people are unable to be truthful with themselves, and helps them develop greater internal honesty by considering in what manner they fall short of it when they try.

Psychoanalysts speak of 'resistance' and of patients 'defending' themselves, sometimes in a way that makes these sound like sins against the work of analysis. It is interesting that, just as with 'repentance', the original New Testament Greek word for 'sin' does not have the loading of culpability that we are used to. *Hamartanein*, the verb we know as 'to sin', in fact means 'to be off the mark' or 'to miss the target'. The compassion of the analytic process is to recognise that, while patients do inevitably defend themselves against it and the ways in which they do so need examining, they are also being as truthful with themselves as they are able, given their present psychic state. To give up a defence is not a matter of stopping some sort of intellectual or emotional misbehaviour. It implies a fresh perception of oneself, a new truthfulness which in its turn makes deeper and more complex kinds of truth available.

Pushing at the frontiers of one's internal honesty like this is hard, and sometimes painful, work. Not for nothing do patients in analysis, and followers of a spiritual path too, seek to protect themselves against what they desire. Becoming more conscious of how one stays persistently off target involves giving up assumptions about oneself that have had a protective, but also limiting, function. In one spiritual tradition these are known as 'buffers' against true self-awareness (Mouravieff 1989–1993, vol. 1: 29; Nicoll 1952: 756). The acceptance of loss, or to be more specific, accepting the *necessity* of loss, is essential to interior growth. Freud said of the Wolf Man:

> Any position of the libido which he had once taken up was obstinately defended by him from fear of what he would lose by giving it up and from distrust of the probability of a complete substitute being offered by the new position that was in view.
>
> (Freud 1918: 115)

All psychological, or spiritual, growth involves leaving something behind, giving up attachments to familiar ways of being. Developing our particular identities involves accepting that we cannot become all of the people that we might have been (Parsons 2000: 81ff). Helping patients sacrifice attachments to outmoded or unrealisable ways of being, helping them give up their narcissistic fantasies in favour of reality: this is the stuff of analytic work. But the sacrificial aspects of religion – 'mortification of the flesh' – can seem, from a psychoanalytic point of view, to be a kind of self-denying masochism. Certain kinds of extreme practice are certainly an opportunity for disturbed, self-torturing personalities, and there are plenty of undoubtedly pathological examples in the history of every religion. But the shift mentioned earlier, between external and internal levels of understanding, is crucially important here. In Marion Milner's (1937) book of psychological autobiography, *An Experiment in Leisure*, she is at first troubled by the moralism and the magical thinking that seem evident to her in Christianity. Then she considers the possibility

> that the Gospel story is concerned, not with morals at all, not with what one ought to do because someone (God, father) expects it of you, but with practical rules for creative thinking, a handbook for perceiving the facts of one's own experience.
>
> (Milner 1937: 135)

She thinks that a kind of internal sacrifice of oneself, in the sense of giving up one's preconceived assumptions, and intentions based on them, may be the only way in which creative psychic growth is possible. She comments:

> the power of the idea of the Crucifixion could be due to two quite different causes. One, to the survival of a magical belief in the power of blood sacrifice to bring actual safety (or 'salvation') to all who sympathetically participated in it, to cause an actual miraculous interference with the course of nature; and the other, to the fact that it was the culminating poetic dramatisation of an inner process of immense importance to humanity, a process which was not an escape from reality, but the only condition under which the inner reality could be perceived.
>
> (Milner 1937: 139)

Easter is the season of the Crucifixion and Resurrection. One of the Church's Easter anthems that celebrate the transition from deadness to aliveness says: 'let us keep the feast, not with the old leaven nor with the leaven of malice and wickedness, but with the unleavened bread of sincerity and truth' (1 Corinthians 5: 8). 'Sincerity' may seem a mundane sort of word to find in this elevated context. There is another milieu where the word makes a similarly unexpected appearance. Ask a Japanese martial arts master what is the most important quality in a student of karate or swordsmanship, and he will probably not reply 'strength', 'speed' or 'determination'. As likely as not he will answer 'sincerity'. This is the Japanese concept of *makoto*. It does not just mean being sincere in the sense of meaning what you say, or being as truthful to the facts as possible. It connotes rather a genuineness of spirit, so that words and actions come immediately from the heart, as a direct expression of a person's true nature. The student of martial arts needs to make his or her practice an embodiment of who he or she is as a person. The Greek word for 'sincerity', in the biblical passage that the Easter anthem quotes, is *eilikrineia*, which means the quality of being 'unmixed' or 'undiluted'. Sincerity in both these contexts refers to a clarity of motivation that derives from truthful self-awareness.

Here again is something that the psychoanalytic process also is very much concerned with. Much of the day-to-day work in an analysis consists of

129

clarifying obfuscations, of elucidating the ways in which, at a deep level, people cannot avoid being insincere with themselves. The complex techniques of the martial arts master are achieved through years of detailed, elaborate training, but the sincerity that they express is simple and unequivocal. The enormous detail of the analytic work, in any individual case, serves to help a person discover internal states that can be emotionally rich and complex, yet have that same clarity and simplicity.

Behind the Japanese martial arts lies Zen Buddhism. One of the classic texts of Zen is the *Shobogenzo*, written in the thirteenth century by Dogen, who says in it: 'The way of the Buddha is to eat rice and drink tea' (Nishiyama and Stevens 1975: 17). Another Zen teacher, when asked what enlightenment consisted of, replied: 'When hungry, eat. When tired, sleep'. The point is that such direct simplicity can be full of meaning if it issues spontaneously from the heart (meaning in Zen terms something like the Sufi *qalb*) without the interference of what psychoanalysts might call idealisations, projections and defensive fantasies. Exactly the same insight in western spirituality appears in the work of the eighteenth-century French Jesuit Jean-Pierre de Caussade, author of a famous mystical treatise whose English title is *The Sacrament of the Present Moment* (de Caussade 1981). His advice for progress in the spiritual life is to give oneself willingly to the tasks life puts in one's way, letting them have whatever meaning they have, without imposing one's own significance on them or using them to bolster any image of oneself: simply to fulfil what the present moment requires. De Caussade expresses this in his own Christian language of duty to God and acceptance of His will, but essentially he is saying, 'When hungry, eat. When tired, sleep'.

Such simplicity calls for the relinquishing of all sorts of habitual attachments, not so much to material things as to ways of thinking and, particularly, ways of thinking about oneself and one's own significance. This is the same call that the psychoanalytic process makes on patients (not to mention on analysts as well, but that is another story): to question and be willing to give up the ways of thinking about themselves on which they have unconsciously relied thus far in their lives. The necessary complexities of clinical theory in psychoanalysis revolve around the fundamentally simple idea that if one can give up the attempt to resolve internal conflicts by struggling to be someone that one is not, this may allow space in which to begin to discover who one really is and who one can become.

Psychoanalysis is not concerned either to generate religious thinking or to avoid religious thinking. Whether someone is interested in religion, antagonistic to it, or simply gives no thought to it, the analytic concern is with what either the interest, or the rejection, or the gap, signifies for the person, and that meaning must be as fully understood as possible. If what then remains is a non-engagement with religion, what matters psychoanalytically is that it should not be a cramped refusal, originating from a cramped interior space. If an interest in religious experience sustains itself, then the larger a universe within themselves that people can be helped to discover, the larger will be the ways available to them of relating to the cosmos.

References

Attar, Farid ud-din (1961) *The Conference of the Birds*, trans. C.S. Nott. London: Routledge and Kegan Paul.

Bollas, C. (1987) *The Shadow of the Object: Psychoanalysis of the Unthought Known*. London: Free Association.

Burckhardt, T. (1959) *An Introduction to Sufi Doctrine*. Lahore: Muhammad Ashraf.

Daniell, D. (1989) *Tyndale's New Testament*. New Haven, CT and London: Yale University Press.

Daniell, D. (1994) *William Tyndale: A Biography*. New Haven, CT and London: Yale University Press.

de Caussade, J-P. (1981) *The Sacrament of the Present Moment*, trans. K. Muggeridge. Glasgow: Collins.

Eigen, M. (1996) *Psychic Deadness*. Northvale, NJ: Aronson.

Freud, S. (1912) Recommendations to physicians practising psycho-analysis. SE 12.

Freud, S. (1918) *From the History of an Infantile Neurosis*. SE 17.

Freud, S. (1927) *The Future of an Illusion*. SE 21.

Green, A. (2002) *La Pensée clinique*. Paris: Odile Jacob.

Guntrip, H. (1975) My experiences of analysis with Fairbairn and Winnicott. *International Review of Psychoanalysis* 2: 145–156.

Milner, M. (1937) *An Experiment in Leisure*. London: Chatto and Windus (under the name of Joanna Field); Virago (1986).

Milner, M. (1950) *On Not Being Able to Paint*, 2nd edn. London: Heinemann (1957).

Mouravieff, B. (1989–1993) *Gnosis: Study and Commentaries on the Esoteric Tradition of Eastern Orthodoxy, vols 1–3*. Newburyport, MA: Praxis Institute Press.

Nicoll, M. (1952) *Psychological Commentaries on the Teachings of G.I. Gurdjieff and P.D. Ouspensky*. London: Robinson and Watkins.

Nishiyama, K. and Stevens, J. (1975) *A Complete English Translation of Dogen Zenji's Shobogenzo (The Eye and Treasury of the True Law), vol. 1*. Sendai, Japan: Daihokkaikaku.

Ogden, T. (1995) Analysing forms of aliveness and deadness of the transference-countertransference. *International Journal of Psychoanalysis* 76: 695–709.

Parsons, M. (2000) *The Dove that Returns, the Dove that Vanishes: Paradox and Creativity in Psychoanalysis*. London: Routledge.

Shree Purohit Swami and Yeats, W.B. (1937) *The Ten Principal Upanishads*. London: Faber.

Tao Te Ching (1963) *Tao Te Ching*, trans. D.C. Lau. London: Penguin.

Ware, T. (1997) *The Orthodox Church*. London: Penguin.

Winnicott, C. (1989) D.W.W.: A Reflection. In D.W. Winnicott, *Psychoanalytic Explorations*. London: Karnac.

Winnicott, D.W. (1971) *Playing and Reality*. London: Tavistock.

7

PSYCHOANALYSIS
AND SPIRITUALITY

Jeffrey B. Rubin

In itself psycho-analysis is neither religious
    nor nonreligious.

Freud to Pfister, 9 February 1909

Psychoanalysis is a religion in which you are not
    allowed to believe in God.

Adam Phillips 1993

Several times in the past few years prospective patients have indicated in the initial consultation with me that they seek a 'spiritually oriented' therapist. During a recent consultation, a patient informed me that she was seeking therapy because she would like to encourage the 'spiritual side' of herself to emerge. Joan indicated that 'spiritual' for her referred to an outlook on the universe that was not materialistic and that valued the uniqueness of the individual and greater authenticity, personal centeredness, balance and wisdom.

There has been a resurgence of interest in religion and spirituality in our world. The word 'spirituality' appears with increasing frequency in books, in the media and on television. And even in that bastion of Enlightenment science and rationalism, psychoanalysis. The word 'spirituality' has arisen with greater frequency since the mid 1980s in psychoanalytic articles, conferences and books (Ulanov 1985; Symington 1994; Roland 1996; Rubin 1996, 1998, 2004; Spezzano and Garguilo 1997; Eigen 1998; Grotstein 2000; Marcus 2003). But these writings have not been integrated into psychoanalysis. They are more like stray notes than a central motif.

Even though I have practiced meditation and yoga since the early 1970s and written a book on psychoanalysis and Buddhism (which Joan apparently did not know about), I was taken by surprise by the spirituality that she sought. The surprise was not because psychoanalytic treatment can't aid contemplative pursuits, but because her quest to experience spiritual facets of herself was so incongruent with the tendency to pathologize religion and shun spirituality in the first one hundred years of psychoanalysis.

Lest this seems an extreme assertion consider three examples: Helene Deutsch considered her treatment of a nun less than a complete cure because she couldn't convert her. And Otto Fenichel maintained that every successful psychoanalysis results in the termination of religious belief. Sorenson's (2004) analysis of

> the nearly 7,000 occurrences of the word religious in psychoanalytic journals between 1920 and 1994 found that analysts disproportionally pathologized being religious, although this practice decreased dramatically once Freud died. During Freud's lifetime, the number of pathological portraits of being religious surpassed more integrative appraisals by a ratio of 9 to 1. After Freud's death this dropped to a ratio of 3 to 1.
>
> (Sorenson 2004: 155)

While not all psychoanalysts have pathologized spiritual experiences, all-too-many still do. While the climate within psychoanalysis has certainly become more hospitable to religion and spirituality, it is still too often assumed that spirituality is delusive or misguided; a regressive urge for unity with the pre-oedipal mother, a wooly search for false and illusory salvations, a self-centered withdrawal from the world or voluntary self-hypnosis (Alexander 1931).

An experience I had playing basketball in the early 1970s, as well as subsequent personal and clinical experiences I have had, suggest the essential inadequacy of the taken-for-granted tendency within psychoanalysis to neglect or pathologize spiritual experiences.

The memory over three decades later remains vivid: it was February 1971, Riverdale, New York. I was a senior point guard on my high school's basketball team. We were playing an away league game against a team whom we were favored to beat. In order to remain in contention for the league title we had to win the game. When we scored a basket with about ten seconds remaining in the game our victory appeared, like our adolescence, invincible. Our one point lead seemed to be sealed. But when someone on the opposing team hit a shot with six seconds to go we suddenly felt buried alive.

A great calm descended upon me and I called time out.

Five seconds remained. Our huddle was like a UN meeting without an interpreter. I moved next to my coach and asked him to tell my teammates not to panic and to get me the ball. He did. The other team lined up about ninety feet down the court near our basket. One of my teammates took the ball out of bounds and rolled it to me near mid court, approximately forty-five feet away. The clock didn't start until I touched the ball. As I scooped the ball up, turned and began dribbling up the left side of the court I seemed to enter a realm where the game and I were not-two. Time appeared to slow down and elongate. The gym seemed silent. I didn't hear the roar of the crowd or feel the cold of the gym. I felt no pressure. I also felt no fear. Hope and dread, victory and defeat did not exist. As I approached the top of the key I sensed it was time to shoot. I squared my shoulders to the basket, bent my knees, and jumped in the air. I scanned the basket with a dispassionate gaze like an archer studying the target before releasing the arrow. Just as my left hand released the ball and my left wrist waved to the rim, the arms of my 6'2" defender enveloped me. I could no longer see the rim. As my feet touched the wooden gymnasium floor there was a cavernous silence. A deafening roar broke my spell and spectators from our side of the gym mobbed the court. It was only then that I glanced at the scoreboard and realized that my shot had gone in and that we had won the game by one point.

The locker room was noisy but I was strangely quiet, unmoved by the dramatic win and my personal heroics. I wasn't numb. Nor was I indifferent to winning. The victory did not lose its luster because I was upset by the transience of the sweetness of victory. No. I was unemotional about our comeback because victory paled compared to what I had internally experienced.

I remember standing alone in the dim, smelly high school locker room after my teammates had showered and changed, replaying what I had experienced the last five seconds of the game: the heightened attentiveness, focus and clarity. The way time seemed to expand. The absence of thought, pressure and fear. The serenity.

Before those last five seconds of the game I would have called my childhood irreligious. While my teammates were celebrating our narrow victory at the end of the game I was preoccupied with the tantalizing glimpse I had of another domain of being, what I would later term spirituality or the sacred, in which I was open to the moment without a sense of time, un-self-conscious but acutely aware, highly focused and engaged yet relaxed and without fear.

What I experienced at the end of that game became a defining moment in my life. I knew directly and viscerally that there was a radically different way of relating to the world. The vice-like grip of ambition, victory, competitiveness and succeeding at all costs – the divinities I worshiped until the last five seconds of that game – was loosened. While winning still felt better than losing, the joy of just playing the game became as important as winning. I still valued and recognized the importance of trying to make things happen. But it was now clear to me that surrendering to and flowing with life is no less important than planning and goal-directed behavior.

In this chapter I shall reflect upon how spiritual experiences might enrich psychoanalysis and how psychoanalysis might enlighten spiritual seekers. My thesis is twofold: first, both psychoanalysis and the spiritual quest have been impoverished by the lack of contact between them, and second, both could be enriched by a *dialogue of reciprocity* in which there is mutual respect and a willingness to learn from each other. Insights from spiritual experiences could expand psychoanalytic conceptions of the nature of self-experience, empathy and compassion. But there is a tendency outside psychoanalysis to idealize spiritual experiences as blissful and inherently positive. Psychoanalysis reveals the fallacy of romanticizing these experiences and can elucidate *pathologies of spirit*.

My strategy will be to first discuss spiritual dimensions of psychoanalysis, and then to explore psychoanalysis' neglect of the spiritual and the cost to psychoanalysis. Then I shall examine pathologies of spirit. Next I shall consider some clinical implications of valuing spiritual experiences. In the concluding section I shall point toward some of the ingredients of a contemplative psychoanalysis, a psychoanalysis that would at once be receptive to, yet unafraid of being properly critical of, spirituality.

Defining and explaining what we mean by the words 'spirituality' and 'sacred' is a difficult task. The dictionary defines 'spiritual' as 'not tangible or material', that is, beyond sense impressions and perhaps ineffable. The 'spiritual' is often contrasted with the psychological as well as the material, the mundane, and the flesh.

The meaning of a word, Wittgenstein (1953) reminds us, is its 'use in the language'. Several years ago, I began jotting down the variety of ways patients in treatment used the word 'spirituality'. It was used in five different ways. One was to express a deeply felt sense of unity and connection with the universe. A second use depicted deeper, more sustaining values guiding one's life – higher meaning and purpose than self-aggrandizement – and a more balanced and tolerant attitude towards life. The cultivation of particular qualities that are ordinarily neglected in western culture such as awe, humility, joyousness and compassion were closely linked to the third use of the word. It was also used by patients to refer to a more humble, alive and loving self; or an unconditioned and uncorrupted, authentic core of one's being and a more natural and organic way of living. And finally, spiritual paths referred to practices designed to foster any of these four experiences.

There are various reasons why spirituality has been so often pathologized or neglected in psychoanalysis. It is most frequently spoken about in religious contexts. Religion, according to Freud (1927), offers illusory consolations in the face of the vicissitudes of life. It has also been guilty of numerous 'crimes' (p. 27), including acts of intolerance and oppression toward dissenting viewpoints and alternative religions.

There are more personal reasons why Freud dismissed religion. As I discuss in detail elsewhere, there is compelling evidence that Freud had a deeply problematic relationship with his mother, which he completely denied and disavowed (Stolorow and Atwood 1979; Rubin 1998; Breger 2000). Consciously he idealized her. He described the mother–son relationship (in a strikingly un/preFreudian formulation) as completely free of conflict and ambivalence. The disavowed dimensions of his struggles with his mother perhaps shaped and skewed his views on women. There is evidence that Freud unconsciously connected and conflated religion and the feminine (Rubin 1999). His dismissal of the former was, I believe, deeply influenced by his negative and mystifying experiences with the latter.

The third reason for spirituality's dismissal in psychoanalysis was that Strachey's translation of Freud's German was shaped by positivistic assumptions, which 'scientized' Freud's humanistic insights and made the spirit seem even less germane to psychoanalysis (Bettelheim 1982). A soulless version of Freud's work could not address nor illuminate the spiritual. And finally, exploring the domain of spirituality foregrounds the question Winnicott (1951) recognized that psychoanalysis, with its essentially 'tragic' world view (Schafer 1976), has rarely addressed: the question 'of what life is like apart from illness' (Winnicott 1951: 98).

Psychoanalysis has suffered because of this neglect of spirituality. The cost is that psychoanalysis embraces a secular modernist/postmodernist world view in which the individual is alienated from larger sources of meaning and solace. Individuals are left unmoored and disconnected when they are not embedded in something beyond the isolated self. The individual, in a secular world, is a god-term – the ultimate ground of being and source of meaning. Freud (1927) claimed that to question the meaning of life is a sign of emotional illness. But the search for meaning may enrich one's life, and be life-affirming rather than defensive (Corbett 1996: 168).

To not question the meaning of life can inadvertently lead to being attached to meaninglessness, thereby fostering alienation and compromising emotional health. From such a perspective life is disenchanted and emptied of wonder. The alienation of many patients (and therapists) may not be unrelated to such a disconnection. Various substitutes are then consciously or unconsciously recruited to ground the disconnected individual. The self and the theories and organizations we are affiliated with, for example, may become idols. When the isolated individual is the ultimate source of meaning then altruism and self-centeredness are seen as dichotomized rather than intimately interpenetrating.

To see the self-centered psychoanalytic view of self, reflect for a moment upon the differences between Martin Buber's (1970) view of relationships and those of many post-classical relational thinkers (Benjamin is a notable exception). The latter view the 'other' in terms of what it does or does not provide the self. The other is then seen not as a subject with its own unique needs but as a need-gratifying object. The relationship between self and other is reduced to an instrumental one, with the crucial question being: 'What did I get (or not get) from the other?' Buber, on the other hand, stresses a *moral* relation with the other; asking what can I give to the other, not simply what the other can do for me. The other is seen as a subject or a thou with his or her own needs and ideals.

With the notion of the depressive position, Kleinian thought offers a vision of the other as a whole and separate person. One experiences guilt and the urge for reparation toward other people because of the damage or hurt one has inflicted.

Let us return for a moment to my experience playing basketball. As barriers between self and not-self erode in the 'non-self-centered subjectivity' (Rubin 1996, 1998, 2004) experienced in such moments, one feels a self-expansive connectedness with the world characterized by a sense of engagement, not escape or detachment. In this being-at-oneness one experiences the world from a more inclusive perspective in which self and other are seen as mutually interpenetrating facets of the universe rather than as polar oppositions. Experiencing the world and one's self from this perspective casts a different, more benign light on such perennial human struggles as anxiety, guilt and the possibility for happiness. Experiences of non-self-centered subjectivity are, as Grotstein (2000) suggests, a fourth state of being that is different from and transcend the autistic/contiguous, paranoid/schizoid, and depressive positions of Klein and Ogden.[1] Self and other exist in a non-dualistic relationship that may be devoid of conflict, guilt and fear. While afflictive states of mind are often absent in moments of spiritual experience, negative experiences such as self-nullifying fusion with and compliance to another may be present.

The profusion of analysands and analysts who are exploring spiritual practice and the increasing number of articles on psychoanalysis and spirituality suggest that we may be witnessing a return of the spiritually repressed in contemporary psychoanalysis (Rubin 1998). Might increasing numbers of analysands and analysts turn to the meditative cushion or the yoga ashram, because psychoanalysis does not fully nurture their spiritual needs or hunger?

The spirit(uality) of psychoanalysis

While psychoanalysis has certainly been tardy in appreciating spirituality, spiritual experiences have been present in psychoanalysis since its inception.[2] Let me briefly mention several examples. Horney (1987), Kelman (1960), Bion (1970) and myself (Rubin 1985, 1996) have noted the resonances between meditation and psychoanalytic listening. Freud's (1900, 1912) delineation of the optimal state of mind to listen – 'evenly hovering attention' – shares two important features with eastern meditative practices (Rubin 1985, 1996). In Freud's method one gives oneself over to experience to which one attends with all one's being. In her posthumously published *Final Lectures* Horney (1987) discusses how Buddhism can train one in 'wholehearted attentiveness' which is a prerequisite for doing sound analytic work. Harold Kelman (1960) recognized this feature of psychoanalytic method when he asserted that carried to its logical conclusion it is eastern in technique but not in theory. According to Kelman, the theories underlying psychoanalysis and eastern thought are different, but eastern meditative techniques can enrich psychoanalytic practice.

Bion (1970) attempted to elaborate on Freud's perspectives on listening in his recommendation that analysts listen without 'memory', 'desire' or 'understanding' (pp. 51–52). He believed that this kind of listening promotes being a *real* self. It also resonates with Buddhist meditative practices; embodying what contemporary Buddhists term 'beginner's mind'. In the mind of the 'beginner there are many possibilities,' notes Zen teacher Shunryu Suzuki (1970: 21) 'but in the expert's there are few'.[3]

Lacan's obscure and elusive style of writing may function, as Mitchell and Black (1995) aptly note, like Zen koans (p. 195), those rationally unsolvable conundrums that Zen teachers give to their students in an attempt to foster the open receptivity of 'beginner's mind'. Challenging habitual preconceptions, as Lacan's writing does, can generate a transformed perspective and new emotional insights and understandings.

In my own clinical and personal experience, an ongoing practice of meditation fosters an uncongealed mind which cultivates a greater capacity to free-associate and to be attuned to the nuances of one's inner experiences including counter-transference. Greater personal freedom and creativity are byproducts. Ferenczi (1927) intimates the salutary facets of these subtle and not always tangible free-associational experiences when he suggestively remarks that you don't free associate in order to be cured, you are cured when you can free associate (p. 79).

Ghent (1990) usefully distinguished between 'submission' and 'surrender'. Submission is a self-negating 'submergence of self' in the other (p. 125). It is a masochistic corruption and distortion or 'perversion' and 'defensive mutant' of surrender (p. 111). Surrender is not resignation or 'defeat', but a self-enriching liberation and expansion of self as one opens to the larger world one is embedded in.

The 'religious' attitude, according to Jung (1938), involved not belief in a 'creed', but 'careful and scrupulous observation' of the 'numinosum' (p. 7), an awe-inspiring experience that fills one with exaltation. It is an encounter with an unsurpassable value to which absolute respect is due. Religion designates, for Jung (1938), 'the attitude peculiar to a consciousness which has been altered by the experience of the numinosum' (p. 8). And spirituality is the search for meaning in one's life. With its careful examination of an analysand's life in the service of generating meaning and facilitating his or her uniqueness, psychoanalysis embodies this quest.

Winnicott's (1951) 'transitional phenomena' and 'transitional space', a fertile, creative state of being and environment that is neither self nor non-self, but both, depicts (without exhausting) the psychic space in which spiritual experiences occur. A transitional phenomenon is not an internal or external object or possession. It is a third part of a human being, an 'intermediate area of *experiencing*' (1951), between the 'subjective and the objectively perceived' (p. 231), that is neither inner psychic reality nor external reality but to which each contributes. From Winnicott we might learn that moments of spiritual experience are not possessions or achievements of the self, but arise in the intersection and interaction of self and world. Such experiences partake of both but belong to neither.

And finally, psychoanalysis can be a sacred space, a sanctuary for raising the deepest sorts of questions about how we might live (Rubin 1998). Having the opportunity of hearing another person's deepest sufferings and yearnings is sacred. There are certain moments in treatment – perhaps when the analytic dyad is highly attuned, playing emotional or mental jazz – when it feels as if something sacred is happening in the consulting room (Ulanov 1985).

The psychoanalysis of spirit: psychopathology of spirituality in everyday life

even of Holiness
there is offal:
Just as there is sweat
and hair and excrement,
So Holiness too
has its offal.
    Nachman of Bratzlav
    (Bratzlav 1996: 270)

Spirituality is usually presented as an antidote to the rampant narcissism in personal, corporate and political relations that permeates our world. Going 'beyond narcissism' (Epstein 1995) is unreflectively accepted by many people as a viable solution to the egocentricity that afflicts us individually and as a culture.

The plethora of scandals in spiritual communities in recent years involving esteemed 'masters' illegally expropriating funds from the communities and sexually exploiting students (Boucher 1988) suggests that the idealization of spiritual experiences can be psychologically naive because there are sometimes hidden dangers to spirituality (Rubin 1996, 1998).

There are illusions, obsessions and pitfalls on the spiritual path. The pursuit of spirituality may be used to bypass emotional trauma. It can allow us to avoid conflict that we would be better off dealing directly with, or forestall growth by masking developmental lacunas or arrests.

Spiritual literature acknowledges hazards on the spiritual path ranging from sloth to pride and anger. The classical (Narada 1975) and contemporary Buddhist literature (Goldstein 1976; Goleman 1977; Kornfield 1977; Walsh 1981) has delineated many of the conscious interferences to meditation: 'hindrances' (such as sense-desire, anger, restlessness, sloth and doubt); 'impediments' (e.g. excessive involvement with projects and theoretical studies divorced from practice); and 'fetters' (including attachment to blissful non-ordinary states of consciousness, adherence to rites and ceremonies, ignorance and self-centered thinking). The unconscious psychological and interpersonal obstacles to meditative practice, however, have not been systematically elaborated (Rubin 1996).

A great many people in Occidental civilization excessively worry about the future or torture themselves about the past and feel disconnected from the actual texture of their lives in the present. A heightened capacity to reside in the moment can lessen these destructive tendencies. But glorifying the wisdom of the moment, or blissful oceanic experiences, do not solve ethical dilemmas or the challenges of growing up and becoming a unique individual. The spiritual quest can be a defense against embodied living, against tackling life's basic issues and everyday problems. A psychoanalysis of spirit would attend to the hidden motivations and secondary gains of the spiritual quest as well as its exalted dimensions. Psychoanalysis could show that spirituality, like all human experience, serves multiple functions ranging from the adaptive and transformative to the defensive and psychopathological. In working psychoanalytically with many Buddhists, students of yoga, and numerous non-denominational spiritual seekers, I have observed a variety of pathologies of spirit including using the spiritual quest to narcissistically inflate oneself, evade subjectivity, deny emotional losses, shield oneself from the painful vicissitudes of everyday experience and neglect ethical responsibility. The spiritual path has allowed its devotees to engage in masochistic surrender, schizoid detachment and obsessional self-anesthetization, and to pathologically mourn traumatic experiences. I will briefly discuss several of these. Since my focus is highly selective and there are some space constraints, I will provide illustrative examples rather than more fully fleshed out clinical interactions or vignettes.

In *Psychotherapy and Buddhism* I discussed the attraction for one Buddhist of the no-self doctrine of Buddhism.

Albert was an affable humanities professor in his late twenties who suffered from conflicts over individuation and success, and a pervasive sense of directionlessness and meaninglessness. Albert was an only child who was raised as an agnostic. In the beginning of treatment he described his mother as caring and devoted. As treatment proceeded, he saw her as a rigid person who was more concerned with everyone conforming to her view of reality, which included how her son should act and be. She was scared of feelings and deeply committed to banishing all aspects of internal, subjective life. Albert felt that she lived in a 'fortune cookie' universe in which her 'shoulds' were idealized. Cliché responses ('You must have felt badly when you got that rejection') replaced genuine emotional engagement. Albert felt impactless and non-existent in her presence. He described his mother as like a 'fencer who parries everything I say'.

Albert had a distant relationship with his father, whom he experienced as intelligent and detached, critical and passive. His father submitted to his wife's way of relating and never sustained an interest in Albert. Albert never felt understood or supported by him.

In Albert's view, his parents did not see themselves as subjects capable of introspecting, feeling, desiring or playing. Rather, he was coerced into accommodating to their pre-existing viewpoint on reality. To stay connected to his parents he had to hide his subjective life. He 'harmonized' with his parents' view of reality, so as to not feel 'like an astronaut cut off from home base in outer space', because that was the only hope of being emotionally related to them.

His parents were sorely unresponsive to his inner reality and failed to encourage his uniqueness from emerging or flourishing. In fact, they encouraged compliance with their narrow mode of being by rewarding submissiveness and conventionality and discouraging authenticity and individuation.

Albert developed a private subjective world of depth and richness, but he had great difficulty believing in its validity. The price of conforming to his parents' wishes was to bury his own sense of how he should live. He kept alive the tenuous hope of being accepted by them by banishing huge parts of his self through subverting and obscuring his 'voice'. This led to an excessively limited view of himself and his capabilities. What he wanted lacked significance to him and he felt that his life was not his own.

Albert was attracted to the no-self doctrine because it resonated with his experience of self-nullification in his family. The self-evasion that Buddhism fostered for Albert was a defense against his own sense of non-being. Believing in the doctrine of no-self also rationalized away and disavowed his sadness and grief about an unlived life. It is not that he didn't live or missed out on life; there was no subject to experience subjective existence.

Self-emptiness is often masked by the idealization of spiritual teachers. From self psychology we learn that one momentarily derives strength by an identification with and a submission to an idealized teacher who is presumed to be unconditionally accepting and loving, never harsh, judgemental or abandoning. Here a spiritual teacher or cause provides vital and missing functions to the self such as the guidance or identification with idealized strength, calmness, or wisdom that one lacked from parents or surrogate caregivers. One's own personal deprivation and bereftness is thus denied and avoided. In its extreme versions such surrender can take the form of masochistic submission in which one may become pathologically deferential toward a spiritual teacher or in a spiritual community. Initially, uncritical devotion may feel relieving as it seems to offer connectedness and even direction about how to live. But this often leads to the person not thinking for him/herself, and rationalizing disturbing behavior on the part of the teacher or members of the community. When the spiritual teacher is immune to feedback and the student has no impact, authoritarianism is operative (Kramer and Alstad 1993). Questions that cannot be asked about the teacher, or spiritual doctrines that are supposed to be completely taken on faith, may signal the presence of a teacher or a spiritual community that is autocratic rather than liberatory.

Sometimes spiritual experiences rather than spiritual teachers are idealized. Experiences of oneness and bliss offered one meditator, a competent and successful middle-aged professional man, a way of avoiding, rather than confronting and coping with, the excruciating pain and sadness of his divorce.

Ron initiated therapy after his wife of twenty years announced that she wanted a divorce. He was stunned and felt that he was falling apart. Intelligent and articulate, Ron was a successful lawyer, highly regarded in his field. He was an intense man, with a commanding presence and an incisive intellect. I felt there was little margin for error in our interactions. He treated me as if I was a hostile witness in a courtroom whenever I attempted to explore the realm of his feelings.

Ron had been experiencing severe stress since his wife's sudden announcement, which he had been trying to handle by meditation. An experienced meditator, Ron had developed an unusual facility for cultivating states of deep focus and prolonged concentration. He said he felt peace, rather than sorrow, while experiencing these non-ordinary states of unity and bliss. While this immediately translated into a feeling of confidence and a detachment from his stressful emotions, he acknowledged that the underlying issues that contributed to his wife's decision to end their relationship, remained untouched. The feelings of fragmentation had recently escalated and Ron could no longer escape them by meditating.

Ron grew up in a home in which there was a facade of 'love' without the substance. His parents were more comfortable in the realm of logical thought than feelings, and Ron's emotions were rarely engaged and never validated by them. Ron learned at an early age that he would have to take care of himself because his parents were not available for emotional support. Logical thought became a kind of 'foster parent'. Ron lived in a realm of pure thought and viewed the world through the prism of his intellect. Emotional conflicts or issues became problems that he strove to solve with logic. But the onslaught of feelings unleashed by his impending divorce overwhelmed Ron's highly developed capacity for rational thought. One of the benefits he got from meditation was a concrete strategy for managing his emotional life without the benefit of other resources. In therapy he eventually realized that meditation anesthetized powerful feelings of loneliness and grief, which resulted in his avoiding and prolonging the necessary process of mourning and healing.

Spiritual experiences of oneness offered another patient, a depressed woman in her late forties, a way of avoiding the agony of her life.

At the beginning of our first session, Eileen immediately launched into a recitation of her spiritual insights. A successful entrepreneur, Eileen nevertheless felt that she was a failure, that life had passed her by. She had no children or husband and was involved in an on-again, off-again relationship with a married man. She renounced normal emotional attachments, claiming that ordinary relationships were unnecessary evils, obstacles to a more important and greater, selfless, spiritual love for humanity. 'Real love is not possessive,' she informed me, with a coercive tone of voice. 'We are one. Fear is an illusion. We are God, we are Love, we are Sacred. If everyone felt the way I feel at this moment there would be peace on earth.' Unfortunately there was not much peace in her soul.

Eileen was disconnected from people and the world. Her contacts with other people usually devolved into ongoing battles rather than loving friendships. Her belief in and assertion of boundless love and freedom was belied by the acrimony and distance that characterized most of her relationships. But it also enabled her to keep at bay profound and shattering loss: the premature death of both her parents when she was a young adult, and her regret at not getting married or having a child. Feeling connected with the sacred allowed Eileen to believe that her life was not a failure, that it had deep, even transcendental significance. It was not that she was abandoned and betrayed and might never love or be loved; in her periodic experiences of 'cosmic consciousness' she experienced the greatest and only really substantial love. Eileen had a glimpse of something visionary – the interconnection of people, the power of love and the holiness of daily life. But since her spiritual experiences were utilized in the service of defensive self-protection they never led to a genuinely self-transformative experience.

In my work with Ron and Eileen I saw the way spiritual experiences can all too often be an unwitting form of pathological mourning, in which traumatic experiences of loss, abuse or neglect are sealed off and the person's current life is endlessly shaped by these disavowed, unconscious experiences. Mourning is arrested as one enacts rather than remembers, experiences, integrates and works through one's past.

The spiritual quest too can be recruited to enhance one's stature or self-esteem. Many spiritual aspirants fall victim to what the Tibetan Buddhist teacher Chogyam Trungpa termed 'spiritual materialism'. I have observed the way 'spirituality' becomes, for many spiritual seekers, a badge of specialness in two ways: first, spiritual experiences or attainments lead to self-inflation, and second, spiritual asceticism is utilized to make one feel more pious or evolved than others.

'It is very remarkable,' notes Wittgenstein (1980)

that we should be inclined to think of civilization – houses, trees, cars etc. – as separating man from his origins, from what is lofty and eternal, etc. Our civilized environment, along with its trees and plants, strikes us then as though cheaply wrapped in cellophane and isolated from everything great, from God, as it were. That is a remarkable picture.

(Wittgenstein 1980: 50e)

Many of us are ontological dualists: we divide the world into the ordinary and The Extraordinary, the profane and The Holy. We take the first term in each binary opposition for granted, hardly noticing it. We treat the second one with reverence. When we do this we desanctify ordinary existence. We imagine that the special region is beyond or divorced from ordinary existence. Getting to this realm or having experiences associated with it ('spiritual' experiences) makes us feel we are part of something larger and justifies our existence. While Zen offers a counter-pressure to this – emphasizing the importance of this-(as opposed to other-)worldliness, many spiritual seekers, like Eileen, are prone to this devaluing and desanctifying of the quotidian world. But the ordinary does deserve our gratitude. We need, as Ozick (1983) suggests, to 'sanctify the ordinary' (p. 203); for it is a 'treasure and a gift' (p. 202).

Our modern English language, including psychoanalytic discourse, offers a rather impoverished vocabulary for evoking non-egocentric states of subjectivity and spiritual experiences. In such experiences of 'the sublime in the pedestrian' (Kierkegaard 1843: 52), we can be un-self-preoccupied yet highly attentive, receptive to the moment but without a sense of time, attuned to otherness but without necessarily being neglectful of the self (Rubin 1998, 2004).

My clinical work suggests that there are at least five aspects of healthy spirituality: an experience of profound unity with the universe, the cultivation of virtuous character, the experience of a pure, uncorrupted sense of self, leading one's life based on deeper meaning and purpose and the path to any of these experiences. Drawing on Winnicott's view of transitionality, Grotstein's reflections on the transcendent position, Eigen's reflections on spirituality and my own personal experiences I'll elaborate and extend these reflections.[4]

When you least expect it – walking on a country road, meditating, making love – it just happens. You didn't cause it or expect it, although you were open to it. When it first happened to me in a basketball game when I was 18, I didn't even know it existed.

Sometimes it is spawned by pain. Other times by silence and beauty. You see glory in the flower, grace in the slithering animal in the grass, wonder in the starry skies. Time may elongate. You feel centered and balanced. Intimate with the universe. You feel the self and the universe are sacred. The sense of yourself expands – at least momentarily – beyond a cohesive, integrated self to a communion and homecoming with the universe. The universe feels more alive and wondrous and less (or non-) conflictual. Life has a deeper meaning.

Such spiritual experiences, from my Winnicottian-inspired perspective, are not possessions we have/own or ends to which we strive or even facets of our personalities, but ever-present possibilities of being involving the intersection of self and the larger world in which we are embedded.[5] In such moments – that arise in the moment (yet often feel timeless) – there is an intersection of human beings and the world they live in, leading to a sense that there is more than meets the I. These moments and experiences represent an opportunity for expanding our sense of identity and overcoming our separateness.

Spirituality is often presented as the antidote to the egocentricity fostered by secular, individualistic culture. Symington (1994) argues, for example, that psychoanalysis needs religion and spirituality, which contain those core values such as compassion and wisdom that give life meaning. But these issues may sometimes be complex and elusive. Can spiritual experiences ever be amoral? Oneness in the moment allows some spiritual seekers to avoid ethical responsibility. Zen's emphasis on a whole-hearted being-this-moment can lead to immersion in oppressive nationalistic policies, as was the case with the Samurai's service to whomever was in power (Barry Magid, personal communication, 12 May 1998).

Psychoanalysis and spirituality: clinical considerations

> It remains to be considered whether analysis in itself must really
> lead to the giving up of religion.
> Freud to Eitingon, 20 June 1927

I suspect that an increasing number of patients, like Joan, seek a life of greater spirituality. Where does this leave the psychoanalyst, who was trained in an analytic culture that valued reason and science and may not have been entirely hospitable to religious and spiritual concerns? A moment of Freud's own undogmatic agnosticism about his atheism in *The Future of an Illusion* (1927) serves as a suggestive reminder for us post-classical psychoanalysts treating people for whom religion and spirituality seem to be of increasing concern. 'If experience should show – not to me – but to others after me, who think the same way – that we have been mistaken,' writes Freud (1963: 16), 'then we will renounce our expectations.' Traditionally, the spiritual path and psychoanalysis have been segregated. Then spiritual teachers and seekers all too readily assume that the spiritual path uniquely possesses the truth about human experience. Psychotherapeutic disciplines are devalued and neglected. There needs to be a rapprochement of psychoanalysis and spirituality in which they each are more receptive to what light the other might shed on the art of living. A contemplative psychoanalysis would appreciate the constructive as well as the pathological facets of spiritual experiences. If it is anti-analytic to treat spiritual experiences as inherently psychopathological, as some psychoanalysts have done, it is unanalytic to take spiritual claims at face value, without inquiring into the complex and multidimensional meanings and functions they uniquely possess in the mind and heart of a particular person in psychoanalytic treatment. There needs to be a close encounter of a new kind between psychoanalysis and the spiritual quest, in which each can learn from the other and they are neither segregated from each other nor assimilated into one another. Psychoanalytic imperialism emerges when it tries to conquer spiritual experiences; when it has a 'nothing but' attitude toward them; when everything spiritual is explained by and reduced to psychoanalytic categories. But spiritual traditions need to avoid their own brand of intellectual (or spiritual) imperialism in which a spiritual text or meditational practice is treated as if it is the final truth about reality. Psychoanalysis and the spiritual quest have different, although at times overlapping concerns. If they are too separate and autonomous then fruitful contact is precluded. If they are too merged then important differences are eclipsed. The task for psychoanalysis and spiritual disciplines, like the challenge for individuals in a committed relationship, is to balance autonomy and connectedness (Jones 1996) so that there is intimacy that preserves and enriches the uniqueness of each.

What are the clinical consequences of my perspective on spirituality and psychoanalysis?

Therapists rarely talk about their spiritual life and its impact on treatment. There are sound reasons for this, ranging from not wishing to shape the transference to not wanting to infringe upon the patient's autonomy. But then the impact of an analyst's spiritual views and spiritual life – which may include his or her atheism – may be rendered unconscious. In the spirit of bringing to consciousness something that could enrich psychoanalysis I shall offer some very tentative reflections on this subject. My remarks are provisional speculations rather than fully formed conclusions.

Spirituality affects my theory and practice of therapy in explicit and implicit ways. While it is rarely a topic of explicit discussion – usually only when it is brought up by the patient – it has an indirect impact in ways that I can only sometimes articulate. I shall artificially divide my remarks into theoretical and clinical considerations. I realize the lines between them are, in practice, more blurry.

My spiritual experiences have influenced my view of the world as well as my conception of human nature and human relationships. This affects how I think of the therapeutic relationship and the possibilities of treatment to generate change in implicit and explicit ways. Ever since I had the spiritual experience I mentioned toward the beginning of this chapter, I have experienced the truth of the French surrealist poet Paul Eluard's remark that 'there is another world and it is in this one'. There is more to life than is dreamt of in our psychoanalytic psychologies. While psychoanalysis is skilled at revealing the fallaciousness of illusory hopes, there is a mirror opposite danger in psychoanalysis that we will normalize a tragic and melancholic view of the universe. I see life as a dialogic movement of change and stasis with personal evolution an ever-present possibility.

Patients have, I believe, definite biological, existential and psychological constraints. But they also have undreamt-of creative potentials. This gives me more hope than I might have if I subscribed to the kind of tragic view that permeates psychoanalysis.

Psychoanalysis lacks compelling visions of the self after analysis, as Bollas (1997: 48–49) notes. Spiritual experiences have convinced me that psychoanalytic conceptions of health are too limited and dispirited. There is more to life than achieving common human unhappiness or the depressive position. Having spiritual experiences gives me a different – I believe fuller – sense of human possibilities. There may be capacities for empathy and compassion that psychoanalysis has not yet mapped. A story about Gandhi is illustrative. A man attended one of Gandhi's spiritual talks with the goal of assassinating him. But he was so moved by the power of Gandhi's teachings that he scrapped his plan. After Gandhi's talk the assassin prostrated himself in front of Gandhi and tearfully informed him that he had been hired to kill him but after hearing him speak he no longer could carry out his original plan. Gandhi looked the assassin in the eyes with deep compassion and said: 'How are you going to explain to the people who hired you about your failure to carry out the plan?' In empathizing with his assassin's plight even when his own life had been threatened, Gandhi may be depicting a quality of compassion that psychoanalysis has not fully articulated.

'It is impossible to escape the impression', notes Freud (1930) in the opening sentence of *Civilization and its Discontents*, 'that people commonly use false standards of measurement – that they seek power, success and wealth for themselves and admire them in others, and that they underestimate what is of true value in life.' While spiritual traditions each have their own world view they tend, in general, like Freud, to critique conventional societal values. Not only do they challenge the egocentricity and materialism of secular world views, but also they tend to offer an alternative system of values based on selflessness, compassion and wisdom. Many people in our culture – even those who scoff at the vacuousness of conspicuous consumption – live as if wealth directly correlates with happiness. But while there is no inherent virtue in poverty, and financial struggles obviously do not foster inner peace and contentment, economic prosperity does not resolve our fundamental psychological and spiritual questions or problems. What I have observed clinically is that people often suffer because of the search for fame and material goods as well as because of the panoply of causes that psychoanalysts have so ably elucidated. While critiques of the commodification and alienation of modern life have come from various quarters, my spiritual background has contributed to my capacity to question patients' values such as consumerism – especially the correlation between wealth and happiness.

My spiritual experiences have led to a less dualistic view of the relationship between people, by which I mean, I see self and other as deeply connected and irreducibly interrelated. I have a deep and abiding sense that patient and analyst are not-two and that we are both in the treatment together. While I am not responsible for their life, their choices, even for how they use the treatment – I feel a deep responsibility for fully engaging the process.

The second crucial way that spiritual experiences shape my work is non-specific and personal; it affects who I am in the treatment – my being, that is, the quality of my presence in the room. I have periodically been told by certain patients that something healing is transmitted in the treatment – a quality of deep attentiveness, non-judgementalness and serenity.

Spiritual experiences have fostered in me a deeper sense of the mystery of the universe and human development and treatment. Aware of the more than what I currently know and believe, I am more able and willing to surrender to the therapeutic process and let go of beliefs of how treatment should unfold.

I feel that my patients are potential supervisors (Langs and Searles 1980), which breeds, I suspect, a less defensive attitude about my theories or the correctness of my insights or interpretations. It makes me hold my theories lightly rather than tightly.

Hope, connectedness and non-defensiveness may create a different kind of intersubjective space between me and the patient – one which is infused with a spirit of safety and curiosity, openness and respect. Therapy is then a 'sacred space' in which shame may be decreased. Patients are encouraged to say and experience what they had not been able to say before, and to be heard in ways that they didn't expect and had not previously known.

Spirituality and wholeness

In this chapter I have attempted to depict what spirituality is; how it might enrich psychoanalysis, and how psychoanalytic understandings might aid spiritual seekers in avoiding a variety of potential pitfalls.

Spirituality plays an incredibly vital role in our culture; expanding and enriching human subjectivity; connecting us to a larger reality in which we are all embedded; re-enchanting the world; disclosing undreamt of dimensions of being; and infusing our lives with mystery and vitality and wonder. A world without spirit is impoverished.

The neglect of spirituality in psychoanalysis and the culture at large may contribute to the enormous alienation that permeates the lives of many people. Psychoanalysis, like the larger culture it is embedded in, suffers because it only intermittently realizes that there is more than meets the I. Wholeness of being necessitates an openness to and an experiencing of broader dimensions of existence that can be revealed in spiritual experiences.

But the notion of spirituality has become in our culture what the literary critic Kenneth Burke (1950) termed a 'god-term', a universal category beyond examination. It is central to our existence, but it also seems the site of numerous illusions and abuses.

Psychoanalysis is traditionally viewed as an atheistic science of human subjectivity, or more recently, intersubjectivity. The atheism is often taken-for-granted and unconscious. It tends only to emerge when religiously committed patients are in treatment. It then all-too-often generates countertransference, as many analysts view religion and spiritual experiences through the distorting lens of assuming them to be neurotic.

But psychoanalysis can also appreciate spiritual experience without the mystifications of organized religion. Psychoanalysis offers tools to elucidate pathologies and pitfalls on the spiritual path. If contemplative traditions temper the egocentricity of psychoanalytic accounts of self-experience and thereby deabsolutize the self-centered self, then psychoanalytic attention to psychological complexity might deprovincialize the non-self-centered, contemplative self (Rubin 1996, 1998).

There is no guarantee that blissful absorptive union leads to intimacy, self-understanding, or moral action. Fusion experiences are no guarantee of goodness, as survivors of sexual abuse know all too well. Since spirituality can sometimes lead to self-evasion or even immorality it needs to be integrated with psychological wisdom and moral sensitivity.

Spirituality lives in the everyday; where the profane (including immanence as well as transcendence, carnality no less than compassion) is sacred and the sacred is profane. Spiritual seekers often devalue ordinary existence when they segregate the sacred and the profane. Immanence, passion and carnality can get eclipsed. Because of its attention to the moment and to mundane, embodied existence, as opposed to other-worldly, disembodied transcendence, psychoanalysis can sacrilize the ordinary, and foster this-worldly spirituality and morality.

Karl Marx revealed our social unconscious. Sigmund Freud illuminated our personal unconscious. I wonder if in the twenty-first century we need to become aware of the 'sacred unconscious' (Smith 1982: 178). If we get in touch with the personal unconscious we are less driven and imprisoned by the past. We are more liberated from the demons that have haunted us. If we get in touch with the social unconscious we are aware of social conditioning and exploitation and we are more individuated from our culture and its values. If we got in touch with the sacred unconscious we would see the world as more holy; we would see it whole. The world would be experienced as more magical and enchanted. We would celebrate life in all its inexhaustible vibrancy and diversity. We would feel more serenity and joy and live in a civilization with less discontent.

Acknowledgements

This chapter, a revised version of an earlier investigation along compatible lines (Rubin 2004), was inspired by Mark Finn and benefited from discussions with Diana Alstad, Neil Altman, Emma Anderson, Claude Barbre, Jim Barron, David M. Black, Mark Branitsky, Lou Breger, Peter Carnochan, Paul Cooper, Doris Dlugacz, Mark Finn, Jerry Garguilo, Jim Jones, Don Kalshed, Joel Kramer, Barry Magid, Esther Menaker, Louise Reiner, Alan Roland, Tony Schwartz, Mary Traina, Ann and Barry Ulanov and Avi Winokur. I am especially grateful to Neil Altman, David M. Black and Barry Magid, whose feedback on a penultimate draft greatly enriched this chapter.

Notes

1 I read Grotstein's (2000) writings on a fourth position, a 'transcendent position', characterized by serenity and reconciliation with the universe, as I was preparing to submit this manuscript. Spirituality is, for Grotstein, 'the latent capacity within imperfect subjects for attaining full development' (xxvi). He terms the 'state of serenity' in which one becomes 'reconciled to the experience of pure, unadulterated Being and Happening' – with an obvious nod to Melanie Klein and the post-Kleinian revisions of Thomas Ogden – the 'transcendent position' (p. 282).
2 I am indebted to Neil Altman, who first inspired this way of thinking about psychoanalysis.
3 While Bion did not speak explicitly about spirituality his thinking and theorizing are compatible with it. Bion's 'O' refers to ultimate, unknowable reality; including the ineffable mystical. His theorizing is an attempt to depict and not reduce actuality.
4 Eigen's (2001) poetic expression of spirituality and mysticism aided me in articulating my own sense of spiritual experiences, particularly their bliss and radiance.
5 Winnicott's (1951) reflections upon transitional objects and transitional phenomena played a seminal role in my conception of spiritual experience. Creativity, not spirituality, was emphasized by Winnicott in his reflections upon transitional experiencing. My work could be viewed, at least in part, as a spiritualizing of Winnicott's.

References

Alexander, F. (1931) Buddhistic training as an artificial catatonia. *Psychoanalytic Review* 18: 129–145.
Bettelheim, B. (1982) *Freud and Man's Soul.* New York: Random House.
Bion, W. (1970) *Attention and Interpretation.* New York: Basic Books.
Bollas, C. (1997) Interview with Anthony Molino. In *Freely Associated: Encounters in Psychoanalysis with Christopher Bollas, Joyce McDougall, Michael Eigen, Adam Phillips, and Nina Coltart.* London: Free Association Books.
Boucher, S. (1988) *Turning the Wheel: American Women Creating the New Buddhism.* San Francisco, CA: Harper and Row.

Bratzlav, N. (1996) The Torah of the Void. In C. Milosz (ed.) *A Book of Luminous Things*. New York: Harcourt Brace.

Breger, L. (2000) *Freud: Darkness in the Midst of Vision – An Analytical Biography*. New York: John Wiley and Sons.

Buber, M. (1970) *I and Thou*. New York: Simon and Schuster.

Burke, K. (1950) *A Rhetoric of Motives*. Berkeley, CA: University of California Press (1969).

Corbett, L. (1996) *The Religious Function of the Psyche*. New York: Routledge.

Eigen, M. (1998) *The Psychoanalytic Mystic*. Binghamton, NY: ESF.

Eigen, M. (2001) *Ecstasy*. Middletown, CT: Wesleyan University Press.

Epstein, M. (1995) *Thoughts without a Thinker: Psychotherapy from a Buddhist Perspective*. New York: Basic Books.

Ferenczi, S. (1927) The problem of the termination of the analysis. In *Final Contributions to the Problems and Methods of Psycho-Analysis*. New York: Brunner/Mazel (1955).

Freud, S. (1900) *The Interpretation of Dreams*. SE 4–5.

Freud, S. (1912) Recommendations to physicians practicing psycho-analysis. SE 12.

Freud, S. (1927) *The Future of an Illusion*. SE 21.

Freud, S. (1930) *Civilization and its Discontents*. SE 21.

Freud, S. (1954) *The Origins of Psycho-Analysis: Letters to Wilhelm Fliess, Drafts, and Notes*. M. Bonaparte, A. Freud and E. Kris (eds), E. Mosbacher and J. Strachey (trans.). New York: Basic Books.

Freud, S. (1960) *The Letters of Sigmund Freud*, E. Freud. (ed.). New York: Basic Books.

Freud, S. (1963) *Psychoanalysis and Faith: Dialogues with the Reverend Oskar Pfister*, H. Meng and E. Freud (eds). New York: Basic Books.

Ghent, E. (1990) Masochism, submission, surrender. *Contemporary Psychoanalysis* 26(1): 108–136.

Goldstein, J. (1976) *The Experience of Insight: A Natural Unfolding*. Santa Cruz, CA: Unity Press.

Goleman, D. (1977) *The Varieties of the Meditative Experience*. New York: Dutton.

Grotstein, J. (2000) *Who is the Dreamer, Who Dreams the Dream? A Study of Psychic Presences*. Hillsdale, NJ: Analytic Press.

Horney, K. (1987) *Final Lectures*. New York: W.W. Norton.

Jones, J. (1996) *Religion and Psychology in Transition: Psychoanalysis, Feminism, and Theology*. New Haven, CT: Yale University Press.

Jung, C.G. (1933) *Modern Man in Search of a Soul*. New York: Harcourt, Brace.

Jung, C.G. (1938) Psychology and religion. In *Psychology and Religion: West and East*. Collected Works 11: 3–107. New York: Pantheon.

Kelman, H. (1960) Psychoanalytic thought and eastern wisdom. In J. Ehrenwald (ed.) *The History of Psychotherapy*. New York: Jason Aronson.

Kierkegaard, S. (1843) *Fear and Trembling*. Princeton, NJ: Princeton University Press (1941).

Kornfield, J. (1977) *Living Buddhist Masters*. Santa Cruz, CA: Unity Press.

Kovel, J. (1990) Beyond the future of an illusion: further reflections on Freud and religion. *Psychoanalytic Review* 77(1): 69–87.

Kramer, J. and Alstad, D. (1993) *The Guru Papers: Masks of Authoritarian Power*. Berkeley, CA: North Atlantic Press.

Langs, R. and Searles, H. (1980) *Intrapsychic and Interpersonal Dimensions of Treatment.* New York: Jason Aronson.

Marcus, P. (2003) *Ancient Religious Wisdom, Spirituality, and Psychoanalysis.* Westport, CT: Praeger.

Milner, M. (1973) Some notes on psychoanalytic ideas about mysticism. In *The Suppressed Madness of Sane Men: Forty Four Years of Exploring Psychoanalysis.* London: Tavistock (1987).

Mitchell, S. and Black, M. (1995) *Freud and Beyond: A History of Modern Psychoanalytic Thought.* New York: Basic Books.

Molino, T. (ed.) (1998) *The Couch and the Tree: Dialogues in Psychoanalysis and Buddhism.* New York: North Point Press.

Narada, T. (1975) *A Manual of Abhidhamma.* Columbo, Sri Lanka: Buddhist Publication Society.

Ozick, C. (1983) *Art and Ardor.* New York: Knopf.

Phillips, A. (1993) *On Kissing, Tickling, and Being Bored: Psychoanalytic Essays on the Unexamined Life.* Cambridge, MA: Harvard University Press.

Phillips, A. (1994) *On Flirtation: Psychoanalytic Essays on the Uncommitted Life.* Cambridge, MA: Harvard University Press.

Roland, A. (1996) *Cultural Pluralism and Psychoanalysis: The Asian-American Experience.* New York: Routledge.

Rubin, J.B. (1985) Meditation and psychoanalytic listening. *Psychoanalytic Review* 72(4): 599–612.

Rubin, J.B. (1996) *Psychotherapy and Buddhism: Toward an Integration.* New York: Plenum Press.

Rubin, J.B. (1998) *A Psychoanalysis for our Time: Exploring the Blindness of the Seeing I.* New York: New York University Press.

Rubin, J.B. (1999) Religion, Freud, and women. *Gender and Psychoanalysis* 4: 4.

Rubin, J.B. (2004) *The Good Life: Psychoanalytic Reflections on Love, Ethics, Creativity, and Spirituality.* Albany, NY: State University of New York Press.

Rubin, J.B. (n. d.) *The Art of Living.*

Schafer, R. (1976) *A New Language for Psychoanalysis.* New Haven, CT: Yale University Press.

Smith, H. (1982) The sacred unconscious. In *Beyond the Postmodern Mind.* Wheaton, IL: Theosophical Publishing House.

Sorenson, R. (2004) *Minding Spirituality.* Hillsdale, NJ: Analytic Press.

Spezzano, C. and Garguilo, J. (eds) (1997) *Soul on the Couch: Spirituality, Religion, and Morality in Psychoanalysis.* Hillsdale, NJ: Analytic Press.

Stolorow, R. and Atwood, G. (1979) *Faces in a Cloud: Subjectivity in Personality Theory.* New York: Jason Aronson.

Suler, J. (1993) *Contemporary Psychoanalysis and Eastern Thought.* Albany, NY: State University of New York Press.

Suzuki, S. (1970) *Zen Mind, Beginner's Mind.* New York: Weatherhill.

Symington, N. (1994) *Emotion and Spirit: Questioning the Claims of Psychoanalysis and Religion.* New York: St Martin's Press.

Ulanov, A. (1985) A shared space. *Quadrant* 18(1): 65–80.

Walsh, R. (1981) Speedy western minds slow slowly. *Revision* 4: 75–77.

Winnicott, D.W. (1951) Transitional objects and transitional phenomena. In *Through Paediatrics to Psycho-Analysis*. London: Hogarth Press (1978).

Winnicott, D.W. (1971) *Playing and Reality*. London: Tavistock.

Wittgenstein, L. (1953) *Philosophical Investigations*. New York: Macmillan.

Wittgenstein, L. (1980) *Culture and Value*. Chicago, IL: University of Chicago Press.

8

REFLECTIONS ON THE PHENOMENON OF ADORATION IN RELATIONSHIPS, BOTH HUMAN AND DIVINE

Francis Grier

Day after day, O Lord of my life, shall I stand before thee face to face?

With folded hands, O Lord of all worlds, shall I stand before thee face to face?

Under thy great sky in solitude and silence, with humble heart shall I stand before thee face to face?

In this laborious world of thine, tumultuous with toil and with struggle, among hurrying crowds shall I stand before thee face to face?

And when my work shall be done in this world, O King of kings, alone and speechless shall I stand before thee face to face?

Rabindranath Tagore: from *Gitanjali*,
LXXVI (1909; Tagore's English translation 1913)

When an infant is about 3 or 4 months old, he or she can be observed from time to time to stop its other activities, and to gaze adoringly into the eyes of the mother (or other primary care-taker). The quality of this gaze is heart-stopping. Although apparently gentle and expressive of deepest love, it is also searching and penetrating. It is felt to penetrate deep into the very marrow of the mother's soul. The mother feels compelled to respond. But how? She may well feel no doubt about how she *should* respond. She would like to feel she could return the gaze spontaneously, communicating a love no less profound and searching than that of her baby. If she is able to do this, this will be, for her, a most profound, deeply satisfying and fulfilling emotional interaction. During these moments the relationship is intensely dyadic, cutting out any awareness in either party of a third person. Should a third person be present, he or she may well feel uncomfortably like an intruding presence when this wordless expression of exclusive mutuality occurs.

What is happening is of great significance for the infant's development. He (for the sake of brevity I will refer to the infant as 'he') is learning not only that his love is accepted by the other, but also that that other loves him. Through repeated interactions of this kind, he will, over time, internalise an image of himself as both loving and lovable. Fairbairn wrote:

> the greatest need of a child is to obtain conclusive assurance (a) that he is genuinely loved as a person by his parents, and (b) that his parents genuinely accept his love. It is only in so far as such assurance is forthcoming in a form sufficiently convincing to enable him to depend safely upon his real objects that he is able gradually to renounce infantile dependence without misgiving.
>
> (Fairbairn 1941: 39)

This interaction with the infant's mother forms part of that 'conclusive assurance'.

This kind of intercommunication is vital if the child is successfully to build up a store of 'goodness' at the core of his being. And yet, for all its beauty, it also contains and expresses hostility to any third party, either actually present or in his or the mother's mind. During those moments, the mother must attend to him, and only to him. The child also splits off any awareness of his mother as being annoying, unsatisfactory or nasty. She is ideal, and so is he. And yet no one who has experienced these moments can doubt that the dominant feelings are of love, goodness and beauty. The child who can express this adoration and inspire an adoring response in the mother is building up a core of ontological security; and, by so forcibly attracting his mother into the interaction and drawing out the desired response in her, he is also making even stronger the attachment she has for him, which he needs for his future development.

Complementary things are happening for the mother. She may be able to respond spontaneously and confidently only if she has an internalised image of herself as being both lovable and capable of loving. Otherwise, the penetrative force of the infant's gaze may make her all too aware of an internal judgement on herself as unworthy, or unlovable. Or her wish to respond lovingly may be seriously inhibited by an anxiety that, if she were to do so, she would not only spoil the baby but she would herself gain too much pleasure from the interaction. See, for example, Winnicott (1948):

It took me years to realize that a feeding difficulty could often be cured by advising the mother to fit in with the baby absolutely for a few days. I had to discover that this fitting in with the infant's needs is so pleasurable to the mother that she cannot do it without moral support . . . she is scared to do as she deeply wants to do.

(Winnicott 1948: 165)

Being drawn into this exclusive twosome challenges the mother's own unconscious internal Oedipal situation. She may need the reassurance Winnicott speaks of, to offset an anxiety that she risks being seduced into what can almost feel like a 'sinful' twosome. There are so many subtle variations on this theme. She may intuit that she really does have unconscious magnets attracting her to a stronger connection with her child than with her spouse, perhaps simultaneously satisfying an old grievance against a father and an old seductive wish to form an ideal couple with a mother, aggressively excluding the father. She may be unconsciously affording refuge, in her own infantile self, to an old desire to coerce the mother to 'drop' any other children and concentrate purely on her. So the 'good', Winnicottian figure reassuring the mother may, unwittingly, sometimes be experienced internally as colluding with her unconscious phantasies of Oedipal triumph. More often, however, as Winnicott implies, such reassurance from a third party can confirm for a mother that, notwithstanding any such menacing anxieties hovering on the edge of consciousness, it is fundamentally good for the child if the mother can enthusiastically participate in an age-appropriate, temporarily exclusive love-affair.

A mother may feel inhibited and fail to respond to her baby for other, more obvious but painfully guilt-provoking reasons, such as how the child arouses not only the jealousy of others, but, in addition, her envy, perhaps for its beauty. The child may also stimulate her hatred, perhaps for the baby's overturning and threatening what may have been a prized, independent adult lifestyle and career. She, and particularly her partner, may also feel that the baby has aggressively come between them sexually.

But if she can find her way to responding to her baby with a corresponding adoration – and she may interpret the baby's gaze as potentially healing as well as truth-searching – she will feel fulfilled and satisfied. This experience will be the vehicle for her falling even more deeply in love with her baby than before, which in turn will mean that she will find mothering him more enjoyable, and so she will probably carry out her maternal duties more freely. This pattern of building up the mother's and baby's mutual attachment for the benefit of the development of the baby is one of the crucial threads of Bowlby's ethological investigations into the nature of the healthy mother's complex relation to her baby (Bowlby 1969).

A lot may depend on how much the father, if present, can tolerate being excluded from this twosome, especially as this may well mean that what he had been receiving from the mother really does get, to some extent, redirected towards the child. In a partnership in which jealousy can be known about and tolerated to some extent, and in which it is more than balanced by trust and generosity, the man may even be able to appreciate what is happening, through identification with both parties, especially if he feels that his wife or partner can also be sympathetic to the exclusion he has to discipline himself to endure. But many couples flounder over this very issue, particularly with their first child, experiencing such acute pain and disappointment that the longed-for birth can feel as if it actually delivers more cruel separation of the parental couple than united joy. It is not uncommon for such pain to part a couple effectively for good. Many couples, presenting for psychotherapy, trace their mutual disappointment and antagonism to the birth of their first child, and to their failure to negotiate and repair their intensely hurt, triumphant and bitter feelings, arising from the mother's and child's mutually amorous possessiveness and their exclusion of the father.

Two couples I have seen come to mind.

Mr and Mrs A were completely disunited by the birth of their child. They had undergone a catastrophic period, in which Mrs A was utterly taken over by her mutual adoration and idealisation of her baby, and Mr A felt he had lost both his wife and his baby. He embarked upon a passionately sensual affair at this point, in which he seemed to be trying desperately to retrieve the adoration that he no longer received from his wife, and to grasp triumphantly the sensual and blissful aspects of the mother–baby relationship from which he felt so cruelly excluded. When Mrs A discovered her husband's extramarital activities, she adopted a position of complete moral outrage. In their therapy, the couple slowly found the courage to face up to their own unconscious parts in their near-disaster. Mrs A had to face how she had quite actively and triumphantly turned her back upon her husband, thereby triumphing, in unconscious phantasy, over her own father, whom she bitterly resented for, as she had experienced it, constantly and coercively claiming her mother's attentions away from her. At other times, however, Mr A symbolised her mother, whom she had experienced as greedily taking her father away from her, when she wished to enjoy an exclusive and exciting twosome with him. And, at an earlier stage in her life, she had felt her mother to have been infatuated with Mrs A's younger brother, born two years after her, virtually annihilating her own significance.

In the course of the therapy, Mr A, who had hitherto prized an image of himself as a highly independent and autonomous man, rather patronisingly protective of his wife, had to come to terms with the fact that this self-portrait was, in large part, defensive and brittle. It camouflaged a much more exposing and more truthful image of himself as an anxious man, perhaps more accurately an anxious boy, very dependent upon receiving regular supplies of narcissistic adoration from his symbolic mother. His affair expressed, among other things, his hatred and punishment of his internal version of his actual, historic mother, who had outraged him by daring to turn her back on him and give the three sisters born after him the adoration which he felt should be his possession, and his alone. Without it, he felt he would collapse, internally. Mr and Mrs A found the courage to begin to face these extremely challenging and unflattering images of themselves, some of which were very similar to each other, and which we could now understand were part of the shared anxieties and defences that had unconsciously been binding them together. In the course of their therapy, they began imaginatively to understand these jagged issues from each other's point of view. This brought them closer together again, and they united in their love for their child, and even managed to reclaim some of the adoring feelings they had felt for each other before her birth, as well as becoming wiser and more disillusioned. At this point they had a second child, which brought them great joy, and gave them a chance to do things differently from the first time round.

By contrast, the emotional atmosphere created by an older couple was much more riddled with cynicism.

Mr and Mrs B had conceived their first child by mistake in the early days of their courting, and had felt forced into marriage by the unwanted pregnancy. They actively shared this grudge against each other and against life throughout the rest of their marriage, which included the births of several more children. They sought couple psychotherapy when their children started to move on to university, when they feared they no longer shared much in common. I began to perceive that their marriage had actually been marked by many instances of friendly and creative collaboration between them, and they seemed to share a genuine love for their children. But a menacing undertone had already sounded constantly and dissonantly in the background of their marriage, the feeling of something unforgivable, which seemed to get gathered up into the grudge about the unwanted pregnancy. It was only when we went into how they were uniting in protecting their eldest child from their combined hostility, that we discovered there were many other people and issues from each of their individual histories as well as their current lives about which they were each nursing intense grievances. We could see that they were gathering their strong feelings about their other grievances into this one grudge about the unwanted pregnancy, apparently in an attempt to keep other highly invested relationships conflict-free. This one emotional pocket was marked by cynical and implacable unforgiveness. Once they were able to look at and release some of the intensity from this particular knot, albeit at the expense of knowing about their grievances in other areas, this couple began to rediscover each other, and found, to their embarrassment, that they were beginning to fall in love with each other again. It was as if the energy emanating from their combined grievances had put a deadly spell on the potential development of their mutual love. Now they could even begin to enjoy an experience of adoring each other, although this also entailed going through bitterly depressing feelings about all the opportunities for a more passionate love of life and of each other that they had spoiled and wasted throughout so many years, through their active, unconscious, cynical collusion.

Searles points out how children between the ages of about 2 and 8 years often have 'crushes' on both their parents (Searles 1958: 232). This is an aspect of the child's, and his parents', working through not only their individual Oedipal situations, but also what one might refer to as the family's joint, or composite, 'family romance'. What happens, and its importance, is similar to the earlier adoration-episodes, and is again partially expressed nonverbally, through behaviour and looks, but it is nevertheless usually more conscious for all concerned, and is sometimes, at least in part, verbalised. Whereas an adult's infantile mother-adoration is virtually always entirely absent from his conscious memory, some of this later father- and mother- (in turns) adoration might more easily be recalled. The situation is also fraught with negative possibilities arising from adoration. If the young child's adoration fails to inspire an adequate parental response, the immediate result may be panic and shame, followed by a sense of betrayal and rage. This may lead on to highly aggressive rivalry, and a desire for retaliatory conquest and triumph over the parent.

These pleasurable and intensely painful variations on the theme of adoration reoccur at the times of falling in love, during adolescence and adulthood. The other is perceived as the ideal Other, who is to be adored, whose eyes – the windows of the soul – are gazed into, in a peculiar mixture of timidity and confidence, and who is desired – and required – to gaze in a similar response back into one's own soul. Romeo and Juliet might serve as prototypes for this stage of adoration, as the herald of sexual love. Later in the life-cycle the adoring relationship may thereafter be repeated, many times, including across the generations, this time as adult father or mother with children or grandchildren.

If it is mutual and fulfilling, and inhabited more by love and generosity than by envy and jealousy, whenever it is experienced during the life-cycle, adoration marks a special moment of intense and yet reflective and quiet relating, imbued with a numinous quality of feeling for both participants. There is a strange paradox at the heart of the experience. On the one hand, it can be experienced by the participants as a meeting between two separate people, who adore each other, and feel known by each other. Yet, simultaneously the opposite can be true: each partner is required to take into themselves and personify the ideal image the other partner is projecting. When this second dynamic is in the ascendant, there is no relationship between a subject and a real, other, separate object – what Martin Buber (1923) would refer to as an 'I' and a 'Thou'. Instead there is a narcissistic coercion of the other partner – via projective identification (Klein 1946: 8), and through what Winnicott referred to as the use of 'an object subjectively perceived' (Winnicott 1971: 45) – to play a role enacting an idealised part of the 'I', rather than to be allowed to exist in their own, different, right as 'Thou'.

At the beginning of life, adoration is clearly a natural process, leading to a healthy degree of symbiotic bonding; yet, if it persists, it can become pathological in that projections are not withdrawn, and thus the reality, the 'otherness', of the other person is not perceived, but is actively and aggressively denied. In this aggressively narcissistic frame of mind, that other is continually to be used as an extension of the subject's self. One danger is that those loving parts of the subject which are being located in the object may, over time, become effectively lost to the subject, whose personality will then become seriously diminished in its emotional scope. This danger is quite frequently exhibited in those couples in which one partner cannot bear to acknowledge his (or her) own capacity to love, and insists, with the active, albeit unconscious, collusion of the partner, that the partner be the designated 'loving one'. After a time, this unconscious strategy can go drastically wrong. The relationship gets stuck: one partner greedily grabs all the adoration; the other, equally greedily, hoards all the capacity for adoring. If either starts to move into the other's territory, perhaps motivated by hunger rather than greed, the status quo of the dynamics of the stable, pathological relationship becomes threatened. If all goes well, however, adoration between couples appears to be one of the channels through which we humans get to know ourselves, by being known in this way by an other and by then evolving from this initial mutual adoration to a further developmental level in which we come to discover the ways in which we are similar and different from that other. This organic process calls to mind St Paul's words, 'For now we see through a glass darkly; but then face to face: now I know in part; but then shall I know even as also I am known' (1 Corinthians 13).

Life moves on, and the moment of adoration cannot be infinitely extended, especially if what is happening is primarily a collusive and coercive narcissistic projection by each partner of an unrealistic, idealised image which that other cannot, over time, sustain in reality. Over time, indeed, the partner is bound to become experienced as different from the projected romantic illusion. The question then becomes whether the partners can sustain their relationship as the basis for its foundation becomes increasingly an awareness of similarities, differences and complementarities rather than the illusion of identity, however sweet and seductive the illusion. If the partners can adapt satisfactorily enough from illusion to reality, the memory of the moments of mutual adoration will remain precious, albeit sometimes painful; if they cannot, they may attempt to imprison each other in an artificial mutual adoration, which may become a torment rather than either an inspiration or a stepping-stone to a deeper, if less seductive and more rugged, reality.

One of my patients experienced this problem acutely.

From two completely contradictory parts of himself he wanted two completely contradictory responses from his wife. In his adult self, he wished to appreciate his wife's complementarity to himself; her different, separate self. The trouble was that, when his wife, who was indeed very different from him, excited his adult, sexual love, he became very troubled and disturbed on quite a different psychic level. Here he was a very young boy, who demanded that the mother should be utterly and adoringly in love with him, completely under his narcissistic control. For this boy, his wife's (=mother's) separate, different self spelled nothing but trouble. It was not only that she threatened not to be focused exclusively on him, but also that she was successfully attracting a different part of himself. When the man in him got together lovingly with his wife, particularly when sex was involved, the boy in him not only hated the woman for abandoning him, but also hated the sexual couple who, he felt, annihilated him from their minds and were hell-bent on conceiving his replacements. My patient became quite split, psychologically, and would attack his wife and their marriage vigorously. Subsequently he would feel intensely persecuted by anxiety. It was only through understanding the split way in which he related to me in the transference, that he could begin to get more of a grasp of these different, and highly conflictual, quite unintegrated currents of intense love and hatred.

Adoration and idealisation, as narcissistic illusions, need gradually to be replaced by the realistic, non-narcissistic, critical perception of the real qualities of the other person, now experienced as separate from the self. While this seems true and clear enough, it risks becoming a seductively overclear, oversimplified road map to maturity. It implies the value-judgement that, in terms of Kleinian theory, the depressive position is 'better' than the paranoid-schizoid position, whereas, as Britton (1998) has emphasised, these two states of mind are co-dependent, and, for the individual's psychological development to occur, they need to oscillate, moving forward in what can be pictured as a kind of spiral progress. This more complex, less linear and less clear picture approximates to a more truthful description of the maturational process. A mind which resolutely turns away from experiences of adoration and idealisation risks losing a crucial, vital quality, becoming somewhat desiccated and moralistic.

Many marriages come to grief in this way. Partners often find they have become friends, respectful of each other, but losing the vital spark of their earlier relationship. Similarly, in the relationship between individuals and their work, they can realise, depressingly, that they have lost the spark they used to feel for their work, which used to be as strong a motivation as, say, their intellectual curiosity: their work has perhaps now become worthy, but not inspiring. The question becomes, was the initial honeymoon feeling merely a narcissistic illusion, which, though painful, it is better (in the name of truthfulness) to know, leading perhaps to the ending of a relationship and to the possibility, through learning from experience, of forming a new, different and, it is hoped, better one? Or might the present, rather dulled relationship still actually contain hidden, repressed seeds of inspiration, and might trying to understand what has been desiccating and inhibiting it, open the door to its regeneration?

This can be an exceedingly painful problem.

One patient's character was marked by a particularly dry and mean, envious disposition. When, in the course of her analysis, she began to get in touch with more generous drives and aspects of herself, she began to perceive, particularly through her dreams, how she immediately attributed her own more vital and fruitful engagement exclusively to myself, while she stepped back into her dry and barren, critical position. She would then accuse me of getting narcissistically overexcited by my own analytic success and of robbing her of what was hers, in so superior and convincing a manner that, to begin with, I regularly believed her, feeling quite undermined and unsettled by my narcissistic shortcomings. These attacks were particularly venomous if she herself had just been in danger of being touched and moved by an interpretation. It was possible eventually to speculate that she was repeating what she had started doing so many years before as a child, backing her mean impulse to attack her mother's mothering, which brought about its own sadistic gratification, rather than backing her own, quite different capacities for generosity and interested, loving engagement. It was extremely painful for this patient to have to face not only that she was doing this with me in the present, but also that this mean and depriving style of relating, in which the target of this spoiling action was her own love as much as the love of others, was indeed characteristic of her current and past relationships. She had given over much of her life to desecrating any relationships that threatened to evoke an adoring response in herself, and to insist on enviously usurping the place of the one she felt the impulse to adore.

The adoration experience is rarely simple and purely 'good'. Organic hunger for adoration is indissolubly linked with greed and envy. It is difficult, if not impossible, not to envy the person one so adores. The mother has, after all, wonderful qualities, just by being the mother, which the infant adores her for having; and this emotional movement is bound to stimulate the infant's envy of the mother for the very qualities that he adores her for and craves. If his natural generosity is strong, the infant's envy for the mother may well be more than counterbalanced by his love for her, and this shadow-side of the numinous adoration experience may hardly disturb the deep waters of his love. But if his in-born psychological qualities tend towards a more narcissistic disposition, his loving adoration may well be very disturbed, and truly spoiled, by his envy. The same is true for the mother. It is very crucial to the encounter how generous she is towards her child, as compared with how enviously she may react towards his capacity for stirring up the impulse to adore him.

As if these two-person difficulties were not enough, they always occur within the context of a relationship between at least three people. There is always a father involved, even on those occasions where there is no external father, symbolically and in unconscious phantasy in the minds of the mother and infant. It is crucial whether this father is generous and supportive towards the adoring pair, being prepared temporarily to exclude himself, or whether his jealousy drives him to punish them for their passionate and exclusive coupling. Nor is this problem located only in the actual father's mind. There can still be severe problems of jealousy if, say, the mother is convinced that her actions will stimulate her husband's jealousy. Every family has to struggle with this, and no two families' positions and responses will be identical. In some cases, the wife's conviction of her husband's jealousy will actually stimulate his jealousy; in others, if the father is not prone to too much jealousy, and if his love and generosity and forbearance are fairly strong, the mother may accept that her unconscious phantasy of a jealous mate has been disproved, bringing relief and loving appreciation of him. Very often these developments tend to occur in malign or benign circles, which bears out the suspicion of many – particularly children – that life is unfair. Whatever the parents' emotional disposition, there is also the unknown factor of their young child's loving and destructive impulses. Some infants seem from the start to be particularly successful at stirring up jealousy and rivalries in those around them, just as others seem to have a talent for inspiring loving cooperation in their parents. The situation also often involves the highly potent factor of the unconscious phantasies of the feelings towards the adoring couple provoked in other siblings, alive, or dead, or even as yet unborn, but thought of.

A prominent place is given to the practice of adoration by many religions, or groupings within religions, e.g. Catholic and Orthodox Christians, groups within Hinduism, Mahayana Buddhism and the Sufi tradition within Islam. The practice of adoration often seems to express the emotional core of the religion, and devotees are often expected to practise their adoration both publicly, in the context of group worship, and in their private devotions. Within the Christian tradition, popular examples include the adoration of the child Jesus by his mother, by Joseph and the Magi; the adoration of Mary as Mother of God; Jesus' adoration of his Father, and the devotee's adoration for the adult Jesus, sometimes symbolised, as the focus of adoration, as the transubstantiated bread and wine of the Mass or Eucharist.

When worshippers celebrate the birth of their God and devotees revere and adore the divine child and his mother – e.g. Christ at Christmas or Krishna at Krishna-Jayanti – they are unconsciously reimmersing themselves in their own unconscious experiences of adoring and being adored by the mother. Searles (1958) writes:

> One can have the self-enriching experience of worshipping him [one's own newborn infant] with much the same devotion and joy which a really devout Christian may feel towards the Christ-child; the latter can be seen as, in this connexion, a symbol of the radiant joys which a newborn baby bestows upon those who love him and welcome his arrival.
>
> (Searles 1958: 227)

If our experience of infantile adoration has been satisfactory, we will remember it with tranquillity, but, if it has been unsatisfactory or lacking, we are likely to have a more ambivalent and complex reaction. Perhaps the religious experience will be seized upon as a symbolically idealised substitute for the original unsatisfactory experience. Or this whole aspect of the festival will be feared and hated, perhaps scorned and belittled. With its idealistic picture of the baby Jesus, feted by all creation when the human world would find no place for him, Christmas can seem like a child's ultimate wish-fulfilling fantasy: the child was originally unfairly rejected, particularly by brothers and sisters, but then the parental king and queen (not to mention the angels!) came to their senses, giving the child their utter adoration, placing him over all his rejecting older rivals, and even over them, the parents, themselves. Nor does the child have to face his parents' sexuality and the ubiquitous Oedipus complex: others may have to face this, but not him. His parents never had sex, so father is no rival, and mother is the child's alone. Father gratifyingly volunteers to take third place, serving the primary couple, that of mother and child.

It is not surprising that, particularly for some who feel their life experience has made them wary of trusting and loving a real person, adoration and attachment to a religious figure often serves, at least in part, as a defensive substitute. The Buddha, in particular, taught that emotional attachments, even of spouse to spouse or parent to child, could only lead in the long run to experiences of *dukkha*, sorrow, and thus were best avoided. Sometimes the religious attachment of those who have overtly put religion to the forefront of their lives, perhaps even as a profession (e.g. priests, monks and nuns), turns out to be largely defensive against human attachment.

One such patient sought therapy, undergoing a midlife crisis, realising that she had lived the first half of her life denying her need of human love, idealising religious adoration to the point of idolatry, and only waking up to this self-deception when it was already too late for a more ordinary, less exalted human aspiration – to try and find a sexual partner and have a family. Jesus may have said, 'Render therefore unto Caesar the things that are Caesar's, and unto God the things that are God's', but my patient was one of a group of religious people who appear to have been involved in an unreal rendering to God of that which should belong to their humanity. She had then to travel through a deep depression, a truly dark night of the soul, feeling she now had nothing. She felt that what she had formerly seen as her 'rich' religious attachment had actually deprived rather than enriched her, robbing her of her humanity.

Adoration can be seen to be oriented more to life, when it leads to development. If, for example, an infant and mother couple can respond fairly straightforwardly to an organic hunger for adoration, the result is supportive of the child's development (and the mother's). If an amorous couple adore each other, the organic result is often a child. If scientists adore their work, they may be inspired to work particularly creatively. Flaws arise when the experience is over-idealised and craved for its own sake. A child can demand forever to be adored, resisting the side of growing up which involves losing his place at the centre of mother's attention. Lovers – e.g. Jocasta and Laius – can hate the arrival of a child, as it disrupts their exclusive adoration. A scientist, jealously and possessively in love with his private love affair with his science, may be inhibited from letting other professionals share his work. One could make a similar assessment of whether religious adoration leads to a genuinely human and spiritual development of the devotee, or whether it leads instead to a more static and anti-developmental reaction, perhaps camouflaged by pious observance.

As the father becomes an increasingly important figure for the child, he too may now get adored, and pulled into a mutually adoring twosome. As the relationship with him becomes internalised, he begins to become transformed within the child's inner world into what one might call the child's classical Freudian super-ego. One might speculate that the aspect of the father which is adored becomes one of the principal components of the 'ego-ideal' dimension of the super-ego (Freud 1914, 1923). If all goes well, as it gets added to in life by other benign authority figures, it becomes the guiding light of the mind, the inner voice of conscience, duty, desire and the ambition to achieve moral and ethical ideals.

The ego-ideal tends to be symbolised culturally by a male religious figure, e.g. Jesus, the Buddha, and, for Hindus, a plethora of gods and gurus, including the more contemporary figures of Gandhi and Tagore. As the child grows in knowledge of his cultural inheritance and begins personally to appropriate it, this figure becomes introjected and, as it were, grafted onto the developing structure of his 'ego-ideal'. For many religious groups, loving the religious figure, as earlier the child had adored his mother, is seen as the central route for the child's religious development. Via adoration, the ideal religious figure is taken into the self. The theory is that the self is offered to the idealised paternal god-figure not only submissively but also in a relationship of mutual acceptance, regard and respect. The image of the Holy Spirit expresses the loving, adoring relationship between the Father and the Son. But to contemporary eyes, it exposes a glaring deficiency in Christianity that this central relationship lacks any female element, when all adoration must ultimately be based on the crucial early interaction of adoration between infant and mother.

In the Hindu tradition, this is part of the meaning of *saccidananda*, a composite word meaning a state of the highest contemplative knowledge (*cit*), of being (*sat*), leading to bliss (*ananda*). As Bede Griffiths (1982) writes:

> The Ultimate is experienced in the depths of the soul, in the substance or Centre of its consciousness, as its own Ground or Source, as its very being or Self (*Atman*). This experience of God is summed up in the word *saccidananda*. God, or Ultimate Reality, is experienced as absolute being (*sat*), known in pure consciousness (*cit*), communicating absolute bliss (*ananda*).
>
> (Griffiths 1982: 27)

This word is very often used to describe the ultimate religious goal by the advaitic tradition, which, being utterly monistic, does not believe in the real, ultimate existence of object-relations. See, for example, the conclusion of a poem by Ramana Maharshi, a famous and highly influential twentieth-century South Indian guru of advaita (Abhishiktananda 1974: 216):

Then when the true knowledge of the self is reached,
There is only being,
Without end or beginning,
Infinite delight in the awareness of being!
SAT-CIT-ANANDA

This tradition, therefore, perceives adoration of a God perceived as an Other as essentially a product of *maya*, illusionary ignorance. Nevertheless the term *saccidananda* is also shared by the dvaitic tradition, which is marked by the practice of bhakta or devotion to a God (often a Goddess), very much perceived as a real Other with whom one can be in relationship, the central religious practice being that of adoration. For example, here is the seventeenth-century poet Tukaram writing in praise of an image of Vishnu:

Sweet basil beads
Garland His neck
A yellow silk garment
Girdled around His loins
I love His trance
His forever stance

Crocodile-shaped rings

Gleam at His ears
The *Kaustubha* stone
Glows at His throat

Says Tuka, for me
This is absolute bliss
The loving eyes are mine
The loved face His
(Tukaram 1991: 61)

Many such mystical poets oscillate between singing their spiritual love-songs to a God who is felt to be a separate being from them, and singing of how they experience a sense of feeling at one with God. Tukaram, for example, can sing very playfully, becoming very familiar, even quite mocking, to his God:

I'll fight
You
And I'm sure
I'll hit you
In the tenderest spot.
And at times
You are
A coward

Lord
You are a lizard
A toad
And a tiger
Too
Only the weak
Who
Try to run away

Frantically
Covering
Your own arse

When you face
A stronger-willed
Assault
You just
Turn tail
You attack

Says Tuka
Get
Out of my way
You are
Neither man
Nor woman
You aren't even
A thing.

(Tukaram 1991: 100)

But then Tukaram can express the confusional state, where he is not sure where the boundaries are between him and his God:

Between you and me there is no
   difference
I am simply making fun

You serve yourself out of me

Inside you I stay very still
Inside me is your strong will

You are exactly my shape and size
You stretch me as you will

I am really inside you
With my mouth, it is you who
   speak;
Inside you, I just stay cool

Says Tuka, O God
Our names get so mixed up
(Tukaram 1991: 198)

Tukaram and Michael Balint seem to see things similarly: Balint writes of a

harmonious, interpenetrating mix–up . . . It is an idle question to ask whether the water in the gills or in the mouth is part of the sea or of the fish; exactly the same holds true about the foetus.

(Balint 1968: 66)

Tukaram writes of an even closer sense of fused identity:

The night has passed.
What's sleep? I haven't seen it.

I have built my nest in Narayana.
My joy does not cease.

I have compressed my space.
I have no room for myself.

Says Tuka, we are contained
   together.
We do not split for one moment.
(Tukaram 1991: 188)

167

What is being evoked here is also what Winnicott perceived as one of the two main modes of the infant's relationship with the breast: when the infant is actively engaged with sucking from or playing with the nipple, he is, in Winnicott's opinion, having an early experience of I DO, but when he lies quietly at the breast, at one with it, this may be his first semi-conscious experience of I AM. I AM, therefore, from this perspective, means, at its emotional root, 'I am at one with the (m)other', or even, at an even earlier stage, before there is any dawning recognition of the mother as other, 'I and the mother are one'. Perhaps this is at the root of Jesus' words (St John's Gospel 10: 30): 'I and the Father are one'. Winnicott writes about

> *the baby becoming the breast (or mother), in the sense that the object is the subject* . . . The term subjective object has been used in describing the first object, the object *not yet repudiated as a not-me phenomenon* . . .
>
> However complex the psychology of the sense of self and of the establishment of an identity eventually becomes as a baby grows, no sense of self emerges except on the basis of this relating in the sense of BEING. This sense of being is something that antedates the idea of being-at-one-with, because there has not yet been anything else except identity. Two separate persons can *feel* at one, but here at the place I am examining the baby and the object *are* one.
>
> (Winnicott 1971: 93–94, original italics)

He goes on to say: 'The term primary identification has perhaps been used for just this that I am describing'.

Fairbairn seems to agree:

> I employ the term '*primary identification*' here to signify the cathexis of an object which has not yet been differentiated from the cathecting subject
>
> (Fairbairn 1941: 34, original emphasis)

All this is a part of what resonates behind the dvaitic interpretation and emotional experience of saccidananda. The 'doing', i.e. the act of knowing, leads on (or back? or down?) to the experience of pure 'being', the state of bliss.

Calling to mind the link between adoration and falling in love, it is not surprising to discover that, at the core of the Bhakti tradition, the devotee imagines himself falling in love with the divine figure. The deity can be female, e.g. Kali in this poem in her honour:

When you lie down,
Think you are doing obeisance to Her;
When you sleep, meditate on the Mother.

When you eat,
Think you are offering oblations to the Mother;
Whatever you hear with the ear is Her sacred incantation;
Each one of the fifty letters of the alphabet represents Her alone.
Ramaprasad declares in joy:
The Mother pervades everything;
When you move about in the city, you are walking around the Mother.

(Embree 1966: 244)

If the God is male, however (e.g. Vishnu in his incarnation as Krishna), then one possible outcome is that he will be felt to create an impossible threesome, stirring up intense love, passionate adoration, jealousy and hatred, as in the case of Mirabai, the sixteenth-century poet. Embree explains how her devotion to Gopal (Krishna) led to her abandoning her husband, a Raja, passing her life

in complete dedication to the praise of her God. Once, for example, her husband, hearing her talk in a closed room to a man, rushed in with drawn sword to kill her for her unfaithfulness. But it was Krishna with her, and he transformed her into a multitude of forms so that the king could not tell which one was really his wife . . . Krishna finally revealed himself in his glory and absorbed her soul into his.

(Embree 1966: 252)

Mirabai, still very popular and much sung in India, wrote:

My only Lord is Giridhar Gopal,
None else, none else, in this false world;
I have forsaken my family and friends,
. . .
I have watered the creeper of God's love with my own tears,
Churning the curds of life, I have taken out the butter, and thrown away
    the rest.
The King, my husband, sent me a cup of poison:
I drank it with pleasure.
The news is now public, everyone knows now
That Mirabai has fallen in love with God!
It does not matter now: what was fated to happen, has happened.

(Embree 1966: 253)

Another possibility when the worshipper adores a male God, is that he will imagine himself to be a woman. This leads to the religious transvestite practice, in which a man will dress as a woman to sing his spiritual love-songs to the male God in a Hindu temple. Tukaram clearly sometimes experienced this:

I've got addicted
To it.
I am tight
With arousal.

'She's crazy for God!
She's crazy for God!'

Says Tuka,
Having met Him,

Says the world
Of me.

I made love
So secretly.
But it's come out.
It can't be hid.
One is cut off
From all else.
(Tukaram 1991: 174)

This transformation is also what lies behind the metaphorical trans-sexism of Christian mystics, such as the sixteenth-century St John of the Cross, who imagine themselves to be essentially brides adoring the bridegroom, Christ. See, for example, St John's most famous poem, 'The Dark Night of the Soul' (1991):

Upon my flowering breast,
which I kept wholly for him
    alone,
there he lay sleeping,
and I caressing him
there in a breeze from the fanning
    cedars.
When the breeze blew from the
    turret,
as I parted his hair,

it wounded my neck
with its gentle hand,
suspending all my senses.
I abandoned and forgot myself,
laying my face on my Beloved;
all things ceased; I went out from
    myself,
leaving my cares
forgotten among the lilies.

The human ability, even necessity, to express adoration in these terms is surely a powerful manifestation, within the realms of religion, of the basic human bisexuality described by Freud (e.g. Freud 1913), simultaneously offering the worshipper an opportunity symbolically to express both his normal and inverted Oedipal emotions in a sublimated form. Hinduism seems to express the fluid and infinite varieties of unconscious human relating, i.e. the transference, much more fully than any of the other principal world religions. The semitic religions of Judaism, Islam and Christianity, by contrast, tend to view these possibilities with much greater anxiety and moral suspicion, and tend to outlaw many such manifestations.

Religious adoration is often represented artistically, perhaps because of its deep, preverbal roots. If the visual arts are the best suited for illustrating the crucial adorational quality of the gaze, music may claim to be intrinsically suited for evoking the rapt, emotional quality at the heart of the experience. There are countless examples in secular music for lovers, of which, within western classical music, perhaps the dreamy, rapturous music of Act II of Wagner's *Tristan und Isolde* could stand as an archetypal instance. Within the religious sphere, the devotional Hindu songs of Mirabai and the Tamil Vaishnavite Tiruvaimoli of Nammalvar stand out as exemplars, and, in Christian music, there are the countless radiant settings of Marian antiphons, the entirely adorational Sanctus in the Mass, Christmas texts such as 'O Magnum Mysterium', and, perhaps most self-consciously adorational, virtually all the music written to accompany the receiving and adoration of the Holy Sacrament. In the St Matthew Passion (as in virtually all his sacred works), Bach employs the arias, as opposed to the narrative sections, to express a huge range of the emotional responses of the soul which adores Christ to the particular, current dramatic moment. This is a telling example of how, even after the more Puritanical, morally reforming and rational Protestant theology had triumphantly rejected specifically the emotional excesses of Catholicism, it could not stop its own new tradition developing its own idiosyncratic variety of intense emotional expression.

Tagore's poem (at the head of this chapter) represents the adored ego-ideal at its best: an inner and outer authority which is respected and regarded with awe, but which can be approached with a free love and a certainty of being loved in return. In Fairbairn's terms, this is an illustration of the good object which, when internalised, enables the ego to cope with its internalised bad objects (Fairbairn 1943). What is represented is not only the explicitly stated hope of actually seeing God eventually, but also the symbolic evocation of the image, consciously forgotten but unconsciously forever treasured at the core of the soul, of the memory of the experience of the infant, 'alone and speechless', adoring the mother and being adored by her. Just as the child's adoration of the father is underpinned by the infant's earlier adoration of the mother, so the poem is manifestly addressed by an adult to a male God; and yet, does not the atmospheric tone of the whole poem and, especially, its final words evoke the underlying, unconscious but yet profound and potent, image of the mother?

References

Abhishiktananda (1974) *Saccidananda*. Delhi: ISPCK.
Balint, M. (1968) *The Basic Fault*. London: Tavistock.
Bowlby, J. (1969) *Attachment*. London: Penguin (1984).
Britton, R. (1998) Before and after the depressive position. In *Belief and Imagination*. London: Routledge.
Buber, M. (1923) *Ich und Du*. Berlin: Shocken Verlag.
Embree, A. (ed.) (1966) *The Hindu Tradition: Readings in Oriental Thought*. New York: Random House.
Fairbairn, W.R.D. (1941) A revised psychopathology of the psychoses and psychoneuroses. In *Psychoanalytic Studies of the Personality*. London: Routledge (1952).
Fairbairn, W.R.D. (1943) The repression and the return of bad objects. In *Psychoanalytic Studies of the Personality*. London: Routledge (1952).

Freud, S. (1913) The claims of psychoanalysis to scientific interest. SE 13.

Freud, S. (1914) On narcissism: an introduction. SE 14.

Freud, S. (1923) The Ego and the Id. SE 19.

Freud, S. (1930) *Civilization and its Discontents*. SE 21.

Griffiths, B. (1982) *The Marriage of East and West*. London: Collins.

Klein, M. (1946) Notes on some schizoid mechanisms. In *Envy and Gratitude, and Other Works*. London: Virago (1988).

St John of the Cross (1991) *The Complete Works*, trans. K. Kavanagh (OCD) and O. Rodriguez (OCD). Washington, DC: ICS.

Searles, H.F. (1958) Positive feelings in the relationship between the schizophrenic and his mother. In *Collected Papers on Schizophrenia and Related Subjects*. London: Karnac (1986).

Tagore, R. (1913) *Gitanjali*. London: Macmillan.

Tukaram (1991) *Says Tuka: Selected Poetry of Tukaram*, trans. D. Chitre. New Delhi: Penguin.

Winnicott, D.W. (1948) Paediatrics and psychiatry. In *Through Paediatrics to Psychoanalysis*. London: Karnac (1992).

Winnicott, D.W. (1971) *Playing and Reality*. London: Pelican (1974).

9

PREVERBAL EXPERIENCE AND THE INTUITION OF THE SACRED

Kenneth Wright

When my silent terror cried,
Nobody, nobody replied.
                    Louis MacNeice

See; not a hair is, not an eyelash, not the least lash lost; every hair
        Is, hair of the head, numbered.
                    Gerard Manley Hopkins

Religion, law and the father

In this chapter, I explore the idea that the roots of religious experience lie in the preverbal core of the self. I shall argue that religion offers recognition, and a promise of containment, to elements of the self that have been excluded from the developmental process; and that where it exists, the religious quest is fired by a *need* for containment, and *longing* for a containing object. Finally, I shall attempt to show that the religious process so defined is part of an axis of *love* (*agape*, tenderness) in the human personality, distinct from the libidinal axis (*eros*) described by Freud. In making these assertions, I do not wish to circumscribe the field of religion but to draw attention to a neglected area of psychoanalytic theorising.

Freud himself was deeply interested in religion but for the most part his views were quite negative. His insights were principally concerned with man's unresolved dependence on parental figures and he believed it was the persistence of longing for a strong father that induced belief in an all-powerful god (Freud 1927, 1930). Echoing in part the paternalistic values of his day, Freud regarded this as a failure of development and he might have agreed with St Paul that the 'putting away of childish things' was the essence of 'becoming a man' (St Paul's First Epistle to the Corinthians).

Increasingly, however, it is being recognised that Freud's views were constrained by his own make-up. While he gave brilliant descriptions of those parts of the personality that turned on the axis of the father, the Oedipus complex and its legacy, his formulations concerning the pre-oedipal period, the maternal axis, were far weaker. The argument linking theory to personality was first put forward by Ian Suttie, who claimed that not only Freud's account of religion, but also his entire theoretical opus, was skewed by an anti-maternal bias in his make-up (Suttie 1935). Noting Freud's difficulty in identifying with the *oceanic feeling* and his derivation of love and tenderness from the sexual instinct, he postulated a *taboo on tenderness* in Freud's personality, stemming from a blindness to, or repression of, his early *relationship* with his mother. In a way that prefigured Bowlby's *attachment theory*, Suttie suggested that the infant was born with 'a simple attachment-to-mother', a *primary need* for 'companionship' and contact with her.[1] He considered that feelings of tenderness developed from this early matrix, and had little to do with the *sexual* appetite or instinct *per se*, at least in the way that Freud envisaged.

That Freud's personality was organised along paternal lines (Wright 1991) is further evidenced by his fascination with the figure of Moses. Freud wrote at length about this 'father' of the Jewish people and was deeply fascinated by Michelangelo's sculpture of him with the tables of the Law. This powerful statue relates to Moses' descent from Mount Sinai with 'two tables of testimony, tables of stone, written with the finger of God', and the moment of wrath when he discovered that his people were worshipping the golden calf of heathen neighbours. Freud too was intolerant of those in his circle who advocated 'false gods' in the form of theories different from his own. Indeed, he was so keen to preserve the *paternal* 'truth' of his discoveries that it took two generations to fully instate the *mother* into psychoanalytic thinking. Consequently, psychoanalytic views on religion remained fixed at the oedipal level of understanding – patricidal impulse, incestuous guilt, atonement, and ultimately subservience to the father. Over and above the personality aspect, however, such constructs would have seemed pertinent at the end of the nineteenth century. Not only was the prevailing ethos paternal but also the Judeo-Christian tradition itself was paternally weighted. The God of Abraham was a father ruling over his chosen race and the God of Christianity inherited many of his characteristics: 'Our *father* which art in heaven, hallowed be thy name,' says the Lord's Prayer, '*Thy* kingdom come, *thy* will be done, on earth as it is in heaven.'

Within such a patriarchal society it would have made sense to see the function of religion as the maintenance of good relations with this sky-father (see for example, Suttie 1935: ch. 9), and this involved, as the Old Testament states again and again, conforming to the paternal Law. It is *he* (the father) who has laid down what is right and wrong, what *can* and *cannot* be done, what *can* and *cannot* be thought. And while historically and developmentally such Law involves sub-missive relations with an external father figure, with internalisation, the subject's well-being comes more to depend on the link with a father *imago*. Whether the emotional concerns of such an internal organisation are those of transgression and punishment, or forgiveness and reacceptance as in the story of the Prodigal Son, the key figure remains the father. It will be recalled that in that story, the returning son says: 'Father, I have sinned against heaven and before thee.' And as he welcomes him back, the forgiving father replies: 'This, my son, was dead, and is alive again; he was lost and is found' (Gospel according to St Luke).

The overlapping scenarios I have described present a patriarchal society (nineteenth- and early-twentieth-century Vienna), a patriarchal religion (the Judeo-Christian tradition) and a patriarchal theory (psychoanalysis) that includes a patriarchal *theory* of religion. There is a son (Freud) rebelling against the canons of his society and against his own father; a theory that spells out many aspects of such rebellion (oedipal theory); and the same son, who taking on himself the mantle of authority for the new patriarchy, psychoanalysis, strives, like Moses, to keep its (paternal) beliefs (theories) pure. Patriarchies die hard and as so often, the rebel son becomes the authoritarian father.

Love, tenderness and the maternal

Rebellion against the father in psychoanalysis led to some early expulsions from the movement, notably Jung and Adler; important disputes, notably that with the 'maternal' Ferenczi; and, only *after* Freud's death, to an upsurge of creative theorising about the role of the mother in infant development. From this perspective, Melanie Klein, Michael and Enid Balint and Donald Winnicott in the British Society, Harold Searles, Heinz Kohut and the subsequent protagonists of self-psychology in the United States, were 'protestants' against the paternal bias.[2] They spoke for what had been neglected during the years of Freud's 'rule', and attempted to reinstate the excluded maternal into theory and practice.

Such maternal revisions took different forms. Ferenczi's ideas, for example, revolved round the therapeutic relationship – it was the analyst's *love* that healed the patient (Ferenczi 1926). This theme continues through Michael and Enid Balint to the work of Winnicott and the contemporary Independent Group of the British Psychoanalytic Society. It was the environment, the caring, adaptive behaviour of the actual mother that shaped the course of development. Kleinian revision, by contrast, gave primacy to instinct and phantasy, while 'locating' such phantasy in an overall maternal frame.

175

The tension between such differing views significantly affected the development of British psychoanalysis. This can be seen, for example, in the way infant aggression is understood. While Klein's followers stressed the *inherent* aggressiveness of the infant – an original 'badness', perhaps – those in the line of Ferenczi regarded aggression as *reactive*; it was secondary to maternal or environmental failure. In this view, closer to Suttie's position, what is stressed is the inherent tendency of the baby to be *loving* – the baby is endowed with an original 'goodness' which prevails as long as the environment does not fail excessively.

In this chapter I shall theorise from within this 'softer' maternal tradition. I shall argue that 'love' is in some sense present from the beginning, and will focus on the nature of this love – on what it involves – in a practical and detailed way. First, however, I shall discuss a problem that has dogged psychoanalytic thinking about religion from the beginning. This concerns the way in which love has been predominantly construed from within a male, paternal frame.

Religion, at least in its higher forms (Symington 1994), is deeply concerned with love. However, such love is not primarily paternal – a love of the Law – but a love of the human person. It is this love that I call 'maternal'. Paternal religion wants the Law (the Ten Commandments, for example) to reign supreme. Jesus, a more maternal advocate, wanted to replace this love of the Law with an empathic love of one's neighbour. Indeed, some of Jesus' strongest words were spoken against the Scribes and Pharisees who lived by the letter of the Law, and he shocked and angered such 'fathers' of the tradition by suggesting that empathic understanding might obviate the need for punishment. One example would be his approach to the woman taken in adultery: first identify with the other person, only then judge. Jesus was thus more concerned with a love based on identification than on one that was erotic or lustful: 'We are all human,' he says; 'any one of us could be in this position for we are all adulterers in our hearts.'

But altruistic love (*agape*) is precisely what has troubled psychoanalysis from the beginning. For if you derive such love from a root that is primarily erotic and self-seeking (*eros*, aim-inhibited sexuality), how can it be genuinely other-directed? How can *agape* ever gain ascendancy if it is merely an outpost of self-seeking *eros*?

Suttie's answer was clear: it was the theory – psychoanalytic theory – that needed correction because it shared in the anti-maternal skew of Freud's personality (the taboo on tenderness). If one listened to one's intuition, the problem simply disappeared. Given a *primary* need for contact and social relatedness with the mother, it was obvious that the caring aspects of love were built upon *this*. Religious love could now be seen as the flowering of a developmental line *present from the beginning*. Suttie's (1935) view of a separate relational axis has been amply confirmed by Bowlby's later work (Bowlby 1969) and within this more empirical framework, a rationale now exists for basing altruistic love, or love of the neighbour, on the earliest mother–infant bond.[3]

Institutional and revealed religion

Symington (1993), in a short article on religion and psychoanalysis, divided religions into two major groups. *Revealed religions* are more or less institutionalised and impose a set of mandatory beliefs and practices. They coincide in some degree with the type of religion I have termed patriarchal. However, Symington noted another important group that he called *natural religions*, among which he placed the teachings of Socrates, Buddha and at least some of the teachings of Jesus. *Natural religions*, according to Symington, are not so much concerned with conformity to practice and the letter of the Law as with inward questions to do with the meaning of life: how do humans find fulfilment? How are individuals to find true satisfaction in their lives? Such questions are more subjective, but no less real, than questions of whether or not one has sinned according to the Law, but they involve *intuitive appraisal of the inner person* rather than objective evidence. So within this approach, an action or thought can be said to *feel* right because it *fits* in relation to some inner criterion; another action or thought feels wrong because it does *not fit* and creates a sense of inner discordance. It is clear that such judgements are made according to intuitive, *inner* criteria rather than by reference to *objective* rules.

With their emphasis on inner states of mind and internal criteria of judgement, natural religions place greater emphasis than revealed religions on *the well-being of the self*, and this suggests a structuring round the axis of the mother. Compared with patriarchal religions, they are less involved with *objective* truth and *objective* right and wrong – values of the oedipal period concerned with the 'out there'. They are more concerned with *subjective* truth – the intuitive and empathic appraisal of what is *right* or *good* for the *self* – involving maternal values of the pre-oedipal period. In adult life, the subject makes such appraisals; at the start of life, another person would have made them *on his or her behalf*. Quite clearly, the person who originally *looked after the self* in this caring way would have been the mother, making such appraisals on behalf of the infant.

In this chapter, my concern is with Symington's second group of religions in which self-appraisal and individual experience are paramount. It needs to be noted, however, that revealed religions begin with an individual vision (subjective), and only with the passage of time is this commandeered by a ruling (paternal) group and given institutional (external) form. As Martin Buber (1937) pointed out, the process of institutionalisation ultimately leads to loss of contact with the subjective vision – with god or the sacred – and when this occurs, religion deteriorates into external observance. But then a new cycle may begin, with further breakthrough to the sacred, and at this point the religion is spiritually renewed. Buber's (1937) account is a reminder that the *fons et origo* of religion is always the *individual's* experience of the sacred.

Significant moments, preverbal experience and the sacred

While the great world religions have been based on the insights of a few outstanding individuals, *an intuition of the sacred* falls within the realm of ordinary experience. I am referring to what the ordinary person might call *a significant moment*, a moment outside of ordinary time, when the world, or some part of it, becomes lit up in a different way. The quality of such moments can be understood by thinking of a person's relation to a line of poetry or piece of music. The first contact is fraught with significance – there are shivers down the spine, or the heart misses a beat. But such physical sensations are merely markers; subjectively, the feeling is one of recognition, of being addressed – the poetic or musical phrase 'speaks' or 'sings' to a part of the subject's soul. There is a feeling of validation and reluctance to let the moment go: 'This beautiful form is what I have always longed for! It is almost a part of me!'

Similar moments may punctuate a person's involvement with the natural world. A person may love nature and enjoy contact with it; but from time to time, there is a different experience – a sense of being *struck* in a special way by a seascape, a vista of hills or the rolling dunes of a desert. What is then experienced is no longer ordinary but an epiphany of significance: as with the fragment of poetry or music, the subject has a sense of *living through the forms*, of becoming one with the landscape. This kind of experience is linked, I think, to the creative impulse and to artists' need to *capture* the landscape, or rather their vision of it, within the forms of their medium, thereby making the significant moment more 'real' and more available to them.

To link such ordinary experiences with explicitly religious ones may seem strange, but I believe there is a continuum between these mini-moments that catch at the heart and the great visions that eventually move humankind. And I think the underlying event is essentially the same. In each case, an outer form, created by a shaping perception, or re-created by the artist's skill, *resonates* with a part of the self as yet unformed, giving it, in that moment, a kind of being. The landscape that 'takes form' in the seeing eye, the 'forms' created by the artist, and the religious 'forms' that promise salvation – each provides a 'home' or 'form' for the self, and simultaneously a richer experience of it. In each case there is contact between the discovered or created form (external) and something deep in the subject's nature (internal); the 'self' (secular) or 'soul' (religious) has found in these moments an external recognition or echo.

In whatever setting such moments occur, a further commonality may be noted – they cannot be called forth on demand. There is always a sense of surprise, and usually a sense of grace, of having been 'chosen' in some way for something special. With religion, for example, the significant moment may occur in spite of the person's conscious opposition to religious things, as for St Paul on the road to Damascus. Or it may be the fruition of a search, of being drawn towards something *felt* to be important – reading religious texts, going to places of worship, and so on. But when (and if) the moment comes, it always surprises and is felt to be personal and specific: a *particular* form – religious, artistic or natural – grabs and stirs the subject, and touches *him*. Relationship and recognition are essential features of the experience.

Most important is the nonverbal nature of such experiences – they are seldom mediated through words and are difficult to describe. They are not, however, formless because the perceptual form that shapes the experience is intrinsic to it. When Mahler was asked by an admirer of his music what one of his pieces meant, he replied: 'Madam, if I could tell you in words what it meant I would not be writing music.' The significance thus lies within the form itself. And so it is with significant moments – the moment comes, has its effect, and goes, but it has no existence apart from the containing form.

Some examples from Josephine Klein's (2004) book on psychotherapy and the ineffable serve to illustrate some of the features I have described. The first two examples particularly express the nonverbal nature of the experience; the third illustrates how it may be mediated by, and contained within, a complex of sensory (i.e. nonverbal) forms.

The Spanish mystic, St John of the Cross, in 'Verses written after an ecstasy of high exaltation', wrote of:

> The gift that leaves men knowing nought,
> Yet passing knowledge with their thought.

And St Teresa of Avila, writing of one of her mystical experiences, again emphasises the lack of communicable knowledge:

> There is no sense of anything but enjoyment, *without any knowledge* of what is being enjoyed. The soul realises that it is enjoying some good thing that contains all good things together, but *it cannot comprehend* this good thing.
> (St Teresa of Avila, *The Life of the Holy Mother Teresa*, ch. XXI, italics mine)

Finally, a more secular example, in which the writer uses her facility with poetic language to convey at least some qualities of the experience:

> It is a sunny fall afternoon and I'm engaged in one of my favourite pastimes – picking chestnuts. I'm playing alone under a spreading, leafy, protective tree. My mother is sitting on a bench nearby, rocking the buggy in which my sister is asleep . . . I pick up a reddish brown chestnut, and suddenly, through its warm skin, I feel the beat as of a heart. But the beat is also in everything else around me, and everything pulsates and shimmers as if it were coursing with the blood of life. Stooping under the tree, I am holding life in my hand, and I am in the centre of a harmonious, vibrating transparency. For that moment I know everything there is to know,[4] I have stumbled into the very

centre of plenitude, and I hold myself still with fulfilment, before the knowledge of my knowledge escapes me.

(Hoffman 1989: 41–42)

Religious experience, the aesthetic moment, and maternal containment

If experiences of this kind are indeed contained within a 'language' of *nonverbal* forms, and if as I have suggested, they belong generically to a religious domain that is closer to the maternal, then it may be possible to link them to prototypical experiences of the preverbal period. This is what Christopher Bollas has done in his work on the *unthought known* (Bollas 1987). What I have called 'significant moments', he has termed *aesthetic moments*:

> when a person is shaken by an experience into absolute certainty that he has been cradled by, and dwelled with, the spirit of the object, a rendezvous of *mute recognition* that defies representation . . . [Such moments] are *fundamentally wordless* occasions, notable for the density of the subject's feeling and the fundamentally *non-representational knowledge* of being embraced by the aesthetic object.
>
> (Bollas 1987: 30–31, italics mine)

For Bollas, all such 'aesthetic moments' are a reliving of early experience:

> The uncanny pleasure of being held by a poem, a composition, a painting, or, for that matter, any object, rests on those moments when the infant's internal world is partly *given form* by the mother since he cannot shape them or link them together without her coverage.
>
> (Bollas 1987: 32, italics mine)

They constitute a revival of what Bollas has called *moments of transformation*, brought about by the mother through her ordinary sensitive ministrations of infant care. Not only does she transform painful hunger into comfortable satiation, but also she changes the diapers, turns the baby on his back, smiles, talks, coos and so on. Bollas dates such experiences from a time before the mother was perceived as a separate object. Her appearances are *apparitional-like* (Bollas 1987: 33) and each announces a significant and welcome change in the infant's state. But for Bollas, it is not only *what* she does, but also her special way of doing it, that becomes part of the infant's experience. Her *idiom of care*, as he calls it, becomes *the infant's first aesthetic*, a *pattern* of holding, being and relating that is linked to major transformations of the infant's psychosomatic state. He writes:

Alongside the infant's experience of being transformed is the reality that he is being transformed according to the mother's aesthetic . . . The baby takes in not only the content of the mother's communications but also their form. In the beginning of life, handling the infant is the primary mode of communicating, so the *internalisation of the mother's form* (her aesthetic) is prior to the internalisation of her verbal messages.

(Bollas 1987: 33–34, italics mine)

For Bollas, the aesthetic moment *recreates* the transformational moment with its unique maternal pattern; the earlier moment is glimpsed and re-embodied within the perceived shapes of the present. The aesthetic moment thus constitutes an irruption of preverbal memory, a sense of being drawn again into *iconically remembered* maternal holding.

Bollas is aware of the religious resonance of what he writes for his language is redolent with religious expressions. 'Reverential', 'beseeching', 'supplication', 'transported', 'uncanny', are just some of the words he uses. But the word 'sacred', which occurs repeatedly, is the closest he can get to this earliest experience: 'The sacred,' he says, 'precedes the maternal' (Bollas 1987: 39).

Transformation as provision of maternal form

Bollas' ideas are a creative extension of Winnicott's work on the *environment mother*, a term he used for the pre-object mother who facilitates infant development by her adaptive responses. Winnicott's work in this area is well known, but it is pertinent to emphasise an aspect that in my view is relatively downplayed in Bollas' formulations. Although he speaks of the mother as 'giving form' to the infant's inner world (Bollas 1987: 32), the emphasis lies on her *transformation* of the baby's experience. Winnicott, on the other hand, emphasised the mother's role as *provider of forms*. This is not one of Winnicott's expressions, but I think the idea is implicit in his concepts of *primary creativity*, the *transitional object*, and even more in his later work on *the mirror role of the mother's face* (Winnicott 1951, 1967b).

Primary creativity was Winnicott's way of referring to the baby's experience when the mother provided the 'form' that the baby needed to complete an experience. The sequence was: 'baby's *anticipation* of breast' in terms of both arousal and specificity; 'mother's *provision* of breast' in terms of both timing and manner of presentation. Where these two things came sufficiently together (the baby's anticipation and the mother's answering 'form'), the baby could feel he had *created* the breast: the 'form' of the maternal response matched the 'shape' of the infant's anticipation. The fact that the mother had allowed this experience made it possible for the infant to build upon it, and later to find/create his own forms 'adapted to' (embodying) aspects of his experience. For Winnicott, the *transitional object* is the baby's first achievement of this kind – a sensory form is discovered in the qualities of the bit of blanket, and the infant uses this as needed to *embody* and *recreate* an experience of the mother. In this way the baby becomes able to evoke the mother's presence in her absence – the beginnings of imaginative experience. In a late paper (1967a), Winnicott suggested a direct line from such early creativity to the larger world of culture (including religion), culture for the most part being based on imaginative illusion.

In his work on transitional phenomena, Winnicott was only beginning to appreciate the importance of forms provided by the mother for infant experience. He was still in thrall to the traditional paradigm of the breast as object of instinctual gratification, yet struggling to incorporate into it new insights about the importance of the mother's responsiveness. Sixteen years later (1967a) he is clearer about the mother's provision; the paradigm shifts from instinctual gratification to preverbal *communication* and the mother's facial expressions. I refer to the mirror role of the mother's face and the way he saw her expressions as reflecting forms for infant experience.

In this new paradigm, the baby uses the mother's *face* as a reflective medium. When he smiles, for example, what he sees in the mother's responsive smile is a visual form of his own inner state. Winnicott is not concerned here with what Bollas has termed 'transformation', the changing of 'bad' experience into 'good', but with how the mother's response enables the infant to *appropriate* or grasp its own experience. Through her emotional reflection the baby acquires the wherewithal to become more fully what he already is. Winnicott puts this in existential terms: 'I am seen, so [now] I exist' (1971 [1967a]: 114).

Facial expression as non–material form

The shift in paradigm between Winnicott's earlier and later work has implications for any discussion of religion for it places a non-material experience at the centre of emotional development. The *breast* paradigm clings to Freud's original way of thinking in which love derives from feeding at the breast. The *face* paradigm, which puts the maternal face at the centre of emotional development, makes non-material visual forms (which cannot be touched or physically incorporated) the principal currency.

In typical fashion, Winnicott does not tell us where the new idea fits in his total scheme of things, but arguably it runs in parallel with the earlier view. As attachment theory and infant research have shown, the maternal face provides a major focus of infant attention from soon after birth. Not only is the facial *gestalt* part of the mother's unique pattern (a focus of her 'apparitional-like appearances' [Bollas]), but also it is an *expressive surface*, the screen on which her emotional expressions play. Long before words can be understood, *it becomes the centre of communication between mother and infant*, and a major source of responsive forms in the way that Winnicott describes.

It is, therefore, not difficult to suppose that the mother's face occupies a privileged place in the infant's feelings. At a later date, it will become the visual identity of the mother as *object*. At this early stage, however, it is probably the organising core of the mother's 'apparitional-like appearances' and magical transformations. And if, as Bollas suggests, 'the sacred [transformational object] precedes the maternal [mother as separate object]', then surely the maternal face must lie at the heart of the sacred.

Where does this new understanding leave us in relation to religion? In my view, it provides a platform from which to approach the nature of spiritual love. Spiritual love, I suggest, is related to what Anna Freud might have called a different developmental line from sexuality, with its early focus on excited feeding. It stems from a different place, a different axis of the infant's equipment, related to the earliest bond with the mother, and thus to the earliest issues of security. According to this view, its central object would be the maternal face and its expressions, and its central dynamic to do with maternal empathy and understanding – or the lack of it. Indeed, it could be argued that just as the infant has an in-built propensity to relate to the human face, so also will it have an in-built expectation of response (facial mirroring) that will lead to a search for it. Whether or not that is so, the currency of such response is a distanced 'form', not a tangible object, and this marks a clear divide, even at this early stage, between material and non-material ('spiritual') strivings.

Containment, attunement and the religious quest

Winnicott (1967a) saw the mother's facial expression as giving a new dimension of being to the infant, enabling it 'to feel real rather than existing' (1971 [1967a]: 117). It is, however, possible to see the function of the mother's 'forms' in a number of different, though related ways. First, it is a *recognition and acceptance* of the baby's emotional gesture. Second, it offers potential *containment* of the infant's emotional (psychosomatic) state. And third, it provides an *objectification* of that state, an external form with which to mark it. In this sense, the maternal expression, like the transitional object, constitutes an early symbolic form (iconic, not verbal).

To communicate through facial expressions, however, is like speaking a language with few words; the smile and other expressions are relatively unspecific, and poorly suited to convey the increasing complexity of experience that needs to be shared. It might therefore be asked whether and how this 'language' might develop in the period *before* verbal language makes its appearance. Does it too increase in complexity, thus enriching the possibilities of sharing preverbal experience? Daniel Stern's (1985) work on maternal attunement offers a way of thinking about this question.

What happens in attunement is this. During the course of her ongoing interactions with the infant (Stern says attunements begin around nine months and continue through the preverbal period),[5] the mother intuitively makes responses that constitute a replay, or mini-enactment, of the way she has just experienced her infant. These responses are replays of sequences in the infant's level of arousal and excitement (Stern calls them *vitality affects*), as intuitively discerned by the mother. In effect, such replays constitute a *specific* sharing of the infant's experience, a *specific* appreciation of it. They are graphic, iconic mini-performances, and although not directly mimetic, they follow quite closely, in pattern and rhythm, the sequences the mother has observed. They follow, in Stern's language, the *contours* of the infant's vitality affects, thus making available to the infant the *profiles* and *shapes* of those patterns. Stern defines attunement as 'the recasting of an affective state' (1985: 161), a recasting in perceivable, but essentially nonverbal form. The mother's attunement performance thus phrases and punctuates the infant's flow of experience far more specifically, and within a far greater variety of 'forms', than facial expression on its own can muster. Yet arguably its function is similar: recognition and acceptance, sharing and containment, and incipient objectification. In principle then, attunements offer to the infant a rudimentary *preverbal language of forms* with which to contain, recall and manipulate experience. Its richness and usefulness, however, depend upon the mother's sensitivity and responsiveness.

The preverbal era of human development lasts for up to two years. During this time, many important aspects of personality are organised and much early experience is structured within the infant's developing self. It can seem, however, that psychoanalytic discussions do not go into detail about how such structuring takes place. While it is generally accepted that the processes of projective identification and mirroring are important, the actual way they achieve structuring is glossed over. Bion's concept of maternal containment (Bion 1962; Britton 1998a) is often discussed in this context but the details remain elusive. To say that 'beta elements' are transformed by the mother's 'alpha function' (Bion 1965) does tell us something, but it does not precisely describe *what* the mother gives back, nor the way in which the infant uses it.

Winnicott's concept of facial mirroring goes some way towards addressing this problem because it offers a glimpse of how an internal feeling state might become linked to an external form, the mother's expression. At least potentially, such linkage gives the infant a first handle (primitive symbol) with which to manipulate and mark an inner feeling. At risk of simplification, one could say that the mother's expression provides a visual 'name' for an inner state.

Such considerations become more cogent when one considers Stern's descriptions of attunement. For in attunement, the maternal response is of similar form and shape (isomorphic) to the infant's arousal pattern. That at least is the theory. But without doubt, the mother's activity also *shapes* the infant's experience because the way she sees her infant's experience will inevitably be constrained by her own make-up. If it can be assumed, however, that a sensitive mother can be genuinely in touch with her baby, we can also assume that the patterns she gives back are then sufficiently isomorphic. In this case, the provided pattern has the potential to 'fit' the emerging experience. Because the rhythm (pattern in time) of the responsive form matches the infant pattern of arousal, there will be resonance, enhancement and containment. I am using the term containment loosely for an imagined relation between form and content, based on iconic similarity.

If, however, containment, acceptance and sharing depend on the sensitivity of maternal attunement, there is much scope for the process to miscarry. Stern (1985: 160) even suggests that it may be impossible to attune to certain negative affects such as anger: 'the sense of threat and harm', he writes, 'places a barrier between the two separate experiences such that the notion of communion is no longer applicable'. Even in the best case then, containment may be patchy and incomplete, leading to lacunae in emotional development.

It seems probable that what a person regards as his or her 'self' is closely linked to what has been maternally accepted and contained. The 'contained' is that which has been given a maternal 'blessing' – in the beginning a maternal smile or attuned enactment. The 'contained' is that which has made *a circuit through the (m)other* – a view that Bion might have endorsed. Through this circuit it acquires a form, a resonating and accepting 'shape'. That which is 'contained' is thus *held* by a maternal form within the mother's ambience (now of course, an aspect of experience) – or as Bollas might say, within the ambience of the sacred.

But what happens, psychologically speaking, to that which has not been contained? What is the fate and nature of such unratified material? This is a question that concerned Bion who thought of the 'uncontained' as a place of untransformed beta elements and fragmented bizarre objects. Within the present framework, to be 'contained' is to be wrapped within a maternal form; to be 'uncontained' is to dwell in a limbo of unrecognised selves, away from the shadow of the mother's presence.

To be 'uncontained' is thus to be radically excluded. Moreover, such dis-inherited selves may well be fragmented and unusable, for without maternal recognition, they have no 'name' and no form. They may be terrifying because unnamed, and although not necessarily 'bad', they may *seem* unredeemable, like a caste of untouchables doomed to wander forever.

Now, religion is often a quest for redemption, yet as usually understood, the need for it lies in the badness or sinfulness of humankind. And while it would be foolish to claim that guilt and a sense of badness were insignificant factors in shaping religion, they are not the only cause of human beings' existential distress. While they may be central in an oedipal world of whole objects, in the preverbal world on which I have focused, they are not the main concerns. In this earlier maternal world, the central issue is containment, and in so far as the religious need has its roots in *this* domain, the quest for redemption is driven by a need to be 'found'. In the existential distress of this domain, guilt and sin play little part. A failure of containment is the 'cause' of the malaise, and acceptance and recognition are its cure.

Rilke: transformation and
redemption through poetry

In order to give substance to these notions, I shall briefly discuss the Austrian poet, Rainer Maria Rilke, who lived in a state of continual existential angst, yet believed passionately in the possibility of redemption through his art. It has been suggested (Britton 1998b) that Rilke was the young poet, already famous, who once walked in the Dolomites with Freud. Freud (1937: 297) later described Rilke as 'the great poet, who was a little helpless in facing life', and Lou Andreas-Salome, his one-time lover, as 'his Muse and protective mother'. Rilke was not only a connoisseur of 'significant moments' – bad as well as good – but also deeply interested in the nature of poetic activity, and in his later poetry offered a 'philosophy' of the poetic process.

He had a poignant sense of the precariousness of life and the transience of each created thing. Each unique creature had only one chance to live and only one thing could save it from disappearing without trace – the poet giving voice to its unique essence. Rilke experienced all creatures, including man-made objects, as *dumb* and *in need of a speaker; they had no voice of their own*. Only a poet had the sensibility to get inside them and thus proclaim their unique and vibrant existence. So it was that each thing turned to the poet in silent supplication, urging him *to speak on its behalf*. Only this would make the creature fully 'real', and fulfilling this need was the poet's vocation: 'Are we perhaps *here* just for saying . . .' he exclaims, listing a whole series of quite ordinary objects. 'But for *saying*, remember, /oh for such saying as never the things themselves /hoped so intensely to be' (Rilke 1960: 224).

Now on one level, the similarities with a mother and her infant are striking. There is a dumb creature who needs the poet's voice to articulate and give form to its unique being, and an infant with no words, who, according to Winnicott and Stern, needs the mother to articulate its 'forms' in order to 'feel real' rather than 'merely existing'. But Rilke is not talking about mothers and babies but about a passionate activity in which he feels *compelled* to engage – so much so that he shuts himself in a tower with his writing for weeks on end. He wrote poetry as though his life depended on it – and probably it did.

I have argued elsewhere (Wright 2000) that the artist is frequently someone who struggles through his art to make good an early maternal deficit. Rilke was no exception, having had an appallingly narcissistic mother who had wanted him to be a girl, a fact enshrined in his second name, Maria. When Rilke speaks of the dumb creatures waiting to be brought into real existence by the poet's 'saying', it is surely clear that on a deeper level he refers to himself. It is his own unspoken, un-reflected self that turns in silent supplication to the poet-mother (also part of himself) for redemption.

In pursuing his passionate vocation, the poet thus becomes his own 'sayer', his own self-reflecting and attuning 'other'. He tackles the problem of deficient containment and the consequent sense of being only half-alive, by becoming his own creator of containing forms. He finds and masters a medium — in this case the medium of poetic language — and brings it under his control. Through his skills he now coaxes, or coerces this medium into furnishing the forms he needs. Whereas in infancy he was at the mercy of his mother's whim — perhaps in Rilke's case a highly *selective* attunement — he is now his own provider of resonating forms. He becomes his own therapist — or dare one say it, his own *saviour*.

In writing about Rilke and his redemption of the dumb creatures, I have been drawn, as was Bollas in his discussion of the aesthetic moment, into a quasi-religious terminology. In part this may stem from this particular poet's passionate intensity that blurs the distinction between artistic and religious forms, but I think the reason lies also in the roots of religious need. If the 'environment mother' who brings 'forms' and 'transformations' to the infant is 'sacred', it is easy to see how the longing for such a mother *when she is unavailable* creates the need for a *saviour*. Rilke thus exemplifies in his life, and records in his work, the springs of a certain kind of religious impulse in the ordinary person.

Conclusions and summary

I started this chapter by looking at certain broad divisions that have a bearing on religious phenomena: institutional and personal religion, paternal and maternal elements of religious life, and patriarchal and matriarchal organisations. I touched on the dominance of patriarchal forms within Judaism and Christianity and a similar dominance in psychoanalytic institutions. I followed Suttie (1935) in suggesting that psychoanalytic understanding of religion had been hampered by this patriarchal or paternal bias, both in Freud's own personality, and subsequently within the psychoanalytic establishment.

In trying to redress this balance and open up discussion of maternal elements in religious culture, I have focused on two things: the notion of *forms*, which is closely linked with *mirroring* and *containment*, and the connected idea of *significant moments*. In linking these to a newer understanding of the mother–infant relationship, I have sought to show that a more sympathetic understanding of religion is possible than that provided by traditional psychoanalytic thinking. This has been hampered, not only by paternal bias but also by an outdated view of love that derives the altruistic variety from earlier self-seeking forms. These things were a legacy of Freud's thinking and revision is long overdue. I have discussed work by a number of psychoanalysts and psychotherapists, notably

Suttie, Winnicott, Bowlby and Bollas, that makes it plausible to link religion with the attachment/relational axis of human development. This places the early mother – her face and responsive forms – at the centre of spiritual longing; empirical infant research, particularly the work of Stern, has provided concrete detail of the period in which such longing would originate.

In asserting that the deepest roots of religion lie in the preverbal core of the self, I do not claim that everything about religion can be understood in these terms. I suggest, however, that core elements of religious aspiration are linked to a need for containment and recognition; and that religion, like art and psychotherapy, creates new possibilities of redemption by providing self-containing forms. Since the original containment – the mother's *saying*, in Rilke's terms – is always incomplete, the need for a second chance (*a new beginning*: Balint 1932) is universal. Religion, art and psychotherapy each offer this chance in different, though related ways.

Notes

1 Suttie's (1935) 'primary need for companionship' may sound quaint and old fashioned to those used to a harder and quasi-scientific terminology. But the term has been reintroduced by Trevarthen (1979) who claims that the infant does not merely need an attachment object but someone with whom to engage in 'proto-conversation'.
2 These are merely the more important names in a renaissance of thinking about the maternal, pre-oedipal phases of development.
3 I am not suggesting that the earliest mother–infant relationship is lacking in sexual/erotic elements in the wider sense – clearly the infant is immersed in sensual, bodily experience. What I am arguing for, and trying to clarify, is the coexistence from the beginning of distinct threads or strands: one that is erotic, and to some extent corralled within the excited phases of instinctual activity in the traditional sense (e.g. feeding at the breast); another that from the beginning is relational and has more to do with communication and social contact. The smiling response would be an early manifestation of this second axis, as later, would the need for mirroring and attunement.
4 Hoffman (1989) uses the words 'know' and 'knowledge' in relation to her experience, but clearly she is not referring to cognitive knowledge, but immediate sensed apprehension, mediated through nonverbal sensory forms.
5 It may be surprising to realise that attunement, in Stern's sense, begins so late but this is a matter of definition. For Stern, attunement is linked to the beginnings of subjectivity and the possibility of intersubjective experience. Rich social exchanges occur throughout the first nine months but according to Stern lack the intersubjective dimension. Their focus is behavioural and interactive (games, imitations and so on) rather than affective. Attunement is linked to affect recognition and the first beginnings of (preverbal) symbolic exchange.

References

Balint, M. (1932) Character analysis and new beginning. In *Primary Love and Psychoanalytic Technique*. London: Hogarth (1952).

Bion, W. (1962) *Learning from Experience*. London: Heinemann Medical.

Bion, W. (1965) *Transformations*. London: Heinemann Medical.

Bollas, C. (1987) *The Shadow of the Object: Psychoanalysis of the Unthought Known*. London: Free Association Books.

Bowlby, J. (1969) *Attachment and Loss, Volume 1: Attachment*. London: Hogarth Press and the Institute of Psycho-Analysis.

Britton, R. (1998a) Naming and containing. In *Belief and Imagination: Explorations in Psychoanalysis*. London: Routledge.

Britton, R. (1998b) Existential anxiety: Rilke's *Duino Elegies*. In *Belief and Imagination: Explorations in Psychoanalysis*. London: Routledge.

Buber, M. (1937) *I and Thou*, trans. R. Gregor Smith. Edinburgh: T and T Clark.

Caldwell, L. (ed.) (2000) *Art, Creativity, Living*. Winnicott Studies Monograph Series. London: Karnac.

Ferenczi, S. (1926) *Final Contributions to the Problems of Psychoanalysis*. London: Hogarth Press.

Freud, S. (1927) *The Future of an Illusion*. SE 21.

Freud, S. (1930) *Civilization and its Discontents*. SE 21.

Freud, S. (1937) Lou Andreas-Salome. SE 23.

Hoffman, E. (1989) *Lost in Translation: Life in a New Language*. London: Heinemann.

Klein, J. (2004) *Jacob's Ladder: Essays on the Experience of the Ineffable in the Context of Contemporary Psychotherapy*. London: Karnac.

Rilke, R.M. (1960) *Selected Works, Volume 2: Poetry*, trans. J.B. Leishman. London: Hogarth Press.

Stern, D. (1985) *The Interpersonal World of the Infant: A View from Psychoanalysis and Developmental Psychology*. New York: Basic Books.

St John of the Cross (1542–1591) *Poems*, trans R. Cambell. London: Harvill Press (1951).

St Teresa of Avila (1515–1582) *The Life of the Holy Mother Teresa of Jesus*, trans. E. Allison Peers. London: Sheed and Ward (1946).

Suttie, I. (1935) *The Origins of Love and Hate*. London: Kegan Paul.

Symington, N. (1993) Is psychoanalysis a religion? In *Is Psychoanalysis Another Religion: Contemporary Essays on Spirit, Faith and Morality in Psychoanalysis*. London: Freud Museum.

Symington, N. (1994) *Emotion and Spirit: Questioning the Claims of Psychoanalysis and Religion*. London: Cassell.

Trevarthen, C. (1979) Communication and cooperation in early infancy: A description of primary intersubjectivity. In M. Bullowa (ed.) *Before Speech*. Cambridge: Cambridge University Press.

Winnicott, D.W. (1951) Transitional objects and transitional phenomena: A study of the first not-me possession. In *Collected Papers: Through Paediatrics to Psycho-Analysis*. London: Tavistock (1958).

Winnicott, D.W. (1967a) The location of cultural experience. In *Playing and Reality*. London: Tavistock (1971).

Winnicott, D.W. (1967b) Mirror role of mother and family in child development. In *Playing and Reality*. London: Tavistock (1971).

Wright, K. (1991) *Vision and Separation:Between Mother and Baby*. London: Free Association Books.

Wright, K. (2000) To make experience sing. In L. Caldwell (ed.) *Art, Creativity, Living*. London: Karnac.

—————————— 10 ——————————

RELIGION: THE GUARANTOR OF CIVILIZATION

Neville Symington

Darwin taught us that human beings did not spring out of the hand of God, a new formed species upon the earth with no pre-history. Since *Origin of Species* shattered our arrogant assumptions, enlightened biblical scholars have sifted out the religious truth in the myth of Adam and Eve and separated it from the scientific truth about humankind's biological and historical antecedents. Victorian England had until then smugly believed that we humans were on an entirely different plane from our animal cousins.[1] The human sciences, like psychology, sociology and anthropology, have rooted their scientific investigations upon this premiss: that because we are animals then investigation of them will tell us what we need to know about human beings. This opened a mineshaft to a rich vein of information out of which has come wagon loads of new knowledge about human beings. It has thrown neon lighting into the enigmas of human motivation. To give just one example. We have learned that if you put a food pellet at the end of one pathway in a maze, it does not teach a rat to run down that particular one as well as if you put a food pellet at the end of that pathway only intermittently. This has thrown light on why it is so difficult to divert gamblers away from their addictive sport. The Victorian attitude, prior to Darwin, that we humans had no familial bond with other animals prevented thinkers from even considering that we might learn more about ourselves through studying the behaviour of the brutes, to use a word that encapsulates this prejudice.

The excitement generated by this new perspective blinded a whole generation of social scientists to two huge developmental steps that occurred within the species *homo sapiens*. Modern humans have a brain size of about 1400 millilitres. If we go back to about 2.5 million years ago, our brain size was about 600 millilitres, then in the following million years it had leapt in size to 900 millilitres and from then to now another 500 millilitres. The social scientists left out of their reckoning this huge physiological development together with the mental correlate of this anatomical change: the move from barbarism to civilization. Damasio (1994: 112) makes an important distinction between that part of the brain whose structure *is determined* by the genome from that part which is *to be determined*. The latter depends on the former but its precise determination depends upon what he calls 'individual activity' and 'self-organizing pressures'. I take this to mean that there is within human activity a source that lies within the province of the organism's own planning and that it is this which made the process of civilization possible.

I am making the assumption here that this increase both in brain size and structure are the physiological correlates of that momentous change that occurred when humans created civilization. This could not have happened while our brain size was still half of what it is today. There is a distinct difference between human-kind in the uncivilized state and the same creature in the state of civilization. The boundary between the two states is less like a fence between two farmlands and more like the climate change that occurs meteorologically between a high and low pressure system. The change from one to the other is gradual but the difference between the two is huge. There is also no one moment when the child becomes an adult but although there is an identifiable continuum between the two yet there is a definite difference that we all recognize. So also the difference between humankind uncivilized and civilized is quite distinct. The social sciences, including psychoanalysis, have seriously underrated this difference.

Religion, art and science came to birth with the advent of civilization. So what exactly happened as civilization dawned on our planet? We shall certainly not understand religion or art or science unless we understand in essence what marked the passage from barbarism to civilization. Religion, art and science are all the fruits of civilization. So what was its distinguishing characteristic? I think the ability to create a civilization lies in the capacity to represent. For instance a $100 note may represent an hour of work for a carpenter, the purchase price of a twenty kilo bag of rice, the cost of a mobile phone or a train journey from Washington to New York. Money is a token that represents labour and goods. Think of the chaos that would ensue if suddenly an angel of oblivion swept over the world and removed that vital part of the brain that enables the mind to fashion representations. We would all fall into total chaos because not only would money become meaningless but so also would language, mathematics and the whole art world. We would in a flash all be savage hominids once more. These three mental activities, religion, art and science, must all therefore rely upon this basic capacity to represent. Let us look at them briefly and closely and then concentrate on religion.

The capacity to represent is what enabled *homo sapiens* to create civilization. This has been argued powerfully by the philosopher John Searle (1995) in his book *The Construction of Social Reality*, where he says, the capacity to attach a sense, a symbolic function, to an object that does not have that sense intrinsically is the precondition not only of language but of all institutional reality. The preinstitutional capacity to symbolize is the condition of possibility of the creation of all human institutions.

(Searle 1995: 75)

Religion, art and science are mental axes dependent upon this capacity to represent. Each of these mental axes has a different goal. The role of science is to tailor the environment for the physical, communicative and practical needs of humankind. The role of art is to represent the world as perceived through the senses in a variety of sensual modalities with the aim of giving pleasure through this form of communication. The role of religion however is to enhance representation itself and give it lasting form. When humankind realized this great treasure that had raised our species into a new form of living, it created an axis designed to conserve and develop it.

Representation is intimately linked with communication. Representation is communication with the self within the boundaries of the individual personality. Communication with the outside person is the symbol of this inner state of portrayal. When I use the word 'symbol' it does not just mean that it stands for, though this is one dimension of it, but also that it has an effective function. It brings about within the personality that which it symbolizes. What is external becomes internal but how is this possible? I believe it is because symbolic com-munication is possible only because of a third element in the personality both ontologically and epistemologically.

One of the earliest preoccupations of civilized human beings was a curiosity about our origins. Cosmogonies have a huge part in the mythology of early civilizations and also there is today the scientific correlate of this.[2] Behind this desire to know our origins is a wish to grasp the nature of existence. The first documented evidence of a comprehension of existence is in the writings of the Upanishads. These seers in ancient India, probably in the Indus Valley, reflected upon the character of existence itself. Reflection upon existence was an internal act of judgement and not a registration of sensations through the bodily senses. There are two sources of knowledge for human beings and there is a link between them. The first source of knowledge is that championed by Locke and known as empiricism. Locke had the idea of the mind as a *tabula rasa* – a blank slate – and that all which we know of the world comes through the senses and that this is our only source of knowledge. Later philosophers like Schiller, Schelling and finally Kant modified this by saying that through the imagination this information which comes through the senses is constructed into forms suitable to the mind but the principle was the same: that the source of knowledge is through what is impressed upon our senses either from outside the body or from within it. What is known arises from the stimuli from within or without that impinge upon the bodily senses. So this is one source of knowledge.

There is another source of knowledge which we associate with Aquinas, Spinoza, the Louvain School of Philosophy and Heidegger. I have been careful to leave out of these names the idealists such as Berkeley and Hegel. Essentially Berkeley, who is the purest instance of idealism in philosophy, believed that our contact is only with an idea in the mind. I am talking rather of those philosophers who have believed that there is a contact with the real world other than through the senses. It is that existence itself, shorn of all its myriad forms, is known not through the senses but through an inner act of comprehension. It is through this faculty that a horse in a dream is distinguished from an actual horse, how an hallucinated woman is distinguished from a real woman, how a tree produced by the imagination is distinguished from a real tree independent of my mind. When I state *That horse exists*, or *That woman exists* or *That tree exists* I am making a judgement whose focus is upon the existence itself rather than one of its particular forms. I can imagine the form of a horse or a woman or a tree but this is not what I am asserting. It is the existence that I am concerned to assert and it is an assent that contains certainty in it. This certainty arises through what I call the *faculty of existence*. Existence is a *primum cognitum*. I am going to call this process of knowledge *existence knowledge*. I prefer not to call it existential knowledge because so much is associated with the term 'existential' that may lead us to make false assumptions. I prefer also not to call it rational knowledge because this has become so closely associated in many people's minds with idealism. It is through this *existence knowledge* that I know what is a real horse and what is a horse fashioned in my imagination. I know what is real from what is not real and the practice of psychoanalysis demands that we should be able to distinguish between an hallucination and a real existent. This distinction can never be achieved unless these two sources of knowledge are recognized.

The *faculty of existence* is a form whose object is existence itself. Through this faculty I do not know existence in any particular but the thing itself. I do not know horseness or womanhood or tree-ness through this faculty. I only know existence itself whether it be in the form of a horse, woman or tree. Empirical knowledge is always of the particular, the varied and of what is different between things. *Existence knowledge* is of *One Thing* deprived of all quality, of all variation, of all difference. Rationalists, through failing to grasp this form of knowledge have all focused upon the inner idea but taken its presence paradoxically to have come through empirical knowledge. I say paradoxically because they downgrade the knowledge that comes through our senses just as empiricists scorn the knowledge that arises through the *faculty of existence*. The *faculty of existence* grasps existence in utter simplicity. Once one recognizes the nature of the object then it carries the conviction of utter simplicity. It is *one-ness*, it is *simple*, it cannot be other than a *unity*. Parmenides grasped this but because he could not reconcile it with the diversity which he observed through his senses he believed that the world of change and diversity must be an illusion. The failure to recognize that the mind is limited in its capacity to grasp these antinomies has led philosophers arrogantly to deny one of the two terms of the contradiction. The religious concept of *mystery* asserts the reality while recognizing the mind is unable to grasp how two apparent opposites can be reconciled yet knowing they must be. So *mystery* is an essential piece of equipment if we are to know the world as it is and not distort it because we insist on fitting it into the petty dimensions of our own limited minds.

How does this *faculty of existence* function? It functions on the most simple and elementary of principles. It has been called the *principle of co-naturality*.[3] It is on the principle of there being a sympathy between two objects sharing the same nature – existence knowing existence; of their being a sympathy due to the oneness that exists in the two objects.

So let us just summarize my position so far. It is that there are two sources of knowledge: one through the senses which give the particulars, the qualities of objects, both the primary and secondary characteristics and the other through the *faculty of existence* and that the link between this existence knowledge and empirical knowledge depends upon what I have called the *principle of co-naturality* – a shared nature between the knower and the known. I need to elaborate further upon the nature of *co-naturality*.

If we take the *principle of co-naturality* as the factor making knowledge possible then we posit that it is through this same principle that links the two sources of knowledge: that there is some common denominator between these two sources that demands a connection. *Co-naturality* is a principle in the sphere of knowledge as basic as gravity in the physical world. So just as in the *faculty of existence* there is a process of abstraction through which the existence, shorn of all its forms, is abstracted so a common denominator is reached. So what I posit is that there is *in the form of knowledge* something that is common both to sensory processing and the act through which existence itself is grasped. In both processes there is a taking in. One can think of it this way also: that it is *one* taking in of reality but it functionally bifurcates although it is one act and therefore co-naturality is a finding of itself. It is like the two eyes which each take in a different image but are conjoined in the visual cortex. It is one vision and not two.

I said that in both processes there is a taking in and yet this is not accurate. In *existence knowledge* there is a reflection upon what is. It is not that existence is taken in from outside to inside but that I realize what it is, both internally and externally. I take in that which is in. We shall expand on this in a moment. How am I able to 'realize' it? It must be that realization of itself is of the essence of existence. There is nothing outside of existence so reflective knowledge of it must be one of its characteristics. It is possible however to refute that which we are.

This oneness outside of which there is nothing is the core of all religions. It is that which gives meaning to individual acts and discrete entities. Today we are so influenced by a linguistic philosophy which finds meaning through the place of a word in the structure of a sentence that we have lost what meaning truly is: the unifying element in an array of factors. Wilfred Bion was rooted in this older ontological tradition when he designated the *selected fact* as that which gave sense to a range of elements and brought them into a recognizable pattern. Ultimately linguistic philosophy negates religion. It is profoundly an atheistical doctrine. This core of religion was stated with stark clarity by Tolstoy:

> Every religion is an establishment by man of his relation to the Infinite Existence of which he feels himself a part, and from which relation he obtains the guidance for his conduct . . . True religion is the establishment by man of such a relation to the Infinite Life around him, as, while connecting his life with this Infinitude and directing his conduct is also in agreement with his reason and with human knowledge.
>
> (Tolstoy 1899: 213–214)

All great religions have stressed the centrality of love or compassion. This is so of Hinduism, Buddhism, Jainism, Judaism, Zoroastrianism, Christianity and Islam. The reason is that, as I just said above, the existence which is our task to realize can be put another way. It is that we are called to love it; to love that which is us. It sounds odd to speak this way yet it is possible not to love that which is us. A basic tenet of psychoanalysis is that to deny something which is us, which is true of us, results in ill-health. The word 'denial' is too bland; 'hatred' is what it is. The aim of psychoanalysis is to reclaim split-off parts which means that those parts which are hated need to be loved. So that which is us can either be loved or hated. Moses de León, who is presumed to be the author of the Zohar, a Jewish mystical text, says that something is evil in virtue of it being out of relation with the rest of the personality:

> moral evil, according to the Zohar, is always either something which becomes separated and isolated, or something which enters into a relation for which it is not made . . . The totality of divine potencies forms a harmonious whole, and as long as each stays in relation to all others, it is sacred and good.
>
> (Scholem 1974: 236–237)

This gives expression to the psychoanalytic notion of 'split-off' parts of the personality but placed with a background in which it makes sense both philosophically and religiously. The difference between philosophy and religion is in essence that in the former the observer remains outside the object of scrutiny whereas in the latter the observer is included which is why Tolstoy says that *he obtains guidance for his conduct*.

When it is loved it is embraced and becomes as a consequence represented in the personality; when it is hated it is expelled. The expulsion is the hatred, primitive hatred. This expulsion may be into the body, into sexual activity, into those to whom I am closely attached or any realities to which I am attached be they external institutions, races or cultures or internal ideologies with their external correlates.

I need to insert an emphasis here. The definition which Tolstoy gives of religion does not apply to any one particular cultural religious expression but the heart of the matter that is to be found in all the great religious traditions. We are so imbued with the idea that religion is the particular cultural form of it that we were brought up with, that it is difficult to connect with a concept which is quite different but, at the same time, fundamental. Religion, as Tolstoy defines it, is *natural religion*. This means that it can be arrived at through an act of insight. It does not require faith, or at least faith in the way it is defined in the Judeo-Christian tradition. Natural Religion has been defined thus by C.C.J. Webb (1915):

> Those things in religion, the appeal of which meets a universal response, whether they be statements about the essential and eternal nature of reality, apprehended by the reason as true in their own right, from whatever source they have been learned, or whether they be precepts of conduct, the moral obligatoriness of which, when once propounded, is also perceived, as Kant would say, *a priori*, these will constitute, so it has seemed to some, *Natural Religion*.
>
> (Webb 1915: 33–34)

This is what is being referred to as religion in this chapter.

Representation arises as a consequence of an act of love towards an element within the self. Without representation we simply react in an instinctual way to the external stimulus; we are the playthings of the environment; those ancient hominids from whom we are descended would never have left their ecological niche in the Olduvai Gorge in eastern Africa. This instinctive animal response to an external stimulus is of course exactly the psychological doctrine of what has become known as classical conditioning theory, first championed by Pavlov, but then elaborated and systematized by Clark Hull, J.B. Watson, Skinner and others. This view is closely supported by that other psychological buttress: the homeostatic theory which has been embraced unquestioningly in all psychological circles from Pavlov to Freud.

It is only through representation that those ancestors of ours were able to fashion the environment to suit their needs and therefore spread out and colonize almost every corner of the globe. That ability to fashion our surroundings to satisfy the bidding of our restricted anatomy relies on our capacity to represent. Why so? To answer this we have to look more closely at what occurs when we embrace with love an element in ourselves. The representation is a creation. When our ancestors drew those animals on the ceilings of caves at Altamira and Lascaux 30,000 years ago it was evidence of a capacity to create a form from the animals that they had encountered on their hunting trips but this ability flowed from a more primaeval work that had occurred. These paintings flowed from a representational creature. Self representation occurred before representation of the outer world. The question that confronts us is how is it possible for human beings to turn into themselves and create from elements that are already there? I think the answer has to lie in what I have called above *existence knowledge*. That this knowledge which flows out of that unity of existence creates from the elements of empirical knowledge a new form which we call representation rather in the way in which a composer creates the birdsong in the woods into a piano sonata. Richard Church (1964), who was drawn first to Wordsworth and then to the philosopher who had inspired the poet, Spinoza, says this:

> From my increasing devotion to Wordsworth, I went farther, to the philosopher who had fired Wordsworth's early vision during the creative years . . . Spinoza was that guide. His divine genius flashed over my dark world at that time, a lighthouse in stormy weather. It has never failed me since.
> It still stands as the image of unity, of coherence, of mutual, interdependent and sustaining force in all things, the 'rocks, and stones and trees', the organic creatures from mollusc to Man, the superb and indifferent mathematics of the galaxies within the atom, and the cosmic structures, which in their accumulation and rhythm are the Universe, the Substance, the Father.
> (Church 1964: 96–97)

Existence knowledge is Existence knowing Itself and in Itself are the varied forms which are known through the senses. No ontology, neither the Hindu one embraced in the west by Spinoza nor the Judeo-Christian one is able to reconcile how the diversity is possible within the unity yet the knowledge we have from these two different informational pathways tell us that it must be so. The mind is not capable of reconciling this contradiction. It is a *mystery*. Spinoza's ontology is founded on the basis that there is one substance and it manifests itself in different modes but quite how that is so, it is not possible to explain. The Judeo-Christian ontology is based on the idea that there is an Eternal Unity and that the world of diversity is created by it. It does not explain why this Eternal Unity, or God, created and continues to create the world of variety. So both ontologies are defective but I prefer the one of Spinoza for the following reasons. First, under this dispensation it is not possible to fall back on an outer figure who instructs us, it forces us to reason. Second, it accommodates better to Reality knowing Itself and in the particular manifestation of myself and yourself.

This Reality is the source of representation. As soon as a thinker denies this Reality and the knowledge that is achieved through it then the very basis on which civilization depends is being torpedoed. At the level of mental life therefore the human has sunk back into barbarism. It is not by chance therefore that as the great civilizations developed in Greece, Iran, Palestine, India and China that great religious teachers arose – Socrates, Zarathustra, Isaiah and Jeremiah and Ezekiel, the seers of the Upanishads, Mahavira, the Buddha and Lao-Tzu. These were men who realized what lay at the foundation of the human capacity to create civilization. They realized that this was being undermined and that this endangered the whole project of humankind's civilizing aims. The technological and aesthetic capacities were in evidence but the very basis that made these skills possible were constantly under threat: that they had become ends in themselves. Perhaps the Hebrew Prophets gave the most potent expression to this:

> They are ignorant, those who carry about
> their idol of wood,
> those who pray to a god
> that cannot save . . .
> There is no other god besides me,
> a God of integrity and a saviour;
> there is none apart from me.
> (Isaiah 45: 20–21, Jerusalem Bible)

The 'god of integrity' is that Reality, the Infinite or Absolute that guarantees the capacity to represent. The idol of wood can stand for any scientific invention or aesthetic creation. As soon as it is made into an end in itself civilization collapses and is substituted with savagery. Scientific or aesthetic instruments are no guarantee of civilization. They are products of a civilizing process but function as civilizing agents only if they are servants of thinking and representation whose foundation lies in religion, properly understood. We are shocked by the slave trade with its Middle Passage in the eighteenth century, Armenian genocide, the Stalinist purges in Russia in the 1930s, the Holocaust, the massacre in Rwanda, the genocide in former Yugoslavia. Here the instruments fashioned by civilization have been taken up but used by barbarism. The prime difference between barbarism and civilization is that in the former there is action without thinking or symbolization whereas in the latter there is both. Symbolization is a particular case of representation and thinking is founded upon it.

Rather than base our psychology upon human capacity to represent, it has been built upon the instincts. Instincts are the biological signalling system that drives the animal to seek food, water, warmth or protection. They are those secondary processes that guarantee the survival of the organism.[4] But these are secondary to life itself. What we require is a psychology built upon an analysis first of life and then of human life in its fully developed civilized state.

Instincts are one of the means through which the organism survives, continues living but they do not tell us what life itself is. We need first to define for ourselves what life itself is and then the particular form it assumes in human life. The philosopher Bergson (1919) defined it as *the tendency to act on matter*. This is correct as far as it goes but is, as it were, an outsider's definition. Streeter (1935) came closer to the core of it when he said that essentially life was the autonomous capacity for self creation. The psychology underlying both behaviourism (with its contemporary cognitive therapeutic form) and also psychoanalysis, as formulated in Freud's metapsychological papers, assumes that the living organism is determined by the external stimulus rather than being determined *partly* by the external stimulus and *partly* by a source from within the organism. It is not that what has sometimes been called Freud's clinical theory does not envisage activity that originates within the human organism but that his metapsychology does not encompass this. It is inanimate objects that move only through the agency of an external object but not living ones. What distinguishes a living thing from this dead object is that there is a source of movement from within the organism as well as from outside it. With human life within civilization there is additionally the capacity to represent the existing life within the organism. Psychology urgently needs to base its philosophy upon what essentially constitutes life rather than what is characteristic of the inanimate world. Isaiah Berlin (1979) said:

> If anthropomorphism was falsely to endow the inanimate world with human minds and wills, there was presumably a world which it was proper to endow with precisely these attributes, namely, the world of man. Consequently a natural science of men treated as purely natural entities, on a par with rivers and plants and stones rested on a cardinal error.
>
> (Berlin 1979: 96)

I think Freud in his metapsychology would have been judged erroneous in terms such as Berlin is describing.

I think the present surge of inquiry into the nature of consciousness will ultimately lead us back to religion and away from an areligious scientism and aesthetics and I suspect the inquiry itself is being driven by this search. What is certain is that religion is the guarantor of civilization and without it we collapse into barbarism.

Notes

1   Statements like this are never accurate. There had been thinkers prior to Darwin who had intimated what he elaborated. People such as Lamarck, Erasmus Darwin and Wallace, his contemporary.
2   The Big Bang Theory, for instance.
3   This term was formulated by the Spanish mystic, John of Avila.
4   The primary processes being the neural circuits of the brain stem and hypothalamus that govern the endocrine glands that are indispensable for the maintenance of metabolic function (see Damasio 1994: 118).

References

Bergson, H. (1919) *Creative Evolution*. London: Macmillan.

Berlin, I. (1979) The divorce between the sciences and the humanities. In *Against the Current*. London: Hogarth Press.

Church, R. (1964) *The Voyage Home*. London: Heinemann.

Damasio, A. (1994) *Descartes' Error*. New York: G.P. Putnam's Sons.

Scholem, G. (1974) *Major Trends in Jewish Mysticism*. New York: Schocken.

Searle, J. (1995) *The Construction of Social Reality*. New York and London: Free Press.

Streeter, B.H. (1935) *Reality*. London: Macmillan.

Tolstoy, L.N. (1899) *What is Religion?* In *The Complete Works of Lyof N. Tolstoi*. New York: Thomas Y. Crowell.

Webb, C.C.J. (1915) *Studies in the History of Natural Theology*. Oxford: Clarendon Press.

PART FOUR

Echoes between psychoanalysis
and specific religious traditions

11

PSYCHOANALYSIS
AND JUDAISM

Stephen Frosh

Introduction

Among the complexities involved in any discussion of Judaism is the puzzle created by the varied strands of Jewish life. Jewish 'identity', Jewish 'experience' and Judaism as a religion are interwoven yet also separable strands of Jewish existence: feeling oneself to be Jewish, finding oneself to be the victim of anti-Semitism, and practising and/or believing in the tenets of Judaism are not the same thing. Jews can be secular or religious, assimilated or separatist; 'Jewish' ways of behaving and thinking may be attributes of culture and 'ethnicity' (with all the uncertainties of that notion) or they may be specifically religious, or – quite commonly – both. What this means is that exploration of any 'Judaism and . . .' phenomenon requires careful attention to the question of whether one is describing a set of sociological issues (Jews are involved in this or that way), or religious ones.

In the case of 'Judaism and Psychoanalysis' the separation between cultural and religious affiliations is important in many ways. As is documented briefly below, there can be little doubt that psychoanalysis was profoundly shaped by the experiences of its Jewish originators, especially Freud, and that the 'Jewishness' of these experiences in terms of modes of historical, cultural and ethical awareness left a lasting mark on the discipline and the profession. On the other hand, none of these originators (again including Freud) were religious, and few post-Freudian psychoanalysts have been practising religious Jews. Yet if the influence of 'Jewishness' on psychoanalysis is more obvious than that of 'Judaism', it is nevertheless the case that these things are linked, and that Jewish identity has been forged in the context of religious practices, beliefs and assumptions over many generations. Consequently, it can be argued that 'Judaic' as well

205

as 'Jewish' ways of thinking infiltrate psychoanalysis, or more cautiously, that there are similarities between psychoanalysis and Judaism that are not accidental, and that throw light on both.

In what follows, the cultural influence of Jewish identity (specifically, Freud's) on psychoanalysis is briefly traced before links between Judaism and psychoanalysis are explored. The argument is that because of the cultural factors, psychoanalysis also has a Judaic heritage, and that this can be observed in several ways. Speculations on parallels between psychoanalysis and Jewish mysticism have some force, but are relatively non-specific, in that similar parallels can be made between psychoanalysis and other mystical traditions. What psychoanalysis and Judaism share more deeply, however, is a fascination with depth interpretation, with seeing 'beyond' or 'beneath' what is readily available, and a concern with, even promotion of, the bounding of desire by law. It is upon these shared interests that the final sections of this chapter are focused.

The Jewish heritage

Psychoanalysis has its origins in the mixed experience of Jewish emancipation in the late nineteenth century, and specifically in the life story of one classic 'secular Jew', Sigmund Freud.[1] These origins and the heritage they left to the new discipline resonate in the continuing notion of psychoanalysis as a 'Jewish science', a notion that had its most bitter apogee during the Nazi era, but is maintained in the general association of psychoanalysis with Jews and Jewish culture, despite this being less sociologically true now than at any previous point. What should be noted here is that the 'Jewish science' label may have strong anti-Semitic connotations and was clearly and dangerously derogatory in Nazi times, but there are also many serious Jewish scholars interested in the links between psychoanalysis and Jewish thought (e.g. Bakan 1958; Klein 1985; Roith 1987; Diller 1991; Gilman 1993; Yerushalmi 1991), making any simple repudiation of the 'Jewish science' idea difficult to sustain.

The claimed link between psychoanalysis and Jewish identity depends only partly on the fact that most of its originators in Europe were Jews, although this was certainly the case: as Klein (1985: 93) points out, 'Until March 6 1907, when Carl Jung and . . . Ludwig Binswanger, attended their first meeting in Vienna, every member of the [psychoanalytic] circle – by this time, there were about 20 – was Jewish.' That there were social reasons for this Jewish dominance is attested to not only by the circumstances in Vienna at the time during which psycho-analysis emerged, but also by its rather different history in places where different conditions prevailed – notably in Britain, where the most significant early analysts were intellectual and literary non-Jews, some of them with clear anti-Semitic tendencies (Frosh 2003). More significantly, the claim that psychoanalysis should be considered a 'Jewish science' relates to the idea that Jewish thought, Jewish philosophy and Jewish history flooded its foundations, investing it with the specific inward-consciousness of the Jews, who were newly released in the nineteenth century from their ghettoes and at least some of their traditions. That is, the claim is based on the idea of cultural inheritance: that however atheistic these early psychoanalytic Jews were, they could not but pursue a way of looking at things which was 'Jewish'. What this 'Jewishness' consisted in was not an explicitly religious perspective – not *Judaism* – but an approach to argument and interpretation established over centuries in which debates over the meanings of texts were the main expression of cultural achievement. The claim is therefore not just that Jews became psychoanalysts because they felt comfortable and familiar in this role, but it is also an argument about intellectual history: the *reason* they felt so comfortable was that the psychoanalytic world-view was so much like the Jewish one.

Much of this argument is focused on Freud himself, who epitomised the kind of secular Jew who played such a powerful role in revolutionising western culture at the turn of the twentieth century. This does not depend on the assertion that Freud himself was committed to his Jewish identity, although there is now not much doubt that he was. In a famous exploration of the impact of psychoanalysis, Philip Rieff (1959) credits it with the invention of what he calls (in gender-blind language) 'Psychological Man'. 'Psychological Man' already sounds stereotypically Jewish, characterised as he is with a tendency to be reflexive, introspective, anxious and depressed; for Rieff, this is the nature of the western human subject throughout the first half of the twentieth century, when the influence of psychoanalysis was at its greatest. Yosef Hayim Yerushalmi (1991) takes this further by positing the 'Psychological Jew' behind the 'Psychological Man', with psychoanalysis being a branch of the general cultural explosion that was to a large extent dependent on, and carried forward by, the progressive secularism that arose in the wake of Jewish emancipation.

> Alienated from classical Jewish texts, Psychological Jews tend to insist on inalienable Jewish traits. Intellectuality and independence of mind, the highest ethical and moral standards, concern for social justice, tenacity in the face of persecution – these are among the qualities they will claim, if called upon, as quintessentially Jewish.
>
> (Yerushalmi 1991: 10)

The attributes of the Psychological Jew summarised by Yerushalmi neatly define the ideal mentally healthy character proposed by classical psychoanalysis and in many respects embodied by Freud (at least as remembered and idealised by his followers), although post-Freudian analysts have added a less obviously 'Jewish' emphasis on fulfilling interpersonal relationships. The ideal person of early psychoanalysis is less worried about how he or she gets on with others, than with living an intellectually coherent and ethical life in the face of the immense instinctual and external pressures towards corruption – a rather neat parallel to the secular Jew balancing between inner doubts and external pressures to convert or assimilate.

The secular Jew's combination of commitment to intellectual goals and ethical achievement, alongside resentment at the demeaning effects of anti-Semitism, is very much the story of Freud, although as Yerushalmi (1991) notes there are also ways in which Freud deviates from it. It is also a characterisation of an interior way of being, hovering around questions of belonging and otherness, of historical determination and freedom, which demonstrably influences modern Jewish identities, and perhaps modern identities in general. This 'Psychological Jew' is not a Freudian creation, but it is deeply inflected by, as well as reflected in, Freudianism, with its unsettled, constantly searching, forever-analysing hunt for some elusive truth. Taking this further, what arises is the question of *marginality* as a necessary condition for the emergence and influence of psychoanalysis. Could someone who was surrounded by the comfort of social acceptance, rather than subjected to the ambivalent love/loathe dynamic characteristic of religious and racial anti-Semitism as of all racism, have stood far enough outside that culture to offer the devastatingly ironic critique that Freud offered? Does one have to be an outsider to see *in*? Freud himself thought so: writing in 1926 in a famous letter to the B'nai Brith, he comments that because he was a Jew, 'I found myself free of many prejudices which restrict others in the use of the intellect; as a Jew I was prepared to be in the opposition and to renounce agreement with the "compact majority"' (Freud 1961: 368). The notion of the 'compact majority' here comes from Ibsen's play, *An Enemy of the People*, neatly emphasising Freud's somewhat paranoid, but also well-founded, sense of being a repudiated outsider who nevertheless speaks the truth. A mode of well-founded paranoia (of the form, 'Just because I'm paranoid it does not mean they are not out to get me'), one might hazard, that is not uncharacteristic of Jews as a whole. This also relates to many aspects of Jewish culture emphasising its analytic dimension: Talmudic patterns of exegesis, free thinking within a heavily structured pattern of rules, fascination with words, with reading, with critical commentary, a relentless and unending search for another way of looking at things. 'Intellectuality and independence of mind,' writes Yerushalmi (1991: 10), 'the highest ethical and moral standards, concern for social justice, tenacity in the face of persecution': both Jews and psychoanalysts have needed these attributes, and sometimes they have possessed them.

Freud's relationship with his Jewish identity was notoriously ambivalent and has been the subject of a great deal of historical, psychoanalytic and frankly speculative scholarship. For Edward Said (2003):

> To say of Freud's relationship with Judaism that it was conflicted is to venture an understatement. At times he was proud of his belonging, even though he

was irremediably anti-religious; at other times he expressed annoyance with
and unmistakable disapproval of Zionism.

(Said 2003: 35–36)

Indeed, Freud worked hard to present himself as someone alienated from even
vestigial relationships with a Jewish *religious* identity. In a famous letter of 1930
to A.A. Roback, he comments:

> It may interest you to know that my father did indeed come from a Chassidic
> background. He was 41 when I was born and had been estranged from his
> native environment for almost 20 years. My education was so un-Jewish that
> today I cannot even read your dedication, which is evidently written in
> Hebrew. In later life I have often regretted this lack in my education.
>
> (Freud 1961: 394)

Noting the force of Freud's repudiation of Judaism, and his aggressive critique
of all religion, which he saw as 'illusion', Halpern (1999) suggests that it might
reflect an antagonism towards his father that was projected onto the religion
itself. In this view Freud, disappointed in his father, refuted the claims of all
father-religions to authority:

> He believed that God and religion had no right to demand submission
> because they had not lived up to their promise. God, far from being ideal-
> izable, was seen as the opposite – merely an illusion . . . For Freud, God
> represents the disappointing father whose demands were nonetheless still felt,
> and which Freud needed vehemently to reject.
>
> (Halpern 1999: 1200)

In contrast, Halpern argues, Freud sought out the 'maternal' warmth of Jewish
life through its cultural heritage. (Parenthetically, it might be said that the idea
of Freud as repudiating the *paternal* seems far-fetched, however complex his
relationship might have been to his father.) Even when, as in the letter to the
B'nai Brith organisation mentioned above, he is at his most explicit in acknowledging his continuing links with Jews and Jewish identity, Freud distances himself
from its most characteristic outward forms – religion and Zionism.

> What tied me to Jewry was – I have to admit it – not the faith not even the
> national pride, for I was always an unbeliever, have been brought up without
> religion, but not without respect for the so-called 'ethical' demands of human
> civilisation.
>
> (Freud 1961: 367)

Despite these clear disavowals, Yerushalmi (1991) rather persuasively documents
evidence suggesting not only that Freud's father remained knowledgeable about,

and to some degree at least committed to, Judaism throughout his life (contrary to Freud's assertion about his 'estrangement'), but also that Freud retained at least some knowledge of Judaism. The claim, for instance, that he barely even recognised Hebrew when he saw it seems unlikely, especially given the trouble that his father took to assemble a *melitza* (a compendium of biblical quotations) in Hebrew to write into the flyleaf of his gift of the rebound family Bible on the occasion of Freud's thirty-fifth birthday (Yerushalmi 1991: 71ff). Freud himself, taught religion by the inspirational Samuel Hammerschlag, may have focused on Judaism's ethical principles, but is unlikely never to have come into contact with its forms or its language. Indeed, even though the Freud family 'spoke German and ignored such observances as kashrut and the Sabbath' once they had moved to Vienna when Freud was 3 years old, they still recognised some major Jewish holidays and some scholars claim that Freud would still have heard his father's 'adept . . . Hebrew recitation of the Passover service' (Klein 1985: 42).

Freud's Jewish background has also been claimed to have had a substantial effect on the content of his theories, particularly in relation to mystical traditions (Bakan 1958) and to Jewish ideas on feminine sexuality. Roith (1987), for example, argues that:

> The centuries-long Jewish emphasis on intellectual and spiritual values and the curious relationship that the Jew, partly as a result, has had with the body and its expressions, have important implications for Freud's doctrines, especially for his theories of sex and gender. These values . . . are intimately bound up with the differential perception and treatment of the sexes in Judaism and with patterns of child-rearing in Jewish families.
>
> (Roith 1987: 5)

Carefully documenting traditional religious attitudes towards women, sex and the family, Roith (1987: 140) shows compellingly that religiously infused cultural attitudes (for example, that the sexual instinct must be 'mastered, never denied') are markedly parallel to Freudian conceptions, suggesting a shared world-view if not a direct causal connection. More 'mystically', perhaps, the Jewish connection can be seen in the distinctively self-aggrandising energy which Freud put into his creation of a new vision of how people function which makes it possible for the first time to see as problematic that which might otherwise be taken for granted: people's intentions and motivations, their wishes and, indeed, their dreams. Consequently, in its magical prescience and capacity to bring the hidden to light, to bring 'news of the plague' to those who think they have escaped it, psychoanalysis can be conceptualised as a new form of prophecy.

This image of prophecy, especially in the sense of a special wisdom given only to initiates, is one which hovers over some of Freud's most speculative and penetrating work, as in the famous conclusion (albeit a disavowal of the prophet role) to *Civilization and its Discontents*: 'I have not the courage to rise up before my fellow-men as a prophet, and I bow to their reproach that I can offer them no consolation' (Freud 1930: 339). David Bakan, in his preface to the 1990 edition of his *Sigmund Freud and the Jewish Mystical Tradition*, notes the connections between prophecy and dreaming as worked out in one of the most influential classical Jewish texts, Moses Maimonides' late-twelfth-century book, *The Guide for the Perplexed*. Maimonides himself writes, in a style rather reminiscent of Freud, that 'Prophecy is given either in a vision, or in a dream, as we have said so many times, and we will not constantly repeat it' (1956: 240) and describes the dream state as the only one in which a prophet (with the exception of Moses, the greatest prophet of all) can hear words spoken.

> It appears to me improbable that a prophet should be able to perceive in a prophetic vision God speaking to him; the action of the imaginative faculty does not go so far, and therefore we do not notice this in the case of the ordinary prophets . . . But it is possible to explain the passages in which a prophet is reported to have heard in the course of a vision words spoken to him, in the following manner: at first he has had a vision, but subsequently he fell into a deep sleep, and the vision was changed into a dream. According to this explanation, it is only in a dream that the prophet can hear words addressed to him.
>
> (Maimonides 1956: 244–245)

Freud, similarly, learns the secret of dreams *in* a dream: 'In this House, on July 24th 1895, the Secret of Dreams was revealed to Dr Sigm. Freud' (Freud's letter of 12 June 1900, to Fliess, commemorating the dream of Irma's injection; quoted in Freud 1900: 199). Real prophecy occurs when vision is combined with words, and this happens only through and in dreams. The dream is not, therefore, purely mystical; it is also a space of a certain kind of rationality, in which words are delivered and a message conveyed. Bakan (1990) puts all this together to see Freud in the tradition of Maimonides:

> Freud appreciated just how it was that in the dream there is a rational appre-hension which gets worked over in the 'dream work', in the generation of the dream by the imagination using the images of common human experi-ence, including the sexual. Freud, in so far as he had a therapeutic intention, followed in the path of Maimonides who offered his book as a cure for 'heartache and perplexity', and followed the tradition that being 'anxious in one's heart' is the critical qualification for receiving instruction in the esoteric topics.
>
> (Bakan 1990: xxvii–xxviii)

There is substantial debate over whether or not Freud had detailed knowledge of Jewish sources (Diller 1991) and it is clearly likely that Maimonides' exact ideas on dreams would have escaped him. However, whatever the direct influence of factors connected with Jewish tradition, the tone and content of much of *The Interpretation of Dreams* – one of the founding texts of psychoanalysis – is unquestionably biblical, as if Freud is attempting to use elements of his Jewish background in creating his own book of origins. Moreover, in the context of Freud's explicit recognition that the book was written as a response to his father's death and is much concerned with showing that he has 'come to something' despite his father's warning that he would not (Lear 2005), the book becomes in part an engagement with Jewish patriarchy, and in large part with the ways in which visions and dreams of justification and immortality emerge in the construction of historical movements and systems of belief. While this might not be a uniquely 'Jewish' theme, it is true of Jewish thought throughout history, from the Bible and the Kabbalah to the Messianic stream in Zionism (Rose 2005).

Psychoanalysis as Judaism

The effects on the development of psychoanalysis of these elements of Freud's Jewish identity, of anti-Semitism and of the Jewish make-up of the early psychoanalytic movement has been much discussed and documented in the literature (see Frosh 2005, for a review). As can be seen from the material presented so far, not only is there plenty of evidence that Jewish history and identity were major factors in shaping psychoanalysis in Europe and hence in the United States and many other countries, but also there are indications that assumptions embedded in *Judaism* have found their way into psychoanalytic thought. Some commentators, for instance Yerushalmi (1991), see this as an intentional move: writing a 'monologue with Freud', he concludes,

> I think that in your innermost heart you believed that psychoanalysis is itself a further, if not final, metamorphosed extension of Judaism, divested of its illusory religious forms but retaining its essential monotheistic characteristics, at least as you understood and described them. In short, I think you believed that just as you are a godless Jew, psychoanalysis is a godless Judaism.
> (Yerushalmi 1991: 99)

The idea here is that psychoanalysis replaces Judaism with something that develops its fundamental assumptions and perceptions for a scientific, non-religious epoch. Freud certainly saw himself as carrying on in the traditions of rabbinic Judaism with its concern for intellect and learning, for maintaining culture through promotion of scholarly values over physical ones. In his last major work, *Moses and Monotheism* (1939), Freud argues that Judaism has survived – and is superior to other religions, including or especially Christianity – because of its adoption of an abstract notion of God, not tied to sensuality or iconography. This forces the intellect into operation, constructing a psychological attitude in which analysis is primary and rational thought is the highest ideal. That this is an aspect of Jewish superiority is a claim made explicit by Freud, writing under the shadow of Nazism:

> The pre-eminence given to intellectual labours throughout some two thousand years in the life of the Jewish people has, of course, had its effect. It has helped to check the brutality and the tendency to violence which are apt to appear where the development of muscular strength is the popular ideal.
>
> (Freud 1939: 115)

Moreover, a story he tells in *Moses and Monotheism*, of how the Jewish people transcended their destruction as a nation by the Romans through maintaining knowledge of its scholarly traditions, presented to Freud's mind a strict analogy with the psychoanalytic movement, which he used when leaving Austria after the Anschluss. In his last speech to the Vienna Psychoanalytic Society, on 13 March 1938, he said:

> After the destruction of the Temple in Jerusalem by Titus, Rabbi Yochanan ben Zakkai asked for permission to open a school at Yavneh for the study of Torah. We are going to do the same. We are, after all, used to persecution by our history, tradition and some of us by personal experience.
>
> (Diller 1991: 206)

While the impetus for this quote is one of identification with Jewish *history*, it also embodies the Judaic assumption that 'study of the Torah' is the central component of Jewish life. Now the psychoanalysts are 'going to do the same' – that is study Torah, in their case the holy texts of Freudian psychoanalysis. The 'we' in all this is clearly a reference to Jews; the identity of the Jewish and psychoanalytic experience is seen as pretty exact; and the Jewish *religious* assumption that the key activity for a meaningful life is study, is taken by Freud as the blueprint for psychoanalysis' survival. Freud confirmed this with his greetings to representatives of the London Jewish community on his arrival in that city in 1938: 'We Jews have always known how to respect spiritual values. We preserved our unity through ideas, and because of them we have survived to this day' (Diller 1991: 122).

The intellectual bent to both Judaism and psychoanalysis is picked up by Ostow (1982) in one of the few extended attempts to explore the relationship between these traditions from within the psychoanalytic movement itself.

> Judaism and psychoanalysis therefore share the basic principle that one must acquire knowledge in order to share the benefits that each offers: leading a

life of mitzvah and obtaining its rewards, in the first instance; and freedom from disability and pain of mental illness, in the second. They both posit that special knowledge is a prerequisite for elitist status and for personal mastery over a crucial aspect of one's destiny.

(Ostow 1982: 4)

This particular argument opens into two directions in relation to the Judaism–psychoanalysis parallel. One, to be examined more fully below, is the emphasis that both traditions have on the bounding of desire by law: in the case of Judaism that of the *halacha*; in psychoanalysis, the Oedipus complex. The second direction has become somewhat characteristic of more general links between psychoanalysis and religious *experience*, for example in the work connecting psychoanalysis and Buddhism. This is to see psychoanalysis as linked with the *mystical* elements of the religious (here, Jewish) tradition. Ostow's reference to 'special knowledge' in the quotation given above is reminiscent of Ernst Gellner's (1992) criticism of psychoanalysis as something mystical, in a very strict sense of the term.

Mystical experience can best be defined as follows: an intense emotional experience, which at the same time purports to be and is felt as being the acquisition of knowledge which is important, privileged, and out of the ordinary.

(Gellner 1992: 41)

The suggestion here is that it is the personally transformative quality of psycho-analytic encounters that is central to its action and that attracts adherents, and that this is manifested as a mode of knowledge that has intense emotional effects. It is mystical because it is not characterised by careful examination of knowledge claims, but rather by a powerful subjective experience, after which the person concerned is no longer the same. Ostow's description of psychoanalytic trans-formation can be seen as in accordance with this view, in that he consciously utilises the imagery of mysticism to suggest that psychoanalysis is participating in what is an ancient tradition of self-liberation, shared by Jews, Christians and others.

Both patient and analyst approach the treatment with the conviction that the knowledge to be acquired will liberate the former from inner restraints. It is secret knowledge, unknown to the public, to the analyst, and to the patient. It is esoteric in the sense that it can be acquired only by a certain kind of revelation . . . The patient's attitude toward acquiring the liberating insight suggests the Gnostic principle that learning the names of the existing demons, and techniques for overpowering or evading them, will permit the soul to ascend to the *pleroma*, the fullness of God's life.

(Ostow 1982: 7)

As is clear from various scholarly studies of Jewish mysticism, all of them carried out in the wake of Gershom Scholem's (1941) seminal *Major Trends in Jewish Mysticism*, this type of illuminative experience is characteristic of early 'merkabah' mysticism, in which the initiate is empowered to reach a state of consciousness enabling perception of the glory of God's throne. 'Learning the names' (of God) is one route to such an exalted state, as the knowledge they offer gives the individual access to higher states of being. However, despite Ostow's (1982) analogies, there is little in the writings of Freud or later psychoanalysts to suggest that the transformations produced by analysis are of this magical kind; indeed, as is well known, Freud was pessimistic about how much his 'impossible profession' could achieve (Frosh 1999).

More plausible parallels between Jewish mysticism and psychoanalysis arise out of what should probably be understood as a reductive explanation suggesting that they serve similar psychological functions. A characteristic example here is an article by Lutzky (1989: 449) that claims 'a striking congruence between the Kabbalistic myth of tikkun and the Kleinian concept of reparation, both metaphors of creation, fragmentation and re-creation – of the mystical cosmos on the one hand, of the internal object world on the other.'These two powerful ideas have many similarities, and both are set up as responses (individual and communal) to the operations of a destructive impulse that can be observed in human affairs. *Reparation* refers to 'the variety of processes by which the ego feels it undoes harm done in phantasy, restores, preserves and revives objects' (Klein 1955: 133). *Tikkun* is the term given in the Kabbalah to complex processes whereby the fragmentation of the universe produced at the start of creation is made good by the acts of humans – especially and particularly Jews – who repair the breach in reality and recover aspects of the Divine from the shadowland into which it has fallen. Both these sets of images are responding to what seems to be a very widely felt psychological sensation of guilt arising from a consciousness of destructiveness; both of them also have historical resonance, in Klein to the destructiveness of the first half of the twentieth century, and in Lurianic (that is, deriving from the Jewish mystical teaching of Isaac Luria) mysticism to the historical cataclysm of the expulsion of the Jews from Spain at the end of the fifteenth century, and the continual deepening of the Jewish exile. Lutzky (1989: 457) uses such parallels to suggest that 'tikkun expresses on the mythical, cultural level, the same dynamics that the concept of reparation does on the level of the individual psyche.'

It seems likely that parallels such as these, between specific psychoanalytic concepts and those to be found in the Jewish mystical tradition, have some validity, but perhaps this is mostly because such concepts gain their potency and durability because they refer to widespread experiential dilemmas – in this case, how to deal with guilt, loss and the sense of unreasonable punishment. Whether this is a specific and meaningful link between psychoanalysis and Judaism is another matter: it is very probable that similar parallels can be found with many other traditions, as the studies of Christianity, Buddhism and so on in this book all testify. Psychoanalysis' propensity to seek out hidden knowledge and to imply that gaining it is in some way liberational fits with most mystical traditions, and while Jewish mysticism has its own profound dynamic (especially grappling with issues of exile and *hester panim*, God apparently wantonly turning His face away from those who need Him), mystical striving is a much broader tradition that cuts across many religious perspectives. The more interesting question is whether psychoanalysis, with its Jewish heritage, draws on, corresponds with or antagonises tendencies in Judaism that are specific and that are culturally and religiously meaningful.

Interpretation and law

Perhaps the most striking characteristics of Judaism are its interpretive, 'hermeneutic' approach to holy texts, and its fascination with law. Ostow (1982) again offers a way in to the first of these:

> The feature of both Judaism and psychoanalysis that comes first to mind when one thinks of them together is the principle that the meaning of a matter is not exhausted in its appearance or literal text, but that true knowledge, essential aspects of meaning, can be obtained only by a process of interpretation or exegesis.
>
> (Ostow 1982: 8)

'Hermeneutics' began with biblical interpretation and is now a widespread movement, increasingly influential since the turn to narrative in the social sciences, including psychoanalysis (Frosh 2002, 2006). Its psychoanalytic heritage is somewhat different from that left by Freud, with his insistence on the scientific, causal nature of psychoanalytic inquiry. Instead, the hermeneutic tendency in psychoanalysis is to give priority to meaning-making as the main activity of psychic life, and to use the psychoanalytic method to elaborate meanings rather than determine some specific causal wish. For some writers, most famously Habermas (1968), the interpretive power of psychoanalysis is 'emancipatory', linking the subject with her or his split-off meanings; that is

> The interpretation of a case is corroborated only by the successful *continuation of a self-formative process*, that is, by the completion of self-reflection, and not in any unmistakeable way by what the patient says or how he *behaves*.
>
> (Habermas 1968: 266, original italics)

Emancipation is expressed in a kind of becoming-real, as the analysand recognises the meanings generated dialogically and takes them in so that they have causal impact, promoting an enrichment of felt experience and a process of enhanced self-reflection. While this is a more ambitious statement than many, it illustrates the general hermeneutic idea that what distinguishes psychoanalysis as a practical as well as intellectual activity is its generation of meanings that are 'true' in that they are creative and effective in promoting psychological growth, rather than necessarily accurately naming any specific underlying reality. The debate about the relationship between these two different kinds of truth – performative truth, that has an effect because it speaks powerfully to a person's self-understanding, and 'objective' historical truth, that 'really exists' – is one of the liveliest debates not just within psychoanalysis, but in much of the human sciences.

Judaism shares many of these same issues. The Torah, we are told, has seventy explanations – the number 'seventy' here representing an infinite amount. On Mount Sinai, at the moment of revelation, each member of the Jewish people had her or his own experience, interpreting things in her or his own way. The Written Law, expressed in the Pentateuch, was accompanied by the revelation of the Oral Law, which took thousands of years to codify, and the Talmud, which draws the Oral Law together, is maintained as a history of debates rather than simply a book of legal instructions. Rabbinical Judaism turned firmly away from the Karaite challenge (which was genuinely 'fundamentalist' in taking the Pentateuch literally) and argued that it is not possible to comprehend the Torah without interpretation, but rather that its truth lies beneath the surface, in every word, letter and space, and that this truth – legal and homiletic – turns its very many faces to human understanding. The point here is not that truth is 'relative'; far from it: Judaism certainly posits the existence of an absolute God with many attributes, one of which is specifically 'truth'. Rather, humans' capacity to comprehend this truth is halting and partial, and each layer of interpretation – guided as it is by revelatory and scholarly knowledge vouchsafed to the rabbinical leaders of the Talmudic periods – deepens this knowledge without exhausting what is to be found out.

The interpretive tendency in Judaism expresses a surprisingly liberating ideology, given that orthodox Judaism in particular is more often than not characterised as reflecting the rigid application of constraining laws. Despite the existence of indubitable orthodoxies, and a very large, indeed all-encompassing, set of regulations for the activities of daily life, understanding meaning – most centrally, the nature of God and the intentions and purpose of His laws – is a personal activity, in which people can find their own way. Even the possibility of meaninglessness is allowed, though it would be wrong to constitute it as 'orthodox': God does not necessarily intend everything, as sometimes there are self-imposed limitations on His power, the most potent being human beings' free will; moreover, it is always likely that humans will run up against the incomprehensibility of God, His absolute otherness, making the full significance of His actions impenetrable. Nevertheless, the attempt to act in accordance with God's law, and to strive to understand it even in the knowledge that at some point its meaning will escape comprehension, is effectively what life is about.

There are some obvious parallels with the psychoanalytic mission here, although the latter's search for understanding is of a decidedly secular kind: self-knowledge is the medium for enhanced mental health, yet that which has most centrally to be known, the unconscious, is effectively unfathomable. It shifts all the time, tripping us up and making full knowledge untenable; even the desire for knowledge has unconscious determinants, so not only can we not know fully the thing that we seek, but also we cannot really know the reasons why we seek it. It is important, of course, not to push parallels like this too far: that way the trap of seeing psychoanalysis as analogous to religious mysticism lies, and that is a travesty of the truth. Psychoanalysis is materialistic, founded on the notion of the human as a bio-psychosocial system out of which meanings emerge and into which they feed, devoid of any notion of spiritual, divine causation. Judaism is also a set of practical actions and regulations, out of which meanings arise: the classic, indeed biblical, acceptance of God's word by the Jews is *na'aseh venishma*, 'we will do and we will hear' – in that order, the doing coming first and the understanding following, usually derived only through great effort. But Judaism is also a *religion*: it assumes the existence of a God who acts historically and personally, who is neither perfectly abstract (as Freud might have liked Him to be, for the sake of his argument about Judaism's superiority over other religions) nor a holistic world-force. The God of the Jews is irascible, a stickler for justice and truth, sometimes (but not always) merciful, a judgemental patriarch rather than a maternal container. Many Jews reject this vision and remain Jews, sometimes staying orthodox or at least traditional in their practices; but *Judaism* undoubtedly postulates the existence of this specific, un-psychoanalytic God.

Despite this, the link between Judaism's hermeneutic tradition and psychoanalysis is not accidental. As described in the first section of this chapter, psychoanalysis has a very particular set of origins in the experience of European Jewish emancipation during the nineteenth century; while this emancipation produced secular Jews like Freud (as well as Reform Jewry and a new breed of orthodox Jews such as Samson Raphael Hirsch), it carried over from earlier times the idea that interpretation and argument is the most human of enterprises, and the route to knowledge. This hermeneutic activity was free and individualistic, with no constraint on criticism even of God; but it was also bounded by law and by deference to authority. The famous 'Kaddish' of Rabbi Levi Yitzchak of Berdichev is exemplary here (Leftwich 1939: 864–865). In this poem or prayer, Rabbi Levi Yitzchak complains to God of his injustice and of the persecution of the Jews, calling into question God's good faith in 'choosing' the Jews at all; yet the piece ends with the submission of Rabbi Levi Yitzchak to God's power. This Jewish tension between free-thinking and a sense of the rights given to people to consider and challenge their position in the world, on the one hand, and acceptance of the authority of forces beyond them on the other, is a key tension within psychoanalysis itself. Knowledge of the unconscious may depend on free association, but as free association is itself determined by the unconscious, there is nothing really free about it at all.

Psychoanalysis, like Judaism, is mightily concerned with the question of bowing one's head to authority. In psychoanalysis, this is firmly expressed in the structures of training, in which incorporation into the values, mores and authority structures of the psychoanalytic movement often seem to count for more than the talent of the individual trainee (Frosh 2006). More to the point, psychoanalysis makes the relationship with authority absolutely central to its practices through its understanding, and manipulation, of the transference. Conventionally, starting with Freud (1905), transference has been understood as that mysterious phenomenon that underpins the excessive relationship the analysand has with the analyst: its passionate combination of hatred and love that seems out of all proportion to the often banal reality of the actual contact between the participants. Transference is an explanation of the *investment* that each has in the other; in particular, it describes the way the analysand gives potency – authority – to the analyst, hoping this will produce some kind of 'cure', yet also rebelling against it. Lacan (1972–1973: 139) refers to the psycho-analyst in the transference as 'the subject supposed to know', implying by this that there is a common way of relating to the analyst as if she or he possesses a particular knowledge or truth, and that part of the process of analysis is discovering that this is a fantasy, that no one owns the kinds of truths we all look for. Whatever the broader merits or otherwise of this position, it usefully directs attention to the ambivalence surrounding authority embedded in psychoanalysis itself, at every point of its personal and organisational structure. For Freud and his early followers, this was an aspect of the break with the past that they thought they were making: the continuing 'Copernican revolution' (Laplanche 1999) that completed the decentring of the human being begun with the discovery of heliocentrism was also a way of establishing something completely new and shocking, hence subversive of authority. Later, as the institutions of psychoanalysis emerged, schisms and other conflicts arose, conservatism entered into the structure, and people's actions were increasingly understood as signifying loyalty or treachery to the movement. Within the individual psychoanalytic treatment too, with its shifting sands of relational ambiguity, the analysand never knows quite how much her or his emotional responses to the analyst are 'realistic', appropriately attuned to the analyst's capacities and actions, and how much they are transferentially induced, built out of the ambivalent wish both to be subjected to authority and to rebel against it.

This ambivalence towards authority can be seen as part of the 'Judaic' heritage of psychoanalysis. God and the rabbis have always wielded power in the orthodox community, and even nowadays there are many members of the strictly orthodox Jewish population who will take no decisions or actions without the approval of their rabbi. Nevertheless, from Abraham (who argued with God over the destruction of Sodom and Gomorrah: 'should not the judge of all the Earth act justly?' – Genesis 18: 25) onwards, Judaism has always demanded of its leaders that they warrant the authority vested in them, and Jews have never fought shy of challenging authority when it did not suit. The entire *haskalah*, the Jewish enlightenment, can be understood as a kind of psychoanalytic process whereby the authority invested in tradition and its representatives comes to be owned by individuals, at last thinking for themselves and weighing up their experience against received wisdoms, finding the latter lacking. That is, using the Lacanian formulation mentioned above, the Jewish experience out of which psycho-analysis itself emerged was one of discovering that 'the subject supposed to know' was only acting in the place of knowledge, and that moving forward – as Jews, as psychological subjects – meant falling back more on one's own resources.

With all the argumentativeness and challenge of Judaism, however, there is something else about authority that holds it in place and that finds its own echo in psychoanalysis. This is the primacy given to the place of law. In psychoanalysis, the law is central to the notion of acceptance of reality, commonly coded through the exigencies of the Oedipus complex. The Oedipal father is a representation of what society allows in terms of the expression of desire and through this also of sexual difference, of what is masculine and feminine: one pattern of identifications is promoted in the boy, another in the girl. This is why so many writers emphasise the *legal* function of the Oedipus complex: it regulates, differentiating between the many biologically and psychologically possible things a person may wish and do. Juliet Mitchell (1982: 14), for example, states that it 'governs the position of each person in the triangle father, mother and child; in the way it does this, it embodies the law that founds the human order itself.' For Laplanche and Pontalis (1973: 286), the Oedipus complex describes the trian-gular configuration 'constituted by the child, the child's natural object, and the bearer of the law.' The real father slips away in this; what emerges instead is a description of the impossibility of interpersonal relationships that are not already structured by something outside them, this being the 'law' by which society operates.

For Judaism, the principle of boundedness within the law hardly needs to be stated: it is the absolute bedrock of what constitutes Jewish life. As noted earlier in this chapter, this law is twofold: the written Torah and its oral interpretation, rigorously debated in the Talmud and coded in the regulations of the *halachah*, especially as laid out in the *Shulchan Aruch*, the definitive sixteenth-century exposition of what is allowed and what not, what should be done at all times, and what should be avoided. This law is not only the glue that has held the Jewish people together, but also the primary expression of religious life, the mode through which Judaism is expressed. It is much more important, for example, than religious experience, despite the genuine impact of mystical ideas on the Jewish people. What matters above all in Judaism is whether one acts in accor-dance with a law that divides the biologically possible – the animalistic – from the socially, culturally and religiously acceptable. The Torah is thus, generically speaking, a law exactly like the Oedipus complex: it represents the founding principle of culture created through the postulation of a third term (God), the break between narcissistic wishfulness and acceptance of reality. Freud's (1939) notion of the psychological gains of Judaic patriarchy might be transparently misogynist, but in his own terms something important is recognised here: that the interpretive freedoms both of the psychoanalytic subject and of Judaism, including their capacity to revolt against authority, are limited by the law; and that without this, as both Freud and the rabbis believed, culture crumbles. Judaism and psychoanalysis have many parallels, and the former has influenced the latter to a profound extent, but the central connection is thus over the ubiquity and potency ascribed to the law. The 'transformational' capacities of Judaism and psychoanalysis, indeed, depend on acceptance that there is no absolute, immediate connection with the other (in this sense, that mystical unity is impossible); but rather that it is by negotiation with and through symbolic structures (the Torah, the transference) that their specific truths are approached.

Note

1   The first section of this chapter is based on Chapter 1 of S. Frosh (2005) *Hate and the 'Jewish Science'*. London: Palgrave.

References

Bakan, D. (1958) *Sigmund Freud and the Jewish Mystical Tradition*. London: Free Association Books (1990).

Diller, J. (1991) *Freud's Jewish Identity: A Case Study in the Impact of Ethnicity*. London: Associated University Presses.

Freud, S. (1900) *The Interpretation of Dreams*. SE 4.

Freud, S. (1905) Fragment of an analysis of a case of hysteria. In *Case Histories*. Harmondsworth: Penguin (1977).

Freud, S. (1930) *Civilization and its Discontents*. In *Civilization, Society and Religion*. Harmondsworth: Penguin (1985).

Freud, S. (1939) *Moses and Monotheism*. SE 23.

Freud, S. (1961) *Letters of Sigmund Freud 1873–1939* (edited by E. Freud). London: Hogarth Press.

Frosh, S. (1999) *The Politics of Psychoanalysis*. London: Macmillan.

Frosh, S. (2002) *After Words: The Personal in Gender, Culture and Psychotherapy*. London: Palgrave.

Frosh, S. (2003) Psychoanalysis in Britain: The rituals of destruction. In D. Bradshaw (ed.) *A Concise Companion to Modernism*. Oxford: Blackwell.

Frosh, S. (2005) *Hate and the 'Jewish Science': Anti-Semitism, Nazism and Psychoanalysis*. London: Palgrave.

Frosh, S. (2006) *For and Against Psychoanalysis*, 2nd edn. London: Routledge.

Gellner, E. (1992) Psychoanalysis, social role and testability. In W. Dryden and C. Feltham (eds) *Psychotherapy and its Discontents*. Buckingham: Open University Press.

Gilman, S. (1993) *Freud, Race and Gender*. Princeton, NJ: Princeton University Press.

Habermas, J. (1968) *Knowledge and Human Interests*. Cambridge: Polity (1987).

Halpern, J. (1999) Freud's intrapsychic use of the Jewish culture and religion. *Journal of the American Psychoanalytical Association* 47: 1191–1212.

Klein, D. (1985) *Jewish Origins of the Psychoanalytic Movement*. Chicago: University of Chicago Press.

Klein, M. (1955) The psychoanalytic play technique. In *Envy and Gratitude and Other Papers*. New York: Delta (1975).

Lacan, J. (1972–1973) God and the *Jouissance* of The Woman. In J. Mitchell and J. Rose (eds) *Feminine Sexuality*. London: Macmillan (1982).

Laplanche, J. (1999) *Essays on Otherness*. London: Routledge.

Laplanche, J. and Pontalis, J.-B. (1973) *The Language of Psychoanalysis*. London: Hogarth Press.

Lear, J. (2005) *Freud*. London: Routledge.

Leftwich, J. (1939) *The Golden Peacock*. London: Robert Anscombe.

Lutzky, H. (1989) Reparation and Tikkun: A comparison of the Kleinian and Kabbalistic concepts. *International Review of Psychoanalysis* 16: 449–458.

Maimonides, M. (1956) *The Guide for the Perplexed*. New York: Dover.

Mitchell, J. (1982) Introduction – I. In J. Mitchell and J. Rose (eds) *Feminine Sexuality*. London: Macmillan.

Ostow, M. (1982) *Judaism and Psychoanalysis*. New York: Ktav.

Rieff, P. (1959) *Freud: The Mind of the Moralist*. Chicago: University of Chicago Press (1979).

Roith, E. (1987) *The Riddle of Freud: Jewish Influences on his Theory of Female Sexuality*. London: Tavistock.

Rose, J. (2005) *The Question of Zion*. Princeton, NJ: Princeton University Press.

Said, E. (2003) *Freud and the Non-European*. London: Verso.

Scholem, G. (1941) *Major Trends in Jewish Mysticism*. New York: Schocken.

Yerushalmi, Y.H. (1991) *Freud's Moses: Judaism Terminable and Interminable*. New Haven, CT: Yale University Press.

12

THE STRUCTURE OF NO STRUCTURE

Winnicott's concept of unintegration and the Buddhist notion of no-self

Mark Epstein

Much of the fascination that Buddhism holds for psychoanalysis stems from its assertion of the emptiness of the self. This is a strong psychological message to be found at the heart of one of world's most prominent religions and it has not failed to capture the imagination of psychotherapists for whom the study of the self is a central aspect of their profession. Buddhism affirms a paradoxical truth that psychoanalysis, after one hundred years of investigation, has at times come close to agreeing with: that the self which seems so real becomes less so upon analytic inquiry. Where once psychoanalysts seemed sure that the self existed, they now, more often than not, qualify this belief: couching the self in the framework of intersubjectivity, relationality and relativity. Buddhism, however, has contended from its inception that the self, as we conventionally understand it, is empty of intrinsic reality.

Of course, the problems of language and concept creep in immediately to this kind of discussion. What is the self that Buddhism says does not exist? Is this the same self that is explored in psychoanalysis? Is it the self of ego psychology or object relations? Is it the self of healthy or pathological narcissism? A review (Falkenstrom 2003) articulated several different selves that have emerged in the analytic literature of relevance to Buddhist psychology: self as experience, self as representation, and self as system.

The self that does not exist

Self as experience describes our phenomenological selves: our subjective experience through time. The representational self is an internalized concept of who or what we are, made up of a shifting amalgam of intrapsychic representations that coalesce in varying ways into our repertoire of self-images. And self as system is what might be termed the structure of the self, the architecture or hierarchy of the entire constellation of self-representations. It is a way of talking about the overall shape of an individual person's psychic structure, a description of a person's general capacity for both intimacy and self-awareness.

The Buddhist view of the self that does not exist is relevant, in different ways, at all of these levels, although it does not stress any single one of them to the exclusion of the others. It must be remembered that the Buddha's investigation preceded psychoanalysis by 2500 years and came in a culture in which different questions were being asked, where the notion of soul was much more tied to the concept of self than it is nowadays. Yet given these vast differences in time, place and culture, it is remarkable how relevant the Buddhist contributions can be to the psychoanalytic model (Epstein 1995).

In the Buddhist view, all notions of self are held to be potentially imprisoning because of our inherent tendency to cling unproductively to whatever gives a sense of security. This clinging to self may be thought of as a form of narcissism. The Buddha put forth a radical proposition: that identification with *any* concept of self, while tempting, is actually unnecessary. It is possible, he declared, to free the mind from its tendency to believe in the ultimate reality of any version of self.

Self as experience is indeed the starting point of the Buddhist investigation, but things get complicated rather quickly when the subjective self is made an object of contemplation. First, it becomes obvious that the self that is experienced can be both subject and object. There is experience and the experiencer of the experience, and they are not the same. But then it gets even more complex. As the Buddhist psychotherapist Jack Engler (2003) has pointed out, meditation reveals that there is a source of awareness, consciousness itself, which can never be observed completely in the act of being aware. We can observe it in retrospect, and therefore turn it into an object, but we can never truly know it as it occurs. Meditative efforts to observe awareness are always eventually frustrated: the very effort of searching for it removes us from it so that we are always backing up from ourselves, caught in the duality of subject and object. The effort to trap the self ultimately founders on this shore. Self as experience reveals the presence of a self that can never be truly experienced; yet this self, the self of awareness, is clearly an essential and vital aspect of who or what we are. From a Buddhist perspective, observation of self as experience deepens the mystery of our being rather than clarifying it.

On a conceptual level, the sharpening of introspective awareness that takes place in what is known as 'insight' or 'analytic' meditation brings the various self-representations into focus. Images of self are revealed in all of their variety, yet they are also observed to be images rather than reality. They are acknowledged to have a relative reality: they do appear in the mind and can be identified with, but they do not demand to be identified with and they are clearly only conceptual in nature. In fact, meditation seems to increase the potential for disidentification from such concepts and, while the self does not become any clearer as a result, the relative nature of the self-representations becomes obvious. The hold that such representations have over us is loosened as an appreciation is gained for an awareness that is vast, ungraspable, and simultaneously immediate and yet out of reach.

Finally, self as system is radically reorganized under the influence of meditation. From one perspective, of course, nothing is changed at all. The self is not destroyed. It is seen to have never existed in any of the ways we imagined. The Dalai Lama compares this realization to that of someone who knows he is wearing sunglasses. The very appearance of the distorted color, he says, is a reminder that what is perceived is not real. On a structural level, the psychologists Daniel Brown and Jack Engler (1986) found that when they gave projective tests to experienced meditators that there was no diminution of internal conflict as compared to controls, only a greater willingness to acknowledge the presence of this conflict. Nothing changes, and yet something is reorganized. Awareness is empowered. The balance between self-observation and self-identification shifts. Narcissistic defensiveness is diminished while the holding power of awareness is strengthened. As identification with the various self-representations fades, awareness fills more and more of the available psychic space.

One important thing to keep in mind in any discussion of Buddhist psychology is that the Buddhist negation of self is not a negation of personhood. In no way does the Buddhist concept of *sunyata*, or emptiness, imply that people or things do not exist at all. The etymological root of the word *sunyata*, in fact, has the meaning of a pregnant womb, not of an empty void. *Sunyata* derives from the Sanskrit verb 'to swell'. It suggests the generative swelling of a seed that contains within it the potential of a whole organism, just as emptiness contains within it the diversity of phenomenal existence.

While disputing the reality of an ongoing self with its own intrinsic nature, the Buddha's emphasis on self-observation and self-awareness had the effect of affirming what in today's language is called personal subjectivity (Epstein 2005). Self as experience was the Buddha's starting place. He was interested, within that vast field, in what could be discovered about the nature of the self as it is directly perceived. This brought him into a deepening exploration of emotional experience, because it is in emotional experience that the self (as we think about it conventionally) becomes most apparent. When we are angry, hurt, anxious or afraid, or when we really want something or someone, the self comes more into focus. It is a fundamental tenet of Buddhist psychology that in order to understand the emptiness of the 'object of negation' (Epstein 1988) the conventional self must first be seen as clearly as possible. In order to understand the emptiness of self, we first have to find the self as we experience it. This is one of the primary challenges of Buddhist meditation, at whatever structural level it is practiced.

The four noble truths

The Buddha laid out his psychology in his famous teachings of the Four Noble Truths (Rahula 1959). His first truth affirmed the presence of a feeling of pervasive unsatisfactoriness in all of experience. A gnawing sense of imperfection, insubstantiality or unrest disturbs even pleasurable experiences. He defined the problem in several different ways. First, physically, birth, decay and death are all painful experiences, as are physical and mental illnesses. Second, emotionally, not to obtain what one desires is suffering, to be united with what one dislikes is suffering, and to be separated from what one likes is suffering. Third, psychologically, our own selves are troubling. They never seem quite right. There is a discrepancy, as the psychology of narcissism has made clear, between the wishful concept of the self and the self-representations.

The Buddha's second truth gave the cause of this dissatisfaction as thirst or craving. He defined three kinds: for sense-pleasures, for existence and for non-existence. The thirst for sense-pleasures causes anguish because all such pleasures are fleeting. The objects of our desire are never real enough or lasting enough to give us the ongoing satisfaction that we crave. We are trying to extract an essence from them that they lack and so we suffer. The thirsts for existence and non-existence relate to a contemporary understanding of the psychology of narcissism: they can be seen as compensatory self-inflation and compensatory self-negation, the two tendencies of a mind that is searching for certainty in the face of insecurity. This is, in fact, a duality that is typical of both Buddhist psychology and the theories of narcissism. The mind sets up extremes: of existence and non-existence, absolutism or nihilism, reification or annihilation, or grandiosity and emptiness, and then oscillates between them in a furious attempt to find some solid ground to stand on. In Buddhist psychology, the central motivation for these dualities is 'the false idea of self arising out of ignorance' (Rahula 1959). There is a thirst for certainty, a craving for identity and a resulting misapprehension of self.

The Buddha's third truth, of cessation, is that there can be freedom from unsatisfactoriness. It is possible to extinguish thirst, reconcile polarities, and eliminate false ideas of self. The paradox of the Buddha's psychology, however, is that the only way to accomplish this is to find the self that does not exist. In the Tibetan tradition (Hopkins 1987) this is described as ascertaining the 'appearance of a substantially existent I'. In psychoanalytic language, we would call this process an unrelenting excavation of narcissistic identifications. In scanning the field of experience, as is encouraged in Buddhist meditation, the primary focus is on this elusive object: the sense of self as it actually appears. At times, it may be in the form of self-representations, at other times it may be less conceptual and more of a feeling. However, and whenever, it appears, it is meant to be examined. And this examination yields an appreciation of emptiness and a concomitant respect for the mystery of awareness, essential antidotes to the unsatisfactoriness that the Buddha pointed out in his first truth.

The Buddha's fourth truth is the way leading to the cessation of suffering. It is described as the Middle Path, that which avoids the two extremes of indulgence and repression. The former the Buddha described as 'low, common, unprofitable and the way of ordinary people', and the latter, which he put in the general category of asceticism, he called 'painful, unworthy and unprofitable' (Rahula 1959). The Middle Path, also known as the Eightfold Path of Right Understanding, Thought, Speech, Action, Livelihood, Effort, Mindfulness and Concentration, is designed to highlight and force a confrontation with increasingly subtle psychic manifestations of narcissistic impulses. Meditators, at every stage, have the tendency to use their insights and revelations in a narcissistic manner, to reinforce the sense of their own specialness, and the path actually consists of continually uncovering those tendencies in order to free the mind from clinging.

As the various self-feelings, self-images and self-representations are uncovered and observed, there is a corresponding appreciation for just how much of our psychic experience is outside of the domain of the conventional self. As Engler (2003) described, there is an increasing regard for the power and mystery of an awareness that is felt to infuse subjective experience. The situation that evolves is much like that of the narrator of one of Wallace Stevens' (1923) most famous poems, 'Thirteen Ways of Looking at a Blackbird':

> I do not know which to prefer,
> The beauty of inflections
> Or the beauty of innuendoes,
> The blackbird whistling
> Or just after.

Western psychology emphasizes the beauty of inflection: the self's whistle as it appears. But the Buddhist psychologies dwell on the beauty of the self's innuendo: the space around the self. The effort that Buddhist meditation requires is not just about searching *for* the self, but also about learning to leave the self alone. This latter effort is toward permitting oneself to simply be, without worrying about keeping oneself together (Epstein 1998). The appreciation of emptiness depends as much on this capacity as it does on the excavation of narcissistic identifications.

227

Unintegration

Within the psychoanalytic literature, one person whose work clearly dovetails with the Buddhist approach is D.W. Winnicott. Especially in his championing of a state of unintegration, Winnicott gave great credence to the Buddhist suggestion that it could be salutary for the mind to learn how to relax into itself, instead of being caught by all of the psychic manifestations of selfhood. But the Buddhist understanding also helps clarify Winnicott's attachment to, and interest in, this state. While Winnicott's descriptions are wonderfully evocative, a careful reading of his work shows him groping for a clear way to express what he found so compelling about an unstructured self. At times equating such a self with madness and at other times with a sacred and 'incommunicado' center (Winnicott 1963), Winnicott's thinking about this matter comes into focus when we read it in the light of Buddhism. In both Winnicott's psychology and that of the Buddha we find the discovery that the less sure we are about the self the greater our mental health. Both meditation and Winnicottian psychoanalysis open up uncertainty, not to provoke anxiety but to evoke tolerance, humility and compassion.

'In thinking of the psychology of mysticism,' wrote Winnicott (1963),

> it is usual to concentrate on the understanding of the mystic's withdrawal into a personal inner world of sophisticated introjects. Perhaps not enough attention has been paid to the mystic's retreat to a position in which he can communicate secretly with subjective objects and phenomena, the loss of contact with the world of shared reality being counterbalanced by a gain in terms of feeling real.
>
> (Winnicott 1963: 185–186)

When Winnicott wrote of communicating secretly with subjective objects and phenomena, he was alluding to a mode of being that he described over and over again in his work, one that ties together the worlds of emotional development and meditation. His description is important because of the way he articulates something true about meditation while using the developmental language of psychoanalysis. Communicating secretly with subjective objects is a different, and more accurate, way of describing meditation than withdrawal into a world of introjects. Meditation opens up subjective experience and makes it into a field of contemplation. It shows us that self as experience is more than the sum of self representations and that the self as system has to include the unfathomable awareness that illuminates each of us.

'The opposite of integration would seem to be disintegration,' commented Winnicott (1962),

> [But] that is only partly true. The opposite, initially, requires a word like

unintegration. Relaxation for an infant means not feeling a need to integrate, the mother's ego-supportive function being taken for granted.

(Winnicott 1962: 61)

Opposing such a state to one of either ego integration or disintegration, Winnicott wrote instead of the experiences of letting go. Unintegration, for him, meant a time when the usual needs for control could be suspended and where the self can unwind. He meant losing oneself without feeling lost, hearing the self's innuendo rather than just its inflection. In Buddhist terms, this is a meditative capacity, one that has to be practiced if it is to flourish and one that eventually opens into the freedom of the Buddha's third noble truth.

Unintegration ran through close to thirty years of Winnicott's writings. Commencing in a paper entitled 'Primitive emotional development' (Winnicott 1945) almost as an aside, the concept grew in importance as he integrated it into all of the major themes of his work: creativity, feeling real, the true self/false self dichotomy, and the function of therapy. At first, Winnicott's tone was rather sinister: he wrote of unintegration as the underlying truth that we shy away from but are perversely drawn to. At times equating it with a madness that lurks within, Winnicott challenged conventional assumptions of a 'healthy' personality that has progressed, evolved or developed beyond its infantile origins. The healthy individual is not always integrated, declared Winnicott. In fact, it is unhealthy to deny or to fear 'the innate capacity of every human being to become unintegrated, depersonalized, and to feel that the world is unreal' (1958: 150).

As unintegration became more central to Winnicott's thinking, he began to tie it in more directly to his all-important notion of the 'capacity to be'. The infant who can be, as opposed to one who can only do, has the capacity to feel real (Winnicott 1971). Out of the unintegrated state, she starts to 'gather experiences that can be called personal', and she begins 'a tendency towards a sense of existing' (Winnicott 1962: 60). Throughout a career that was always focused on how his patients felt unreal to themselves, Winnicott never tired of pointing out how that unreality stemmed from a child's reaction to a parent's inability to leave her alone without abandoning her.

As the psychoanalyst Michael Eigen (1991) has written,

Winnicott's therapy created an atmosphere in which two people could be alone together without all the time trying to make sense of what was or was not happening. Developing a capacity for play (transitional experiencing) went along with tolerating unintegration and madness.

(Eigen 1991: 78)

Or as Winnicott (1971: 55) put it, 'The person we are trying to help needs a new experience in a specialized setting. The experience is one of a non-purposive state, as one might say a sort of ticking over of the unintegrated personality.'

In this view of therapy we find an immediate overlap with the Buddhist approach. For in Buddhism, also, the ticking over of the unintegrated personality is the key to successful practice. Meditation, like Winnicott's psychotherapy, is a way of introducing (or reintroducing) a person to this possibility. In both cases, it is the holding function of awareness that is being developed, sometimes through the participation of the therapist or meditation teacher, and sometimes through the individual's own practice. The self-representations and self-feelings are observed instead of identified with; conflicts are noted without attempts having to be made to solve them. But this holding is not what we usually imagine it to be – it is not a holding on, but is more like juggling. Keeping a number of balls in the air, we hold all and none of them. In so doing, the experience of self is opened up, deepened, made more transparent, and transformed.

The scenario that I am describing is explored in depth by Winnicott in his penultimate paper, 'On communicating and not communicating leading to a study of certain opposites' (1963). 'In the best possible circumstances,' he says, 'growth takes place and the child . . . possesses three lines of communication', first, communication that is forever silent, that he called the 'incommunicado element' present at the core of each individual, second, communication that is explicit, indirect and pleasurable, that he linked to verbal and symbolic communications, and third, an intermediate form of communication 'that slides out of playing into cultural experience of every kind'. When there is a failure, however, and a child is forced to develop a reactive self to manage the demands of the intrusive or abandoning environment, 'the infant develops a split'. Partly compliant and partly in hiding, the child isolates a secret and impenetrable private world, the remnant of the incommunicado element, to concentrate on managing what we might call the external world. Christening the split-off dimension a 'cul-de-sac communication', Winnicott suggested that this isolated bubble 'carries all the sense of real' (1963: 183–184). Rather than enjoying free access to it in a state of unintegration, such a person isolates her truest self in an inaccessible fortress, hidden, even to the self.

The task of the healthy personality is to re-establish contact with this cul-de-sac, to heal the split and open up the capacity for unintegration that was aborted earlier. The mature person has access to a kind of silent communication that permits an intensity and a personal subjectivity that is lacking when the thinking mind is always trying to maintain control.

Meditation and psychotherapy

To me, Winnicott's descriptions of 'good enough' parenting and non-intrusive therapy are powerful evocations of what I learned, in different language, from meditation. A child who can be lost in play with the knowledge that her parent is present but not interfering is a child who has access to her subjective self. This is a scenario that meditation seems to facilitate. The usual needs for control are suspended, and the self floats. It does not dissolve into nothingness but it is not maintained in its usual form, either. There is the possibility for what Winnicott called silent communication with subjective objects. This temporary dissolution of ego boundaries is both satisfying and enriching. It feeds a sense of continuity and trust that is implicit in Winnicott's notion of what it takes to feel real. A person without enough of that experience has gaps in what Winnicott called the capacity to go on being, with an artificially rigid self to show for it and an inability to relax into the self's innuendo.

The self that Buddhism finds to be unreal is remarkably similar to the 'false self' of Winnicott's psychology. The caretaker self that develops when a child is forced to deal with parental intrusion or abandonment is a self that, in Buddhist language, has no inherent reality. It is a construction, albeit a necessary one at times, that tends to become more and more restrictive the more often it is needed, squeezing the capacity for spontaneity and authenticity into what Winnicott described as a cul-de-sac.

In Buddhist meditation, the dismantling of this false self is encouraged through the deliberate meditative cultivation of unintegration. This is not the endpoint of Buddhism, but it is an important portal of entry. Once comfortable in a state of unintegration, Buddhist psychology contends, we can begin to see clearly how compulsively we cling to the various images of self that present themselves in our minds. Unintegration, the importance of which Winnicott recognized so clearly, is the platform upon which Buddhist insight grows. Without some grounding in the state of unintegration, it is impossible to disidentify enough to see clinging clearly. But when enough subjective expertise is gained, clinging to self becomes very obvious, because it is the clinging itself that disrupts the state of unintegration. From a Buddhist perspective, it is not a single 'false self' that is uncovered, however, it is a multiplicity of such selves. The thrill of Buddhist meditation lies in seeing how possible it is to be free of clinging to all such selves, be they experiential, representational or systematic.

My Buddhist teacher, Joseph Goldstein (1994), tells a story about a moving encounter with one of his teachers that, to my mind, illustrates how central this capacity for unintegration is in both meditative and therapeutic capacities. Joseph was doing a retreat, called a *sesshin*, with a very powerful Zen teacher named Sasaki Roshi and was working with a form of meditation known as koan practice, in which he was forced to struggle with a problem, or riddle, that has no rational answer. The *sesshin* was structured very tightly and Joseph saw the Roshi, or teacher, four times a day for interviews. But each time he tried to solve the koan the Roshi would ring his bell very quickly and dismiss him, saying things like, 'Oh, very stupid', or 'Okay, but not Zen', leading Joseph to feel more and more ill at ease. Finally the Roshi seemed to relent and he gave Joseph a simpler koan, 'How do you manifest the Buddha while chanting a sutra ?' Joseph understood that the point was to come in and chant, but it was more complicated than that for him.

As Joseph describes it,

> I do not think Sasaki Roshi knew, although he might have known, that this koan plugged in exactly to some very deep conditioning in me going back to the third grade. Our singing teacher back then had said, 'Goldstein, just mouth the words.' From then on I have had a tremendous inhibition about singing, and now here I was, having to perform in a very charged situation. I was a total wreck. In the pressure cooker of the sesshin, which is held in silence except for the interviews, everything becomes magnified so much.
>
> I rehearsed and rehearsed two lines of chant, all the while getting more and more tight, more and more tense. The bell rang for the interview, I went in, I started chanting, and I messed up the entire thing. I got all the words wrong: I felt completely exposed and vulnerable and raw. And Roshi just looked at me and with great feeling said, 'Very good'.
>
> (Goldstein 1994: 21–23)

The therapeutic implications of the encounter were not lost on Joseph. Sasaki Roshi helped him open up to the very fragility that he was struggling to avoid. He helped him to be open and vulnerable and insecure, not confident, controlled and coherent. By bringing the false self that developed in the third grade into the meditative arena, Roshi helped Joseph release himself from its particular grip. The meditative demands of the koan practice brought that particular self-representation into the foreground and its acknowledgement allowed Joseph to deepen his meditation. This is the model that Buddhist meditation works with. Relaxing into unintegration empowers an impersonal quality of awareness that takes as its object whatever clinging to self makes a further opening impossible. Once this obstacle is turned into an object of meditation, a further release is allowed.

In psychoanalytic language, the change that is brought about through the cultivation of unintegration is akin to the empowerment of the synthetic aspect of the ego, that which must continuously re-establish contact with the object of awareness. This is an aspect of the self, albeit an impersonal one, that is not weakened by meditation but is strengthened, changing the entire equilibrium of the system conventionally known as self. As the analyst Hans Loewald (1951: 14) has written, 'To maintain, or constantly re-establish, this unity . . . by integrating and synthesizing what seems to move further and further away from it and fall into more and more unconnected parts', is the essential aspect of the synthetic function of the ego.

In Buddhist practice, this synthetic ego function is strengthened by meditation. The more comfortable we become in permitting a state of unintegration, the more bits and pieces of self we become aware of. Awareness fulfills its holding function by becoming the swollen and empty container within which the entire process unfolds. Eventually, the still, silent center that Winnicott called incommunicado begins to speak. Sometimes, as Joseph found in his retreat, it even sings.

References

Brown, D. and Engler, J. (1980) The stages of mindfulness meditation: A validation study. Part 1: Study and results. In K. Wilber, J. Engler and D. Brown (eds) *Transformations of Consciousness*. Boston, MA: New Science Library (1986).

Eigen, M. (1991) Winnicott's area of freedom: The uncompromisable. In N. Schwartz-Salant and M. Stein (eds) *Liminality and Transitional Phenomena*. Wilmette, IL: Chiron.

Engler, J. (2003) Being somebody and being nobody: A reexamination of the understanding of self in psychoanalysis and Buddhism. In J.D. Safran (ed.) *Psychoanalysis and Buddhism: An Unfolding Dialogue*. Boston, MA: Wisdom.

Epstein, M. (1988) The deconstruction of the self: ego and 'egolessness' in Buddhist meditation. *Journal of Transpersonal Psychology* 20: 61–69.

Epstein, M. (1995) *Thoughts without a Thinker: Psychotherapy from a Buddhist Perspective*. New York: Basic Books.

Epstein, M. (1998) *Going to Pieces without Falling Apart*. New York: Broadway.

Epstein, M. (2005) *Open to Desire*. New York: Gotham.

Falkenstrom, F. (2003) A Buddhist contribution to the psychoanalytic psychology of self. *International Journal of Psychoanalysis* 84: 1551–1568.

Goldstein, J. (1994) *Transforming the Mind, Healing the World*. Mahwah, NJ: Paulist Press.

Hopkins, J. (1987) *Emptiness Yoga*. Ithaca, NY: Snow Lion.

Loewald, H.W. (1951) Ego and reality. *International Journal of Psychoanalysis* 32: 14.

Rahula, W. (1959) *What the Buddha Taught*. New York: Grove Press.

Stevens, W. (1923/1951) *The Collected Poems of Wallace Stevens*. New York: Vintage Books (1990).

Winnicott, D.W. (1945) Primitive emotional development. In *Through Paediatrics to Psycho-Analysis: Collected Papers*. New York: Brunner/Mazel (1958, 1992).

Winnicott, D.W. (1962) Ego integration in child development. In *The Maturational Processes and the Facilitating Environment*. New York: International Universities Press (1965).

Winnicott, D.W. (1963) On communicating and not communicating leading to a study of certain opposites. In *The Maturational Processes and the Facilitating Environment*. New York: International Universities Press (1965).

Winnicott, D.W. (1971) *Playing and Reality*. London and New York: Routledge.

13

VEDANTA AND
PSYCHOANALYSIS

Malcom Cunningham

Introduction

The need for and pursuit of truth is inherent in human existence and experience. This need impels both psychological and spiritual inquiry. I will attempt to demonstrate the alliance between psychological understanding and spiritual experience and show they not only converge upon the same goal, but also complement each other such that each contributes to the other's development. Psychological equilibrium is prerequisite to receptivity to spiritual experience. In turn, spiritual experience provides perspective that decreases vulnerability to disappointments, frustrations and trauma and supports psychological balance.

For this discussion I choose psychoanalysis and the Indian philosophy of Vedanta to represent psychology and spirituality respectively. While these are very broad fields of inquiry, nonetheless I believe they share as defining attributes an elaboration of a concept of a 'self' and an exploration into the meaning of experience. I will begin with a discussion of some of the basic tenets of Vedanta, particularly the Vedantic idea of Self, and compare and contrast this with various psychoanalytic conceptualizations of the self.

Vedanta, literally 'end of the Vedas', is one of the six systems of Hindu philosophy. (The Vedas are a compilation of hymns, rituals, myths, and philosophical writings of ancient India. The six systems of Hindu philosophy are Vedanta, Yoga, Sankhya, Mimamsa, Nyaya and Vaisesika.) A catholic philosophy, its capacity to accommodate and incorporate disparate ideas while maintaining a core integrity has enabled it to survive and flourish for thousands of years. Perhaps the most central tenet of Vedanta is the supremacy of individual experience as the final arbiter of spiritual truth, with the inner realization of truth being the culmination of Vedanta.

Advaita, a school of Vedanta that embraces a philosophy of non-dualism, translates as 'not two'. Advaita Vedanta holds that there is only one Real Substance and that it is all in all in the universe (Yukteswar 1949). Physical reality, the phenomenological universe, is an illusory manifestation of the *noumenon* of Ultimate Reality and has no intrinsic existence of its own. As a corollary to this, as human beings perceive themselves only as a physical body, an individual ego, and a mind limited to perceiving and interpreting sensual stimuli, they are unaware of their true Self as an eternal part of the one Reality.

Traditional views of the unconscious

Eastern and western thought generally have held contrasting depictions of the unconscious. Western theorists traditionally, though not always, viewed the unconscious with some distrustful apprehension. Freud described it as a repository of the drives and the repressed. Melanie Klein elaborated a theory of unconscious phantasy and its relation to primitive mental states. In these models, the unconscious tends to be principally a source or explanation of potential trouble, and the more it is analysed, modified, and brought under conscious understanding, the more healthy the individual will be.

Alternative conceptions of the unconscious have existed alongside the predominant view even within the same theorist. The structured unconscious of *The Interpretation of Dreams* (Freud 1900) bears little relation to the unconscious of the seething cauldron (Freud 1933). Jung (1936) viewed the unconscious as more potentially beneficent and introduced the idea of a collective, universal, unconscious shared by the group and accessible to each of the group's individual members. More contemporary psychoanalytic thinkers also have recast the unconscious as more salubrious – among other attributes, as the knower of the patient's truth that informs the patient and analyst through the analytic dialogue.

Different conceptualizations of the unconscious create different approaches to psychoanalytic treatment. The view of the unconscious as a repository of drives and conflicts lends itself to a symptom targeted approach, and reciprocally, a symptomatic approach to treatment reinforces this view of the unconscious. Unconscious conflict and phantasy are analysed with the desired outcome of reducing anxiety and increasing psychological flexibility. Psychological health and development are concomitant with the strengthening of the conscious ego. In contrast, the more contemporary view of the unconscious allows a less symptom targeted focus, one more centred on personal and even spiritual growth, however vaguely defined. While conflict is still analysed, there is a shift toward increasing the capacity to tolerate the unknown, to bear anxiety, and to follow the guidance of an inner subjectivity.

The Self of Vedanta

In Vedanta the unconscious is a superconscious, the true Self that informs the ego or conscious self. (Throughout this chapter I will designate the Vedantic Self with a capital 'S' to indicate its association with Ultimate Reality.) While it includes the traditional unconscious, it also incorporates what in western tradition would be the idea of the soul. This Self is a manifestation of, and in its essence equal to, Ultimate Reality Itself. Because of this, the Vedantic Self cannot be a subject of analysis. It is not transformable, nor is it knowable in the sense of understanding its vicissitudes, it having none. It can only be realized or become. The self and the Self are not on a continuum, in that the self does not evolve into the Self. The Self always exists as a Reality undistorted by identification with the physical body or individual mind.

While the Self is pure consciousness and of the same essence as Ultimate Reality, in the phenomenological world it manifests itself as an individualized being. The personalization of the Self, analogous to the personalization of Ultimate Reality as God, occurs due to the perception of separateness and otherness between the conscious ego and the superconscious soul. Isherwood's (1963) explication of the dualistic God serves equally well to describe the personalized Self:

> The dualistic God – the God-who-is-other-than-I – is an aspect of the Reality but not other than the Reality. Within the world of phenomena – the world of apartness, of this and that, of we and you – the God-who-is-other-than-we is the greatest phenomenon of all. But, with the experience of unitive, nondualistic knowledge, the God-who-is-other-than-me merges into the God-who-is-myself. The divine phenomena are seen to be all aspects of the one central Reality.
>
> (Isherwood 1963: 27–28)

While not diminishing the value of a more flexible, loving, and courageous personality – in fact, I will posit that it is both necessary to spiritual growth as well as a marker of the same – the Vedantic view is that because the personality, as well as the reality in which it is constituted, is fundamentally in flux, unstable, and subject to the thrall of duality, psychological understanding can never be a sufficient end in itself. To the degree one is identified with even a healthy ego and its perceptions of reality, one suffers inevitable consequences. In fact, from a Vedantic perspective, the acceptance of the reality of the ego and the physical world is a delusion, or a kind of collective psychosis, and is the root cause of all other difficulties.

However, even though the Vedantic Self is not transformable, the experience of the Self is transforming. This transformation, however, occurs in the self that is subject to change as a result of experience. An increasing, conscious realization of Self provides an experience that is separate from and untouched by inconstancies. While not cancelling the laws of duality, this new perspective diminishes the exclusivity of phenomenological experience and the concomitant suffering inherent in it. Contact with this aspect of the unconscious, therefore, promotes psychological balance in and of itself.

The Vedantic Self and Winnicott

Traditional psychoanalytic distinctions between true and false selves occur within the individualized consciousness of what from a Vedantic perspective is ultimately a 'false self'. For example, the true self described by Winnicott (1960) is biologically determined and emerges from the soma. Associated with instinct, drive and sensory-motor aliveness, this self emerges spontaneously at a time when the infant lacks a sense of cohesion. It requires a maternal response to support an omnipotent demand that reality conform to the infant's creation. Support of this illusion allows for the development of further spontaneity and initiative. With enough experience of imagining itself to create the world according to its own will, the true self is able to abrogate omnipotence and accept an external reality it believes it can impact upon sufficiently to ensure its safety and provide for its needs. If maternal response is inadequate, the infant becomes compliant with a reality that does not conform or yield to his or her demands and initiatives, and a consequent false self substitutes for and protects the vulnerability of the true one.

While it is the case that the Vedantic Self manifests through the consciousness of the infant, and that the will, initiative and enjoyment of the infant is a reflection of that Self, nonetheless, the need to believe that reality conforms to his or her wishes arises from the anxiety created by the infant's identification with him- or herself as infant. In contrast with the Vedantic idea of Self, the omnipotence of the Winnicottian self is an illusion – a necessary illusion, even a healthy one, but an illusion nonetheless. The Self of Vedanta is part of the Substance of creation and cannot be harmed or deprived. Only as infants perceive themselves as separate, small and helpless do they face a reality that is dangerous and overwhelming, and in response adopt a phantasy that this reality is of their own creation and conforms to their desires and needs. This experience is required to develop confidence that they can impact reality and, more importantly, cohere around a self that can be an agent of its own development. But this is not the same as the Vedantic realization of a Self that is both never and always infant and has no need for such an illusion.

Vedantic Self and Bion's 'O'

I believe the place in psychoanalytic theory where the depiction of the unconscious most approaches the eastern idea of Self is in Bion's concept of 'O' (Bion 1965). O is the designation for the unknowable thing-in-itself. It can be represented phenomenologically but remains distinct from any representation. Therefore, Bion describes it by what it is not:

> Its existence as indwelling has no significance whether it is supposed to dwell in an individual person or in God or Devil; it is not good or evil; it cannot be known, loved or hated. It can be represented by terms such as ultimate reality or truth. The most, and the least that the individual person can do is to be it. Being identified with it is a measure of distance from it . . . [It] is not a relationship or an identification or an atonement or a reunion. The qualities attributed to O, the links with O, are all transformations of O and *being* O.
>
> (Bion 1965: 139–40)

Bion's enunciation rings with Vedantic truth.

'Man possesses eternal faith and believes intuitively in the existence of a Substance, of which the objects of sense – sound, touch, sight, taste, and smell, the component parts of this visible world – are but properties' (Yukteswar 1949: 1). I believe Bion's O is a designation of the Substance of Vedanta. This Self, or Substance, or O, can only be intuited and is independent from the relationships with others and the relationship with the physical universe. Truth cannot be apprehended by a mind that is inherently informed by, and itself constrained by, that which is ultimately not real. One cannot *think* one's way to Truth. However, although O cannot be known in the sense of knowing about it, it can emerge or be met in an encounter with another or in an act of understanding.

The primacy of Self-experience

To realize the primacy of the Self shifts the vertex from which psychic mechanisms, functions and relationships are seen. From the Vedantic perspective, the fundamental or primary split that is inherent in the individuation of the Self is that between the aspect of the Self which perceives itself and the aspect which is perceived. The perception of physical reality proceeds from this initial split. It is also the primordial relationship – the Self's experience of itself. It is manifest in all subsequent relationships as well as in the ego's apprehension of the phenomenal world.

There is a psychoanalytic tradition that holds that the quest for a relationship with God, or the state of Self-realization, is a phantasy of returning to the idyllic relationship the infant is imagined to have had with his or her mother (Freud

1930). Vedanta argues that this view of religion is a reversed perspective, and instead the relationship between infant and mother is a model for the relationship of the self to the Self, or of the soul to God. In reality, it is God as infant who perceives and enjoys Himself through the experience of Himself as mother. The Indian psychoanalyst Kakar (1991) questions whether the postulated blissful, perfect, nursing relationship is an infantile reality or an adult myth. If the infant–mother relationship is an allegory for the relationship of the soul to God, then the loss of the self's awareness of its unity with the Self is depicted in the caesuras of early experiences. The rupture of the basic union is mythologized in the psychoanalytic elaborations on the birth experience, weaning, and the attainment of the depressive position.

As with other religious myths, that of the infant–mother relationship is informed by a real but ineffable experience. Interestingly, this is analogous to Romain Rolland's famous response to Freud's *The Future of an Illusion* (1927). Rolland was familiar with Vedanta through his interest in Ramakrishna, a Bengali mystic, and his disciple Vivekananda, who travelled and taught Vedanta in the west. He expressed to Freud that an oceanic feeling, a subjective feeling of something limitless that was experienced within the self, was the source of the illusions of religion (Freud 1930). Freud rejected this and believed that if an oceanic feeling existed, it was a vestige of an infantile experience. Perhaps both the religious 'illusions' of Rolland and the 'vestiges of infantile experience' of Freud are attempts to organize and give coherence to an inchoate awareness of the Self.

Vedantic Self and inner perfection

In one of her last papers, Klein (1963) discussed loneliness as inherent in the depressive position due to a ubiquitous yearning for an unattainable inner perfection. She follows Freud in believing the desire for this perfection is a remnant from the perfect, wordless, understanding that the infant experiences at times with his mother. She believes, however, that due to the death instinct, these experiences are always under threat of persecutory anxieties. The infant attempts to maintain these states by splitting and projection. Integration, while creating a more real and whole experience, brings the loss of the possibility of reclaiming what is felt to be a lost paradise. Klein interprets glimpses of inner perfection as split-off experiences that cannot be maintained, rather than as beckonings to a timeless, inner beatitude.

This is where psychoanalysis and religion have frequently diverged. However, psychoanalysis need not culminate in the resigned acceptance of an alienation from inner perfection. On the contrary, the analysis of psychic mechanisms, structures and phantasies can promote openness to the experience and influence of the Self. For example, at this point it will be clear that the Self of Vedanta is not created by projection. However, this is not to say that one cannot project into an *image* of the Self. Torwesten (1985) reminds us that as long as the 'I' is experienced as real, the 'Thou' of God must be real as well. In other words, as long as the ego exists, a separate and clouded vision of the Self exists. Therefore, psychoanalysis may yield understanding of unconscious phantasies that may be projected into the image of the Self and pollute Self-experience. (In truth what is polluted is the phantasy of Self-experience or the interpretation of Self-experience, the Self's actual experience of itself being unpollutable.)

Psychoanalysis as a spiritual practice

The practice of psychoanalysis as a spiritual discipline will be considered from two complementary approaches. Spiritual progress, as with progress in any endeavour, may be impeded by psychopathology and psychic conflicts that can be treated psychoanalytically. But in addition to its generic meliorative benefits, psychoanalysis may more directly facilitate spiritual advancement by addressing particular states of mind that cloud Self-experience and Self-expression. Specifically, I will explore the Self's turning toward restrictive, narrow identifications and its tenacity in maintaining them. In addition, I will postulate that psychoanalysis can directly foster attitudes which are Self-promoting, particularly *virya* and *sraddha* – the courage to face experience and the active love and reverence for the Self as manifest within the individual and others. (I have attempted to avoid Sanskrit words in this chapter. In some cases, however, an English translation prevents the consideration of the concept as a new idea. In such cases the Sanskrit has been retained. The first of these terms is *sraddha*. *Sraddha* is the energetic tendency of the heart's natural love (Yukteswar 1949). It is a manifestation of the attractive force, as will be described later. *Sraddha*, as distinguished from attachment or object love, is specifically associated with spiritual development. I believe it is closely related to reverence. The other Sanskrit term I have maintained is *virya*. *Virya* is moral courage. I use *virya* to designate the courage required to tolerate frustration and face direct experience.) In so doing psychoanalysis becomes not only a treatment for psychological barriers but also an integral component of spiritual practice.

Rather than examine specific psychic conflicts, I will conceptualize *en masse* what these conflicts may represent. In so doing, a commonality in the origins and purposes of psychological maladies might be recognized. A look at some religious parallels to psychological restrictions may help organize the two analogously.

Hindu philosophy, like psychoanalysis, emphasizes the states of mind that underlie behaviour more than the prescriptions and proscriptions of behaviour itself. Vedanta posits eight meannesses of the human heart as particular obstacles to *sraddha*. These are anger, fear, shame, grief, condemnation, pride of pedigree, race prejudice and a narrow sense of respectability (Yukteswar 1949). While these are presented as darknesses of heart, they also may be seen as states of mind, a conception more useful to the psychoanalyst. What is noteworthy is that these are attributes rather than behaviours.

The parallel in western religion might be the seven deadly sins: pride, envy, lust, avarice, sloth, wrath and gluttony. Again, although they are referred to as sins, they are more accurately states of mind. In fact, they are ubiquitous states of mind, occurring in varying degrees at varying points in time within all of us. Whether it be the seven deadly sins or the eight meannesses of the human heart, what are deadly and mean are the consequences of these states of mind – not only the actions that are harmful to oneself and others, but also the fostering of pettiness and smallness, and the expression of a narrowly circumscribed ego. These states of mind or meannesses of heart preclude expansiveness, nobility, courage, and the expression and experience of the Self.

Having considered impediments to authenticity from a religious or philosophical vertex, psychological symptoms and conflicts may be viewed comparably. They are myriad in form but have in common a restriction of self. Symington (2001) has suggested that all psychiatric illnesses can be simplified down to processes or patterns that interfere with the capacity of the person to have understanding and freedom. (I would make a distinction between psychiatric illnesses and psychological maladies, my focus in this chapter being on the latter.) Neurosis is a narrowing of self-perception; it is pettiness.

Tenacity toward egotism and restriction of Self

From this understanding psychoanalysis explores how individuals restrict their sense of self and, more importantly, why this occurs. First, restriction and misidentification are acknowledged as inherent consequences of the structure of creation as delineated in Vedantic philosophy. A darkening quality or force exists from the beginning, ontologically following from the original split between perceiving and perceived, resulting in a duality that manifests as a repulsing and attracting force.

The attracting force manifests as *sraddha*. The repelling force is *maya*, literally 'the measurer', the manifestation of the essential law of polarity by which the illusions of change and differences appear in what is ultimately Unity. The repulsing force may be physically manifest in the theorized dark energy of physics, an active force causing everything in the universe to push away from everything else (Perlmutter et al. 1999). The importance of recognizing the existence of this force is that it acknowledges the individual's experience of being placed into a struggle not of his or her making. However, it remains an existential backdrop that supports individual experience. Being therefore a fact, it cannot be a subject of clinical analysis.

What is amenable to psychoanalysis is the subjective experience that impels the turning toward pettiness. Vedantic philosophy considers such experience principally to be underwritten by tenacity to life, i.e., the tenacity of the ego to its conviction that only the physical world exists and that the ego is vulnerable in its relationship to it (Yukteswar 1949). Because the ego sees nothing beyond the physical world, a fundamental anxiety toward survival arises. A limited perception of what is real, and the belief that personal existence is wed to that reality, creates fear that to consider an alternative cosmology is to put existence itself at risk. Tenacity prevents a letting go of pettiness for fear of there being nothing outside of one's restricted experience of self and the world. A claim is staked around a constrained psychological terrain and this restriction protects against a more genuine feeling of vulnerability that arises due to the insufficient experience of a Self that is not vulnerable but sustaining. Consequently, what is familiar is idolatrously clung to and the unknown is eschewed.

The relinquishment of egotism and its attachments is espoused by all major religions. Some psychoanalysts have also recognized the need for detachment as both necessary to spiritual development as well as a marker of psychological well-being (Symington 1994). However, while attachment is antithetical to Self-knowledge, it is experienced by the ego as its anchor to individual existence. Non-attachment carries with it fear of loss of individual identity or existence and this anxiety is unbearable for most people.

Cohesiveness and limitlessness in Self-experience

Grotstein (2000) has described how the paranoid-schizoid and depressive positions are filters for an experience of a reality that cannot yet be borne. He postulates that the infant's fear of death is brought about by the spontaneous activation of his death instinct in response to initial experiences of O. I believe that in this context death signifies the inability to create or maintain an experience of a cohesive, individual self. Without a coherent self, the limitlessness of O cannot be perceived as an infinite Presence but only as an infinite absence. This is organized into persecutory phantasies, as described by Symington (2001):

> I am pretty certain that when you get people who are full of the most awful internal objects, real monsters inside them, it is their way of representing an *absence*, because there is no way within the human equipment to produce an image of an *absence* . . . the only way the human psyche can represent an absence is by some form of savage monster in one form or another.
>
> (Symington 2001: 66)

Regardless of the form, phantasy or narrative that gives symbolic meaning to dread, anxiety primarily is experienced in terms of time and space, and psychically, time and space tend to be interchangeable. This is understandable as both are illusions based upon the polarity of the initial split between perceiving and perceived. This polarity or vibration creates the illusion of change in that which is changeless and of division in that which is indivisible (Yukteswar 1949). Bion (1970) further connected time to space by locating past to 'within' memory and the future to 'outside' memory or possession. The permutations of the building blocks constituted by the ideas of time and space support the illusion of individual existence, and tenacity to this perception precludes tolerance for the realization of Unity. Self-experience requires a weakening of tenacity and an opening of time and space. However, the openness of space engenders paranoia, and the openness of time engenders depression. Thus existence outside the individual ego is imagined to be either dangerous or empty. These anxieties are translated into the phantasies associated with the paranoid-schizoid and depressive positions theorized by Klein.

The negation of time and space associated with omnipotence or mania *vis-à-vis* the paranoid-schizoid and depressive positions is not at all the same as the timelessness and spacelessness of Ultimate Reality. In omnipotence and mania time and space are denied when the limits they impose produce intolerable anxieties regarding dependence upon others and vulnerability in relation to the physical world. These anxieties and defences are well described in the psycho-analytic literature. I suggest there is yet another reason for intolerance of time and space. Time and space have been presented as illusions of change and division in that which is changeless and indivisible. Ultimate Reality is only 'centre' and eternally 'now'. The endurance of limits portends a focused present that is the portal to timeless, spaceless Existence. The previously described anxieties of loss of individual existence associated with approaching this realization compel the obliteration of temporal limits, not because they are restricting, but because they usher toward a dreaded Infinitude.

The psychological acceptance of limits requires the capacity to suffer frustration. As described by Bion (1962), intolerance of frustration precludes the development of thought. In addition to being the adaptive means by which the limitations and vulnerabilities of the self in relation to the physical world are addressed, thought is also the agency by which one questions the reality of the physical world and initiates inquiry into truth. While thought is necessary to both psychological and spiritual progress, it also can be a means of filtering, attenuating and evading pure experience. Bion (1970) warns, therefore, that knowledge and understanding can be both an impetus toward and a defence against Infinity. Thought is motion and therefore subject to time and space. Like language, thought represents distance between Reality and the thinker. Not only is the experience of Ultimate Reality ineffable, but also it requires no language because it vouchsafes no distance or separation. When the salt doll of the individual self dissolves into the ocean of Reality it no longer speaks or thinks (Kakar 1991).

243

The psychoanalytic dialogue is accompanied by a silent, invisible metamorphosis and it is the latter that is the apotheosis of the analysis. Eigen (1998) points out that Bion's writings on faith approach the idea of psychoanalysis without words. The verbal or understanding aspect of psychoanalysis (transformations in K) is the precursor to a nonverbal emotional experience or reality (transformation in O) (Bion 1965). Symington (2001) also describes an expansion of the capacity for emotional experience, as well as the development of psychological understanding, occurring during periods of contemplative silence within psychoanalysis.

Direct, unfiltered experience of Reality is difficult to sustain and is therefore evacuated, evaded or psychically manipulated into something that gives the illusion of more manageability, such as unconscious phantasy or conscious thought. The capacity for experience can be strengthened through interpretation of the thoughts and phantasies associated with unbearable experience. In addition, I believe psychoanalysis can facilitate directly the experience of Reality, not only by analysing impediments to this perception, but also by actively promoting qualities necessary to spiritual growth. I specifically will address faith, courage and reverence as attitudes which promote *sraddha* and which can be developed through psychoanalysis.

Faith

Faith is first in that it is the aperture that determines the quantity of pure experience permitted. Something must be given up for something new to be attained, and this relinquishment engenders fear, loss and mourning. Thus, the will to progress requires faith in its value. Through psychoanalysis, an accrual of the experience of tolerance engenders faith that one can bear openness to unknown experience. This is a prerequisite for psychological change as well as for Self-realization.

In Bion's writing on faith, he asserts it to be a scientific state of mind (Bion 1970). He describes the 'act of faith' as a scientific procedure, distinguishing it from its conventional religious meaning. It is the suspension of the sensual and the known so that tolerance of experience is developed. In the vernacular, faith has come to stand for the very thing it repudiates. Faith is misunderstood to be the evasion of experience by filling in the unknown with a god, a dogma, or a doctrine. However, this view is an adulteration of the true religious meaning of faith. Consider the definition in *Letter to the Hebrews*: 'Faith is the *substance* of things not seen, the *evidence* of things hoped for' (Hebrews 11: 1, emphasis mine). Here, faith is distinguished from hope or belief in being the experiential and active realization of that which is not sensually apprehended, remembered or desired.

For Bion, sensually rooted mental functions can understand derivatives of O, but faith is the state of mind where Ultimate Reality or O is met. Faith requires the abandoning of memory and desire. As previously discussed, memory and desire pertain to inside and outside – aspects of space, which are connected to past and future, or aspects of time. The abandoning of the sensual, along with memory, desire, time and space, appears also to be an abandoning of the reality principle and, therefore, is imagined to be an abandoning of the individual ego and of life itself. The anxiety generated by this renunciation is unbearable unless a sustaining experience of faith is cultivated.

Virya, or moral courage, is supported and reinforced through the acquiring of faith. The patient endurance of experience, which can be facilitated through psychoanalysis, allows for courage to be rooted in conviction. *Virya*, born of faith, combats the grip of tenacity to life and the sensual experience of the ego. It is important to understand that Reality or Pure Experience is only *imagined* to be empty or dangerous; consequently, it is in phantasy that courage is required to face it. However, this realization is reached only through *virya*, which is required before the fearlessness of perfect faith can be attained. An aphorism of Vedanta is '*neti, neti*', which translates as 'not this, not that', and refers to rejecting what is not real, and searching for what is. Although it is framed as a rejection, it can also be viewed as an invitation to openness, never being complacent or satisfied with what is known or understood. It is an exhortation to *virya*, the courage to face O constantly.

Kakar (1991) concurs with Bion that the ability to experience Being is the culmination of analysis. He uses the Sanskrit word *bhava*, meaning 'being' or 'existence' in an ontological context, recognizing it as the ground for all creativity:

> The capacity for *bhava* is what an ideal analysis strives for. All the other gains of analysis – insight into one's conflicts, the capacity to experience pleasure without guilt, ability to tolerate anxiety without being crippled, development of a reliable reality testing, and so on – are secondary to the birth of the analytic *bhava*.
>
> (Kakar 1991: 19)

Bion maintained that in order for this type of analytic process to occur, psychoanalysts themselves need to have faith, not only in the analytic process, but also in their own openness to transformation through the analytic experience. By the suspension of memory, desire and sensually derived understanding, the analyst *becomes infinite* so as to be able to become one with the patient's transformations in O (Bion 1970).

Reverence

In considering reverence it first needs to be contrasted with idealization. In idealization, safety is bestowed by a perfect object phantasized as able to afford protection, sustenance and knowledge. Omnipotence, as it is conceived in Kleinian psychoanalytic theory, is a related phantasy. Here, there is an unconscious identification with the idealized object so that one shares in its power and is protected against persecutory anxieties that arise from awareness of smallness, dependency and vulnerability. If the feeling of exposure is too great, one is reduced to a *phantasy* of omnipotence where one *imagines* oneself to be invulnerable. Idealization and omnipotence persist to the degree that the anxieties engendering them continue to be experienced as intolerable.

Klein (1963) believed the realization that the good object could never be as perfect as the ideal led to the painful corollary that no truly ideal part of the self existed. However, in spite of this, she believed the need for idealization was never completely given up and contributed to recalcitrant feelings of loneliness. Klein did not consider the possibility that the persisting desire for the ideal emanated from an intuition of an inner, immanent perfection. As has been discussed, the Self postulated by Vedanta is complete and inviolable. Such a Self does not seek a phantasy of omnipotent control over others, knowledge, or physical reality. It therefore represents a different type of perfection, a different type of omnipotence.

Reverence differs from idealization in that it is an attitude ultimately directed toward the truest Self, rather than a phantasy of protection being provided by an object. Reverence emerges spontaneously toward the experience of one's inner divinity or when in contact with something that brings one's divinity or divine potential to awareness, be it another person, art or an ideal. The object of reverence is esteemed because of what it evokes within individuals rather than what it provides to them. Reverence is attunement with love as the universal attractor. Envy, omnipotence and persecution are not born from reverence, rather reverence is the attitude by which these obstacles to *sraddha* are surmounted. This is not to say that idealization and reverence cannot exist side by side, or that idealization cannot contaminate or cloud reverence. Consequently, the psychoanalytic identification and interpretation of idealization and its origins can facilitate a deeper and clearer experience of reverence.

Similar to Grotstein's (2000) thesis that the paranoid-schizoid and depressive positions are filters for an experience of a reality that cannot yet be borne, awe is an experience of reverence beyond that which can be symbolized or contextualized. Awe is an unfiltered experience of a non-symbolic reality. Awe is intolerance of the O of reverence in the same way as persecution is intolerance of the O of dread. These states of mind are the polarity of the experience associated with openness to faith.

The experience of awe is beautifully described in the Bhagavad-Gita when Arjuna has the 'vision of visions' and perceives Krishna, who symbolizes the Self, as the formless God, or the God encompassing all forms. In other words, he has the perception of Reality beyond the cloak of a symbolic representation. Arjuna is overwhelmed by awe and beseeches Krishna to reassume his human – his symbolic – visage. Here, the Reality of Krishna is more than Arjuna can contain. Krishna reassumes his familiar form but assures Arjuna that his true Self can be arrived at and entered into with perseverance – not that he can be translated into a symbolic reality, but that this filtered reality can be transcended through an expanding capacity to bear Pure Experience. Awe is then transmuted into deeper realizations of reverence.

The analysand's need for reverence presents itself for the recognition and sanction of the psychoanalyst. If psychoanalysis is able to provide an experience of faith, reverence will manifest toward the Self that is experienced in the analysis as well as for the analyst and the psychoanalytic process. Kakar (1991) sees a parallel between the analytic relationship and the guru–disciple relationship. He describes how when the disciple forms a relationship with the guru, he is in fact forming a relationship with his own best Self. His description of the guru–disciple relationship is applicable to the relationship between analyst and analysand, provided it is understood that we are speaking of analyst *qua* analyst or *qua* guardian of the analysis. In other words, the analyst of reverence is the Self of the analyst, or the inchoately perceived Self of the analysand, the Agency that oversees the person of the analyst, the person of the analysand, and the analytic process. While the analyst does not attempt to inspire reverence directly, any more than he would attempt to gratify other perceived needs of the analysand, if reverence in the transference is interpreted as idealization, the analysand will feel that which is most valuable in him and to him is not recognized, understood, or appreciated (Bion 1992).

In the depressive position, love for the object develops as one appreciates its uniqueness and its capacity to provide something one cannot provide for oneself. One appreciates the object in spite of or along with its shortcomings and inflictions of frustration. Strictly speaking, the 'object' is a mental representation of a relationship that provides a function or enables a function to be performed. Consequently, love for the object is not love of another separate individual. Instead, love matures as one relinquishes the object as an object and it becomes a subject in its own right (Grotstein 2000; personal communication 2002). In this process, anxieties arise in response to awareness of the separateness and independence of the other on whom one depends. One may defend against these anxieties with phantasies of omnipotence, fusion with the object, possession of the object, and others, all of which in one way or another deny the separateness of the object and impede the experience and expression of love. Love for the object, and later love for a separate subject, is born from and rooted in separateness.

Whereas love is conceived in the appreciation of separateness, it finds fulfilment in the realization of unity. Only after having established the uniqueness and separateness of the other can there be a vertex from which a truly common essence shared with the other is appreciated. The Essence of the other is the same as the Essence of the self. An expansion of self accompanies the recognition of the commonality with the other, both in terms of a shared divinity as well as the shared misperceptions and misidentifications that lead to the conflicts and suffering inherent in life. The realization of the mutuality and universality of the human condition leads to empathy, love and the desire to give and receive help (Yukteswar 1949). Psychoanalysis can catalyse and support the process of separation and reunification with the accompanying maturation and purification of love and reverence.

'As mortal beings, you offer your fellow men your goodwill. As temples containing the Reality you offer them your reverence' (Isherwood 1963: 27). Love is transmuted into reverence with the appreciation that the Self of the other is the same as the Self of the self. Reverence transcends object relationships by being directed toward a Self that exists independently from them. Reverence leads to an expansiveness of heart and a deeper identification with one's true Self. It both instils the desire to become like unto its attractor, and through its promotion of *sraddha*, is also the means by which the metamorphosis occurs. St John of the Cross (1990) describes this aspect of reverence, here designated as love:

> the property of love is to desire to be united, joined, and made equal and like to the object of its love, that it may perfect itself in love's good things.
>
> (St John of the Cross 1990: 144)

I believe it is clear that the saint is not describing a defensive possession or fusion, but rather the becoming of what one reveres or allowing what one reveres to become oneself.

Yoga and psychoanalysis

Related to Vedanta is the system of yoga as expounded by the ancient Indian sage Patanjali. Whereas the authors of the Vedas and the sages of Vedantic tradition have testified both to the Self's existence and its potential realization, yoga postulates that one can directly know and experience his true Self, increase his identity with it, and ultimately realize his unity with the all-pervasive Spirit or Ultimate Reality through a disciplined practice of concentration and meditation. (Strictly speaking, the Self cannot be identified with or known but only realized or become. However, for the purpose of discussion, it can be helpful to refer to experiences of Self-awareness that impress upon the ego as a process of 'knowing' or 'identification'.) Through the practice of yoga, the anxiety associated with

Infinity is mitigated by the expanding experience of Self. *Virya* and faith reinforce and advance each other.

Freud (1930) briefly addressed yoga and saw it as a means by which the ego tries to defend itself from a threatening external world. He understood yoga to be an attempt to kill the power of the instincts and saw its fulfilment as a negative state of desirelessness. To Freud, yoga enjoined a negative giving up, with no positive attainment other than an illusory remnant of an early, less demarcated ego state. The desire to attain freedom from suffering through an expanding sense of Self, espoused by Buddha, Vedantists, and most religions in one form or another, was seen by Freud as an example of primary process thinking not compatible with reality.

On the other hand, practitioners of yoga often do not recognize the value of psychological development primarily because it attends to what, at the healthiest, is still a misidentified individual ego. Psychoanalysis, it has been argued, cannot bring one to an ultimate truth (Torwesten 1985). This view, however, neglects the *process* of spiritual unfoldment. By acknowledging only the absolute, it fails to recognize the preconditions for Self-realization. I am in agreement with Coltart (2000) that embarking upon the spiritual path, particularly the discipline required for the practice of yoga, requires a strong sense of personal identity. She points out that the ego first has to be strong and secure before it can allow itself to be seen as illusory and unreal.

I suggest that recognizing the value of psychological health for spiritual development is adumbrated in the aphorisms of Patanjali themselves. Patanjali defines yoga as the neutralization of the turbulence of the mind (Prabhavananda and Isherwood 1953). The Self is intuited when the mind is still. A mind in conflict, even unconscious conflict, is in turbulence and Self-experience is clouded. But paradoxically, and somewhat ironically, the mind is the employer of the methods by which it quiets itself. Consequently the executive function of the mind, the healthy ego, is the practitioner of yoga and the conductor of spiritual discipline.

The Yoga Aphorisms of Patanjali delineate an eight-step path for the attainment of placidity of mind and realization of the Self. The system is hierarchical with each step building upon the previous one. The first two steps are prescriptions and proscriptions regarding moral behaviour. The third step is *asana*, which in almost all exegeses of Patanjali's yoga is deemed to denote a steady physical posture. Hatha yoga, with its various exercises and poses, is an elaboration of this step with its goal being to promote health, flexibility, and stamina. While this may be advantageous, I do not believe it can be the real meaning of *asana* as it is located in Patanjali's epigenetics. Moral behaviour is not a precondition for physical discipline, and the higher steps of yoga can be practised in spite of an unsound body. Primarily, *asana* must refer to mental posture, a steady state of mind, the prerequisite for the practice of concentration and meditation that follow in Patanjali's system.

This definition of *asana* brings it into alignment with the attributes of mind delineated by Bion as the foundation and necessary mental posture for meeting and bearing the experience of O. *Asana* is the mental posture of non-attachment, tolerance of frustration, as well as faith. Seen in this light, *asana* is related to psychoanalysis both in practice and as its goal. Psychoanalysis ultimately leads to the attainment of *asana*, a steady and open state of mind, and in this capacity serves as an integral part of yoga, Vedanta, or any spiritual discipline.

Conclusion

When mind broods placid, soothed with holy wont;
When Self contemplates self, and in itself
Hath comfort; when it knows the nameless joy
Beyond all scope of sense, revealed to soul,
Only to soul! And, knowing, wavers not,
True to the farther Truth; when, holding this,
It deems no other treasure comparable,
But, harbored there, cannot be stirred or shook
By any gravest grief – call that state 'peace,'
That happy severance Yoga; call that man
The perfect Yogin!
(E. Arnold (trans.) Bhagavad-Gita VI: 20–23)

Virya is the courage to bear direct experience – Bion's O – without modification or filtering. Having attained *virya*, one can face physical and psychological reality for what it is and not for what it is not. The *sine qua non* of psychopathology is the inability to accept reality on its own terms. This can be consequent to two related causes. First, is an intolerance of O leading to the omnipotent re-creation of reality as a phantasized construct that is imagined to be more comprehensible, safer or more providing to one's needs. In this case, pathology is maintained in an effort to prevent a breakthrough of the reality that cannot be faced. Second, is a lack of experience of Ultimate Reality, or the Self, leading to an over-valuation of sensual reality as a thing in itself.

In this chapter, I have attempted to demonstrate the alliance between psychological and spiritual development and how they complement and facilitate each other in addressing these twin sources of misery. I have attempted to show how psychological equilibrium is necessary for the capacity to be receptive, not only to life experience, but to spiritual experience as well. I also have attempted to show the correlate, which is that spiritual experience provides a perspective that decreases vulnerability to the inevitable duality, frustrations, and trauma associated with physical existence. Finally, I tried to address some common misunderstandings between advocates of psychoanalysis and metaphysics and to suggest that what they have in common transcends their differences.

References

Arnold, E. (trans.) (1975) *The Song Celestial or Bhagavad-Gita.* Los Angeles: Self-Realization Fellowship.

Bion, W.R. (1962) *Learning from Experience.* London: Karnac.

Bion, W.R. (1965) *Transformations.* London: Karnac.

Bion, W.R. (1970) *Attention and Interpretation.* London: Karnac.

Bion, W.R. (1992) Reverence and awe. In *Cogitations.* London: Karnac.

Breuer, J. and Freud, S. (1893–1895) *Studies on Hysteria.* SE 2.

Coltart, N. (2000) Psychoanalysis and Buddhism. In *Slouching Towards Bethlehem.* New York: Other Press.

Eigen, M. (1998) *The Psychoanalytic Mystic.* Binghamton, NY: ESF.

Freud, S. (1900) *The Interpretation of Dreams.* SE 5.

Freud, S. (1927) *The Future of an Illusion.* SE 21.

Freud, S. (1930) *Civilization and its Discontents.* SE 21.

Freud, S (1933) *New Introductory Lectures on Psycho-analysis.* SE 22.

Grotstein, J.S. (2000) *Who is the Dreamer, who Dreams the Dream? A Study of Psychic Presences.* Hillsdale, NJ: Analytic Press.

Isherwood, C. (1963) *An Approach to Vedanta.* Los Angeles: Vedanta Press.

Jung, C.G. (1936) *The Archetypes and the Collective Unconscious.* Collected Works of C.G. Jung. Princeton, NJ: Princeton University Press.

Kakar, S. (1991) *The Analyst and the Mystic.* New Delhi: University of Chicago Press.

Klein, M. (1963) On the sense of loneliness. In *Envy and Gratitude.* London: Vintage (1997).

Perlmutter, S., Aldering, G., Goldhaber, G., Knop, R.A., Nugent, P., Castro, P.G. et al. (1999) Measurements of *Omega* and *Lambda* from 42 High-Redshift Supernovae. *Astrophysical Journal* 517: 565.

Prabhavananda and Isherwood, C. (1953) *How to Know God: The Yoga Aphorisms of Patanjali.* Los Angeles: Vedanta Press.

St John of the Cross (1990) *Dark Night of the Soul.* New York: Image.

Symington, N. (1994) *Emotion and Spirit.* London: Karnac.

Symington, N. (2001) *The Spirit of Sanity.* London: Karnac.

Torwesten, H. (1985) *Vedanta, Heart of Hinduism.* New York: Grove.

Winnicott, D.W. (1960) Ego distortion in terms of true and false self. In *The Maturational Processes and the Facilitating Environment.* Madison, CT: International Universities Press.

Yukteswar (1949) *The Holy Science.* Los Angeles: Self-Realization Fellowship.

14

A SIMPLE QUESTION?

Rodney Bomford

For much of the twentieth century psychoanalytic theory was seen as a major threat to religion. Freud and God did not readily coexist. One criticism of Christianity was that it was bad for you. In *The Future of an Illusion* Freud (1927) described religion as an obsessional neurosis. There has undeniably been a tendency in the Christian Church to identify God as an oppressive divine Father, insisting upon the observance of rituals and of rules of conduct. Such an image of God might well be considered a projection of the super-ego causing untold damage through demanding the surrender of the ego to the super-ego. Religion, furthermore, can propagate a wish-fulfilling fantasy that diverts its adherents from coping with much that life − and death − throws at humanity and thus blesses childish evasions.

Such criticisms have been addressed by a number of apologists for religion. Meissner (1984) for example, while conceding that the Church has often been guilty of such charges, yet argues that theology has its own critique of these distortions and that they are definitely not of the essence of faith. I shall not repeat these arguments here, but rather try to address a more fundamental difficulty that Freud and many others have found in the Faith. I refer to the question of the existence of God. To many the very idea of God is an absurdity and when Christians are asked to explain just what it is they say exists, they can seem very evasive. 'No, we do not believe in an old man with a beard sitting on a cloud', they may say. Yet the idea seems to persist that there is Someone somewhere 'out there', with a superhuman mind, and a very remarkable consciousness that can encompass the thoughts and concerns of every individual human and even scan both the past and future of the universe. It seems that the veracity of that idea is asserted when God is claimed to exist.

As a Christian priest who claims to be a believer I shall try to address this question − does God exist? − with as little evasiveness as possible. Yet the more one thinks about it the more complex appear to be the issues underlying it. One soon finds oneself mired in a philosophical bog, into which I shall now try to enter as cautiously as possible.

Existence

What is it that is asserted when anything is said to exist? And what can we say with certainty does exist? Descartes (1637, section 4), conceiving that we might be deluded by a malicious demon about everything else, yet concluded that he himself must exist while remaining thus far doubtful about everything else. Bishop Berkeley (1710, sections 33ff) in a similar solipsistic reverie concluded that things exist only through our minds. Famously, Dr Johnson (Boswell 1791, vol. I: 471) refuted him by kicking a stone and thereby expressed a view which the post-Enlightenment western world has generally not doubted. Solid material things surely exist and are indeed our paradigms for what existence is. What I shall call the empiricist view of reality is founded upon this. What can be observed by the eyes, heard with the ears or touched by the body is the bedrock of our knowledge. Such is the common sense understanding of the universe and upon it is built our scientific civilisation with all its achievements. Only a lunatic or a philosopher, surely, can doubt the reality and veracity of this.

Yet science itself at some of its frontiers stretches this simple view to breaking-point as becomes clear when questions about existence are raised. The Roman philosopher-poet Lucretius observed that a statue is worn very gradually away by the touch of millions of passers-by and, rejecting the possibility of an infinite divisibility, concluded that matter consists of very small indivisible atoms.[1] One might imagine that such atoms were simply minute pieces of the stuff of the statue as it appears to be. The early twentieth-century explorations of Neils Bohr and others led to a quite different picture. There were sub-atomic particles and the atom became somewhat like a miniature planetary system, with a nucleus and circling electrons. But it was mostly space. The solidity of matter disappeared. As one took in this picture, one might imagine oneself as a much tinier Alice in Wonderland exploring the interior of the atom, handling the protons or whirling around with the electrons: presumably scientists working in this field held in their minds a picture of the atom as such an Alice might have found it.[2] She might have kicked the sub-atomic particles to establish their reality and then she would have had no doubt that they actually existed – if she belonged to Dr Johnson's school of thought. There can be no such Alice and the picture of the atom can never be more than a picture, a model which assists an imaginative grasp of what otherwise would be a wholly alien world. The existence of electrons and protons can never be established by the kind of tests that we apply to the existence of the objects of our observable universe. Once a model is established, questions of existence can be answered within its terms. For instance, if it is agreed that electrons and protons exist, then neutrons must too, for the model requires them if it is to represent adequately the results of calculations based on observation. But the meaning of 'existence' as applicable to any such particles is a metaphysical, not an empirical, matter. In the course of time other sub-atomic particles were required also. The model became rapidly more complicated, but also less like the little planetary system first described. Electrons did not rotate predictably like planets: they came and went in quite counter-intuitive ways, so that it was no longer possible to establish both their place and their velocity at the same moment. They no longer behaved like the larger objects of our world at all. More recently we find the whole theory dislodged from its prime role as the ultimate truth about matter: now there are vibrating strings.[3] It is not that the older model is wrong and it still allows correct predictions of how atoms join into molecules and doubtless many other things. But it is no longer seen as the uniquely true account of the sub-microscopic world. If we ask of any such account, 'Are things really like that?', 'Do electrons or strings or whatever may follow them really exist?', then we are moving beyond the range of empirical discourse: we are making judgements about what we count as reality. Questions about the existence of whole new categories of phenomena take us out of the empirical into metaphysics or some other field.

There are other forms of existence. Historians tell us that at a certain date in the eighteenth century, Poland ceased to exist. It was not swallowed up by an earthquake but appropriated by its greedy neighbours. Houses, churches, potato fields and other material constituents of Poland remained unchanged. The empiricist would not be too bothered about existence in this case since legal edicts and treaties could be examined to establish the matter. What is meant by the existence of a nation is established by convention and there are criteria for deciding whether it meets them. A nation exists through a certain ordering of people and things whereby the whole is more than its parts when viewed in a particular light. What makes it a whole is not necessarily the addition of a new entity but a certain way of looking at it: this is not irrelevant to the question of the existence of God.

Psychoanalysts deal with entities whose existence is of a kind even more elusive than that of sub-atomic particles. Does the super-ego exist? If the existence of id and ego is accepted then certain processes are not explicable without a third 'entity', but that presupposes the existence of id and ego first. No kind of Alice can even be conceived who might wander around the mind and empirically test the reality of its parts. Again, the question of the *existence* of a mental structure is one that takes debate out of empirical discourse. I propose to call such debate 'trans-empirical' discourse.

In both sub-atomic physics and psychoanalytic theory trans-empirical discourse arises from the use of models which facilitate the imagination in grasping highly elusive phenomena. Sub-atomic particles were seen as existing somewhat like the solid objects which in ordinary discourse we may describe as 'existing'. Freud proposed a model of the mind that divided it *spatially* – topographically – into different departments, although of course the 'space' was not like the physical space in which solid objects exist. Empirical discourse may encompass the processes and phenomena which these imagined entities are used to explain, but questions of their existence, reality and perhaps nature lead into the trans-empirical. That conclusion coheres with Immanuel Kant's argument (1781, Second Part, First Division, Book 2, Chapter III) that there is reality behind the phenomenal (i.e. empirical) but we can know nothing about it.

Levels of discourse

The empirical

I have argued elsewhere (Bomford 1999) that religious language may properly be seen as constituted by a number of different levels. Assertions made at one level have a quite different kind of truth and validity from assertions made at another. The first of these levels is simply that of empirical discourse. God does not fit easily into this level at all, for all the excellent reasons that an atheist may typically present. The empirical aspect of religion is most clearly seen in ethical discourse. The establishment of justice, for example, is for the most part something that can be assessed empirically. Because it is empirical the genially disposed of any faith or of none are likely to agree broadly about ethical questions or at worst to disagree within shared terms of reference. The obvious exceptions to this are the debates about abortion and euthanasia, where those of certain religious opinions are likely to differ from non-religious humanists. They differ, however, primarily because of belief in the existence of an immortal soul, which is not an empirical question.

   Talk about God clearly moves into the trans-empirical and typically into a mythological version of the trans-empirical. The existence of entities not belonging to the solid universe is presupposed. Here the ethical atheist and the believer part company. The Christian talks of a tri-une God, apparently a strange being beyond the universe of ordinary life and yet present everywhere in it, an influence everywhere active, yet nowhere empirically detectable. This is the arena of the trans-empirical, particularised in religion as the mythical.

The mystical

Before discussing that further, another area of discourse must be mentioned. Beyond the mythical, there is the mystical. The mystical is notoriously hard to define and no definition adequately covers the experience even of acknowledged Christian 'mystics'. I shall, perhaps arbitrarily, take as normative the stream of mystical writers that constitutes the apophatic tradition. That is to say they approach God primarily through denying his likeness to other beings or concepts – rather than by approaching God through affirming symbols or analogies. This tradition was powerfully influenced by the first-century Jewish writer Philo, by the pagan third-century philosopher Plotinus and among its leading figures are the theologians Origen, Gregory of Nyssa, Dionysius the Pseudo-Areopagite, Meister Eckhart, the anonymous author of *The Cloud of Unknowing* and St John of the Cross. In this tradition it is denied that God is *a being*: rather, he is Being itself, or even beyond the distinction between being and non-being.[4] The pictures that lie behind the mythical are abandoned in the mystical: all imagery has to be transcended. God is darkness, emptiness, absence of any specific content. Mystical discourse is characterised chiefly by paradox and self-contradiction. Stimulated by the theories of Ignacio Matte Blanco (1975, 1988), I have argued elsewhere (Bomford 1999) that the mystical journey may be seen as an attempt by the conscious mind to enter the unconscious. This claim is supported by the fact that mystical writings very often display the five characteristics that Freud attributed to the unconscious – timelessness, non-contradiction of opposites, the loss of the distinction between reality and fantasy, condensation and displacement. Furthermore such writings very generally speak of entering into the depths of the soul. Whether 'the soul' in such writings is the same as 'the psyche' in Freudian tradition could of course be disputed. Theologians who wholly reject psychoanalytic theories might well do so, as might analysts who see no meaning or value in the mystical endeavour. Ultimately it is probably a matter of choice: those interested in both disciplines are likely to see creative parallels between them, but not such as the force of argument can compel others to accept. If it be allowed that the mystical journey is an exploration of the unconscious, then the unconscious entered is not the repressed consciousness – that would be a diabolic byway and dead end on the mystical journey – but the unrepressed unconscious, which Freud described as timeless (1933: 74). Matte Blanco saw this unconscious as the source of emotion, a mode of pure being from which unfolds the creative imagination (1988: 96–99). Quoting Freud's description of it as the true psychical reality Matte Blanco described it as mute silence (1988: 103) and deep peace (1988: 105), as a mode of being, rather than of thinking or feeling.

The mythical

Even if it were to be accepted that there are clear parallels and points of contact between the mystical theologian's God and the Unconscious of psychoanalytic theory, much theological language would still need to be explained. The God of mysticism is experienced as an unknowable, still void at the heart of certain experiences. He, she or it seems remote from the notion of an omnipotent creator believed to be the source and governor of the universe – of matter as well as of mind. The whole biblical narrative from creation, through the choice of the nation of Israel, the narrowing of that choice to the man Jesus, conceived of as an incarnation of God himself, through his ministry death and resurrection, to his ascension, the sending of the Spirit, and his session at the right hand of the Father until his return at the end of the world, this whole narrative appears to come from a conceptual field quite different from that of the God of mysticism. Indeed the theologian cannot sensibly deny that its origins are of a different nature. I shall refer to this narrative, without prejudice to its veracity, as the mythical dimension of Christian theology. It appears to presuppose the existence of a divine being who is distinct from his creation, of a mind over against the minds of his human creatures, of an exterior agency acting among creaturely agencies. In the Bible, and in the imagination of most believers, this mythological God appears to be corporeal, although theologians generally have denied this, and although his corporeality is of a quality different from that of the material of other bodies. In Stoic philosophy God was indeed corporeal, being constituted of an element higher and finer than the four elements (earth, water, air and fire) of which other bodies were made (see for example Armstrong 1967: 124–125). The Manichaeans too conceived God as a kind of bodily substance enfolding that part of the world which was not in the power of his evil adversary.

The Christian myth was apparently formed in wholly – or very predominantly – Jewish circles. As the Church moved into the Gentile world and gradually became the dominant religion of the Roman Empire (and was accepted beyond it also), theologians employed the language and to some extent the concepts of Greek philosophy to come to terms with the apparent crudity of the myth. Out of this marriage of cultures came the established theology of the Church, expressed in creed and doctrine – the Trinity of Three Persons in One Substance, the two Natures of Christ, divine and human, united in one Person, and so forth. The doctrine of God came to include an account of his 'attributes', as eternal, incorporeal, immaterial, infinite, ubiquitous, simple (i.e. without parts or qualities) and so forth. Most of these were couched in negative terms, as denials that God had a body, or changed through time, or was restricted to certain places. While the early theologians accepted the Bible literally, they generally regarded the literal meaning as a platform upon which were erected other equally significant levels of meaning, such as, for example, the allegorical, the tropological and the anagogic. The last of these is the understanding of Scripture as a guide to the ascent to God in what might today be called mystical experience. This was not some rarefied and optional addition to normal faith, as later ages have often seen it, but the central calling of the faithful to that unity with God which was widely called deification, particularly in the Greek-speaking writers whose way of understanding has survived better in the Orthodox churches than the western Catholic or Protestant traditions. The anagogic interpretation assisted theology to reconcile the mythology of Scripture with the demands of a sophisticated philosophical culture, which through current interpretation of its Pythagorean and Platonic inheritance had a decidedly mystical inclination.

A uniquely personal and revealing account of this reconciliation was left to us by St Augustine of Hippo in his *Confessions*. Monica, his mother, was a devout Christian who longed ardently for his conversion to the faith. He grew up estranged from it by, among other obstacles, his sense of its mythological crudity. As a young man he was drawn to the Manichaean beliefs, to which I have referred above (see Augustine, *Confessions*, Book III, Chapters 7–10). An important stage in his development came through reading certain philosophers, whom he does not name but are generally assumed to be such Platonists as the great Plotinus. In studying them he came to reject the corporeal God of the Manichaeans (Book V, Chapter 10). For Plotinus the ultimate reality is the One (not named as God) from whom everything emanates.[5] Ascent to the One is achievable by stripping away all sensations, images and thoughts, moving from particulars to the total abstract unity which he believed underlies all other reality. To Augustine this notion of God as the summit of a mental ascent dispelled the more material concept of Mani. In his new vision, it was necessary to go in to the soul in order to ascend to God (Book VII, Chapter 10). A further decisive development occurred when he came to believe that the One was not remote and blissfully unaware of creation (which was Plotinus' belief) but was passionately and lovingly concerned to inspire a reciprocal love in his human creatures – and thereupon Monica's prayers were answered and Augustine was baptised.

Reality and 'nous'

This ancient history may seem very remote from the world of the twenty-first century yet in that period the Christian faith became essentially what it is nowadays and to understand it we may profitably revisit the world of thought of the time. One particularly pertinent consideration concerns the nature of reality. To modern humanity – I use the term in a general sense to refer to the assumptions of the past two or three centuries – the real is the material. Dr Johnson kicked a stone and thereby disproved the arguments of the solipsists and perhaps of idealists in general. In the Platonic tradition, however, the material was real in so far as it participated in those ideal Forms which are accessible only mentally. To engage with reality, one needed to move away from the material. In Plotinus' famous account of his meditation in *The Enneads*, one stripped away the accidental qualities of matter, such things as colour, shape, extension, in order to draw closer to the real. In those Christian theologians influenced by Platonism a hierarchy is often described in terms of mental activity.[6] At the lowest level is sensation, touching, seeing, hearing actual material objects. The next level is imagination, by which is meant the internal picturing of the material, as when we remember a particular object for example. Then there is discursive reasoning, when the material is described and discussed in conceptual terms – a material object, for example, would not be internally pictured (as at the imaginative level) but would be defined by its construction, mode of operation etc. Beyond these levels, and of supreme philosophical and theological importance, is the level of understanding. Here the word 'understanding' must be taken in a somewhat technical sense, since the meaning of the words traditionally used in this whole tradition has been adulterated and debased. The Greek word used was *nous*, usually translated as 'mind', but that explains very little. Since a technical sense is intended, I will use the word Understanding with a capital U.

Nous, Understanding, had a synthetic, holistic quality which was not found in discursive – analytical – reasoning. In Platonic terms it referred to apprehending the ideal Forms in which the particulars participated, for example, in apprehending Beauty itself through an object of beauty. In theological terms this might mean apprehending the working of God in any of the particulars of creation, and indeed through creation itself as a whole. More specific instances of 'nous' are not easily found in the literature of the time, but in a modern context such can plausibly be suggested. For example, in that fascinating book *Zen and the Art of Motorcycle Maintenance* (Pirsig 1974), the writer – a keen motorcyclist and philosopher – knows the detailed workings of the parts of his machine intimately, but he also cultivates a more intuitive sense of the state of the machine's well-being, a kind of fellow-feeling for it which warns him, for example, of a possible developing problem long before any specific symptoms emerge. It might be called a free-floating, hovering attention which apprehends the machine as a whole, coherent, synergic system, rather than as an aggregation of related parts. Free-floating attention has been compared by psychoanalysts to Buddhist techniques of meditation (for example this is implicit in Eigen 1998: 32–33); these are closely parallel to Christian contemplation, which was supremely the operation of the faculty of Understanding. Nicholas of Cusa, a great mystical theologian of the fifteenth century CE, commends 'learned ignorance' as the way to draw near to God.[7] Everything possible must be learned in a discursive and analytic way, but then this must be recognised as total ignorance if a more unitive understanding is to come to one. I compare this with the motorcyclist's detailed knowledge of the parts of the machine which must be left behind if a synthetic and intuitive sense of its coherence is to be achieved. Perhaps similarly the psychoanalyst in the state of free-floating attention must forget for the time theories of the structure and dynamics of the mind, though knowledge of these is an essential preparation for the task, and that knowledge will be used again at a later point in the therapy. I suggest this kind of attention to another human being might be seen as the work of the Understanding which apprehends the totality of that to which it attends in an intuitive gazing.

Understanding, to the philosophers of the Platonic tradition and the theologians influenced by them, gave access to reality.[8] Reality was not to be found in matter through the senses, but through thought, thought that abstracted the essence from the material shell in which it was expressed. It would be wrong to describe that reality as 'a thought', but it would be more accurate to call it a thought than a thing. This view is startlingly at odds with the general view of the educated western world since the Enlightenment. The scientific outlook is taken to depend upon the observation and measurement of the material. On the frontiers of some of the sciences that perhaps is beginning to change, but the outlook of modern humanity thus far has not. The real is the empirically ascertainable. The implication for religion is very great, since if God is to be real he must surely be material. Since his presence is not materially evident, he must consist of some rarefied material not open to general observation. Such was the Manichaean concept and such is the view of God which many a modern atheist holds – and rightly denies the existence of. Unfortunately for the good of religion such an atheist may well be right to claim that many Christians in point of fact do believe in just such a God – even though officially his corporeality is denied. The desire of believers to take the myth seriously often leads to a tendency to take it literally, and the desire to see God as real often causes him to be seen as quasi-material. If one suggests, to either the atheist or many theists of that kind, that as thought is to matter so God is to thought one is likely to be told that therefore one does not believe in a real God at all. Yet such a view is nearer to historical orthodox Christianity's official beliefs than the quasi-material concept of God which is often taken to be the traditional one.

There is another important point about Understanding in the Platonic tradition. A thing is what it is because it *participates* in a reality beyond it in, so to speak, a higher sphere. A beautiful object, for example, is beautiful because it participates in Beauty, the Form of the Beautiful, to use the usual expression. Understanding grasps this higher reality. The Forms are spoken of as though they existed in an ideal world beyond this one, but how literally that should be taken is debatable. Plato himself at times used relatively crude mythological ways to explain his ideas. Plotinus and others took the Forms to be essentially thoughts. I suggest there is a strong echo of this way of thinking in psychoanalytic concepts. A person who is experienced as motherly, for example, *participates* in The Breast. The Breast is manifest in that person and this manifestation may be perceived with the eye of Understanding. To the Christian theologians influenced by Platonism everything participates to some degree in God, in whom are the true realities of every created thing. If, as I shall shortly propose, one model of God is the organically related totality of things, then to understand a particular thing will be to grasp how it participates in the whole scheme of things, to perceive its place in the universe. That kind of understanding is surely as valid and valuable as is the understanding acquired by analysing a thing purely as it is in itself. It is particularly important in understanding people, since people can be understood only by taking account of their mutual relationships.

Levels of language and God

I presented above the suggestion that to understand religious language one needs to categorise rather carefully. When one attempts to net God, so to speak, in empirical discourse one finds one has caught nothing very much, a fate I have suggested that he shares with the Unconscious. Empirical discourse is very different from mystical discourse and for that reason the empiricist may be brought to tolerate it more readily than he or she can tolerate the mythical. The mythical seems to make claims about the real world that the mystical is supremely unconcerned to address. One facet of the appeal of Buddhism to the intelligent westerner is that it does not depend upon belief in a divine being. It is often said to be atheistic and its mystical practice (if that is what it is) may be pursued without infringing upon the world as known empirically.

From the empirical perspective the Christian God may well be dismissed as non-existent, as nothing. Alternatively — and this is the view I espouse — He (I will use the customary masculine pronoun for simplicity of expression) might be seen as everything, the totality of the cosmos. At first sight this view may seem pantheistic and to attribute a grossly corporeal nature to God. I would hope to avoid these ancient errors by the qualification that God is Everything, but only Everything as seen by nous, Understanding. Furthermore, I emphasise that this is what can be said of God *from the empirical perspective*. Theology has always claimed that God is not knowable empirically and to the ancient concept of nous the real is only dimly glimpsed in the material. The empirical perspective is, after all, based upon what the observer can observe and must therefore observe piecemeal. It must struggle in vain with notions of 'the totality' or 'Everything', not least because such notions include the observer and so transcend the distinction between subject and object. The observer can observe everything that is 'over against' him as observing subject, even his own body and the workings of his mind, but he cannot observe that in himself which itself observes.

I have proposed therefore that 'God' may be interpreted as a word for the totality of the universe — the observer included — seen as a unity by the faculty of Understanding. That at least is how 'God' might be understood from an empiricist perspective. This model will particularly relate to the mythical level of religious language, somewhat as the model of God as the ultimate Unconscious relates to the mystical level.[9] To illustrate how this model of God (as totality) coheres with some traditional notions of God, consider the doctrine of Providence. According to this doctrine whatever happens to the believer in some sense comes from God and forms part of his overarching plan. Positivist philosophers have scoffed at this because it seems to make no definite claim that can be either verified or falsified (see Ayer 1946), for nothing that actually happens can either support this view or refute it. It is, therefore, such have said, just a way of seeing things and has no justification other than received tradition. The sense that whatever happens *is part of an overarching plan* is precisely what Understanding might be expected to induce, for while Understanding makes no particular claim it imparts a sense of unity and coherence to whatever is its field of vision. It sees a person as a person, not a set of processes: the world as a unity, not an aggregation of independent entities accidentally reacting upon one another.

Consider next the doctrine of the Fall of humanity through the disobedience of Adam and Eve. Though Understanding may impart a sense of unified purpose to the cosmos, our experience very often presents an opposite appearance. The cosmos manifests itself as divided and often at war with itself. This brokenness might be dismissed by those mystically inclined as mere illusion. If, on the other hand, it is taken more nearly at face value, as Christianity generally has, then an account of its nature or origin is needed. Understanding directed at this fallenness has seen a struggle between good tendencies in the cosmos which cohere with the unity of the whole and bad tendencies which detract from that unity. The mythological struggle between God and the Devil expresses this insight. It has given risen to many perplexities, since if all comes from God – the God of mystical vision – where does evil and the Devil come from? Such questions point to the necessity of bearing in mind the distinction between mystical and mythical levels of discourse. Understanding at its most extreme level points to the total unity expressed in mystical discourse: at a less extreme level, in which is recognised the brokenness of the cosmos, mythological discourse expresses the conflict between the unifying good and the dislocating evil.

A parallel and related perplexity concerns the nature of humankind, and again the doctrine of the Fall is used to elucidate it mythologically. Humankind was created good and yet is known often to be bad. The book of Genesis (1: 26) affirms that humankind was made in the *image* and *likeness* of God. In Hebrew I understand that these two words have indistinguishable meanings, but those who formed the doctrine of the Church used 'image' to describe humanity's original and real nature in the purpose of God, and 'likeness' to describe humanity's, now lost but still potentially real similarity to God. In the Fall the likeness was lost, the image preserved. This mirrors in the (human) microcosm the macrocosmic distinction between the mystical vision of God and the myth-ical. In the mystical vision the world has indeed that unity which Understanding confers, but in the mythical account, because of conflict and division the cosmos has lost its likeness to the God of the mystics, while retaining an image of the One. In the mystical vision humankind truly reflects the nature of God, while in the mythological vision this image is not realised and the likeness lost, but potentially recovered.

The Creation and Fall form the beginning of the whole Christian mythological cycle and space prevents an examination of the entire corpus. Very briefly, the story of salvation begun in the life, death and resurrection of Christ expresses how the brokenness of the world may be overcome. The sacrificial love of the willing victim who absorbs undeserved violence and death is the means by which the likeness of humanity to God becomes actual and the unity of the cosmos restored through the willing cooperation of those who accept injustice in the pursuit of a universal well-being. Eschatological myths, such as the New Testament book of Revelation, express the triumph of this endeavour in an imagined future.

The place of myth

From an empirical standpoint mythology may well be seen as no more than a collection of fairy tales for adults.[10] It may be seen as true only in so far as it points to the obvious evils of the world and to ways of handling them which many without belief would nevertheless recognise as admirable and sometimes effective. To the believer who sees him- or herself as participating in the myth this is an inadequate account of faith. Believers of literalist or fundamentalist tendency claim that such events as the Resurrection of Christ are true empirically and will argue for their historicity. I believe this is a mistaken approach. Despite such arguments most believers if pressed would defend their belief in the myth, not because it might be verified historically or empirically, but because it coheres with their present experience. Whenever unexpected good comes out of evil, for example, belief in the providence of God is confirmed. When joy comes out of the endurance of injustice, it is felt as a participation in the Resurrection as a present reality. The myth not only expresses such experiences, but also is the means by which the believer is led into them. It is therefore – to the believer – not merely a picturesque way of expression, it is the key which gives access to such experiences. Ideally, the believer finds the myth as the supreme guide to the faculty of Understanding, the faculty which indispensably gives a sense of reality overall, a sense of the unity of the world prevailing through its brokenness. It thus adds much to what mystical experience may offer, for the mystical can be seen as a flight from the reality of the world into a private experience of unity which might remain as just a private experience. The mythical is theologically described as a revelation of God. The mystic tries to experience God directly in himself. The mythical reveals the nature of God through a narrative based on events in the world of common experience. The mythical is intended to give insight into how the diverse multiplicity of the world comes from the mystical One, and of how it may return to it. It addresses the ancient problem of the relationship between the One and the Many, whereas the mystical is concerned only with the One. From a psychoanalytic point of view, the mystical is an attempt to enter the deepest unconscious. The mythical is obviously at a more conscious level but still reflects some of the characteristics of the unconscious. For example, although the myth may be known to express events that happened at a particular date in history, it is essentially a story that is endlessly repeated: the believer in baptism dies and rises with Christ. In the Eucharist the Church believes that it is present again at the Last Supper, Crucifixion and Resurrection of the Christ. The myth thus has a timeless quality. Furthermore, the unimportance of the empirical truth of the narrative parallels the equation of reality and fantasy in unconscious process. The myth might therefore be described as an unfolding of the deepest unconscious into consciousness, a term used by Matte Blanco to describe intermediate levels in the spectrum between the two.

The unity of the world

The mystical vision apprehends the world as total unity and the mythical narratives understand the world as endowed with a unified purpose, the purpose of God. But is the world a unity, and is all the emphasis I have put upon the sense of its unity in any way justifiable? Perhaps it is all a wish-fulfilling fantasy. The empiricist might well share these doubts, and we have all been empiricists for some centuries. In that frame of mind one may look at the world and see good bits and bad bits and some things improving and others getting worse, and may look in vain for either overall unity or any hint of triumphant progress. The unity of the world is not something that is empirically verifiable, or for that matter a concept that makes any empirical sense. It is outside the scope of empirical discourse.

Wide generalities, by contrast, are the meat and drink of Understanding. A doctor on encountering a new patient is, I am told, often given an awareness of 'how the patient is', long before any factual information is available to form a well-founded diagnosis, and I imagine a psychoanalyst may often have such insight too, although he or she may be particularly careful not to make prejudgements. The business of Understanding is to apprehend the whole, how someone is, or how the world is. If the insights of Understanding are expressed verbally it is often narrative that is found to be appropriate and most of the great faiths of humankind have been expressed in narratives. Likewise, if someone is to tell 'how they are', it is probably through a story that they will do so. Mythological discourse unfolds the unitive insights of Understanding about the world as a whole.

Empirical discourse has difficulties with 'the world as a whole'. I have already argued that since it presupposes an observer, it presupposes one who is outside that which is being observed. Understanding tries to understand the subject as within the whole that is being understood. The author of *The Cloud of*

Unknowing instructs his disciple to be aware only of his own existence and of the existence of God.[11] Having reached this point the disciple is then urged to forget even his own existence and be aware only of God. The dichotomy of subject and object is thus overcome and the individual is lost in the totality – the totality understood as unity.

Parallel universes and purpose

The empiricist might argue that nevertheless the world remains what it is, a brute something that is simply unchangeably there, like Dr Johnson's stone, and the mystical endeavour is a mere whimsical entertainment giving no real knowledge. The world we know, however, is not a wholly objective, brute something. It comes to us in piecemeal phenomena that are largely shaped by our own capacity to receive information, by our interests and needs. Wittgenstein (1963: 223) remarked that if a lion could talk, we would not understand him. Leonine language would presumably be full of observations and concepts incomprehensible to us. Eskimos are said to have thirty different words for kinds of snow and a lion might have thirty different words for stalking antelopes. But much more incomprehensibly, not only might a lion have innumerable words for smells undetectable to us, but also there might be concepts built upon chains of olfactory experience that were wholly beyond us. The objective world is only one component of the world that we experience for much comes to us clothed in language which cannot be stripped away.

While language is a communal phenomenon, the world of each of us is necessarily our own. Nuclear physics has begun to use the concept of parallel universes, universes alongside ours whose existence is required to explain certain phenomena. This is a startling conception, yet commonplace in another frame of reference. It is a humbling and strange thought that when one is travelling in a crowded Underground train, for example, one is travelling close up against hundreds of parallel universes, one pertaining to each of one's fellow travellers. Communication between these universes is possible only through an implicit trust in the efficacy of a partly common language.

My neighbour on the Underground may experience 'her' universe as fragmented and she may lack any sense of 'the totality'. It may seem purposeless to her and talk of It or of the One, or of God may be meaningless. To another neighbour the opposite may be the case and some kind of mythological narrative may be how he expresses it to himself. He may imagine there to be some entity, a God, who is the source of this sense of meaning. If his God is the God of Christian orthodoxy however, that imagining will be hedged about by warnings that this God is not an entity in the sense of an extra being within the universe at all. It is on the contrary both most intimately within him – somewhat as psychoanalysts have imagined the Unconscious to be within us – and also something most transcendently inclusive of both him and his universe as seen in the light of Understanding. In describing God thus, I have tried to keep as far as possible within the limits of what empirical discourse can describe. If, on the other hand, I try to express to myself what this sense of the unity of the inmost and the outmost might be, I shall have to use trans-empirical language, mythical or mystical. If an empiricist is listening to me, he or she may well think I am telling fairy stories, or babbling just plain nonsense.

The Christian faith proposes that the world is purposive, that is to say that whatever happens to me, I can make sense of it, or at least accept that for the moment I cannot. In a merely wish-fulfilling faith that purpose would be my own purpose. The Christian journey involves a struggle to move from that to a mature and realistic faith that understands 'my' universe as not mine at all, but as charged with meaning and purpose of its own, or in the preferred language of myth, of God's own.

It seems to me that that kind of faith is very like the maturity that psycho-analysis might seek to bestow, a trust that whatever the contingencies and vicissitudes of life, one is able to find some kind of coherence, or, failing that, a provisional acceptance of incoherence. Both approaches involve attempts to 'Understand', and therefore both implicitly assume that Understanding is possible, understanding of our world, inner and outer, as a whole. There is an important similarity between religious faith and psychoanalytic practice which distinguishes both from the empirical approach of most scientific thinking.

I hope to have drawn out some other links between Christian and psycho-analytic understandings. The purely empiricist view of the world as something objective, which can be viewed by a subject standing outside it, is not a uniquely privileged view, however useful it has been scientifically. As such it is philosoph-ically, theologically and psychoanalytically inadequate. Trans-empirical language of some kind is a necessary complement to it. It is only if individuals see themselves as detached observers that empiricism may seem to offer a complete account of the universe. The world as we each experience it has also much to do with our inner worlds, the outer world mirrored within us. Psychoanalytic and theological disciplines both look for what I have called Understanding, a faculty which encompasses both inner and outer. Both disciplines require something like the Platonic doctrine of participation, by which meaningful events and entities are seen as participating in some wider or deeper or more primordial reality lying behind them. Finally, in both disciplines a coherent understanding of our inner and outer worlds is one aim of personal growth.

One aim of this chapter has been to dispel some misunderstandings of what orthodox Christian faith means by the word 'God'. Such misunderstandings have been current in the Church itself ever since the impact of empirical science has been felt. They are fostered by the strong tendency in many parts of the Church nowadays to take the Bible literally and thus to offer simplistic certainties unjustified by reason or tradition. Over against these I have proposed a way of accommodating to the apparent nonsense of much theological language by distinguishing different levels of discourse. Some of the apparent contradictions of doctrine belong essentially to the expression of mysticism and are paralleled in other faiths, particularly Buddhism. Other apparent contradictions arise from confusing the different levels of discourse. I put forward two models of God – first, the model provided by the unrepressed unconscious as described by Freud and elaborated by Matte Blanco, and second, the model of the world as a whole apprehended by 'Understanding'. These models are intended to dispel the notion that Christianity stands or falls by the existence of an unseen being standing outside or alongside the universe. Both Christianity and psychoanalysis are subject to criticisms from an empiricist standpoint and both have a vital part to play in offering humanity a vision of itself more complete and more true than the materialistic reductionism that holds so great an influence today. Both seek an understanding of life as a totality. I believe they should be seen, not as rivals, but as allies in holding a humane vision of humanity and of reality. Each now has need of the other.

Notes

1   Lucretius, who lived c. 98–55 BC, derived his atomist philosophy from the Greek philosophers Leucippus and Democritus, for which see Kirk and Raven (1957).
2   However, of Neils Bohr himself, the Encyclopaedia Britannica states that he stressed the tentative and symbolic nature of the atomic models (1979 edition, Volume 2: 1203).
3   Perhaps the most readily available account of these will be found in Stephen Hawking 1988 – though of course science will have progressed since its publication.
4   Pseudo-Dionysius in *The Mystical Theology*, p. 141 in the C.W.S. edition of his writings, '<God> falls neither within the predicate of nonbeing nor of being'.
5   Plotinus, *The Enneads*, available for example in Penguin Classics 1991 (translated Stephen MacKenna). Plotinus lived from AD 204 to 270.
6   Richard of St Victor's is perhaps the clearest such exposition in *The Mystical Ark*, Chapter 6.
7   Nicholas of Cusa (1401–1464). His most famous work is indeed entitled *De docta ignorantia* – *On Learned Ignorance*.
8   Plato himself initiated the concept of 'Understanding' – see *Timaeus* 51 b–e.
9   I am proposing therefore two models of God. First, the unrepressed Unconscious, the inmost part of the soul sometimes described as a Void, and second, the Universe (comprehended through nous), the outermost totality conceivable. There is a parallel here with Bion's concept of O, which on the one hand is an inmost state of being, and on the other is the brute reality of impinging events. I rely here on interpretations of Bion by Bleandonu (1994) and Grotstein (2000). In St Luke's Gospel (17: 21) it is said that 'the kingdom of God is within you', but the Greek preposition can equally deliver 'among you'. This ambiguity suggests again a double siting of 'the place where God is'. The first-century Gospel of Thomas puts it more sharply still: 'the Kingdom of God is within you and it is outside of you' (Saying 3a).

10 A comparison I drew out in *The Symmetry of God* (Bomford 1999: 119f). The analogy is based on Bettelheim's work *The Uses of Enchantment*.
11 *The Epistle of Privy Counsel*, Chapter 8 (Anonymous n.d.).

References

(Since there are many editions of the works of the great philosophers and theologians quoted, I have given some references by chapter, section etc. rather than by page numbers in a specific edition.)

Anonymous (n.d.) *The Cloud of Unknowing*, to which is usually appended *The Epistle of Privy Counsel*, both believed to be the work of a fourteenth-century English writer.

Armstrong, A.H. (ed.) (1967) *The Cambridge History of Later Greek and Early Medieval Philosophy*. London: Cambridge University Press.

Ayer, A.J. (1946) *Language, Truth and Logic*, 2nd edn. London: Victor Gollanz.

Berkeley, G. (1710) *Principles of Human Knowledge*.

Bleandonu, G. (1994) *Wilfred Bion*, trans. C. Pajaczkowska. London: Free Association Books.

Bomford, R.W.G. (1999) *The Symmetry of God*. London: Free Association Books.

Boswell, J. (1791) *Life of Johnson*.

Descartes, R. (1637) *Discourse on Method*.

Dionysius the Pseudo-Areopagite (1987) *Pseudo-Dionysius, The Complete Works*, trans. Colm Luibhéid. New York: Paulist Press. Dionysius is believed to have written in the late fifth century AD.

Eigen, M. (1998) *The Psychoanalytic Mystic*. London: Free Association Books.

Freud, S. (1927) *The Future of an Illusion*. SE 21.

Freud, S. (1933) *New Introductory Lectures*. SE 22.

Grotstein, J. (2000) *Who is the Dreamer, Who Dreams the Dream?* Hillsdale, NJ: Analytic Press.

Hawking, S. (1988) *A Brief History of Time*. London: Bantam.

Kant, I. (1781) *Critique of Pure Reason*.

Kirk, G.S. and Raven, J.E. (1957) *The Presocratic Philosophers*. London: Cambridge University Press.

Lucretius (c. 50 BC) *De Rerum Naturae* (published posthumously).

Matte Blanco, I. (1975) *The Unconscious as Infinite Sets*. London: Duckworth.

Matte Blanco, I. (1988) *Thinking, Feeling and Being*. London: Routledge.

Meissner, W.W. (1984) *Psychoanalysis and Religious Experience*. New Haven, CT: Yale University Press.

Nicholas of Cusa (Nicolo Cusanus / Niklaus von Cues) (1997) Selected spiritual writings are available in The Classics of Western Spirituality series, trans. H.L. Bond. New York: Paulist Press.

Pirsig, R.M. (1974) *Zen and the Art of Motorcycle Maintenance: An Inquiry into Values*. London; Bodley Head.

Plotinus (AD 204–270) *The Enneads* were written by his disciple Porphyry from lecture notes and an abridged version is available in Penguin Classics, trans. S. MacKenna. London: Penguin.

Richard of St Victor (c. 1130–1173) *The Mystical Ark* may be found in *Richard of St Victor* in the Classics of Western Spirituality series, trans. G.A. Zinn. New York: Paulist Press (1979).

St Augustine (AD 354–430) *The Confessions* was written in about the year AD 400.

Wittgenstein, L. (1953) *Philosophical Investigations*, trans G.E.M. Anscombe. Oxford: Blackwell (1963).

Index

Black, David M. 1–20, 46, 63–79
Black, Margaret J. 138
Blake, William 92
Blass, Rachel B. 6, 16, 23–43, 73
Bloom, Allan 34
Bohr, Neils 253
Bollas, Christopher 125, 147, 180–1,
    182–3, 185, 187
Bomford, Rodney 12, 19, 252–69
Bonhoeffer, Dietrich 74
Book of Jeremiah 119
Book of Job 16–17, 83–96
Bowlby, John 156, 174, 176
brain: cognitive/psychoanalytic
    interpretations 66; contemplative
    position 75, 76; emotional interaction
    70, 73; evolutionary development
    191–2; implicit relational expectations
    68; memory 72; scientific conception of
    religious experience 64; verbal
    consciousness 65, 67, 70, 74
Bratzlav, N. 139
breast 59, 100, 168, 181, 182, 260
Britton, Ronald 14, 16–17, 83–96, 100,
    161
Brown, Daniel 225
Bruno, Giordano 74
Buber, Martin 136, 159, 177
Buddha 125, 130, 165, 177, 199;
    emotional attachments 164; Four Noble
    Truths 226–7, 229; freedom from
    suffering 249; view of the self 224, 225
Buddhism 5, 15, 18–19, 133, 223–33, 267;
    adoration 163; appeal of 261;
    attentiveness 137; Enlightenment 64;
    free-floating attention 259; Fromm 8–9;
    Horney 7; love 196; martial arts 130;
    meditation 75, 138; mystical experience
    214; no-self doctrine 76, 140–1; Rubin
    17; spiritual hazards 139–40;
    westernised 29
Burke, Kenneth 148

Cabasilas, Nicolas 122
Caesar, realm of 44, 45, 46, 51, 52, 58, 60
Catholicism 85, 171, 257
cave paintings 197–8
Christianity 19, 85, 252, 266–7; adoration
    163; Augustine 258; Book of Job 90;
    Christmas 17, 97–103, 163, 164; the
    Fall 262, 263; Freud on 212; God's
    existence 260, 261, 265; Holy Spirit
    165; love 196; Milner on 129; music
    171; mythical dimension 257;

paternalism 174, 187; St Paul 119;
    trans-empirical discourse 255;
    trans-sexism 170; Tree of Life 125
Christmas 17, 97–103, 163, 164
A Christmas Carol (Dickens) 17, 101,
    103–13
Church, Richard 198
civilisation 18, 143–4, 192, 198–9, 200
classical conditioning theory 197
clinical examples: adoration 160–2, 164;
    couple therapy 157–8; early experiences
    72–3; God 46–8, 51–2, 54–6;
    judgement of super-ego 92–5;
    spirituality 140–1, 142–3
co-naturality 195
cognitive science 77
Coltart, Nina 15, 249
communication 66, 67–8, 69, 73, 181, 182;
    facial expression 182–3; representation
    193; Winnicott 230, 231; *see also* verbal
    interaction
Communism 7
compassion 76, 77, 135, 147, 196
confession 126
connectedness 143, 146, 148
consciousness 65–7, 75, 77, 200; Loewald
    12; meditation 224; myth 264; Vedantic
    Self 236, 237; verbal 65, 67, 68, 69–71,
    72, 74
containment 56, 85, 173, 183, 184–6, 187,
    188
contemplative position 16, 75–7
conversation 67, 69; *see also* verbal
    interaction
convictions 6, 16, 39, 72, 73–4, 77; *see also*
    faith
countertransference 149
creativity 181, 182
Crucifixion 129, 264
culture 7, 10, 182, 221
Cunningham, Malcom 4, 11, 19, 234–51
curiosity 59

da Vinci, Leonardo 34
Dalai Lama 225
Damasio, A. 192
Darwin, Charles 1, 2, 74, 191, 200n1
Davids, M. Fakhry 16, 44–62
de Caussade, Jean-Pierre 130
death 3, 57, 63
death drive (instinct) 2, 9, 84, 239, 242
delusion 25, 27, 28, 30, 36, 236
depression 54, 55, 243
depressive position 76, 77, 101, 137, 161,

Roshi, Sasaki 231–2
Rubin, Jeffrey B. 11, 15, 17, 132–53
Russell, Bertrand 85–6

saccidananda 165–6, 168
the sacred 18, 27, 134, 139, 143, 149;
 Buber 177; intuition of 178; maternal
 containment 185; preceding the
 maternal 181, 183
sacrifice 128, 129
Said, Edward 208–9
St Augustine of Hippo 258
St John of the Cross 170, 179, 248, 256
St Luke 98–9
St Matthew 44, 99, 120
St Paul 119, 120, 127, 160, 174, 178
St Teresa of Avila 179
Satan 87–92
Schafer, Roy 84
Schelling, Friedrich 193
Schiller, Friedrich 193
Scholem, Gershom 196, 215
Schopenhauer, A. 71
Schore, Allan 70, 76
science 1–2, 15, 64, 191, 192, 253–4;
 conservatism of scientists 71; Klein 10;
 neuroscience 69, 70, 77; religion
 contrast 4; representation 193
Scripture 257, 258
Searle, John 192–3
Searles, H.F. 159, 163, 175
secularism 136, 145, 207
Segal, H. 101
self 67, 136, 147; Atman 122, 165;
 Buddhism 223–7, 231; containment
 173, 185; false 71, 231, 232, 237;
 natural religions 177; omnipotent 100,
 101, 103; Other relationship 136–7,
 147–8; religious ego-ideal 165;
 significant moments 178; spirituality
 144–5, 149; unintegration 18, 228, 230,
 232; Vedantic Self 235, 236–40, 241–2,
 246, 247–8, 249, 250; *see also* ego
self psychology 141, 175
self-experience: new psychoanalytic
 approaches to religion 26–7, 28;
 spirituality 135, 149; time and space
 243; Vedanta 236, 238–9, 240, 249
self-preservation 2
self-reflection 216–17
separation 55, 97, 248
sex 2
sexuality 176, 183, 210; *see also eros*
siblings 71, 163

significant moments 178–9, 180, 187
silence 244
Simurgh 123–4
sin 128, 185, 241
sincerity 129–30
Skinner, B.F. 197
Smith, Margaret 49, 50
social interaction 69
social unconscious 149
Socrates 177, 198
Sodre, I. 107
Sophocles 112
Sorenson, R. 133
soul 85, 236, 255, 256; Augustine 258;
 Bach's music 171; Gnosticism 214; God
 relationship 239; significant moments
 178
space 242–3, 245
Spero, Moshe Halevi 15
Spinoza, Benedict de 194, 198
spirituality 17, 27, 117, 127, 132–53; de
 Caussade 130; definition of 135;
 psychoanalysis as spiritual practice
 240–1; spiritual teachers 141–2;
 therapist's 146–8; transformational
 object 125–6
splitting 84–5, 161, 239
sraddha 240, 241, 244, 246, 248
Stern, Daniel 68, 183–5, 188
Stevens, Wallace 227
Stoicism 3, 257
Strachey, James 86, 136
Streeter, B.H. 199–200
subjectivity 144, 148, 149, 235; faith 77;
 natural religions 177; non-self-centred
 137; self-awareness 225; unintegration
 230
submission 138, 141
suffering 226, 227, 249
Sufism: adoration 163; God 49, 50, 52,
 53–4, 60; mysticism 5; *qalb* 127;
 Simurgh 123–4
Sulloway, Frank 71
sunyata 225
super-ego 14, 84–5, 86–7, 101, 252, 254;
 Book of Job 17, 83, 86, 87–92; *A
 Christmas Carol* 104, 106, 107, 108, 110,
 111–12; clinical example 92, 95; ego
 relationship 85, 86, 99–100; father as
 165; punitive/moralistic 56, 87, 119,
 126–7
the supernatural 6, 15, 39
surrender 138, 140, 141
Suttie, Ian 174, 176, 187, 188n1